SS ELITE

SS ELITE

THE SENIOR LEADERS OF HITLER'S PRAETORIAN GUARD

VOLUME I (A–J)

MAX WILLIAMS

FONTHILL

This book is dedicated to the memory of my good friend
Roger Forrow, one of the four 'Jolly Boys'

Fonthill Media Language Policy

Fonthill Media publishes in the international English language market. One language edition is published worldwide. As there are minor differences in spelling and presentation, especially with regard to American English and British English, a policy is necessary to define which form of English to use. The Fonthill Policy is to use the form of English native to the author. Max Williams was born and educated in the United Kingdom; therefore British English has been adopted in this publication.

Fonthill Media Limited
Fonthill Media LLC
www.fonthillmedia.com
office@fonthillmedia.com

First published in the United Kingdom and the United States of America 2015

British Library Cataloguing in Publication Data:
A catalogue record for this book is available from the British Library

Typeset in Minion Pro 11pt on 14pt
Printed and bound in England

CONTENTS

ACKNOWLEDGEMENTS

I am indebted to the following individuals for their help over the years:

James Townsend†
Rod Tidnam
Stuart Russell†
Gary Merlie
Todd Gylsen
Nikolaus von Lindenow†
Caron Cadle
Mark C. Yerger
Entasis
B. C. West†
Ian Sayer
Markus Wicke
Wilfried Beer
Hans Houterman
Dieter Zinke
Andreas Seeger
Norman 'Harry' Harrison
Roger Forrow†
Hans Joachim Lang

I am also particularly grateful to the following, who extended assistance above and beyond what was considered normal:

Kurt Gamer
Martin Bogaert
André at Flanders Militaria
Philip Nix†

Michal Sika
Ulric Woodhams
Andreas Schulz
Stephen Tyas
Michael Butler†
Andrey Bespalov
Michael D. Miller
Peter Etherington

A number of private individuals, who wish to remain anonymous, provided images. To them, I also extend my heartfelt gratitude.

INTRODUCTION

ANY SCHOLAR of history will have recognised the similarities between Ancient Rome and the National Socialist movement of the 20th century. Aside from the obvious expansionist policies of empire governed by a single autocratic leader, the Nazis adopted the Roman-style extended arm salute, the verbal greeting of hailing the leader, and the eagle-adorned banners and standards. Another parallel was the introduction of a modern Praetorian Guard, easily recognisable by their unique attire and consisting of the largest, strongest and fittest men available.

The term 'Praetorian' is derived from the hut of the commanding general. The Praetorian Guard was an elite unit individually selected from the imperial cohorts, initially used as a bodyguard for Roman Generals since around 275 BC. When Augustus became the first ruler of the Roman Empire in 31 BC, he determined that such a formation was useful not only on the battlefield, but also in politics. Thus, from the ranks of the legions throughout the provinces, Augustus recruited the Praetorian Guard. The troop that was formed initially varied to an extent from the later guard, which came to be a crucial influence in the power politics of Rome. While Augustus understood the need to have a protector in the turbulent politics of Rome, he was careful to uphold the republican facade of his regime. He allowed only nine cohorts to be formed, originally of 500, eventually increasing to 1,000 men each. While campaigning, the Praetorians were the rival of any formation in the Roman legions.

An avid follower of events throughout history, Adolf Hitler arrived at the same conclusion as Augustus after realising his physical vulnerability when participating in demonstrations or speaking at public meetings in the early 1920s. Leading Nazis were often physically attacked when attempting to deliver their message of the Nazi gospel, and although the SA storm troopers provided an element of protection by fighting back, they were generally disorganised. Meetings often ended prematurely amid chaotic scenes of violence, broken glass and damaged furniture.

Hitler discussed the situation with his bodyguards, Julius Schreck, Emil Maurice and Josef Berchtold. The resultant directive issued by Hitler in March 1923 was the establishment of the Stabswache (*staff guard*). Led by Schreck, it consisted of a small group of eight SA men, formed as the embryonic Praetorian Guard for Hitler. As in the Roman model, Schreck introduced unique insignia and clothing for his men—the silver Totenkopf emblem appeared on black coffee-can hats. The deaths head insignia, signifying danger and fatality, was an old emblem used by elite troops, significantly by the Prussian Hussar Regiment number 5 of Colonel von Ruesch, formed by order of Frederick the Great. The Hussars adopted a black uniform with a Totenkopf emblazoned on the front of their mirlitons and the symbol continued to be used on Prussian headgear until the end of the Great War.

The Stabswache developed into the Stosstrupp Adolf Hitler in May 1923 and grew in size. Now placed under the command of Josef Berchtold, it participated in the abortive Nazi attempt to seize power by force in Munich in November 1923. It was dissolved as a result. On his release from Landsberg prison, Hitler strove to rebuild the NSDAP and in April 1925 he ordered Schreck and Berchtold to form a new Praetorian Guard. It was given the title 'Schutzstaffel' which was abbreviated to 'SS'. Thus was born the organisation which would grow into a vast political and military machine. It wielded hitherto unknown levels of power and influence and gained an appalling opinion of the German nation for years to come.

Never before has an organisation engendered wide-ranging emotion as on the scale of Hitler's SS. Its tentacles reached into everyday life throughout the German Third Reich, including those territories overrun by Hitler's military might. It achieved this by infiltration into the police and secret services and eventually the military. The SS struck fear into the armed forces that opposed the German spread of influence across Europe and into the civilian population by reputation alone. Those that came into contact with it soon discovered that the reputation was well-founded.

By selecting the pedantic Heinrich Himmler as the head of the infant SS in January 1929, Hitler fused two elements both desperately seeking a direction. Although an undoubtedly able and dedicated party worker, it is doubtful Himmler would have achieved more than moderate success in the political arena. His presence was not conspicuous; his appearance was nothing short of disappointing and his ideals and opinions often provoked ridicule. His only hidden talents, which surfaced after he was given free reign in the SS, were his organisational and administration abilities. The SS was crying out for such guidance and when the two came together it was the dawn of a new era for both.

Himmler immediately set in motion the measures required to advance his own position and that of his SS organisation in the Nazi hierarchy. He introduced new regulations for applicants, behaviour, uniform, insignia and administration. His plans for expansion of SS membership soon bore fruit and numbers grew steadily. His predecessors were often in dispute with the SA leadership and although he wanted autonomy, the SS remained subordinate to the larger SA—but Himmler's opportunity would come. In the meantime, Himmler engaged the services of the clothes designer Hugo Boss to design new SS uniforms that would set them apart. He also used the design talents of Professor Karl Diebitsch to design new SS insignia.

In order to promote the SS within the NSDAP, Himmler invited high-profile members to take advantage of honorary membership of the SS, including senior rank positions. Many Party men who would not be normally entertained as SS members (had their applications been diverted through the usual channels) therefore gained senior ranks in the SS. They simply would not have met the appearance, dental and health requirements now needed to join.

Himmler encouraged the membership of important economists and the Circle of Friends of the Reichsführer-SS was formed from the nucleus of the Keppler Circle. This consisted of a group of bankers and economists which met to discuss and formulate economic policy. The SS tentacles extended into various businesses and senior SS men were often found to own or be directors of numerous companies, such as the Dresdner Bank, the Apollinaris water concern, and the Allach porcelain manufacturer.

Another avenue that Himmler explored for desirable members of the SS was the royal and aristocratic families of pre-Weimar Republic Germany. Many young male members of noble heritage fostered strong nationalistic beliefs. The elite SS, with its smart black uniforms, was an attractive option. Hitler's policies were proving successful and many aristocrats rushed to join the NSDAP. In terms of royal blood, the most senior SS recruit was Josias Erbprinz zu Waldeck und Pyrmont, who was closely related to the Dutch royal family and linked to many royal houses throughout Europe.

Himmler dreamed of a day when his SS would replace the police in Germany. To achieve this he would consolidate his power by taking control of the police in each region and then combine them under one umbrella. After he was appointed as chief of the German police in 1936, many police officers were offered SS rank. The vast majority of those offered, willingly accepted. They became not only answerable to Himmler as chief of the police, but now also loyal SS men. Himmler's power grew even more when he was appointed as Reich Minister of the Interior in 1943.

A similar situation existed with the military. The SA Chief of Staff Ernst Röhm had envisaged his SA hordes replacing the Army with him in control. The events of 30 June–1 July 1934 unfolded without the interference of the Army high command, which was pleased to see the threat of Röhm removed. Himmler realised that Hitler needed the Army and planned to infiltrate the Wehrmacht by other means; he introduced the SS-Verfügungstruppe, designed on military lines and commanded by military-trained personnel. Evolving into the Waffen-SS during the early war years, it expanded to include foreign recruits and grew into a fourth armed service to rival the Army.

Himmler used the SS to implement the racial policies of Hitler, who entrusted his loyal Reichsführer-SS with the abominable task of expunging the adversaries of

Nazi policy and the Jewish threat. Himmler achieved these goals by the introduction of the concentration camp system, ghetto-ization, deportation, resettlement and liquidation. It is in this capacity that the Nazi regime—and in particular Himmler's SS—is judged by posterity. In most cases, the inhumanity displayed by the participants cannot be equated to normal human behaviour. The vast majority of the crimes attributed to the senior SS officers were committed by family men, many of whom would return to their homes and family life just as an office employee goes home after work. The mere stroke of a pen or a verbal instruction was enough to alter the lives of hundreds, sometimes thousands. Some physically took part or personally witnessed their orders being carried out.

Their actions illustrate that hatred of one's fellow man can deliver a normal human being to the brink of the abyss, even into it. Whether by virtue of professed duty or pure loathing of those perceived to be non-Aryan sub-humans, many SS men of all ranks were guilty of inhuman acts of cruelty and murder. The excuse of legality by order of the Führer cannot and does not detract from the imorality of such actions. Many of the subjects in this study were guilty of crimes—some more than others. A few paid with their lives; a few chose to take their own lives, some with their families; many were imprisoned for various terms behind bars; and others walked away from the war with nothing more than memories.

Today there is a historical interest in the period of the Third Reich through books, films, the internet and collecting. The SS attracts more interest than other branches of military or politics, be it the Allgemeine-SS, the Waffen-SS, or the crimes and personalities of the vast organisation. Heinrich Himmler and his chief lieutenants administered a system of government, the like of which has never been seen before and is not likely to be seen again.

This study turns the spotlight upon those characters at the pinnacle of the pyramid that formed the SS. Adolf Hitler, as the supreme commander of the SS, delegated responsibility of practical leadership to the Reichsführer-SS. He, in turn, appointed his select candidates to the positions he dictated and further delegated mandatory powers to them. However, Hitler retained final authority over the most senior promotions and appointments—his signature alone approving elevation to and above the General rank of SS-Brigadeführer—whilst also exercising the power of veto over superior SS and police postings in occupied territories. Everything else was the domain of the Reichsführer-SS and his senior subordinates.

Without the benefit of the camera lens, these powerful men would remain as names in books and reports or as simple signatures on documents. We can now put faces to names and gaze upon the features of the men mainly responsible for administering the policies of the Führer, many of which were often brutal and required blind obedience.

The collection of images and information presented in this study has been my life's work. I bestow them to these pages in an effort to contribute to the great tapestry of history. Some images were donated by a number of individuals who are mentioned under the separate acknowledgements section. Others were obtained from press photographs of that period and printed contemporary publications and newspapers. Certain subject personalities were profusely photographed, whilst others remained elusive to the camera. This resulted in large numbers of surviving images for some people and a distinct lack for others. The science of photography was also still developing and professional photographers were experimenting with types of cameras, light and exposure. Many images reproduced here are also the consequence of what is known today as amateur snapshots and, given their age, are in a delicate condition. The results provide a selection of photographs of every man who held the rank of SS-Obergruppenführer or above. Some are well-known, while others are more obscure, but all had one thing in common—they all belonged to and administered an organisation which is vilified by the vast majority of historians, students of history and the law-abiding members of society.

MAX WILLIAMS
London, 2015

Der Oberste Führer der Schutzstaffel:

Der Führer

ADOLF HITLER

FRIEDRICH LUDWIG HERBERT ALPERS

FRIEDRICH ALPERS was born on 25 March 1901 in Sonnenberg, near Braunschweig. His father, also Friedrich Alpers, was a teacher, and his mother, Marie (born Pehnt), originated from an old trading family in Wolfenbüttel. He spent four years at the elementary school in Sonnenberg and then attended the high school Martino Katherinen in Braunschweig from 1911 to 1919. From 1920 to 1923 he studied law and political science at the Universities of Heidelberg, Munich and Griefswald, qualifying as a trainee lawyer in spring 1923.

Alpers was too young to see military service in the First World War, but he became actively involved in post-war politics. From 13 May 1919 to 1 March 1920 he was a member of Freikorps Märker. He worked as a salesman from early 1923 to autumn 1924; first in Braunschweig for the firm Grotrian and Steinweg, then for the firm C. W. Hartrodt in Liverpool and London, and finally for the Foetisch Brothers in Lausanne. He learned to speak excellent English. He underwent judicial training from 1924 until 1928 and passed his second State law examinations in early 1929, qualifying as an assessor. From mid-1929 he returned to his law career in Braunschweig, working as a lawyer until May 1933.

Alpers married Elizabeth Charlotte Wittmaack (born on 8 December 1900 in Berlin; NSDAP membership number 265 712) on 12 April 1930. They had two sons and two daughters, born between 1931 and 1943.

He joined the NSDAP on 1 June 1929 and was allocated membership number 132 812. On 1 May 1930, he joined the SA with the rank of SA-Sturmführer. On 1 February 1931, he enrolled in the SS, with membership number 6 427, as a member of 1st Sturm of the 2nd Sturmbann 12th SS-Standarte in Braunschweig. He was promoted on 26 October 1931 to SS-Scharführer, on 15 December 1931 to SS-Truppführer, and on 5 January 1932, he was promoted to SS-Sturmführer, taking charge of the Sturm. On 14 March 1932, he was promoted to SS-Sturmhauptführer and placed in command of the 2nd SS-Sturmbann. Further promotion to SS-Sturmbannführer followed on 8 October 1932 and he was transferred to the command of the 49th SS-Standarte, based in Braunschweig, retaining this post until 3 May 1933.

He fell foul of the SS-Abschnitt IV commander, Berthold Maack, for entering a dispute with Dietrich Klagges and Friedrich Jeckeln, and he was suspended from SS duty on 28 February 1933. The same year he was appointed as Gau Hunt Master of Gau Südhannover-Braunschweig, a Prussian State Councillor, chief of the Auxiliary Police in Braunschweig, and, on 8 May, he was appointed as a State Minister. Apparently, he emerged from the dispute with Klagges and Jeckeln unscathed and was subsequently promoted to SS-Standartenführer on 3 May 1933, transferring to the staff of SS-Oberabschnitt Nord on the same day. He was appointed State Minister for Justice and Finance in Braunschweig on 8 May 1933 and held this post until 1939. Another transfer to SS-Gruppe Nordwest followed on 15 September 1933, and more promotion ensued: SS-Oberführer on 9 November 1934 and SS-Brigadeführer on 30 January 1936. On 1 April 1936 he transferred to the staff of SS-Oberabschnitt Mitte, and on 19 October 1936 the Alpers family withdrew from the Church. Alpers was a member of Lebensborn from 1937.

From 15 January 1937 until 1 April 1937, Alpers served as a Luftwaffe reserve officer as an observer at Fliegerhorst Braunschweig, followed by an attachment until 31 May 1937 with the Luftwaffe long-range reconnaissance unit also based in Braunschweig. He was back with the Luftwaffe on 15 June 1937, in Prenzlau Saxony, until 31 July 1937.

On 1 November 1937, he was placed on the staff of the Reichsführer-SS, and was appointed as Prussian General Forest Master and Huntmaster to the State Secretary in the Reich Forestry Office and State Minister for all Forestry and Hunting Matters. A further Luftwaffe attachment for one month in August 1938 was with the 22nd Reconnaissance Group at Prenzlau. A favourite of Göring, Alpers became a Reichstellenleiter and a member of the Prussian State Parliament.

His Luftwaffe reserve service paid dividends as he gained an attachment to the 22nd Reconnaissance Group during the Polish campaign in September 1939. From 1940 until April 1944 he was the leader of the Forest Industry Group as the Führer's authorised representative for the Four Year Plan. He was also a member of the Four Year Plan Advisory Office. In 1941 he was the leader of the Raw Materials Staff of Hesse Industry Inspection and was promoted to SS-Gruppenführer on 20 April 1941. On 17 January 1942 he was appointed chief of the Landwacht and Stadtwacht, which were forms of auxiliary police. He also headed the Special Flight Section of the Reich Air Ministry Technical Office.

On 10 May 1940, he rejoined the Luftwaffe as a Reserve Captain and was posted as staff officer with 22nd Reconnaissance Group and commander of a reconnaissance squadron. He was promoted to Reserve Major on 1 June 1942. From January 1942 until October 1942, he commanded Long-Range Reconnaissance Group 4 on the Eastern Front. Alpers transferred to the 3rd Parachute Division on 1 March 1944 and commanded the 9th Parachute Regiment from 21 August 1944 until

3 September 1944. His military service gained him the German Cross in Gold on 8 April 1942 and the Knights Cross of the Iron Cross on 14 October 1942.

Alpers was promoted on 21 June 1943 to SS-Obergruppenführer on the staff of the Reichsführer-SS.

Alpers was reported as missing in the area of Lille by his adjutant, SS-Obersturmbannführer Franz Wurm, on 3 September 1944. Apparently he shot himself when captured by Allied troops at Quevy le Grand, Belgium.

Above: Friedrich Alpers as a member of the 12th SS-Standarte.

Left: SS-Sturmbannführer Alpers.

Opposite page:

Alpers in State Forestry uniform.

Alpers far right, with Göring and Sir Nevile Henderson, British ambassador to Germany.

Göring listens to Alpers speak at a hunt. In the group are Himmler and Wolff.

Clockwise from top left:

Alpers left, with another State Forestry official.

Alpers' official State Forestry portrait.

SS-Obergruppenführer Friedrich Alpers.

A Luftwaffe portrait of Alpers, who is wearing the Knight's Cross.

Alpers (second left) with Luftwaffe comrades.

Alpers (far right).

Alpers questions a prisoner.

The grave marker of Friedrich Alpers.

MAX AMANN

M AX AMANN was born into a Catholic family on 24 November 1891 in Munich. He was educated in Munich from 1898; first at an elementary school, before spending three years at a business school whilst working as a commercial office apprentice in the law firm of Warmuth and Heckelmann, until 1911. Next he became a salesman, but then, on 24 October 1912, he enlisted in the 6th Company of the 1st Bavarian Infantry Regiment (König). Following the outbreak of hostilities in 1914, he transferred to the 16th Bavarian Reserve Infantry Regiment. Here he first met Adolf Hitler, who was a member of the same regiment, and Amann served as his company sergeant. Amann saw active service in France and Flanders as a Vizefeldwebel and Offizierstellvertreter before being demobilised on 5 December 1919. He then worked in the disarmament office and the war pensions office of the Bavarian War Ministry, prior to finding employment as a bank clerk with two banking firms in Munich until 1921.

He married Anna Frichs (born in St Johann im Tyrol on 10 May 1895) on 3 February 1919 and they produced eight children between December 1919 and June 1941—five boys and three girls. The marriage did not last and the couple later separated. His oldest son, Rudolf, was killed in action in June 1941.

He was a founder member of the NSDAP, joining on 1 July 1921 with Party membership number 3. He became the first business manager of the Party and from 1922 was the Director General of the NSDAP Central Publishing House, Eher Verlag. This was the sole publishing house of the NSDAP and responsible for the *Völkischer Beobachter*, the *Illustrierter Beobachter*, *Der SA-Mann*, *Unser Wille und Weg*, and many other Party newspapers and magazines.

He participated in the 8–9 November 1923 Beer Hall Putsch in Munich and as a result, on 28 April 1924, he was sentenced to four and a half months in Landsberg Prison with Hitler. When Hitler wrote a book entitled *Four and a Half Years of Struggle Against Lies, Stupidity and Cowardice*, Amann shrewdly shortened the title to *Mein Kampf* (*My Struggle*). The result was a best-seller, outselling every other book published during Hitler's time—with the exception of the Bible—and providing Hitler with a substantial personal fortune. On his release from custody, Amann collaborated with Hermann Esser, Franz Xaver Schwarz and Julius Streicher to form the Grossdeutsche Volksgemeinschaft, a secret cover organisation for the now prohibited NSDAP. This lasted until March 1925 when it was dissolved in favour of the resurrected and rehabilitated NSDAP.

On 9 November 1924 Amann was elected as a city councillor in Munich and he held this position until April 1933. On 27 February 1925 he re-enrolled in the NSDAP, keeping his original Party number. From 9 June 1928 until 12 June 1930, he was a member of the Upper Bavarian District Parliament. On 11 September 1931, whilst on a shooting trip with Franz Ritter von Epp, Amann sustained a serious wound to his left arm as a result of an accidental firearm discharge. The doctors could not save the arm and it was amputated above the elbow.

He joined the SS on 15 March 1932 and was immediately given the rank of SS-Gruppenführer, with SS membership number 53 143, attached to SS-Gruppe Süd on the staff of the Supreme SA Leadership Office.

On 2 June 1933, he was appointed as Reichsleiter for the entire German press, and from 11 May 1933 until 14 November 1933 he was the chairman of the board of directors of the Association of German Newspaper Publishers. On 15 November 1933, he was elected as a deputy to the Reichstag for Upper Bavaria-Schwabia and appointed as President of the Reich Press Chamber, a post he held until he was succeeded on 15 January 1938 by Dr Otto Dietrich.

On 22 April 1934, he was listed as an honorary SS-Führer in the redesignated SS-Oberabschnitt Süd. On 20 April 1935, he was at the special command of the Reichsführer-SS, and transferred to his staff on 30 January 1936 on promotion to SS-Obergruppenführer.

In November 1935 he was a member of the Senate of Reich Culture. On 1 May 1941, he was named as a pioneer of work and the same year he was awarded a dotation by Hitler.

Amann was arrested by US troops at Tegernsee on 4 May 1945 and was subsequently used as a prosecution witness at the International Military Tribunal in Nuremberg. On 8 September 1948, a court in Munich sentenced him to two and a half years in prison for his personal ill-treatment of the anti-Nazi news editor Fritz Gerlich. Retried on 6 December 1948 by a de-Nazification court in Munich, he was sentenced to ten years in a labour camp and had his property, business holdings and pension rights confiscated in July 1949. He was released in 1953. A shrewd and astute businessman, described by some as rough and uncouth, Amann died alone and in poverty on 30 March 1957 in his hometown of Munich.

A youthful-looking Max Amann.

Amann before he lost his left arm.

SS-Gruppenführer Amann.

Amann, the NSDAP publisher.

Amann (right, seated) with early NSDAP members.

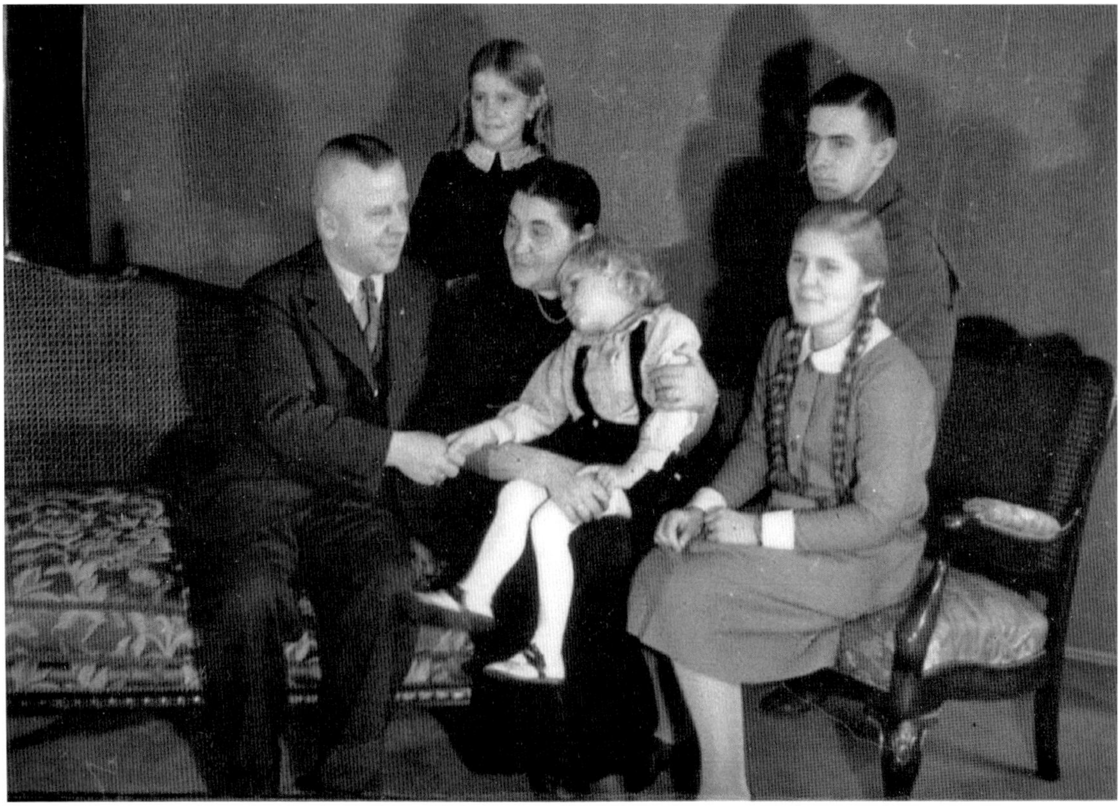

Amann at home with his family.

SS-Obergruppenführer Max Amann. Seen here in his SS uniform greatcoat.

NSDAP Reichsleiter Max Amann.

At the 1942 funeral of Adolf Hühnlein. Left to right: Kurt Daluege, Max Amann, Robert Ley, Heinrich Himmler, Viktor Lutze, Konstantin Hierl and Bernhard Rust.

SS-Obergruppenführer Max Amann.

Amann wearing his Blood Order in SS uniform.

Amann chats to Bormann at one of the Putsch anniversaries.

Clockwise around the table: Rosenberg, Amann, Frick, Buch, Bouhler, Fiehler, Weber, Schwarz and Ley.

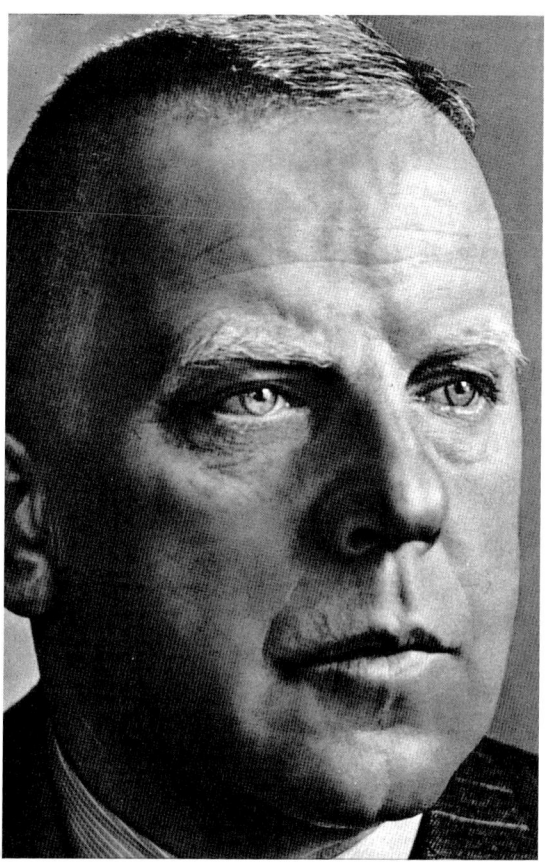

Clockwise from top left:

Amann.

Amann speaks before a post-war de-Nazification hearing in Munich.

The grave of Amann.

ERICH JULIUS EBERHARD VON DEM BACH-ZELEWSKI

ERICH VON DEM BACH-ZELEWSKI was born on 1 March 1899 in Lauenburg, the son of a public welfare official and farmer, Otto Johannes von Zelewski (born on 20 May 1859) and his wife, Amalia Maria Eveline (born Schimanski on 16 April 1862 in Thorn). The young Erich's father died in Dortmund on 17 April 1911 and he was subsequently adopted by estate owner von Schickfuss in Trebnig Silesia (*today Trzebnik*).

From 1905 until 1914 he attended schools in Biala, Neustadt, Strasburg West Prussia and Konitz. As a fifteen-year-old volunteer, the youngest in Germany, he enlisted on 9 November 1914 at the recruit depot of Infantry Regiment 176 and went to the front with the 129th Infantry Regiment. He also served at the front with the 2nd Jäger Battalion and the 10th Grenadier Regiment. On 1 March 1916, he was commissioned as a Leutnant. He was wounded twice: the first, a gunshot wound to the shoulder, and the second with gas poisoning. He ended the war as a commander of a machine-gun company and then fought with the Freikorps Silesian Border Protection Detachment as a battalion commander in 1919. In July 1919 he was posted as a member of the Reichswehr 4th Infantry Regiment, and he stayed with this unit until September 1924.

He joined the German People's Freedom Movement in 1919, with membership number 28083, and in 1924 he became a member of Stahlhelm.

Von dem Bach was married on 21 September 1921 to Ruth Apfeld (born in Neisse on 22 September 1901). They had six children—three girls, followed by three boys, between May 1923 and May 1940. The family withdrew from the Evangelical Church in the 1930s and von dem Bach declared his religion as 'God believer' (*Gottgläubig*).

From February 1928 to 1930 he was the estate manager for the manor at Dühringshof (*today Bogdaniec, Poland*) in the district of Landsberg-Warthe. He ran a farm there from 1930. Whilst at Dühringshof he joined the NSDAP and was allocated membership number 489 101.

On 15 February 1931, he joined the SS as a SS-Anwärter, with SS number 9 831, in Sturm 1/III/27. On 15 July 1931, he was promoted to SS-Sturmführer with the

3rd Sturmbann of SS-Standarte 27 and became the administrative officer on 5 October in the same year. On 6 December 1931, he was again promoted, on this occasion to SS-Sturmbannführer.

He was elected as a deputy to the Reichstag for Wahlkreis 5 (Frankfurt-Oder) on 30 August 1932. Further promotion to SS-Standartenführer followed on 10 September 1932, when he took command of SS-Standarte 27 in Frankfurt-Oder. Another leap up the promotion ladder occurred on 6 October 1932 when he was given command of SS-Abschnitt XII with the rank of SS-Oberführer. Retaining his command, he was further promoted to SS-Brigadeführer on 15 December 1933. He transferred on 12 February 1934 to the command of SS-Abschnitt VII in Königsberg, on the staff of SS-Oberabschnitt Nordost, unofficially as the Oberabschnitt commander.

On 11 July 1934, as reward for his participation in the Röhm purge, he was promoted to SS-Gruppenführer and confirmed officially as commander of SS-Oberabschnitt Nordost. He retained this post until 15 February 1936, when he was transferred to SS-Oberabschnitt Südost as a result of serious differences with Gauleiter Erich Koch. In 1935 he was appointed as Deputy Chief of Police in Königsberg and he held this post until his transfer to Breslau. He was returned as the Reichstag Deputy for Wahlkreis 7 in March 1936 and kept this seat until the end of the war. He was also a member of the Land Farming Council in Kurmark and a Provincial Councillor in Silesia. During 1936 and 1937 he toured abroad, giving talks and speeches to political groups in Turkey, Yugoslavia, Hungary, and Greece.

After having completed one month of Army reserve service with the 1st Infantry Regiment in 1935, he was promoted on 1 December 1936 to Hauptmann der Reserve. Other reserve attachments took place in 1937 and 1938.

He was appointed as Höherer SS-und Polizeiführer (HSSPF—*Higher SS and Police Leader*) in Breslau on 28 June 1938, taking the title 'HSSPF Südost'. In October 1939 he was appointed Agent of the Reichskommissar for the Consolidation of German Nationals in Silesia. On 19 October 1939, as HSSPF Südost, he was given responsibility for the strengthening of the Deutschen Volkstum (*German Home Guard*) in Silesia.

With the successful invasion of Holland in May 1940, Himmler considered who to place in command of the SS and police in Den Haag. He forwarded to Hitler the names of Erich von dem Bach-Zelewski and Hanns Albin Rauter as possible candidates. Hitler selected the latter.

Also in 1940, von dem Bach-Zelewski took steps to remove the 'Zelewski' part of his family name as it sounded 'non-Germanic'. He wrote a five-page letter to Himmler in December of that year, explaining his reasons for the alteration and giving a resumé of his family background. From 28 November 1940 he was officially known as 'von dem Bach' by decree of the Regional President of Breslau.

On 1 March 1941, von dem Bach accompanied Himmler and Gauleiter Bracht on Himmler's first confirmed visit to Auschwitz concentration camp, which was within von dem Bach's sphere of responsibility. It was von dem Bach's 42nd birthday and he was present when the Reichsführer-SS ordered Rudolf Höss to drain the marshlands at nearby Birkenau and to expand the camp facilities—in preparation for the anticipated large numbers of prisoners of war.

Von dem Bach was accorded the rank of Generalleutnant der Polizei on 10 April 1941. A further transfer followed on 1 May 1941 to the Staff of the Reichsführer-SS. He was appointed as HSSPF Army Group Centre (HSSPF Russland-Mitte) from 22 June 1941. In this capacity he oversaw the actions of the Einsatzkommandos and personally directed a mass execution on 17 July 1941 in Slonim, Belarus, where 1,100 Jews were shot. He was able to report to Himmler on 7 August 1941 that the death toll of victims of the Einsatzkommandos operating in his zone exceeded 30,000. Approximately 90 per cent of those were Jews. He accompanied Himmler in Minsk on 15 August 1941, when they witnessed the shooting of 100 souls by Einsatzkommando 8 under Otto Bradfisch. As a result of the effect on the men carrying out these actions, von dem Bach took the opportunity to press for a more humane method of execution, and Himmler agreed to investigate alternative methods—culminating in the widespread use of gas. In September 1941, Hitler awarded von dem Bach a dotation of 100,000 Reichsmarks.

From 24–26 September 1941, von dem Bach attended a specialist course on anti-partisan warfare offered by the Army's expert in such matters, General Max von Schenckendorff. During this course, the participants (including Arthur Nebe and Hermann Fegelein) witnessed an action by Einsatzkommando 8 against approximately thirty Jews in the town of Knjashizy. On his return to his duties, von dem Bach ordered the execution of 2,273 Jews in Mogilew on 2 and 3 October 1941.

He was promoted to SS-Obergruppenführer and General der Polizei on 9 November 1941. It was also von dem Bach whom Himmler had selected as HSSPF for Moscow, a post which never materialised.

On 28 January 1942, von dem Bach was hospitalised at the SS hospital in Berlin-Lichterfelde, suffering from an intestinal complaint. Apparently he had an impacted stool which required surgery. The cause has been the subject of much discussion by post-war historians. In his testimony at Nuremberg, von dem Bach declared that he was suffering from nervous exhaustion brought about by the horrors of carrying out orders in the east. Medical evidence does suggest that this could be a cause of his physical problem. Another suggestion is that the lack of fresh drinking water may have contributed towards both diarrhoea and constipation. He had suffered from constipation and haemorrhoids as a child and this continued into adulthood. Whatever the medical reason, he suffered a great deal of abdominal pain and there is a suggestion he became addicted to morphine in an effort to relieve his suffering. Professor Dr Ernst Robert Grawitz informed Himmler by letter on 1 March 1942 that von dem Bach was suffering hallucinations brought about by his experiences in the east. Morphine addiction may have been a reason why he did not return to full duty until May 1942, after a four-week convalescent rest in Karlsbad following his discharge from hospital.

Apparently, Hitler greatly admired von dem Bach and was keen to despatch him to Prague following the assassination attempt on Reinhard Heydrich on 27 May 1942. It was only after further discussion with Himmler that he settled upon the more-suitable Kurt Daluege.

Von dem Bach attended another anti-partisan course as a lecturer between 20 and 24 May 1942. He was also a participant at the conference held on 9 July 1942 where Himmler discussed Aktion Reinhard (*the extermination of the Polish Jews*) and the SS policy in the east. On 23 October 1942, he was officially recognised as the special authority of the Reichsführer-SS on anti-partisan warfare. He took temporary command of 1st SS-Infantry Brigade (motorised) on 1 December 1942, but this lasted for just a few days.

From 3 April 1943 until 21 June 1944 he was the HSSPF Russland Mitte und Weissruthenien, based first in Mogilew and then in Minsk. On 21 June 1943, he was appointed chief of the Bandenkämpfverbande (*anti-partisan forces*), holding this post until 10 November 1944.

From 20 January 1944 he commanded 'Group von dem Bach' under Army Group South, but was flown out of the operational area around Kowel on 15 March 1944, suffering from painful haemorrhoids.

From 2 August until 2 October 1944, he was the commanding General of Corps Group von dem Bach during the Warsaw insurrection. For his part in the defeat of the Warsaw uprising, Hitler awarded him the Knight's Cross of the Iron Cross on 30 September 1944. Following his success in this short campaign, he transferred on 10 November 1944 to the command of the XIV SS-Corps on the Western Front. He was appointed as commander of X Waffen-Armeekorps der SS on 26 January 1945. This was followed on 5 March 1945 by his final command—that of the Oder Corps, an *ad hoc* unit which ceased to exist on 24 April 1945.

Arrested by the US military police on 1 August 1945, von dem Bach quickly realised his precarious position, having been named on the 'most wanted' list of war criminals. He bargained with the Americans and agreed to give prosecution evidence against his former comrades in exchange for their commitment not to hand him over to the Russians; he would certainly have been hanged had they done so. He appeared for the prosecution at several post-war trials, including that of the major offenders in Nuremberg. On 7 January 1946, after giving evidence at the International Military Tribunal, Göring was so incensed at von dem Bach that he was heard to shout '*Schweinehund und Verräter!*' ('*Pig-dog and traitor!*') at him. During this period, he rediscovered his religious faith and rejoined the Protestant church. He was released from custody in 1950.

Von dem Bach did not totally escape justice and he was sentenced to ten years of 'special labour' by a Munich court on 31 March 1951; however, the sentence was suspended. He found work as a night-watchman and was re-arrested in 1958 for the murders committed in 1941–1942. Living just outside Nuremberg, again under the name von dem Bach-Zelewski, on 25 May 1961 he swore an affidavit in support of Eichmann, who had been seized by Israeli agents and was facing trial in Jerusalem. The same year, von dem Bach was tried for his participation in the Röhm purge, but was released following the suicide in prison of the main prosecution witness. He was tried again from 16 January until 10 February 1961, and received a sentence of four years and ten months in prison. In 1962 he was again indicted, in this instance for the murder of German communists in 1933. For this crime he was sentenced on 3 August 1962 to life in prison by a Nuremberg court. He died in hospital at Munich-Harlaching on 8 March 1972, having been released a few days before on grounds of ill-health.

von dem Bach-Zelewski, wearing the rank insignia of a SS-Oberführer.

Seen here as a SS-Brigadeführer.

Relaxing with a cigar.

A formal portrait of SS-Gruppenführer von dem Bach-Zelewski.

SS-Gruppenführer Erich von dem Bach-Zelewski.

The von dem Bach-Zelewski children.

von dem Bach-Zelewski at a Reichsparteitag with
Fritz Weitzel.

An official SS photograph.

Enjoying a beer with Kurt Daluege.

von dem Bach-Zelewski with Himmler at an event in Silesia.

von dem Bach-Zelewski greets a member of the Sudetenland Freikorps.

Meeting ethnic Germans in the Sudetenland.

In the Sudetenland.

Clockwise from top left:

von dem Bach was a heavy smoker.

von dem Bach wearing his field-grey greatcoat.

von dem Bach on 1 March 1941 in Gleiwitz, with Himmler and Gauleiter Bracht, prior to an inspection visit at Auschwitz concentration camp.

The Polish Home Army surrenders in Warsaw.

Talking to local peasants.

Clockwise from top left:

SS-Obergruppenführer Erich von dem Bach.

von dem Bach proudly wears his numerous decorations.

Prisoner of war.

von dem Bach on the witness stand at Nuremberg.

von dem Bach works as a night watchman.

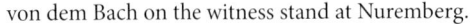

The grave of Erich von dem Bach Zelewski.

HERBERT FRIEDRICH WILHELM BACKE

Herbert Backe was born a German national in Batum, Transcaucasus, Russia, on 1 May 1896. He was the second son of Prussian merchant and retired Leutnant Albrecht Backe. Herbert attended the German Evangelical School in Tiflis from 1902 until 1905, when he entered the Tiflis State high school. He had to work his way through secondary school without the support of his father, who committed suicide in 1907. At the outbreak of war in 1914 he was interned by the Wjatka government in the Urals. He spent the duration of the war in an internment camp, being exchanged via St Petersburg to Germany through the efforts of the Swedish Red Cross in April 1918 on condition that he was not conscripted for military service. On arrival in Germany he volunteered for military service, but saw no action at the front.

Having lost everything during the war, his family was penniless. Backe worked for six months in factories in the Rhineland as a lathe operator, a fitter and a payroll clerk, supporting his sick mother, three young sisters and his elder brother—who was studying engineering. The depression caused the loss of his job and the family moved to Hannover, where Backe found work as a drainage labourer in the moorland and then as a farm labourer. He took up studies for his agricultural diploma at Göttingen University in the winter of 1920, working part-time as a tutor and estate administrator to supplement his income. He obtained good marks in his diploma examination in May 1923 and became a research assistant to Professor Obst at the Hannover Technical High School in the spring of 1924.

Under the influence of Dr Ludolf Haase—then a medical student at Göttingen in 1922—Backe agreed to join the SA, but refused to enrol in any party. Haase apparently paid Backe's NSDAP subscription in secret. In August 1923 Backe resigned from the SA, but his interest in politics remained avid. He officially joined the NSDAP on 1 December, but he resigned from the Party on 24 November 1926. His doctoral thesis was rejected in 1927 on the grounds that it was a work of political science rather than agriculture. He worked as the estate manager of the Gunzelfitz estate in Pomerania from 1 April 1927 until the following year. From

1927 until 1930, he was a member of Stahlhelm. Backe leased the Hornsen estate in Alfeld-Hannover from 1928 and became actively involved with NSDAP politics again in 1930, re-joining the SA in June 1931. On 1 October 1931 he re-enrolled in the NSDAP and held membership number 22 766.

Backe married Ursula Kahl (born on 8 October 1900 in Petersdorf, Schleswig Holstein; NSDAP member 14 667 139), one of his former fellow assistants of Professor Obst, on 6 October 1928. They had a happy marriage which produced four children. The only daughter, Armgard, was born on 16 December 1932. She was followed by three sons: Albrecht on 18 August 1933, Arnulf on 19th November 1934 and Arnd on 10 June 1936.

Sometime during 1931 Backe met both Hitler and Darré. After losing the election as the NSDAP candidate for the Hannover Chamber of Commerce, he wrote an article on the problems of Germany's trade and agriculture which impressed Darré. The same year he was appointed a member of the Ahlfeld district government and retained his post until 1933. He was successful in the April 1932 election to become a NSDAP member of the Prussian State Parliament on 24 of that month. He was also nominated as the NSDAP overseer representative on the agricultural committee of the State legislature and filled several posts on various agricultural and economic committees. Following the National Socialist elevation to power in 1933, he was appointed the leader of Stabshauptabteilung A in the Reich Food Office, in addition to other national agricultural posts. On 27 October 1933 he was also appointed Secretary of State in the Prussian Ministry of Food and Agriculture.

On 1 October 1933, inexorably linked with the 'blood and soil' doctrine of Walther Darré, Backe joined the SS and was allocated membership number 87 882 with the rank of SS-Sturmbannführer. He was placed on the staff of Darré's SS Race and Settlement Main Office. He was promoted to SS-Obersturmbannführer on 29 March 1934 and less than a month later, on 20 April, he rose to SS-Standartenführer. The meteoric advance through the ranks continued: on 9 September 1934 he became SS-Oberführer, and on 1 January 1935 he became SS-Brigadeführer. He was placed at the special commission of the Reichsführer-SS on 13 April 1935. On 21 June 1935 he was appointed head of the Resettlement Office in the SS Race and Settlement Main Office. He remained with this Hauptamt until the end of the war.

In June 1935 Backe was recommended to Göring as a gifted agricultural economist, and he was appointed as the agricultural representative on the Reichsmarschall's committee for the organisation of raw materials and currency. This propelled him into the limelight, and he was subsequently nominated as the agricultural representative to Göring's Council of the Four Year Plan, which convened on 23 October 1936. This demonstrated an obvious shift of power from Reichsminister Darré to his deputy, Backe, from which Darré never sufficiently recovered. In 1937, Backe was appointed chief of the Reich Food Office.

Another SS promotion occurred on 30 January 1938, this time to SS-Gruppenführer. As his boss, Darré, increasingly grew away from National Socialist policies, Backe gained in stature. His disputes with Darré often resulted in heated arguments, Darré extolling the benefits of outlandish ideas with Backe promoting the voice of reason. Mentally exhausted, Backe suffered a breakdown in 1938.

On 1 December 1939, Backe directed that Jews were no longer entitled to special food allocations. From 18 December they were issued with reduced rations. From 1939, Backe was described in the annual agricultural ministry budget as 'acting head of the ministry'. In 1941 he was appointed as the Food Controller for the Economic Staff East. The unfortunate Darré was finally demoted in 1942. From 23 May 1942 until the end of the war, Backe was effectively Reichsminister for Food and Agriculture and Reich Farmers' Leader, but he refused the official title until 1 April 1944. Darré continued to use the title Reichsminister even after his demotion and refused to recognise Backe's new status. On 9 November 1942, Hitler recognised the increased prominence of Backe by promoting him to SS-Obergruppenführer.

Backe was a trusted colleague of Reinhard Heydrich, one of the few men to have gained the security chief's respect—the Backe family even socialised with the Heydrich family. Backe seems to have been genuinely popular with many of his contemporaries. He was captured on 23 May 1945 in Rheims, France, and arrived in Nuremberg prison on 12 October 1946, classified as a witness who would be standing trial himself for war crimes. An honourable man, Backe cheated the prosecutors by hanging himself in his cell at Nuremberg on 6 April 1947, in the belief that he would be handed over to the Soviet authorities.

Left and right: Herbert Backe in brownshirt uniform.

Backe as a Ministry of Agriculture official.

SS-Brigadeführer Backe in a pensive mood.

Backe chatting at a function.

Herbert Backe visits the Reichs Chancellery with members of his staff and a group of ethnic German peasants. Backe is standing front row, second from left. At his right shoulder is Hermann Reischle.

Senior members of the RuSHA (second from left: Meyer-Hetling, third from left: Reischle). Note the RuSHA runic sleeve diamond on Backe's left sleeve.

Backe peers through a microscope.

State Secretary SS-Gruppenführer Backe.

An excellent view of Backe's RuSHA cuff title.

Backe makes a presentation.

Backe at the rostrum.

Backe at his desk.

Backe presenting awards to farmers.

Backe during a visit to a farm.

A smiling Herbert Backe.

Reichsminister SS-Obergruppenführer Backe.

Backe in Obergruppenführer uniform.

JOSEF BERCHTOLD

I no sooner heard Hitler in the Sterneckerbrau than I became a convinced adherent. I resolved to follow this man no matter whither he led ... it gradually became necessary to form a small body of specially-picked men on whom the most absolute dependence could be placed.

(Josef Berchtold, 1933)

BORN A Catholic on 6 March 1897 in Ingolstadt, Josef Berchtold was the son of Josef Berchtold (born in Dorffen on 14 February 1863, died in Munich on 29 April 1935) and his wife Maria (born Schmidt). He attended elementary school and high school in Munich from 1903 until 1915, when he volunteered for frontline service with the Royal Bavarian Army.

On 3 February 1915, he was posted as a Kanonier to 4th Replacement Battery of 1st Bavarian Field Artillery Regiment, and he stayed with this unit until 25 July 1915. From 25 July until 17 November 1915 he was on the Western Front with 5th Battery of 1st Bavarian Field Artillery Regiment, but he was hospitalised for the last week with gastro-enteritis (*possibly dysentery*). This resulted in an extended stay in the field hospital of 1st Bavarian Army Corps until 29 November 1915, when he returned to his unit at the front. He was promoted to Gefreiter on 1 January 1916. He was in hospital again from 16 March until 22 March 1916 with a badly bruised left foot and then reported sick from 19 June until 25 June 1916 with nervous exhaustion. He was promoted to Unteroffizier on 11 June 1916 and he applied for an officer's commission, being granted officer candidate rank on 15 October 1916. He lost this rank on 22 July 1917, but regained it on 10 March 1918.

From 11 February until 8 March 1917, he attended a course at the artillery school of Army Section C and was assigned to battery number 8 of his regiment on his return to the front. Wounded by the effects of poison gas on 17 November 1917, he was declared fit for duty under medical supervision and posted to 4th Replacement Battery of 2nd Replacement Section of his regiment on 22 November 1917. He transferred to 8 Battery of 8th Bavarian Reserve Field Artillery Regiment on 1 January 1918 and went up the line with this gun crew on 31 January 1918. He was promoted to Leutnant on 13 June 1918. He changed to 9 Battery on 9 July 1918, remaining with this gun until 15 December 1918, when he was discharged from military service in Munich. After leaving the military, he studied economics at the University of Munich and then found employment as a journalist.

Berchtold joined the NSDAP in February 1920 as one of the founder members, with membership number 750. From June 1920 until 29 July 1921 he was a member of the Working Committee of the NSDAP, and until 21 January 1921 he was the second treasurer of the Party. Between 21 January and 29 July 1921 he filled the role of primary Party treasurer. He resigned from the NSDAP on 29 July 1921 due to disagreements over policy and then founded the Free National Socialist Association.

By 7 March 1922 he had settled his differences and re-enrolled in the NSDAP and the SA with new membership numbers. He was re-appointed as second Party treasurer. He acquired a business as a tobacco and stationery merchant in 1923.

Berchtold displayed a flair for organising and commanding several SA-Hundertschaften (*units comprising 100 SA men*) in Munich and in March 1923, when a few of the 'old fighters' formed what was called the 'Stabswache' (*headquarters guard*), Berchtold was included. Its brief was to protect Hitler from enemies outside and within the Party. Two months later, the Stabswache was replaced by the Stosstrupp Adolf Hitler and Berchtold was appointed SA-Führer with special responsibility for the Stosstrupp Adolf Hitler. He retained this post until 9 November 1923, the day of the Munich Putsch, when the SA and the Stosstrupp Adolf Hitler were banned. Berchtold commanded the Stosstrupp Adolf Hitler at the Bürgerbräukeller and played a major role in the proceedings. He led the abortive assault on the Police Headquarters in Ettstrasse. Participating in the march to the Reichswehr Ministry, he was present when the column was fired upon at the Feldherrnhalle. He managed to escape back to the Bürgerbräukeller and thence to Austria, where he remained until it was safe to return. He was tried in his absence and sentenced on 23 April 1924 to a term of imprisonment.

From March 1924 until April 1926, he was the district business manager of the NSDAP in Kärnten and simultaneously the SA Leader of the same district until amnestied. In April 1925 Julius Schreck was ordered by Hitler to form a new headquarters unit to act as his bodyguard. Soon after, this unit was given the name Schutzstaffel (SS—*protection staff*). In April 1926, the exiled Berchtold returned to Germany and replaced Schreck as commander of the SS on 15 April 1926, bearing the title 'Oberleiter der Schutzstaffel'. He re-joined the newly re-formed NSDAP and was allocated number 36 003, but was later granted membership number 964. At the same time, he was nominated as chief of the Munich SA. By November 1926, Hitler had appointed Franz Pfeffer von Salomon as Supreme Commander of the SA. Von Salomon issued an order on 4 November 1926 declaring Berchtold as

Reichsführer-SS from 1 November 1926—but subordinate to him. In attempts to retain independence, Berchtold experienced constant problems with the SA and Party officials, and when the SA was allowed to expand further in March 1927, he resigned as Reichsführer-SS.

From 1 January 1927 he was the lead writer of the *Völkischer Beobachter* in Munich, and from 1932 he was the chief editor of *SA Mann*. From 1934 he was chief of the *Völkischer Beobachter* Service and deputy editor-in-chief.

He transferred to the headquarters staff of the SA in 1928. On 1 January 1933, he was promoted to SA-Oberführer. He participated as a member of Hitler's entourage on 30 June 1934 during the arrests of Röhm, Heines, Schneidhuber and other SA leaders at Bad Wiessee.

Berchtold's father died on 29 April 1935 and his funeral in Munich several days later was attended by many 'old fighters' of the Party. Josef Senior had been an early member of the NSDAP, joining in 1920 and participating in the failed putsch of November 1923.

On 1 January 1936, Berchtold received further promotion to SA-Brigadeführer. In 1935 he was nominated as a Town Councillor for the '*Hauptstadt der Bewegung*', the name by which the Party referred to Munich as '*Capital of the Movement*'. Berchtold was elected to the Reichstag on 29 March 1936, representing Baden, and he was promoted to SA-Gruppenführer on 1 May 1937. He underwent reserve military service in April 1940 and held the rank of Hauptmann der Reserve. His final promotion, to SA-Obergruppenführer, took place on 30 January 1942.

Berchtold was an associate contributor to many Party publications. He was the author of the text in the book *Adolf Hitler über Deutschland*, a report of Hitler's air tour of Germany. He was a member of the Reich Culture Senate and the Culture Group of the SA. He died on 23 August 1962 in Herrsching am Ammersee.

Right: Josef Berchtold.

Below: An early photograph of Berchtold (left) admiring Hitler.

Berchtold (far left) leads an early column of SA men.

Berchtold leans on the vehicle cab roof as leader of the Stosstrupp Adolf Hitler. Julius Schreck holds the banner.

Berchtold occupies the seat behind Himmler during a flight in an election campaign.

Hitler entertains members of the Stosstrupp Hitler at the Brown House. Berchtold stands to Hitler's right. Schaub is behind Berchtold and Fiehler is between Hitler and Ulrich Graf.

Berchtold watches Hitler sign autographs in the basement restaurant of the Brown House.

Berchtold (left, partly obscured) listens to Hitler.

A newspaper photograph of Berchtold in SA-Gruppenführer uniform, with a collection tin.

Left to right: Hoffmann, Neurath, Hitler, Brückner, Siebert, Bormann, and Berchtold.

Berchtold in SA uniform (right centre), following the coffin of his father in Munich.

Berchtold bows his head at his father's graveside.

Berchtold stands beside his mother at his father's funeral.

GOTTLOB CHRISTIAN BERGER

GOTTLOB BERGER was born the son of master carpenter and sawmill owner Johannes Berger and his wife Maria (born Moser) on 16 July 1896 in Gerstetten. Two of his brothers fell in the First World War and a third was shot as an enemy agent in the USA in September 1918. Gottlob attended elementary school and secondary school in Gerstetten from 1902 until 1910. He then trained as a teacher specialising in physical exercise from 1910 until 1914 at the Nürtingen Teacher Training College.

On 6 August 1914, he volunteered for duty with the 127th Infantry Regiment in Ulm and was deployed to the Western Front on 18 October 1914 with the 247th Reserve Infantry Regiment. On 31 October 1914, he was wounded in the buttocks and right thigh and was hospitalised as a result, not returning to duty with his unit until 5 December 1914. He received a slight flesh wound to his back, caused by a bullet graze on 18 March 1915 at Ypres, but he was not withdrawn from the front. He attended an officer candidate course at Sennelager from 18 May until 22 August 1915, but returned to the front and was seriously wounded in the stomach on 4 October 1915. At first he was treated in a field hospital at Ledeghem, but was transferred to Kiel on 1 January 1916. He remained in hospital there until 7 April 1916, when he re-joined the Reserve Infantry Regiment 247 as a Leutnant der Reserve—having been promoted on 6 November 1915.

On 17 January 1917, Berger transferred to Infantry Regiment 476 as a supply officer and company commander. From 1 June 1917 until 1 June 1918, he was deputy adjutant of the 3rd battalion. He received another light wound in June 1918, when he was hit by a grenade splinter. From 8 July until 30 December 1918, he was posted as Ordnance Officer of Infantry Regiment 476 and was deputy adjutant of the regiment from 20 August until 26 August 1918. He was posted to the Replacement Battalion of Infantry Regiment 475 from 31 December 1918 until his discharge from military service—with a 70 per cent war disability pension (from 13 July 1919)—on 31 January 1919.

After the war, on 1 March 1919, Berger joined the civil guard Württemberg-Nord in Heilbronn. He attended the Academy for Gymnastic and Sports Teachers,

Tübingen, from 1920 to 1921 and subsequently taught gymnastics in Lichtenstein and Gerstetten. Finally, he was employed as a headmaster in Esslingen. He was appointed Oberleutnant der Reserve on 5 February 1921 and was a member of the Border Troops West from 1 April 1921 until 9 November 1923.

Berger was married on 23 April 1921 to Maria Danzback (born on 20 April 1900 in Grossalt; NSDAP number 1 224 214). They had a daughter on 18 April 1922; she died on 11 November 1942. Their son, Wolf, was born on 23 July 1923 and was killed in action on 11 February 1943 at Kharkov, whilst serving with the Waffen-SS. Two other children blessed the marriage: a girl, on 28 June 1926, and a boy, on 21 December 1938. Berger's son-in-law, Andreas Schmidt, was the leader of the German Volksgruppe in Rumania.

He joined the NSDAP on 6 February 1922 and early the following year he founded the NSDAP Ortsgruppe in Gerstetten. From October to November 1923, Berger was the commander of the Ulm National Socialist Battalion and was briefly arrested for stockpiling weapons for the Munich Beer Hall Putsch on 9 November 1923. From 1 April 1924 until 30 April 1929, Berger was a member of Freikorps Damm.

He obtained employment between 1928 and 1933 as a head teacher in Wankheim, near Tübingen, and for the last three years he was also involved in covert military training.

Berger joined the SA on 15 November 1930 and re-enrolled in the National Socialist German Workers' Party (NSDAP) on 1 January 1931, receiving membership number 426 875. He was SA-Sturmführer of SA-Sturm 10 in Tübingen on 15 January 1931, and was promoted to SA-Sturmbannführer of SA-Sturmbann III/126 on 1 August 1931. On 10 February 1932, he was again promoted, this time to SA-Standartenführer (backdated to 1 January 1931) and was appointed as head of SA training. He was placed in command of SA-Standarte 125 on 1 July 1932, and from 29 July 1932 he was given temporary command of SA-Untergruppe Württemberg. This post was confirmed on 15 October 1932, when he was also promoted to SA-Oberführer. He was elected to the Württemberg legislature in April 1933, subsequently going on to hold a number of local appointments on councils and committees in Württemberg.

He resigned from the SA on 1 July 1933 after a disagreement with younger SA leaders, but he was assigned to the office of chief of SA training services from 15 September 1934 until 31 August 1935.

He attended the infantry school at Döberitz in September 1935 and was attached to an infantry regiment in February 1936. On 1 July 1936, he became a Hauptmann der Reserve. On 10 November 1938, he served with Kavallerieschützen-Regiment 9 in Sorau, and was re-designated as Rittmeister der Reserve.

Berger joined the SS on 30 January 1936 with membership number 275 991 and was placed on the staff of SS-Oberabschnitt Südwest as a SS-Oberführer. He was created head of sport for the Oberabschnitt on 25 February 1936 and on 1 July

1937, he was appointed Director of Physical Training for the Württemburg Ministry of Culture. He transferred on 1 October 1937 to the Staff of the Reichsführer-SS and was nominated as chief of SS sports teams. He was appointed chief of the SS recruiting department, SS Central Office and SS Sports Office on 1 August 1938, and was promoted to SS-Brigadeführer on 20 April 1939.

From 1938 to 1939, he was a department leader in the Reich Ministry for Education and SS liaison officer to the Freikorps Sudetenland. He was elected as a Reichstag Deputy for Wahlkreis Düsseldorf. Among the other State offices he held were District Hunt Master and Member of the Academy for Physical Education.

On 1 October 1939, he was appointed Chief of Amt VI (Registration) and Amt X (Physical Training) in the SS-Hauptamt (*SS Central Office*). He took over complete control of the SS-Hauptamt on 1 April 1940 and simultaneously became Chief of the Reserve Office of the Waffen-SS, retaining this post until the end of the war. He gained the rank of Generalmajor der Waffen-SS on 15 August 1940. From March 1941 until 1945, he was chief of the German Volunteers Bureau and was promoted to SS-Gruppenführer und Generalleutnant der Waffen-SS on 20 April 1941. From 1942 to 1945, he was chief of the Postal Control Office of the Reich Postal Service. From July 1942 until 10 August 1943, he was the Reichsführer-SS personal liaison officer to Rosenberg's Ministry of the Occupied East. He gained diplomatic rank after taking responsibility for the leadership staff for politics from 10 August 1943 until 20 January 1945.

On 21 June 1943, he was promoted to SS-Obergruppenführer und General der Waffen-SS. Berger was appointed Director of Prisoners of War in 1944 and, after 1 October, he was responsible for all prisoners-of-war in German hands.

He was posted to Slovakia on 31 August 1944 as HSSPF and commander-in-chief of German forces, but he relinquished command to the new HSSPF, SS-Obergruppenführer Hermann Höfle, on 20 September 1944—a move which probably saved his life, as Höfle was executed by the post-war Slovakian government. On 7 October 1944, Berger was appointed as staff officer to the Volkssturm.

Berger was captured by French troops in Berchtesgaden and was interned at Augsburg, London, Grizedale Hall in Cumbria, Brussels, Frankfurt-Main, Nuremberg, and Dachau, plus other short stays at various centres. He was sometimes held in solitary confinement. He was arraigned in one of the US trials that followed the International Military Tribunal at Nuremberg. He was found guilty of war crimes and on 11 April 1949, he was sentenced to twenty-five years in prison. He was released from Landsberg Prison on 15 December 1951.

Berger was not trusted by many of his fellow Waffen-SS officers who looked upon him as a spy for Hitler and Himmler. He certainly reported to Himmler on the political reliability and trustworthiness of the Gauleiter. He was well-connected, counting the Croatian Ustascha leader, Ante Pavelitsch, among his friends. He eventually returned to his hometown of Gerstetten, where he answered many letters written to him by genuine researchers and the curious. Gottlob Berger died on 5 January 1975 in Stuttgart and he was buried six days later in the town cemetery at Gerstetten—next to his wife who had died in 1966. Although not popular with many of his contemporaries, several hundred ex-Waffen-SS men nevertheless attended the ceremony. He gained the thanks and respect of various prisoners-of-war for whom he was responsible, evidenced by a plaque on his tombstone which reads:

> IN GRATEFUL MEMORY OF
> GOTTLOB BERGER
> GENERAL OF WAFFEN-SS
> WHO PROTECTED AND CARED FOR
> U.S. AIR FORCE PRISONERS OF WAR
> DURING WORLD WAR II
> DELMAR T. SPIVEY
> MAJ. GEN. U.S. AIR FORCE

Left and right: Gottlob Berger in civilian attire.

An early SS photograph.

SS-Oberführer Berger.

Berger spectating.

SS-Brigadeführer Berger.

Berger in his leather SS greatcoat.

Berger and Himmler accept a posey from a little admirer.

A formal studio portrait of Berger.

SS-Gruppenführer Berger.

Berger enjoys the sunshine.

Left and right: SS-Obergruppenführer Berger.

Obergruppenführer Berger addresses a group of SS men.

Berger in conversation at Feldkommandostelle Hegewaldheim during a visit by the Grand Mufti of Jerusalem (back to camera).

Berger and Werner Best (far left).

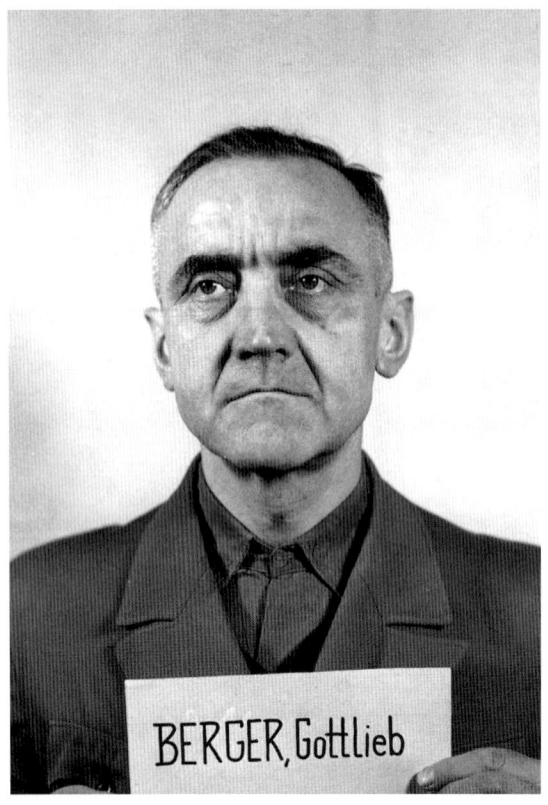

Prisoner of war.

A post-war image of Berger.

The grave of Gottlob Berger.

THEODOR FRIEDRICH WILHELM HERMANN BERKELMANN

THEODOR BERKELMANN was born in Ban St Martin, near Metz, on 17 April 1891. A member of an evangelical family, his parents were customs official Fritz Otto Berkelmann (born on 9 March 1866) and his wife, Marie Luise (born Jung on 26 July 1874). Theodor attended elementary school in Flattershausen from 1900 until 1905, high school in Switzerland between 1905 and 1906, junior high school in Münster from 1906 to 1910, and high school in Colmar from 1910 to 1913, when he graduated.

On 1 October 1913, he joined the 11th Jäger Battalion, and by outbreak of hostilities in 1914 he was a Leutnant der Reserve with the 83rd Reserve Infantry Regiment. He served on the Eastern Front, the South-Eastern Front, and the Western Front with this unit. He also served with the 94th Reserve Infantry Regiment as adjutant, being wounded twice.

Berkelmann joined the Freikorps Hülsen in January 1919 and in September 1919, he was discharged from service. He was unemployed for four months until 18 January 1920, when he found work as a miner. He left this employment in August 1922 to work in a stone quarry for six months, before being employed as a clerk in an insurance office until November 1923.

He was married to Gertrud Josephine Frederike Paul on 29 September 1923 in Köslin. The marriage ended in divorce in Dresden on 27 March 1942, after the couple had produced no children—however, they adopted a daughter, Renate (born 5 February 1933).

From December 1923 until 1 April 1925, he was the commercial manager of an agricultural trading co-operative, but he returned to the insurance industry as an agent for one year from April 1925 until 1 April 1926. Next he was employed as a sports and education teacher in Upper Silesia until 1 February 1930. From 1 February 1930 until 1 March 1931, Berkelmann worked as a farm labourer in Canada.

He joined the NSDAP on 1 May 1929 and was allocated membership number 128 245. On his return from Canada in March 1931, he became active again in National Socialist politics, assisting the leader of SS-Standarte 23 in Oppeln with training. He joined the SA on 15 June 1931. He was immediately promoted to SA-Standartenführer on the staff of the SA leadership, and was posted as a trainer and deputy head instructor at the Reich SA leadership school in Munich. He retained this appointment until 6 March 1932, when he transferred to the SS—immediately gaining the rank of SS-Standartenführer—with SS number 6 019. He was appointed as adjutant of the Reichsführer-SS and relinquished his SA membership and rank.

On 1 October 1932, he was assigned to the post of chief of staff of SS-Gruppe Nord in Hamburg-Altona, and six months later he was selected as commander of SS-Standarte 24 in Oldenburg. On 11 December 1933, he transferred to the staff of SS-Abschnitt VI in Breslau. He was promoted to SS-Oberführer on 30th January 1934, taking command of the Abschnitt. He was again promoted on 9 September 1934, to SS-Brigadeführer.

Berkelmann was elected to the Reichstag as the deputy for Dresden-Bautzen on 29 March 1936, and was then transferred to SS-Oberabschnitt Elbe on 1 April 1936 as Oberabschnitts Führer. On 13 September 1936, he was promoted to SS-Gruppenführer, and was appointed as HSSPF Elbe on 28 June 1938. This was the first of several postings as HSSPF, as a result of reorganisation and redesignation: West on 20 April 1940, Saar-Lothringen on 9 July 1940, Lothringen-Saarphalz on 2 October 1940, Westmark on 3 February 1941, and Rhein on 10 December 1941. He was designated a Generalleutnant der Polizei on 15 April 1941, and was promoted to SS-Obergruppenführer und General der Polizei on 30 January 1942.

Berkelmann was married in Dresden on 8 April 1942 to Gabriele Alexandra Freifrau von Finck (born von Wolffersdorff in Züllichau on 21 January 1918). The couple had one daughter—Heide.

With the two posts of Westmark and Rhein combining on 21 May 1943, Berkelmann was appointed as HSSPF Rhein-Westmark. On 9 November 1943, he received his final posting as HSSPF Warthe in Posen, and retained this post until his death from a brain tumour on 27 December 1943 in Posen. His funeral service was held three days later in the Kaiser-Friedrich Museum in Posen, when Gauleiter and Reichsstatthalter Arthur Greiser represented Hitler and SS-Obergruppenführer Wilhelm Koppe represented the Reichsführer-SS.

Berkelmann (far left, standing) as an instructor at the SA Reich leadership school in Munich.

Berkelmann (far right) and Heissmeyer visit SS-Standarte 51 in Göttingen.

An early photograph of Berkelmann in SS uniform.

A *Das Schwarze Korps* newspaper photograph of SS-Brigadeführer Berkelmann.

Another contemporary newspaper portrait.

SS-Gruppenführer Theodor Berkelmann.

A formal studio study of SS-Gruppenführer Berkelmann wearing the Elbe cuff title.

Berkelmann with Himmler in 1940. Behind are Jüttner and Peiper.

In Metz, 1940, with Himmler and Peiper.

Clockwise from top left:

Berkelmann wearing the SS-Oberabschnitt West cuff title.

The full-length photograph for Berkelmann's SS-RuSHA file.

SS-RuSHA file photos also included a side-profile image.

SS-Obergruppenführer Berkelmann.

Right: Berkelmann as part of the reception committee for an inspection visit by Himmler and Wolff at Wiesbaden on 31 August 1942. Himmler chats with Gauleiter Sprenger.

Below: Wiesbaden airfield, 31 August 1942.

KARL RUDOLF WERNER BEST

W ERNER BEST was born on 10 July 1903 in Darmstadt, the first of two sons born to Georg Konrad Best, a post inspector and Oberleutnant der Reserve, and his wife, Karoline (born Nöhl). Georg died on 4 October 1914, in Trier, of wounds sustained with Infantry Regiment 115 on the Western Front.

Werner attended elementary school and high school in Liegnitz from 1909 to 1912, when he transferred to the Südwall High School in Dortmund until 1914. Following the death of his father, the family moved to Gonsenheim, near Mainz, where the young Werner attended the local high school to study classics until February 1921. During this period, Best used the alias 'Hagen' to join the Korps Adelphia, a student union. In the summer of 1919, he founded the local branch of the German National Youth League in Mainz and joined the German National Peoples' Party as a youth leader. He studied law at Frankfurt-Main University, Freiburg University and at Giessen University from March 1921 until May 1925. During his university education, he actively participated in numerous youth polit- ical groups. Best also took part in various acts of sabotage against the occupying French authorities, for which he received a prison sentence of three years from a French military court in Mainz on 12 July 1924. He was released on 12 September 1924 following a clemency plea by his mother, backed by the German government. In March–April 1923 he volunteered for the Marburg Jäger Battalion.

He continued his law studies, this time at the University of Hannover, from October 1924 until 1925, successfully passing his first state examinations as an articled clerk in Giessen on 14 May 1925. From 1925 until 1928, he was a judicial court civil servant in Mainz, in preparation for his legal qualification. He wrote a political essay in 1926 entitled *'International Nationalist Politics'*, which became a focal point for German nationalist circles and gained Best a reputation as a high- ly-respected theorist. In the spring of 1927, he was expelled from the German National Peoples' Party for his extremist views.

Best obtained his doctorate in law at Heidelberg on 21 December 1927 with a thesis on the question of failures of deliberate collectives. On 2 November 1928, he passed his assessor examinations in Darmstadt, qualifying him as a judge's assistant. From November 1928 to 1 December 1931, Best was employed as a court lawyer and then a judge in the judiciary of Hesse.

He joined the NSDAP on 1 November 1930 and was allocated membership number 341 338. He was appointed as legal advisor to the Gau leadership in Hessen-Darmstadt. The following year he was involved in a political scandal, based on what became known as the *'Boxheimer document'*—this comprised of secret emergency measures only to be introduced if the communists became involved in civil unrest. They included action to seize power and introduction of the death penalty for possession of weapons and opposition to the National Socialists. The contents were publicised by a Party member, Hermann Schäfer, and Best—suspected of being the author—was suspended from his official posts on 28 November 1931. The ensuing investigation was finally terminated on 12 October 1932, on orders of the Advocate General in Leipzig, due to insufficient evidence. Schäfer was found shot to death on 18 July 1933 in a wood near Frankfurt, and Best was suspected of ordering his execution.

Werner Best married Hildegard Regner (born 23 May 1909 in Mainz) on 24 December 1930. They had three daughters and two sons between 5 March 1932 and 19 June 1942.

Best was elected as a NSDAP member of the parliament of Hesse in 1931, and was also the Honorary Kreisleiter for Mainz from 1932 until 1933. On 6 March 1933, he was nominated as the Special Commissioner for the Hesse police, and seven days later he was appointed State Commissioner. From 10 July 1933 until 9 November 1933, he was the Landespolizei President for Hesse and the Leader of Abteilung IA (Police) in the Hesse State Ministry.

Best joined the SS as a SS-Anwärter on 13 November 1931, with membership number 23 377. He was promoted to SS-Scharführer on 24 April 1933 and to SS-Truppführer the following day. On 6 May 1933, he was commissioned as an SS-Sturmführer. This rank was superceded by that of SS-Untersturmführer and Best is recorded as such on 22 June 1933, when he was assigned to SS-Abschnitt XI in Wiesbaden. He was brought to the attention of Reinhard Heydrich, chief of the Sicherheitsdienst (SD), by Himmler in late summer 1933. Best was subsequently transferred from the staff of SS-Abschnitt XI to that of the SD, becoming SD leader of SD-Oberabschnitt Südwest on 15 October 1933. He handed over his post in SD-Oberabschnitt Südwest on 9 November 1933, when he was promoted to SS-Obersturmführer and appointed as Director of Administration and Legal Departments in the SD central office.

Best's promotion to SS-Sturmhauptführer took effect on 15 December 1933. He became Leader of Department I (Administration and Justice) in the central office of the State Police on 22 January 1934. On the same day, he was appointed as Commissionary Leader of Department III (Abwehrpolizei) in the SD central office. He was also SD commander of SD-Oberabschnitt Süd from March 1934 until 1 January 1935.

On 15 June 1934, he was promoted to SS-Sturmbannführer, and this was quickly followed by promotion to SS-Obersturmbannführer on 4 July 1934 for his acts of loyalty during the so-called 'Röhm purge'. With Carl-Albrecht Oberg, Best had co-ordinated the arrests of the SA leadership in Bavaria and the ensuing executions.

In September 1934 Best received a two-week attachment with the Geheime-Staatspolizeiamt (*Gestapo*) in Berlin. From 1 January 1935, Best was appointed as deputy commander of the Gestapo and had control of Department I (Administration, Personnel, and Law). He therefore had a desk in both Prinz-Albrecht-Strasse 8 and the SD headquarters at the Prinz-Albrecht Palace.

On 20 April 1935, he was again promoted, this time to SS-Standartenführer. On 17 June 1936, he was assigned to the leadership of the Administration and Justice Department in the Head Office of the Security Police. At the same time, as one of Heydrich's favoured young intellectuals, he was selected as deputy chief of SD head office, retaining this position until 1 October 1939. During this period he received further SS promotion: on 9 November 1936 he rose to SS-Oberführer, and on 20 April 1939 to SS-Brigadeführer.

During the successful years of 1936 to 1940, Best held many official posts. He was a Regierungsdirektor, Ministerialrat, Ministerialdirigent, and Ministerialdirektor in the Reich Ministry of the Interior. He was a member of the Association of German National Socialist Jurists and the Department Head of Police at the University of Greater Berlin. He issued an instruction on 5 October 1938 that all passports held by Jews were to be stamped with a large, red letter 'J'. He also issued the order on 27 October 1938 that all Jews currently held for deportation were to be sent immediately across the frontier into Poland. The latter months saw him constantly at variance with Heydrich. Although he was appointed as chief of Department I (Organisation and Justice) in the new Reichssicherheitshauptamt (RSHA) on 27 September 1939, by 12 June 1940 his position was untenable and he resigned his security department posts.

He volunteered for military training—not with the Waffen-SS, but with the Wehrmacht, and served with the 15th Infantry Regiment in Frieberg-Hessen from 13th June 1940 until July 1940.

He transferred to the Diplomatic Corps and was posted to the office of Chief of the Military Administration in Paris from 1 August 1940 until 1942, with the rank of Ministerialdirektor from 3 August 1940. In August 1942, he was appointed to the Ministry of Foreign Affairs and he became a Ministerialdirektor in the Foreign Ministry on 3 November 1942. Best was appointed as the Reich Plenipotentiary in Denmark on 5 November 1942. He was promoted to SS-Gruppenführer on 9 November 1942 and finally to SS-Obergruppenführer on 20 April 1944.

Best did not impose strict deportation measures on the Jews during his period of office in Denmark. In doing so, he probably saved his own life and that of the

HSSPF Günther Pancke. Best was a strong opponent of Jewish deportations, taking the view that co-operation from the Danish royal family and populace would cease if the deportations were carried out.

Best was placed under house arrest at Rydhave, his residence outside Copenhagen, from 5 May to 21 May 1945. He was formally arrested by Danish authorities on 21 May 1945 at the Citadel in Copenhagen and brought before a temporary Copenhagen court which ordered his further detention. The British arrested him on 21 June 1945 and transported him to the UK, before he was returned to Germany in March 1946. He was held in the witness wing at Nuremberg and gave evidence between 31 July 1946 and 1 August 1946, before being handed over to Danish authorities for trial in Copenhagen. He stood trial between 16 June and 20 September 1948, when he was found guilty of acts of terrorism and complicity in the deaths of 136 Danish Jews. He was sentenced to death. The sentence was reduced on appeal to five years in prison on 18 July 1949, but the Danish High Court increased this to twelve years' imprisonment on 17 March 1950. He was released from Horsens Prison on 29 August 1951.

Best found employment from 1951 until 1953 in the law offices of Dr Ernst Achenbach in Essen. From 1953 until 1971, he was the legal advisor to the Hugo Stinnes Group in Mülheim. He assisted several former colleagues from the RSHA in their defence against allegations of crimes committed during the Nazi years. He was arrested in March 1969 and held in the Moabit Prison in Berlin; he was charged with complicity in the deaths of at least 8,723 people. He was released in March 1971 and further charges were finally dropped on 25 August 1983. From 1972 until 1983, he was the legal advisor to several companies. Werner Best died in Mülheim on 23 June 1989. His body was cremated and his ashes were scattered in the Baltic Sea.

Georg Konrad Best.

The young lawyer.

Best was recruited to the SD by Heydrich, on the suggestion of Himmler.

The deputy head of the SD office.

Best and Heydrich had differing opinions on the rule of law.

Best listens to Himmler speaking.

SS-Oberführer Best.

SD leader.

Best addresses members of the frontier police. Behind him is Dr Hans Trummler.

Right: A rare photograph of Best as Military Administrator.

Below: Best's Ausweis as Military Administrator.

Clockwise from top left:

Hitler's representative in Denmark with Danish Minister of State Eric Scavenius, 6 February 1943.

Best examines a piece of pottery at his home.

Best with Eric Scavenius.

Best visiting Terboven, in Norway.

Another diplomatic duty.

The Reich Plenipotentiary in Denmark.

Best at a memorial ceremony in Denmark.

SS-Gruppenführer Werner Best.

SS-Obergruppenführer Best enjoying himself.

Best delivers an after-dinner speech.

Best's private residence in Rydhave.

The living room.

Best with Gottlob Berger.

SS-Obergruppenführer Werner Best.

Best and his wife leaving Rydhave for the last time.

The couple in captivity.

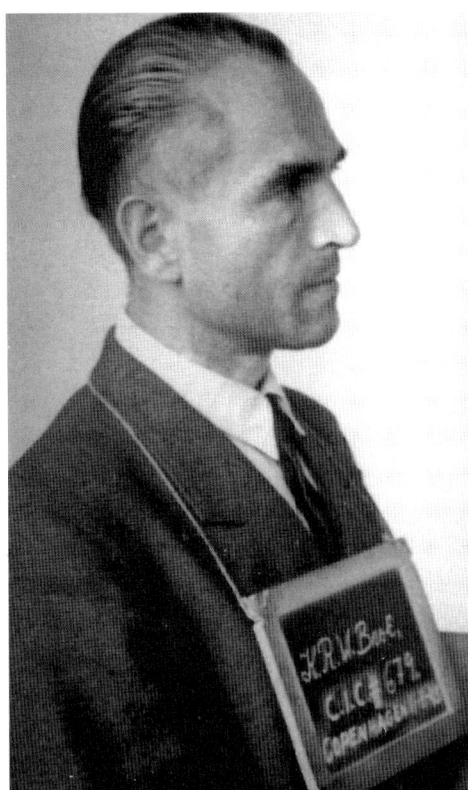

Left and right: Prisoner of War.

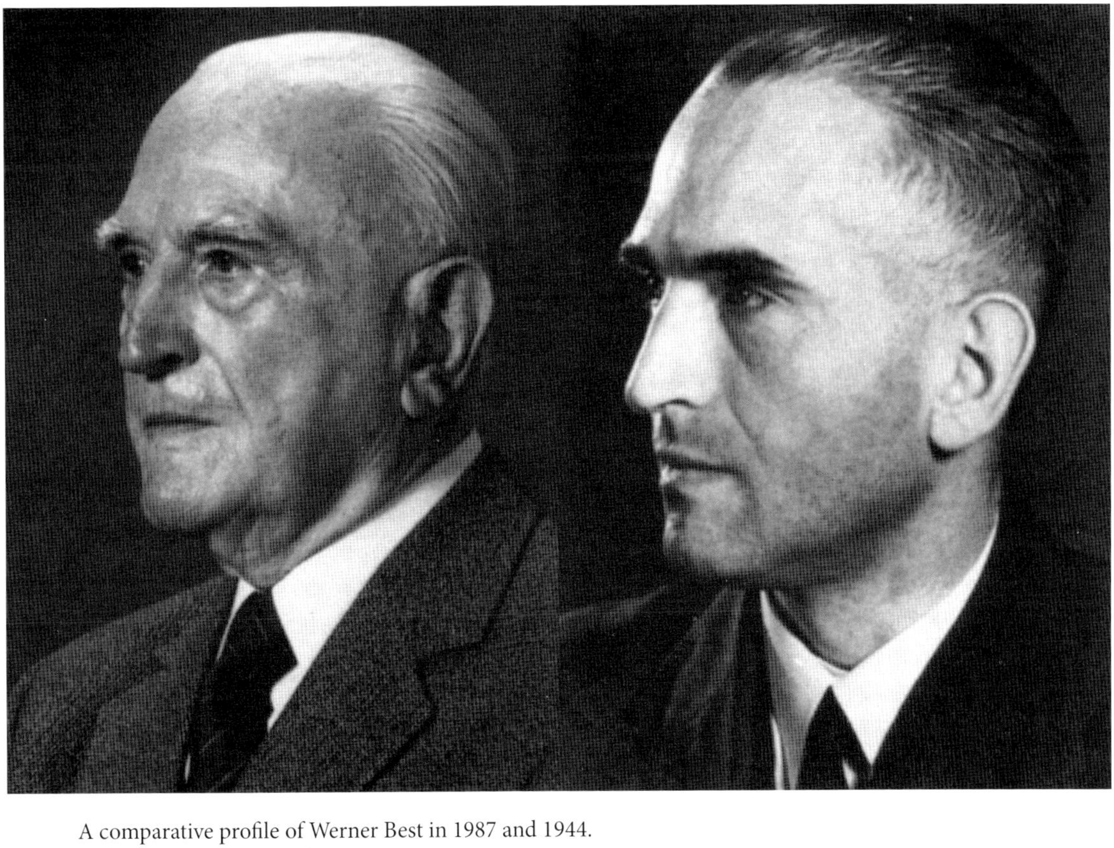

A comparative profile of Werner Best in 1987 and 1944.

WILHELM BITTRICH

WILHELM 'WILLI' BITTRICH was born on 26 February 1894 in Wernigerode, the son of clerk and later commercial traveller Hugo Andreas Bittrich and his wife, Luise Helene Augusta Bittrich (born Bode, died March 1895). Following the early death of his wife, Hugo Bittrich remarried and the young Willi was brought up by a stepmother.

After attending elementary school and middle school from 1900 until 1912, Bittrich trained as a sports and gymnastics teacher, but the desire to become a military officer was paramount. He volunteered for the Army on 30 July 1914, joining the 4th Magdeburg Jäger Battalion. From 10 September 1914 until 1916, he saw active service with Reserve Jäger Battalion 19, Jäger Battalion 8 and the 77th Infantry Regiment. He was wounded in Carpathia on 5 December 1914 and was promoted to Leutnant der Reserve on 15 October 1915. He joined a flying detachment in 1916 and underwent training as a pilot, seeing active service with Field Flight Section 27, Flight Section A266 and Fighter Section 37.

From March to July 1919, he was a volunteer with Freikorps 'von Hülsen' in Upper Silesia. In January 1920, he joined the Erhardt Brigade, remaining with that unit until June of the same year. He also joined the Schutzregiment Grosse Berlin in March 1920, and traded in stocks and shares in his spare time.

Bittrich was married to the actress Käte Blume (born on 16 March 1888 in Bromberg, died on 10 June 1971 in Munsing) on 29 December 1922. They had no children.

On 1 January 1923, Bittrich entered service with the Reichswehr as a flight instructor at the flying school in Oberschleissheim. From August to October 1925, he secretly trained pilots for the German Army at Lipezk in the Soviet Union, returning there again in May–June 1930 in a similar role. He then served in the Reichswehr-Battalion Berlin, and from 1930 until 1932, he was a civilian employee of the Reichswehr at the flight school in Halberstadt.

Willi Bittrich joined the NSDAP on 1 December 1931 and was allocated membership number 829 700. He was a member of the SA from March 1932 until June 1932.

Bittrich joined the SS on 1 July 1932 with SS number 39 177 and was posted to SS Flight Staff East. He became the leader of this unit on 31 October 1932, as a newly promoted SS-Sturmführer, and was assigned as an instructor to SS-Abschnitt XIII in Stettin on 1 November 1933. He was posted as commander of SS-Standarte 74 on 8 March 1934 and was promoted to SS-Obersturmführer on 12 April 1934. Another promotion occurred on 17 June 1936, when he rose to SS-Hauptsturmführer.

On 7 August 1934, he was transferred to the Hamburg Political Squad in the SS-Verfügungstruppe, taking command on 25 August 1934. On 1 April 1935, he was posted to the staff of SS-Standarte 2 'Germania' in Hamburg, transferring once again on 17 May to command the 2nd Sturm of SS-Standarte 1 'Deutschland' in Munich. He was promoted to SS-Sturmbannführer on 1 October 1936, taking charge of 2nd Sturmbann of SS-Standarte 'Deutschland' and retaining this command until 23 March 1938.

On 30 January 1938, Bittrich was promoted to SS-Obersturmbannführer and took control of SS-Standarte 3 in Vienna on 23 March 1938, until 30 April 1938. He was given command of the 1st Sturmbann, SS-Regiment 'Der Führer', on 1 May 1938 and transferred to the staff of the Leibstandarte-SS 'Adolf Hitler' as chief of operations on 1 June 1939, on promotion to SS-Standartenführer.

On 1 February 1940, Bittrich transferred to SS-Verfügungstruppe Inspectorate 'E'. He was promoted to SS-Oberführer der Waffen-SS on 1 September 1940, after being posted to the headquarters staff of the Waffen-SS on 15 August 1940. He transferred to the command of SS-Regiment 'Deutschland' in SS Division 'Reich' (*later 'Das Reich'*) on 1 December 1940. After Paul Hausser was wounded, he took over command of the division on 14 October 1941 and was promoted to SS-Brigadeführer und Generalmajor der Waffen-SS on 19 October 1941.

Another transfer (effective date 1 January 1942) to the Waffen-SS officer reserve list took place on 8 January 1942, as a result of illness. Once fit for duty, a further move to the command staff of the SS-Cavalry Brigade took place on 1 May 1942. He was then selected as the commander of the 9th SS-Panzer-Grenadier-Division 'Hohenstaufen' on 15 February 1943. Further promotion to SS-Gruppenführer und Generalleutnant der Waffen-SS resulted on 1 May 1943. He transferred on 10 July 1944 to the 2nd SS-Panzer Corps as commanding General, and received his final promotion to SS-Obergruppenführer und General der Waffen-SS on 1 August 1944.

Bittrich was one of the most decorated officers of the SS. He was awarded the Knight's Cross of the Iron Cross on 14 December 1941, the oakleaves to the Knight's Cross (*the 563rd recipient*) on 28 August 1944, and the swords to the Knight's Cross (*the 151st recipient*)—awarded immediately by personal order of the commanding General of the 6th Panzer Army (*Sepp Dietrich*) on 6 May 1945. Bittrich participated in the Normandy campaign. He was the commander of the German forces at Arnhem in September 1944, during the Allied offensive code-named 'Operation Market Garden'—the last German victory of the war. Both his men and his opponents respected him. Paul Hausser described Bittrich as '*headstrong*', but a '*good, competent commander*' in a confidential report of 21 June 1944.

He was captured by the Americans on 8 May 1945 and was handed over to the French authorities in 1948 to answer charges of alleged war crimes. He was sentenced to five years' imprisonment on 22 October 1953, but he was repatriated in 1954 having been deemed to have already served his time in detention. He was elected as chairman of HIAG (*the organisation to assist ex-Waffen-SS servicemen*) from 1972 until his death. One of the chief mourners at the funeral of Sepp Dietrich in 1966, Willi Bittrich died in Wolfratshausen on 19 April 1979.

A young Bittrich in civilian suit.

A member of SS-Standarte 74 wearing his SA/SS Flyers' Badge.

SS-Sturmbannführer Bittrich.

Portrait as SS-Oberführer.

Bittrich on horseback, leading a troop of SS-'Germania'.

Bittrich (right) with Hermann Fegelein.

SS-Brigadeführer Wilhelm Bittrich proudly wearing his Knight's Cross.

A signed photograph.

Bittrich (second left) emerges to take up his position in the honour guard for Heydrich's funeral service in Prague, 7 June 1942.

Wearing his field-grey Waffen-SS uniform.

A formal portrait of SS-Gruppenführer Willi Bittrich.

Talking tactics.

Speaking at the funeral of Sepp Dietrich in Ludwigsburg, 1966.

A portrait sketch of SS-Brigadeführer Bittrich.

At a post-war trial.

Bittrich at eighty, wearing his Knight's Cross with
Oakleaves and Swords.

The grave of Wilhelm Bittrich.

ERNST WILHELM BOHLE

ERNST BOHLE was born at 14 Bertram Road, Manningham, in Bradford, England, on 28 July 1903, the fourth child in a family of five children—three girls and two boys (Heinrich, Hermine, Marianne, Ernst, and Hanny). His father was Hermann Bohle (born on 4 October 1876, died in Berlin on 12 July 1943), a university professor and a doctor of electrical engineering. He later became a NSDAP Landesgruppenleiter der Auslands-Organisation (*area leader of the foreign organisation for NSDAP members*) in South Africa from 1932 until 1935, and also a NSDAP Gauamtsleiter für Technik (*NSDAP area office leader for technology*). His mother was named Antonie (née Knode). His elder brother, Heinrich, later became an Oberregierungsrat (*government councillor*). At the age of three, Ernst moved with his family to Cape Town, South Africa, where he attended the local primary school, followed by the English Grammar School from 1908 until 1919. Ernst held dual Anglo-German nationality and when the family returned to Germany after the war, he studied political science and economics at Cologne University, Berlin State University and a commercial trading school in Berlin. He graduated in 1923.

Bohle was married on 14 November 1925 to Gertrud Bachman (born in Kassel on 27 November 1904). They had one son, who was born on 15 July 1928.

From 1924 until 1927, Bohle was employed as a business department head and company secretary in various English-speaking import and export companies in Hamburg and the Rhineland. In 1927 he was employed by the Chrysler Corporation in Hamburg, working for that organisation until 1930, when he started his own business dealing in motor parts. He also acted as an interpreter for the Egyptian Consulate in Hamburg.

Bohle was appointed as the honorary consultant for South Africa, South-West Africa, the USA and the UK, for the NSDAP Foreign Section in November 1931. However, he did not join the NSDAP until 1 March 1932, when he was allocated membership number 999 185. The same year he became the adjutant of Dr Hans Nieland, the Gauleiter and Gauinspektor (*regional inspector*) of the NSDAP Foreign Political Regions.

From 26 April 1933, Bohle took control of the NSDAP department which was responsible for Germans living abroad, and on 3 October 1933, he was attached to the office of the Deputy Führer (*Rudolf Hess*). On 1 August 1933, he was appointed leader of the office for German women abroad—a post he would retain until 1 July 1939. He was elected as a member of the Reichstag on 12 November 1933, and was appointed as NSDAP Gauleiter and the Leader of the Foreign Organisation of the NSDAP (*Auslandsorganisation*—AO) on 17 February 1934. From 21 December 1937, he was officially recognised as chief of the AO in the Reich Foreign Ministry. He held the government rank of Under State Secretary, with promotion to State Secretary in 1938.

He joined the SS on 13 September 1936 with the rank of SS-Brigadeführer. He was posted to the staff of the Reichsführer-SS, with SS membership number 276 915. On 20 April 1937, he was promoted to SS-Gruppenführer, and finally to SS-Obergruppenführer on 21 June 1943.

Bohle handed himself in to the American authorities near Falkenau on 23 May 1945 and was interned at the detention centre for senior Nazis in the Palace Hotel in Mondorf-les-Bain, Luxembourg ('*Ashcan*'). He appeared as a witness before the International Military Tribunal in Nuremberg on 25 March 1946, and then appeared before the court as a defendant in the Wilhelmstrasse Case from 1947 to 1949. He was the only defendant to plead guilty to the indictment and was sentenced to five years in prison on 11 April 1949. By the end of the process he was an ill and broken man. He was released from custody on 21 December 1949. Although he found employment as a sales representative in Hamburg, he never fully recovered and died of a heart attack in Düsseldorf on 9 November 1960.

The young NSDAP member Ernst Bohle.

Bohle was appointed as Gauleiter for the NSDAP Auslands Organisation.

Gauleiter Bohle.

A smiling Bohle.

Left: Bohle (second left) with Hess.

Below: von Ribbentrop strains to hear a question from the press.

Bohle, in SS-Gruppenführer uniform (right), arrives with von Schirach and Murr.

SS-Gruppenführer Bohle salutes.

Bohle, von Schirach and Murr inspect a column of Hitler Youth.

Guests of honour Murr, von Schirach, and Bohle.

Gauleiter of the AO Ernst Bohle.

Bohle (front, third from right) visits the AO branch in Hamburg.

Bohle accompanies Hess at Landungsbrücken in Hamburg. In front is SS-Oberführer Georg Ahrens.

The AO sleeve diamond on Bohle's left sleeve.

Bohle with Constantin von Neurath.

Bohle poses in the sunshine.

Bohle follows Sepp Tiefenbacher after arriving at Himmler's Feldkommandostelle Hochwald in East Prussia.

Himmler in conversation with SS-Gruppenführer Bohle.

Bohle acknowledges a reception guard of honour.

SS-Obergruppenführer Bohle chatting with Heinz Harmel and two of his officers.

BOHLE, Ernst-Wilhelm

Above: Prisoner of War.

Left: Bohle receives his sentence at Nuremberg.

MARTIN LUDWIG BORMANN

Bormann, in the beginning a minor Nazi, steadily rose to a position of power and, particularly in the closing days, of great influence over Hitler...

Nuremberg IMT judgement, 1 October 1946

ARTIN BORMANN was born on 17 June 1900 in Halberstadt, the eldest son of a second marriage between Theodor Bormann, a former Prussian cavalry musician and a senior assistant employed in the postal service, and his second wife Antonie (born Mennong on 19 November 1863 in Wegeleben). Theodor's first wife, Louise Grobler, had died in 1898. Martin had a half-brother, Walter, and half-sister, Else, from his father's first marriage. He was baptised in the Lutheran Church—named after the Great Reformer. Soon after, in May 1901, another boy was born, but he did not survive. The third son, Albert, was born in Halberstadt on 2 September 1902 (died in Munich on 8 April 1989), and he was destined to become an adjutant of Adolf Hitler and the chief of his private chancellery. However, the two Bormann brothers detested each other. Theodor did not live long to enjoy his sons' childhood, succumbing to failing health and dying in Halberstadt in July 1903. His widow, Antonie, married bank employee Albert Vollhorn (died March 1923) in January 1904, and the family moved from the family home on Sedanstrasse to Eisenach in August 1906, where the young Martin attended a private school. In 1909 the family moved yet again—this time to Oberweimar, where Martin attended the local high school.

Martin enlisted in 1917 in the 35th Field Artillery Regiment, and in June 1918 he transferred to the 55th Field Artillery Regiment in Naumburg as a Kanonier (*artillery Private*). He remained with this unit until February 1919, but saw no active service.

Once leaving the Army, Bormann looked for employment on a country estate where he could learn farming. He was employed in farm work from 1919 until August 1920, when he took up a position as a supervisor on the Gut Herzberg Estate near Parchim, the seat of the Treuenfels family. He worked there until May 1926 and had to leave as a result of an affair with the estate owner's wife. However, it was this period that had a dramatic influence on the impressionable young Bormann.

From 1920 until 1926, he was a member of various anti-Jewish groups and in 1922 he joined the Rossbach Freikorps. During the night of 31 March 1923, members of the Rossbach Freikorps murdered a man called Walter Kadow. One of the perpetrators was Rudolf Höss, the later commandant of Auschwitz concentration camp. It was discovered that Bormann had issued instructions to have Kadow beaten up, but the deed had gone too far. Bormann was arrested in the summer of 1923 and spent some months behind bars on remand. He was released in September and appeared before the court in Leipzig on 12 March 1924. Bormann and his co-defendants were found guilty of manslaughter, with Bormann receiving a prison term of twelve months. He was released from the Elisabethstrasse prison in Leipzig in February 1925 and returned to his employer, but by May 1926 he had left Gut Herzberg and moved back in with his mother.

Bormann joined the Thuringian Frontbann in 1925 and was active in the leadership. There is confusion over the date that Bormann actually joined the NSDAP; his own account relates the date as May 1927, but his personal file records member number 60 508 joining on 27 February 1927. From April 1927 until 15 August 1930, he was a member of the SA. He became the district NSDAP press chairman for Thuringia on 1 November 1927 until 14 November 1928. From 1 April 1928 until 15 November 1928, Bormann was the NSDAP district leader in Jena and the Gau commercial manager and spokesman for Gau Thuringia. By now he was a full-time employee of the NSDAP. On 15 November 1928, he was appointed to the staff of the Reich SA leadership in Munich. He retained this post until 24 August 1930.

Bormann married Gerda Buch, the daughter of NSDAP judge Reichsleiter Walter Buch, on 2 September 1929. She was born on 27 October 1909 in Ronfleuz and held NSDAP membership number 120 112. Hitler was a guest at the wedding. The Bormanns had ten children: Adolf Martin, born 14 April 1930, Ilse (named after the wife of Rudolf Hess), and her twin sister, Ehrengard (named after his ex-mistress Ehrengard von Treuenfels), born on 9 July 1931. They were followed by Irmgard on 28 July 1933, Rudolf (named after Deputy Führer Rudolf Hess) on 31 August 1934, Heinrich on 13 June 1936, Eva on 4 May 1938, Gerda on 4 August 1940, Hartmut on 3 April 1942 and Volker on 18 September 1943. After the flight of Rudolf Hess in 1941, Bormann distanced himself from his former boss to the extent that he changed two of his children's names; Ilse, Hess's goddaughter, was renamed Eike, and Hess's godson, Rudolf, was renamed Helmut. With the knowledge and forbearance of his wife, Bormann continued a protracted love affair with the actress Manja Behrens, which lasted for many years.

On 1 April 1930, he was a founder member of the National Socialist Automobile Corps, the forerunner of the NSKK. On 15 April 1930, he was selected as head of the NS Aid Bank, and from 25 August 1930 until 3 July 1933, he was appointed head of NSDAP charitable funds. Bormann held the rank of SA-Standartenführer from 18 December 1931. From 4 July 1933, he was designated chief of staff and personal secretary in the office of the Deputy Führer, and the same month he was selected as Leader of the Adolf Hitler Foundation for German Business. On 10 October 1933, he was appointed as NSDAP Reichsleiter, and in November 1933, he was elected as the Reichstag deputy for Thuringia; he also accumulated other functions on various councils and committees.

Martin Bormann joined the SS with the rank of SS-Gruppenführer on 30 January 1937. He was allocated SS membership number 278 267(this was later changed to number 555) and was placed on the staff of the Reichsführer-SS. On 20 April 1940, he was promoted to SS-Obergruppenführer.

Bormann was officially transferred to the personal staff of the Führer in 1938. He was appointed as the last head of the Party Chancellery on 12 May 1941, simultaneously attaining the government rank of Reichsminister without portfolio. From 12 April 1943, Bormann held the title 'Secretary and Personal Adjutant of the Führer', allowing him unrestricted power over direct access to Hitler. On 18 October 1944, he was assigned as the political and organisational leader of the German Volkssturm.

Martin Bormann is best remembered as Hitler's secretary, and is commonly referred to as the 'brown eminence' in relation to his Party position. Most people who came into contact with him disliked him and, towards the end of the war, nobody could get to see Hitler without prior approval from Bormann. He was the second-most-powerful man in the regime, supplanting the likes of Göring and Himmler. He was a shrewd administrator, whose talents catapulted him to the forefront of the Party; it was he who carried the body of Eva Braun up from the depths of the Reich Chancellery bunker to the garden, where it was cremated with that of her husband. He led the group escape from the Berlin bunker during the night of 1 May 1945 and is presumed to have been killed, or to have committed suicide, in the Invalidenstrasse, where his body was seen by Arthur Amann on 2 May. Bormann was sentenced to death in absentia at Nuremberg on 1 October 1946.

Speculation as to his death or whereabouts continued for many years and there were numerous 'sightings' around the world. Two skeletons were discovered in the Invalidenstrasse in 1972 and subsequent forensic examination of the remains and dental comparisons concluded that they were the bodies of Martin Bormann and Dr Ludwig Stumpfegger. Both bodies had glass splinters embedded in the teeth, indicating the strong possibility of self-inflicted poisoning. On 24 September 1973, Martin Bormann was declared officially deceased. The examining judge certified:

The burial of the skeleton of Reichsleiter Bormann, found on 7th–8th December in Berlin (West) on the terrain of the Ulap site in the Invalidenstrasse is authorised. Cremation will not be allowed.

The Frankfurt Public Prosecutor's Office placed the remains at the disposal of the family, on condition that they were not to be cremated. The family did not accept the condition, and the Reichsleiter's mortal remains reposed in a cardboard box in the vaults of the Frankfurt Public Prosecutor's Office until cremation was eventually authorised. The ashes were scattered over the Baltic Sea on 16 August 1999.

Walter Buch, the father of the bride, with his daughter and new son-in-law.

The wedding party. Far right is Martin's brother, Albert Bormann.

The Chief of Staff and secretary of the Deputy Führer, Rudolf Hess.   Reichsleiter Bormann.

Bormann accompanies his boss and wife, the Hess couple.

Reichsleiter Martin Bormann.

Bormann realised that Eva Braun's position was unassailable and that she held a marked dislike of him. A strained relationship of tolerance existed between the two members of Hitler's inner circle.

Martin and Gerda Bormann on the Obersalzberg.

Bormann in the sunshine on the terrace at the Berghof.

Bormann at Hitler's shoulder as he leaves the Führerbau during the Munich Conference.

Relaxing with Dr Karl Brandt.

An attentive Bormann listens to the Führer speak.

SS-Obergruppenführer Martin Bormann.

Clockwise from top left:

Hitler's 'eyes and ears'.

Borman wearing the last pattern rank insignia of a SS-Obergruppenführer.

Reichsleiter Bormann relaxes in the knowledge that he is all-powerful.

Bormann in Hitler's office at the Reich Chancellery, listening to Vidkun Quisling. Far left is Terboven, Lammers is centre and Albert Bormann is at the far right.

Left to right: Kaltenbrunner, Göring, Dietrich, Goebbels, Himmler and Bormann.

Hitler receives a visit from an Italian officer. (Press release photograph). Left to right: Bormann, Hewel, (unidentified), (unidentified), Hitler.

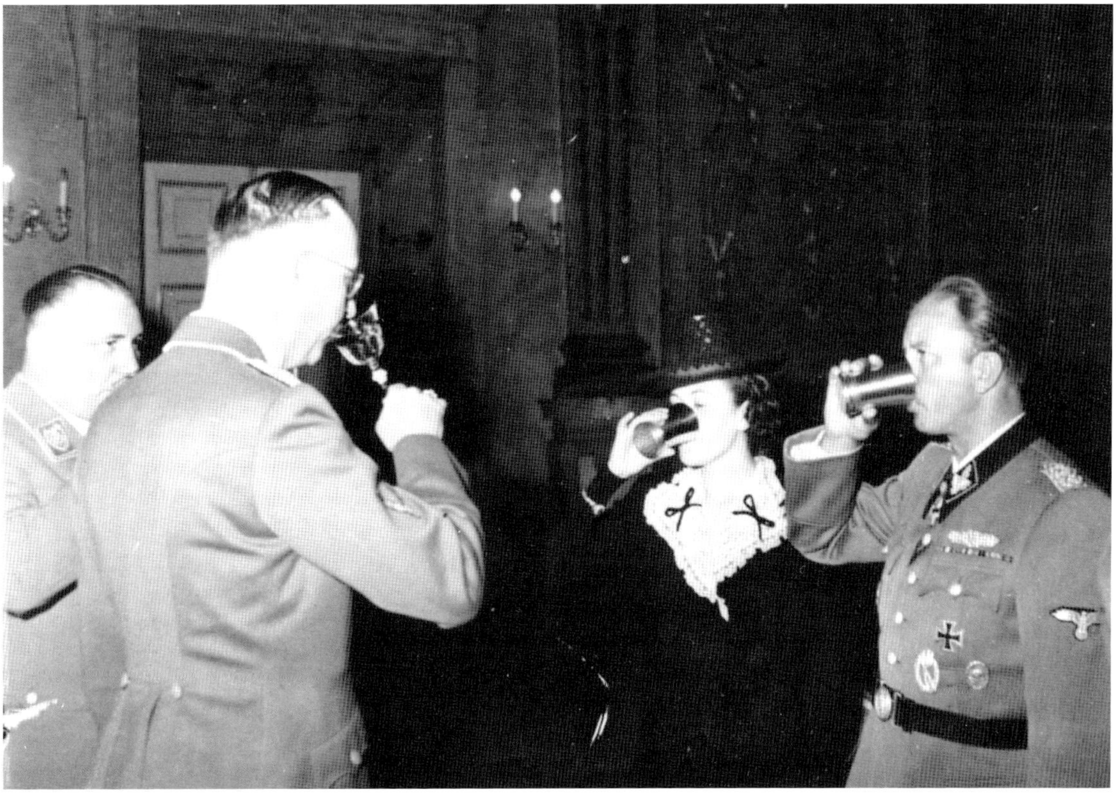

The wedding of Hermann Fegelein and Gretl Braun on 3 June 1944 in Salzburg.

Left to right: Keitel, Göring, Dönitz, Himmler and Bormann.

Bormann, Hitler and von Ribbentrop study
reports at Hitler's field headquarters.

Never far from Hitler's side, Bormann
wears SS-Obergruppenführer rank
insignia.

After the assassination attempt on Hitler's life, Hitler has clearly injured his arm.

Bormann at the side of the Führer.

PHILIPP BOUHLER

PHILIPP 'ANGO' BOUHLER was born into a military evangelical family in Munich on 11 September 1899. His father, Emil Bouhler, was a colonel, and he was chief of the Bavarian War Office. The young Philipp was destined for a career in uniform and after attending an elementary primary school in Munich from 1905 until 1909, he transferred to the Maximilian High School, also in Munich.

He joined the Bavarian Cadet Corps in 1912 and remained there until 15 July 1916, when he volunteered for active service with the Replacement Battalion of the 1st Foot Artillery Regiment. He was commissioned as a Leutnant on 30 July 1917 and on 8 August 1917, after being sent to the Western Front, he was buried alive and sustained serious fractures to both legs. He was still in hospital at the end of the war and remained under the care of doctors until 1920, having been invalided out of the Army.

He studied German literature and philosophy at the University of Munich from 1919 until 1920, and in 1919, his Army career plans in ruins, he turned to politics, joining the German Peoples' Protection League. Bouhler found employment with the publishing firm of J. F. Lehmann and discovered an avid interest in motor sports, something which became a lifelong obsession.

He was a convinced anti-Semite. His beliefs led him to the NSDAP in November 1921, when he worked for the *Volkischer Beobachter* and came under the influence of Max Amann. He joined the NSDAP in July 1922. He became the NSDAP deputy chief business manager, under Amann, in late September 1922. He kept this position until the Party was banned after the November 1923 putsch (in which he participated). During the period of the ban, Bouhler was appointed as the business manager for the Greater German Peoples' Group.

With the reformation of the NSDAP, Bouhler became Party member number 25 on 27 February 1925. He was also appointed as the NSDAP national business manager on 27 March 1925. From 1926 until 1930, he was the editor of the *Illustrierten Beobachter*, a publication which displayed extreme anti-Semitic views under his control. Bouhler wrote a biography of Hitler in 1932. He was elected as Reichstag

Deputy for Westfalen Süd in March 1933 and was appointed as Reichsleiter on 2 June of the same year.

Bouhler joined the SS on 20 April 1933 and was immediately afforded the rank of SS-Gruppenführer, attached to SS-Oberabschnitt Süd. He held SS number 54 932. From 29 August 1934 until 31 October 1934, he was Police President of Munich, but he failed to take up the position as he was posted to the Reich Chancellery staff in Berlin on 28 September 1934. He was chosen as a member of the Academy for German Law on 19 September 1934. On 17 November 1934, he was appointed chief of the Führer's Chancellery and he retained this post until April 1945.

Bouhler married Helene Majer (born in Lauingen on 20 April 1912) on 18 August 1934. They had no children. Frau Bouhler, who was recognised as the most beautiful woman of the Reich Chancellery, killed herself in late May 1945 by throwing herself from a tower window at Schloss Fischorn.

Bouhler transferred from SS-Oberabschnitt Süd on 1 January 1935 and was placed at the special commission of the Reichsführer-SS. From 4 April 1935, he was a member of the Upper National Sport Authority for German Drivers and was the SS representative for motor sports. He was promoted to SS-Obergruppenführer on 30 January 1936 and placed on the staff of the Reichsführer-SS.

Bouhler was a member of the Reich Culture Senate and was Party Commissioner for the Protection of National Socialist Literature. As head of the Führer's Chancellery, the euthanasia programme was placed under Bouhler's direction on 1 September 1939, but the actual operational functioning was administered by Werner Blankenberg and Viktor Brack. Philipp Bouhler's position as head of the Chancellery of the Führer brought him into conflict with Martin Bormann—who viewed him as a rival—and his standing in the NSDAP waned as a result. He attempted to resign his post, but Hitler did not want to lose his competent chancellery chief. In 1942 he was appointed chief of the Special Action Staff for East Africa, probably an indication of his loss of standing.

Bouhler was arrested by US troops at Schloss Fischorn, near Zell am See, on 10 May 1945. Seen by the Allies as a major offender with his connection to the euthanasia programme, he would certainly have trod the scaffold steps at Landsberg am Lech Prison. He cheated the hangman by committing suicide on 19 May 1945, near the US internment camp at Zell am See, whilst being transferred to the internment camp at Dachau.

An early photograph of Bouhler.

Bouhler often favoured bowties.

SS-Gruppenführer Bouhler. An early photograph.

Bouhler wearing his SS civilian pin.

Reichsleiter Bouhler wearing his Golden Party Badge on his lapel.

Clockwise from top left:

SS-Gruppenführer Bouhler.

Bouhler checking an entry.

The beautiful Frau Helene Bouhler.

A signed photograph of SS-Obergruppenführer Bouhler.

SS-Obergruppenführer Bouhler.

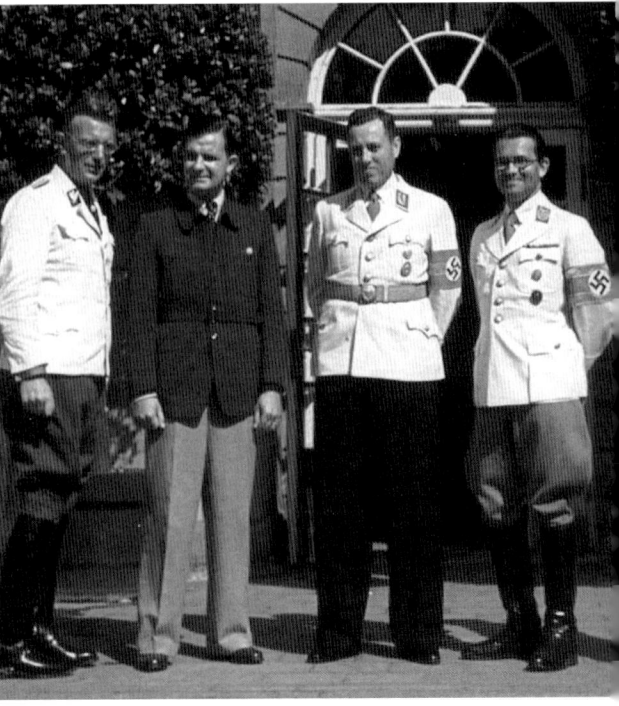

A Christmas present.

Four SS-Obergruppenführer. Left to right: Seyss-Inquart, Bohle, Forster and Bouhler.

SS-Obergruppenführer Bouhler wears the last pattern rank insignia on his tunic.

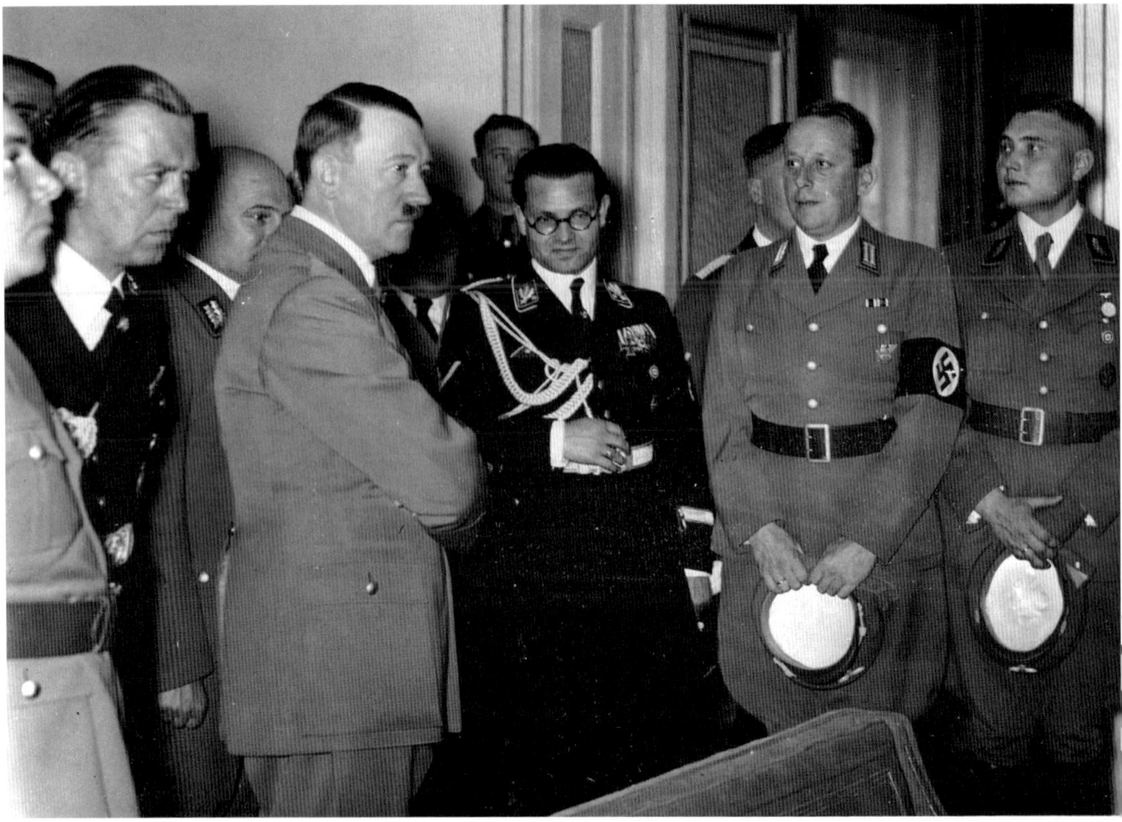

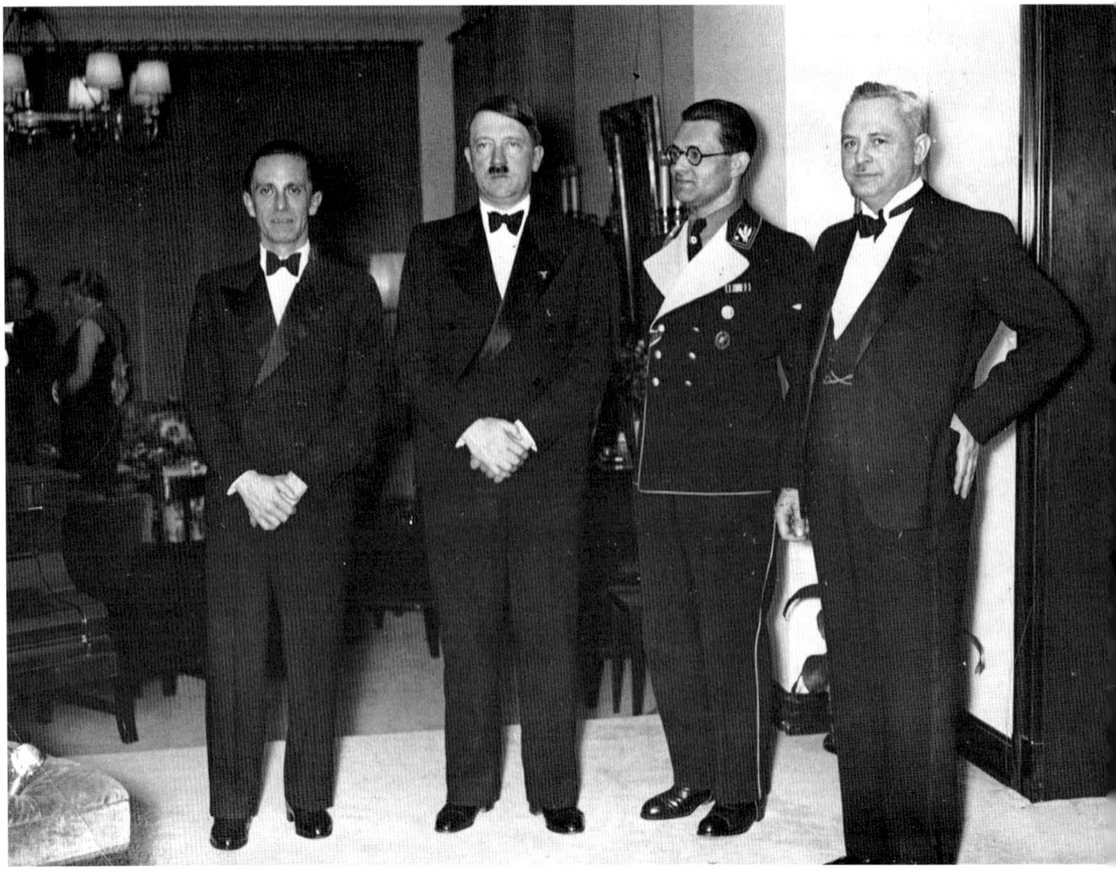

Above: Bouhler waits behind Walter Buch to sign a visitors' book. To the left is Wilhelm Grimm.

Opposite page:

Above: In the Reich Chancellery; Bouhler between Hitler and Giesler.

Below: Goebbels, Hitler and Kerrl, as guests of the Bouhlers.

FRANZ BREITHAUPT

F RANZ BREITHAUPT Senior was a Prussian Army officer who was formerly on the General Staff of the Prussian Army; he died in 1894, when he was commander of the military academy in Anklam. His wife, Maria, gave birth to a healthy baby boy in Berlin on 8 December 1880. Named after his father, the young Franz received a primary school and secondary school education in Rendsberg and Kiel from 1887 until 1891, before attending the Army officer cadet schools at Plön and Gross-Lichterfelde until March 1899.

He joined the 42nd Infantry Regiment in March 1899 as an Ensign and was promoted to Leutnant on 18 August 1900 after attending the military academy in Metz. He became involved in physical education and was an instructor in gymnastics, with promotion to Oberleutnant on 27 January 1910 and to Hauptmann on 20 May 1914. On the outbreak of hostilities in August 1914, Breithaupt was posted to the command of the 5th company of his regiment. He was wounded in the head on 29 August 1914, near Progarts. A month in various hospitals followed before he was assigned as adjutant to the commanding General of the VIII Reserve Corps on 30 October 1914. He experienced brief postings of active service with the 395th, 456th and 364th Infantry Regiments, until his appointment as commanding officer of the 9th Cavalry Division outposts on 24 March 1917—a posting he retained until December 1918. He was then appointed as adjutant to the commanding General of the 2nd Army Corps in Stettin, before transferring in 1919 to the new military physical training school in Wünsdorf. He retired from the Army in November 1919 with the rank of Major.

From 1919 until 1921, Breithaupt was a member of the Freikorps 'Erhardt' and Regiment Gross-Berlin. He was an industrialist by profession, having trained at a factory in Lübbecke from November 1919, before finding employment as director of a business in Godramstein until 1923.

Breithaupt was married in 1923 to Else Hilde Becke (born on 12 January 1893 in Brüstrawe-Schleswig; NSDAP membership number 773 698). Else was Breithaupt's second wife, his first marriage ending in divorce in 1921. This second marriage also ended in divorce on 11 September 1944. They had no children, but Breithaupt had one daughter from his first marriage, born on 4 May 1912.

He was the commercial manager of the German Gymnastics Association from 1923 until 1931. He joined the Stahlhelm on 1 April 1929, but resigned from that organisation on joining the SA on 27 November 1931 as a SA-Sturmbannführer. He joined the NSDAP on 1 August 1931 and was allocated NSDAP membership number 602 663.

Breithaupt transferred to the SS on 1 December 1932 with SS number 39 719. He was assigned to Himmler's staff as an adjutant, holding the rank of SS-Sturmbannführer. He was promoted to SS-Obersturmbannführer on 31 July 1933, and to SS-Standartenführer on 9 November 1933. Another promotion took place on 9 November 1934, when he was appointed as SS-Oberführer and adjutant for special assignments of the Reichsführer-SS in Berlin.

He was placed in command of the Berlin SS garrison on 1 May 1935. On 1 April 1936, he was transferred to the staff of the SS-Hauptamt. The same year he was nominated as leader of Sports District 3 (Brandenburg) of the Reich Federal Physical Training Scheme. He was also the publisher of *Deutscher Sport* and head of the German Trotting Sport Association.

On 9 November 1938, he was promoted to SS-Brigadeführer. As SS garrison commander Berlin—a largely honorary post after 1 November 1935—Breithaupt experienced various attachments to what became the future Waffen-SS. For one month from 1 November 1939, he was attached to the command staff of 8th SS-Totenkopfstandarte; on 28 July 1940 he was attached to 5th SS-Totenkopfstandarte and became commander of the 5th SS-Infantry Regiment (Motorised) on 12 September 1940. This unit developed into part of the SS-Totenkopf Division.

Breithaupt was appointed Police President of Breslau on 25 October 1940, and transferred to the staff of the RFSS on 1 January 1942. From 1 March 1942, he was attached to the Reichssicherheitshauptamt until appointed chief of the Hauptamt SS-Gericht (*legal central office of the SS*) on 15 August 1942, when he was also promoted to SS-Gruppenführer and Generalleutnant der Waffen-SS. He was promoted to SS-Obergruppenführer and General der Waffen-SS on 20 April 1944. He was also a member of the People's Court.

Franz Breithaupt was shot in the back and killed by his driver, SS-Untersturmführer Karl Lang, at Berg-Starnbergersee on 28 April 1945. Lang had hoped to win favour with the approaching Americans by carrying out an 'anti-Nazi' act. Lang was tried for this murder in 1949 and found guilty of manslaughter, resulting in a prison term of just four years. In his defence, Lang declared that Breithaupt had done nothing to reduce the suffering of concentration camp inmates and was corrupt. In complete contradiction, many witnesses testified that Breithaupt had been a decent man, who was always courteous and fair. As the senior SS judge he had always acted with humanity—90 per cent of death sentences were commuted by Breithaupt.

Breithaupt was an army instructor in athletics and gymnastics. He is photographed here in his early army days, with some of his athletics students.

Left and right: Breithaupt photographed in civilian clothes.

Franz Breithaupt.

SS-Obersturmbannführer Breithaupt.

An athletics presentation.

Breithaupt saluting at an event.

Breithaupt with his daughter and grandchildren.

Breithaupt speaking from the orchestra balcony.

SS-Oberführer Franz Breithaupt at his desk. The Tyr rune on his left sleeve denotes his attendance at the Reich leadership school.

Legal minds—Breithaupt with Otto Thierack.

The head of the SS legal office.

SS-Brigadeführer Breithaupt.

SS-Brigadeführer Breithaupt wearing his medals.

An inspection visit during military exercises.

Breithaupt (left) in his SS greatcoat.

SS-Gruppenführer Breithaupt (right).

WALTER BUCH

Walter Buch was born on 24 October 1883 in Bruchsal, the son of Dr Hermann Buch, the Senate President of the Baden District Upper Court (born on 28 July 1854, died on 29 July 1921 in Karlsruhe) and his wife, Hedwig Gertrud Buch (born Heidlauff). Walter Buch had one sister, Hedwig Paula Buch (born on 18 April 1886, died in 1955 in Loerrach).

From 1889 until summer 1902, he attended primary school in Bruchsal and classics high schools in Karlsruhe and Konstanz, where he graduated. On 30 September 1902, he joined the 114th Infantry Regiment in Konstanz as an officer cadet and was commissioned as a Leutnant on 27 January 1904. He was assigned as an instructor and served at the officer aspirant school in Biebrich from 1912 until 1914, gaining promotion to Oberleutnant on 27 January 1913.

Buch was married on 23 September 1908 to Else Pleusser (born on 11 May 1887 in Barmen, died of a heart attack on 29 October 1944; NSDAP number 7 732). They had two sons; the first was born on 11 January 1912, and the second, Hermann, was born on 16 February 1920 in Gernsbach (SS number 357 263). He joined the Waffen-SS and became a SS-Hauptsturmführer and IIa (*Divisional Adjutant*) of the 2nd SS-Panzer-Division 'Das Reich'. Buch and his wife also had two daughters: Gerda, born on 23 October 1909, who died of cancer in the Merano civil hospital on 23 April 1946, and a second, born 10 March 1913. On 2 September 1929, Gerda Buch married the later Reichsleiter Martin Bormann; Walter Buch grew to loathe his son-in-law and fellow Reichsleiter. Under post-war interrogation, Buch stated:

> … I did not get along with him and when the Führer put Bormann in charge of jurisprudence in the Party my job was practically finished … of course I opposed this change, but could do nothing about it because the Führer had stopped listening to me many years ago...

After the war Buch apparently remarried. His new wife was the widow of a dentist who had visited him during his internment.

Buch's war service at the front from 1915 was initially with his original unit, the 57th Infantry Regiment, and then with the 47th Infantry Brigade. This was followed by the Landwehr Infantry Brigade, the 112th Infantry Regiment, and finally the 23rd Machine Gun Marksman Detachment in Infantry Regiment 6. He finished the war in November 1918 attached to the infantry training school at Döberitz on secondment to the War Ministry in Berlin, with the rank of Major. He was registered with a 50 per cent war disability. He left military service of his own volition on 20 November 1918, having refused to swear allegiance to the new Weimar Republic of Friedrich Ebert. Buch took up chicken farming in Scheuern, near Gernsbach, from 1918 until 1923.

He joined the German National People's Party in 1919, eventually rising to the post of local Party secretary in Karlsruhe by 1923. He also joined the Bund Oberland in 1920. Buch's father, a district court judge and right-wing nationalist, wrote a book entitled *Vom Internationalen zum Nationalen Arbeitsstaat,* published by Lehmann Verlag in Munich. In March 1920, he asked his son to personally deliver a copy to Adolf Hitler, whom he greatly admired. In these circumstances Walter Buch first met and quickly came under the spell of Hitler. He officially joined the NSDAP on 9 December 1922 and became Ortsgruppenleiter in Karlsruhe until September 1923, also joining the SA on 1 August 1923. He was appointed as chief of SA troops in Franconia with the headquarters in Nuremberg, a force which numbered approximately 275 men and which expanded to about 800 by October.

Buch was a member of the Stahlhelm from 1 July 1923 until 1 January 1928, and participated in the Munich Putsch of November 1923—albeit in a minor role. From 13 November 1923 until January 1924, he was charged with the temporary leadership of the now-illegal SA, a responsibility he covered with his legal employment as a cigar and wine salesman in Munich until April 1924. From 1924 until 1 January 1928, he was the SA chief in Upper Bavaria and Schwabia. He was arrested in February 1924, accused of attempting to re-introduce the NSDAP. He re-enrolled in the new NSDAP on 15 June 1925 and was given NSDAP number 7 733.

Buch was elected Chairman of the NSDAP Investigation and Arbitration Committee in the Reich NSDAP leadership (USCHLA) on 27 November 1927. From May 1928 until September 1930, he was the Reichstag member for Upper Bavaria-Schwabia. On 11 June 1930 he became Chairman of the NSDAP Youth Office, and he was accorded the rank of SA-Gruppenführer on 18 December 1931. In November 1933, he was elected as the Reichstag Deputy for Hannover East and he held this position until March 1936, when he became the member for Leipzig.

In 1930 Buch was implicated in a plot to remove and murder Ernst Röhm and several members of his staff. Although strongly suspected, no charges were ever brought against Buch due to lack of evidence.

On 2 June 1933, he was appointed as NSDAP Reichsleiter. On 1 January 1934 Hitler selected him as Chairman of the Supreme Party Court, providing him with administration of all Party courts and the responsibility of sitting in arbitration when senior NSDAP officials had disagreements. Buch resented his unhappy position as Nazi supreme judge and constantly requested to be relieved; these requests intensified with the onset of war. He attempted to administer the Party courts along the lines of Army courts of honour, and he insisted that his judges all experienced military service at some point. Although a fanatical anti-Semite, Buch was generally regarded as an honourable man—but with limited abilities.

Buch joined the SS as a SS-Gruppenführer with special duties attached to SS-Standarte 63 on 1 July 1933, and was allocated number 81 353. He provided evidence against Röhm and several senior SA leaders, even warning Hitler of Röhm's homosexual activities as early as 1933. Although an enemy of Ernst Röhm, he did not condone the arbitrary actions of the SS during the Röhm purge of June–July 1934, believing that the accused should have appeared to answer charges before the NSDAP supreme court. He was only informed of the execution of Röhm some days afterwards. He was promoted to SS-Obergruppenführer on 9 November 1934 and was placed on the staff of the Reichsführer-SS on 1 April 1936.

In the aftermath of the 'Night of Broken Glass' in November 1938, Buch contributed to the cover-up by submitting a report in February 1939 which basically excused the actions as 'misunderstandings' by Party members.

Buch was a member of the Academy of German Law and a member of the Information Office for Population and Race Politics in the Ministry of the Interior. He lost favour with Hitler and his son-in-law, Martin Bormann, through a misguided attack on the morals of some senior NSDAP members. Consequently his standing in the Party diminished and by the end of the war his role was superfluous, his significance in the NSDAP evaporating. The sudden loss of his wife added to his misfortune.

Buch was arrested by US troops in Munich on 30 April 1945 and, until 12 August 1945, he was interned at POW Camp 32 (*known as 'Ashcan', the Allied special interrogation and internment facility for senior Nazi leaders at the Palace Hotel in Mondorf-les-Bains, Luxembourg*). Here he was interrogated numerous times concerning his activities during the Third Reich and on the subject of his missing son-in-law, Martin Bormann, who was being tried in absentia by the IMT in Nuremberg. He was then transferred to Nuremberg Jail, where he was held for a time in the witness wing before being transferred to another internment centre (*possibly Dachau*). On 1 January 1947, he was returned to Nuremberg, where he underwent further interrogation. At his first de-Nazification trial in Garmisch on 3 July 1948, he was classified as a 'major offender' and sentenced to five years' hard labour and confiscation of assets up to 2000 marks in value. On 16 February 1949, he attended an appeal hearing before the Weilheim Senate of the Upper Bavaria Judicial Court and was granted a second de-Nazification hearing. At the 29 July 1949 hearing held in Munich, he was again classified as a 'major offender', but was re-sentenced to three years and six months in a labour camp. Deemed to have served more than this amount of time in post-war internment, Buch was released from custody the same day.

The Bavarian State Police reported that Walter Buch committed suicide by slashing his wrists and drowning himself in the Ammersee at Schöndorf on 12 September 1949.

A young Walter Buch.

Buch (left) with two Army colleagues.

A stern-looking young officer.

At the front.

On horseback.

SA-Gruppenführer Buch.

Buch (far left) with early NSDAP supporters.

The chief NSDAP judge, Walter Buch.

Buch being driven with fellow passengers Grimm, Bouhler and Schwarz.

Buch at home with family and friends. Frau Else Buch sitting second from left.

Buch with his daughter at the lake.

Reichsleiter Walter Buch.

SS-Obergruppenführer Walter Buch.

The Obergruppenführer with his son.

The Buch couple with their son and daughter.

Buch (fourth from right) visits the Channel coast defences as part of Generalfeldmarschall Sperrle's party.

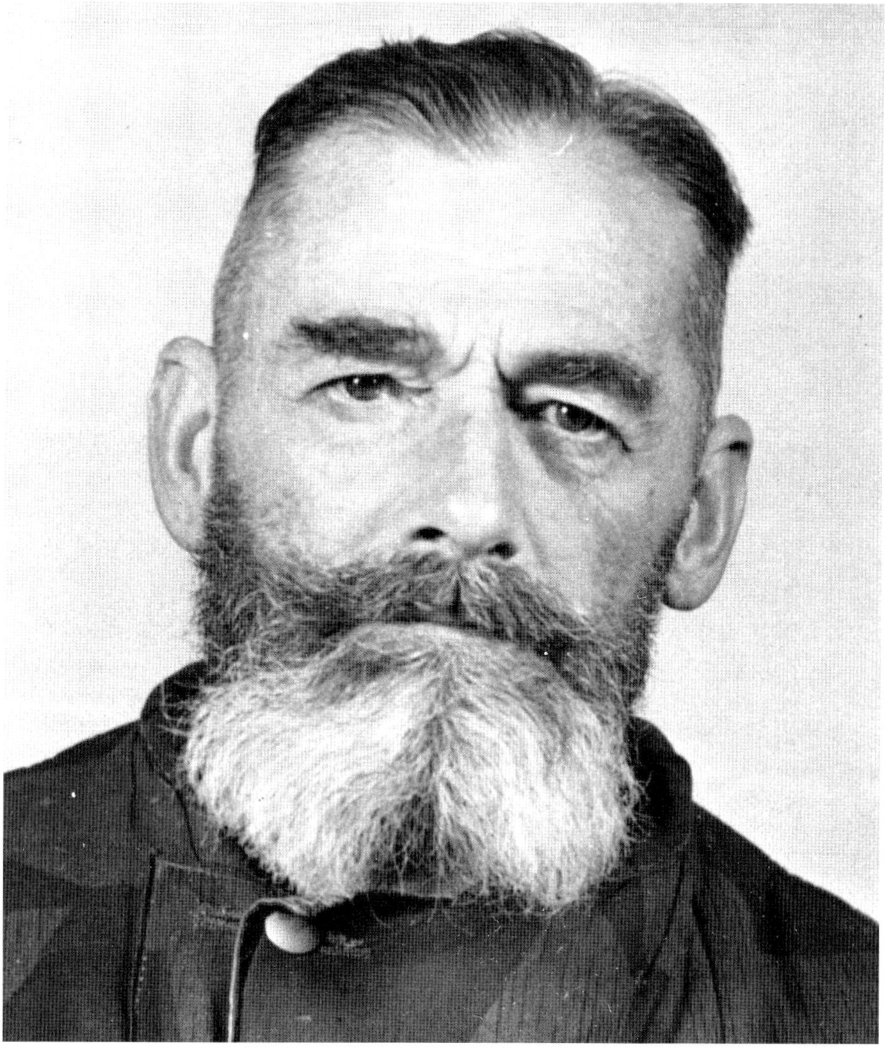

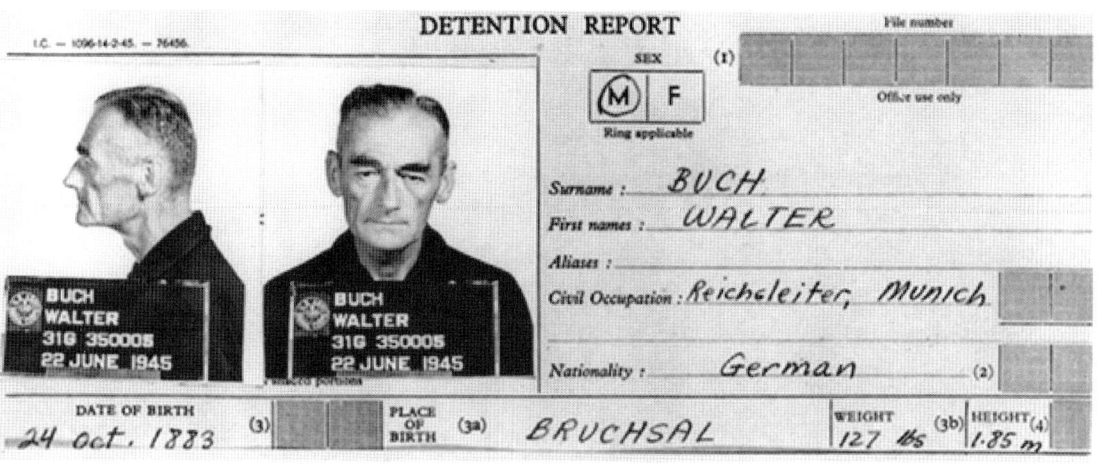

Prisoner of War Walter Buch. Much confusion surrounds his death; various reports suggest he killed himself in a US internment camp near the Ammersee. However, it appears that he committed suicide as a free man in 1949, unable or not wishing to live after the defeat of Germany.

DETENTION REPORT

I.C. — 1096-14-2-45. — 76456.

File number (1)

Office use only

SEX

M F

Ring applicable

BUCH
WALTER
31G 350005
22 JUNE 1945

BUCH
WALTER
31G 350005
22 JUNE 1945

Surname : BUCH

First names : WALTER

Aliases :

Civil Occupation : Reichsleiter, Munich

Nationality : German (2)

DATE OF BIRTH	(3)	PLACE OF BIRTH (3a)	WEIGHT (3b)	HEIGHT (4)
24 Oct. 1883		BRUCHSAL	127 lbs	1.85 m

Walter Buch's detention card.

JOSEF BÜRCKEL

JOSEF BÜRCKEL was the youngest of four children born to Catholic master baker Michael Bürckel and his wife Magdalena (born Zoller, married in Lingenfeld on 9 August 1886). Josef was born on 30 March 1895 in Lingenfeld. He attended the Catholic primary and secondary schools in Lingenfeld from 1901 until 1909, followed by teacher training in Speyer from 1909 to 1914, when he volunteered for active service with the Army.

In August 1914, Bürckel underwent a medical examination for his suitability for the military, but was at first rejected as a result of a recent operation. Unperturbed, he tried again and was accepted for service with the 12th Bavarian Field Artillery Regiment in Landau. He quickly transferred, first to the 20th Bavarian Field Artillery Regiment and then to the recruit depot of the 12th Bavarian Field Artillery Regiment in Landau on 3 November 1914. He was assigned to the 20th Bavarian Field Artillery Regiment on 1 January 1915, and remained in the recruit depot until 3 April 1915, when he was posted to Battery 6 of the same unit, moving up the line to the front on 6 April 1915. He took part in heavy fighting until he was hospitalised with a heart condition on 12 August 1915. He was promoted to Unteroffizier on 4 December 1915, and then saw more active service with various artillery units of the Royal Bavarian Army until he was honourably discharged on 17 May 1916.

On his return to Germany he applied for an assistant teaching post and then worked in Catholic elementary schools in Ramberg, Lingenfeld (his own school), Bellheim and Minfeld until 28 July 1919. He was subsequently appointed as a teacher after passing his state education examinations, and worked at schools in Bobenheim and Rodalben.

Bürckel was married in Lingenfeld on 11 July 1920 to Hilde Spies (born in Landau on 29 December 1899). The couple had two sons: Josef Artur (born on 22 August 1921 in Landau-Pfalz, died of unknown causes as an Unteroffizier 20 km north of Calais on 20 January 1943) and Hermann-Jakob (born on 10 March 1925).

Bürckel was a political activist and supported the National Socialist movement from as early as 1920, joining the NSDAP in 1921. He participated in violent protests against the Pfalz separatist movement during 1923 and 1924. With the re-organisation of the NSDAP in 1925, he became Party member number 33 979 on 9 April that year, and took charge of the NSDAP in the Palatinate and Saar regions. Hitler appointed him NSDAP Gauleiter of Rheinpfalz on 13 March 1926, a post he retained until 28 February 1935.

In August 1927, he became the editor of the NSDAP newspaper *Der Eisenhammer*, and on 1 August he was appointed as head teacher of the Catholic elementary school in Nussbach. He stayed in post until September 1930.

Bürckel was elected as deputy to the Reichstag on 14 September 1930. From 1931 until 1933 he became involved in a bitter dispute with the local SS leader Theodor Eicke, which was only resolved when Eicke was committed to a mental-health sanatorium on 23 March 1933.

On 28 February 1933, Hitler appointed Bürckel NSDAP Gauleiter and Reich Commissioner for the Saarland, effective from 6 May 1935—however, in effect, Bürckel was in control from 31 January 1933. From 25 September 1933, he was granted the rank of SA-Gruppenführer, attached to SA-Gruppe Westmark.

On 11 February 1935, he was appointed as Reich Commissioner for the re-incorporation of the Saarland into the German Reich and on 23 February 1935, he gained the rank of NSKK-Gruppenführer. He was appointed as NSDAP Gauleiter of Gau Pfalz-Saar on 1 March 1935.

Bürckel joined the SS on 9 November 1937, obtaining membership number 289 230, and was immediately accorded the rank of SS-Gruppenführer. He was promoted to SS-Obergruppenführer on 30 January 1942.

His experience in the Saarland qualified him for his nomination by Hitler on 13 March 1938 as head of the commission for the preparation and organisation of the transition of the Austrian plebiscite. He was also ordered to reorganise the NSDAP in Austria. On 23 April 1938, he was assigned the post of Reich Commissioner for the re-unification of Austria with the German Reich. This position ceased to exist on 30 January 1939, when Bürckel became Gauleiter of Vienna, succeeding Odilo Globocnik.

On 20 August 1938, Bürckel ordered the establishment of the Zentralstelle für jüdische Auswanderung (*Central Office for Jewish Emigration*) in Vienna under the leadership of Dr Franz Walther Stahlecker, who delegated the duties to Adolf Eichmann. In the autumn of 1938, Bürckel declared:

> ... Let's not forget that if you want to Aryanize and to deprive the Jews of their means to live, then you've got to solve the Jewish problem in an absolute fashion...

A busy man, Bürckel became chief of civil administration in Bohemia for one month in March–April 1939. From 1 May 1939 until 31 March 1940, he carried out the responsibilities of Oberbürgermeister of Vienna and on 4 May 1939, he was appointed as Reichsstatthalter of the Ostmark.

On 1 September 1939, Bürckel was appointed as Reich Defence Commissioner for Wehrkreis XVII. He relinquished all his posts in the former Austria and the Gau leadership of Vienna on 2 August 1940, when he became chief of civil administration for Lorraine—an appointment he held until his death. He also became the authorised agent for total employment in his Gau. To these he added positions as housing commissioner and Reich defence commissioner for his Gau in November 1942.

On 7 February 1943, at the Wolfsschanze headquarters in East Prussia, Hitler directed:

> Gauleiter Bürckel will be responsible for the line of the Moselle from the boundary of Gau Westmark via the arsenal of Metz-Diedenhofen south of St Avoid [part of the Maginot Line] to Saaralben.

By 8 September 1944, Bürckel was complaining to Martin Bormann that there was a lack of combat-ready troops in his zone and consequently the construction of defensive positions was futile. Borman responded by sending Willi Stöhr to supervise construction work. Following Bürckel's premature death, Stöhr replaced him.

Although holding a very-senior rank in the SS, Josef Bürckel was rarely seen in SS uniform and was often described as anti-SS. He often fell out with senior SS commanders, whom he eyed suspiciously as usurpers to his authority. He vehemently disagreed with the SS theory on race and maintained a personal dislike of Himmler. He antagonised the SS by releasing over 1,000 prisoners from concentration camps in Austria and prevented the incarceration of the later-French Foreign Minister Robert Schumann. He clashed with Heinrich Müller over the question of admitting suspected partisans to concentration camps. He disagreed with the building of some defensive measures within his Gau, arguing that this would turn his area into a war zone. All this gained him the nickname 'the Red Gauleiter of Westmark'. In 1944 the Party Chancellery (*Bormann*) took steps to deplete his power.

Suffering from exhaustion, Bürckel died in Ludwigshafen at 11.04 a.m. on 28 September 1944. The death certificate gave the cause of death as pneumonia and blood failure, but the circumstances of his death have been the subject of discussion. His wife maintained that he was forced to commit suicide, but the official version states that he died after an illness that lasted for two days, which arose from circulatory problems. The Gau medical officer, Professor Ewig, declared that his circulation problems had been brought about by overwork and lack of sleep.

Bürckel speaks.

The Gauleiter in a pensive mood.

Left and right: Gauleiter Bürckel.

Josef Bürckel at home with his family.

Bürckel addresses a crowd which includes nurses and various military groups.

Bürckel had a particular fondness for trench coats.

Rudolf Hess visits Bürckel in Austria. Hubert Klausner is in SS uniform.

Bürckel photographed with Himmler and SS officers including Heydrich, Schmelcher and Schmitt.

Himmler in Vienna in 1938. The SS officers are Wolff, Heydrich, Kaltenbrunner and Fitzthum. Daluege is in the foreground.

Josef Bürckel in SS uniform (centre) behind Göring.

Front, left to right: Seyss-Inquart, Bürckel, Kaltenbrunner and Globocnik.

Bürckel in SS-Gruppenführer uniform.

Left to right: Fitzthum, Becker, (unidentified), Bürckel and Globocnik.

Bürckel's grave.

LEONARDO CONTI

L EONARDO CONTI was born on 24 August 1900 in Lugano, Switzerland, the son of Swiss-Italian postal official Silvio Conti and his wife, Hanna Conti (born Pauli). Conti's parents divorced in 1915 and he was naturalised as a German citizen the same year. His mother, known by the affectionate name of Nanna, subsequently became the female leader of the National Socialist midwife association, was a leading opponent of smoking tobacco.

From 1906, Conti attended elementary school in Switzerland, followed by the humanistic Mommsen High School and the Friedrich-Wilhelm High School in Berlin. In the summer of 1918 he volunteered for military service with the Field Artillery Regiment 54 at Küstrin. However, he was too late to see any action at the front.

Active in the national student movement, he became embroiled in politics and in November 1918 he co-founded the anti-Semitic Fighting League for German Culture. From January 1919 until March 1920, he was a member of the Guard Cavalry Rifle Division; he participated in the Kapp Putsch and was active against the Spartacists. He joined the German National People's Party in 1919, but withdrew in 1922 as he was at variance with its Jewish policy. From 1921 until 1923, he was a member of the Freikorps 'Erhardt' and was also busy with politics in the Berlin branch of the German Protection League.

Conti studied medicine from 1919 until 1923 at the universities of Berlin and Erlangen, passing his State medical examinations in November 1923. He joined the SA in Erlangen in 1923 and gained his medical doctorship at Berlin University in 1924, attaining a licence to practice medicine the following year in Munich. He worked as a voluntary physician at several Berlin children's hospitals, but he was disqualified as a result of his political views, before moving to Munich. From April 1925, he worked there as a general practitioner in the Social Hygiene Academy and as a paediatrician.

Conti was married on 22 August 1925 to Elfriede Freiin von Meerscheidt-Müllgasern (born 27 July 1902 in Berlin; NSDAP number 90 829). They had four children between 1926 and 1935, the last of whom died as a child. The family withdrew from the Evangelical Church in February 1943 and declared themselves as 'Gottgläubig'.

Conti moved back to Berlin in 1927 and joined the NSDAP on 20 December of that year, gaining membership number 72 225. From 1927 he was SA physician for Standarte V. The following year he was tasked with organising the SA medical services in Berlin. At the 1928 Reichsparteitag (*Reich Party day*) he was head of the medical service for the SA and from 1929 until 1930, he was senior physician of SA-Gruppe Ost. In February 1930, he was called upon to treat the fatally injured Horst Wessel, in his capacity as the head of the National Socialist medical section for the Greater Berlin Gau. The following September he was expelled from the SA with the rank of SA-Oberführer after taking an anti-Stennes stance (*Walter Stennes, SA-Gruppenführer Ost*).

Conti joined the SS on 16 November 1930 and was allocated SS number 3 982. He was appointed as senior doctor for SS-Gruppe Ost on 2 December 1930. He retained this post until 9 April 1933, when he was succeeded by Dr Ernst-Robert Grawitz. He was promoted to SS-Standartenführer on 12 June 1933, with special responsibilities in SS-Gruppe Ost.

He held a number of posts on councils and committees connected to medicine and health, including that of honorary commissioner in the Prussian Ministry of the Interior. He was President of the German Red Cross from 1933 until he was succeeded by Grawitz in 1935, and was also assigned to the Public Health Office for Gau Berlin in 1934.

Conti was promoted to SS-Oberführer on 20 April 1935 and was later designated as being on special assignment for the Reichsführer-SS. On 1 April 1936, he transferred to the staff of the Reichsführer-SS and was placed in charge of the medical arrangements for the Berlin Olympics. Promotion to SS-Brigadeführer followed on 30 January 1938.

On 20 April 1939, he was commissioned as Reich Health Leader and chief of the head office of public health; he was accorded the NSDAP rank of Hauptdienstleiter two days later. He was appointed as State Secretary for Public Health and Nursing in the Reich Interior Ministry on 28 August 1939. He was also a member of the Reichstag and the Berlin Provisional Council, and was the advisor on all questions of public health for the Party Chancellery. It was in this capacity that Hitler chose him to administer the euthanasia programme in September 1939. Conti was unhappy about the legality of this task and requested Lammers to obtain written legal authority from Hitler. Upset at Conti's reaction, Hitler immediately replaced him with Bouhler.

Conti was promoted to SS-Gruppenführer on 1 October 1941, and to SS-Obergruppenführer on 20 April 1944. He was a Leutnant der Reserve in the Medical Corps, having performed active military duty in 1935, 1937 and 1938.

Leonardo Conti was arrested by the British in Flensburg on 19 May 1945 and was held as a witness at Nuremberg Jail. He committed suicide by hanging himself with his towel from his cell window on 6 October 1945. His suicide note read:

> I depart this life because I said under oath something untrue. I was not quite all here. I have had heaviest depressions, thoughts of death and sense of fear and visions for months, although I was never cowardly.

The prison commander, Colonel Burton Andrus, was ordered to cover up the circumstances of Conti's death to save embarrassment. He would certainly have been arraigned for his involvement in the euthanasia programme and medical experiments on humans. His estate was fined 3,000 marks on 1 May 1949 by a Berlin de-Nazification court.

An early SS portrait of Conti.

The medical officer of SS-Gruppe Ost.

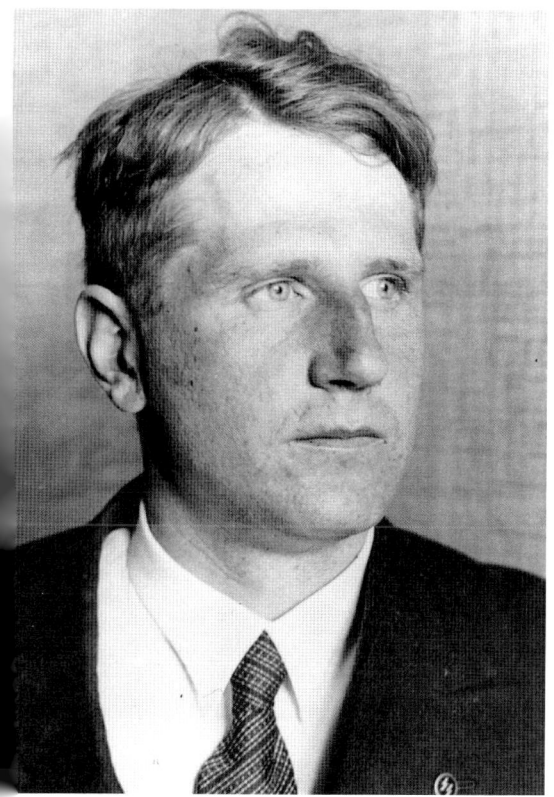

Conti wears his civilian SS pin.

SS-Oberführer Dr Leonardo Conti.

Leonardo Conti in the uniform of a Reich Hauptdienstleiter.

SS-Brigadeführer Dr Leonardo Conti.

Conti visiting a concentration camp.

Left and right: SS-Gruppenführer Conti.

Two doctors converse—Conti in discussion with Dr Karl Brandt.

Conti and an Italian officer overlooking the Berlin Brandenburg Gate.

Left and right: Conti in SS-Gruppenführer uniform.

SS-Gruppenführer Conti examines a man's hand.

Doctors Conti and Gebhardt.

Conti during an inspection visit.

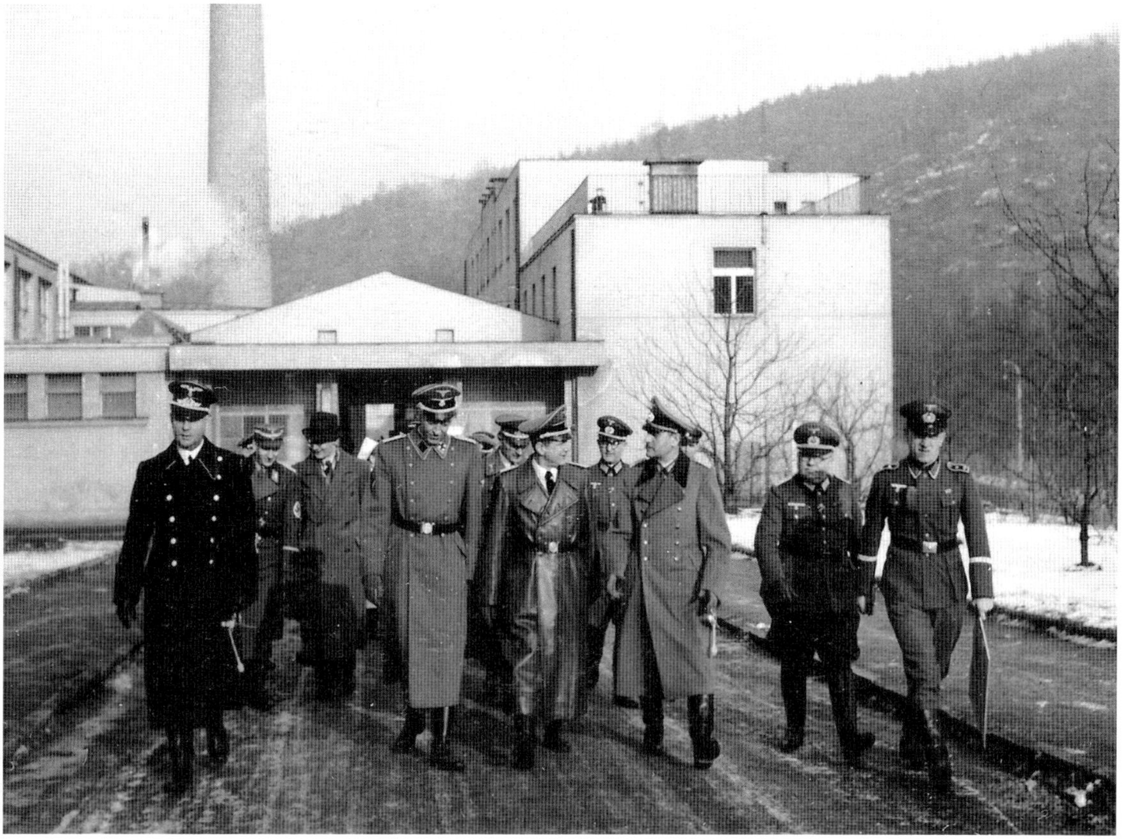

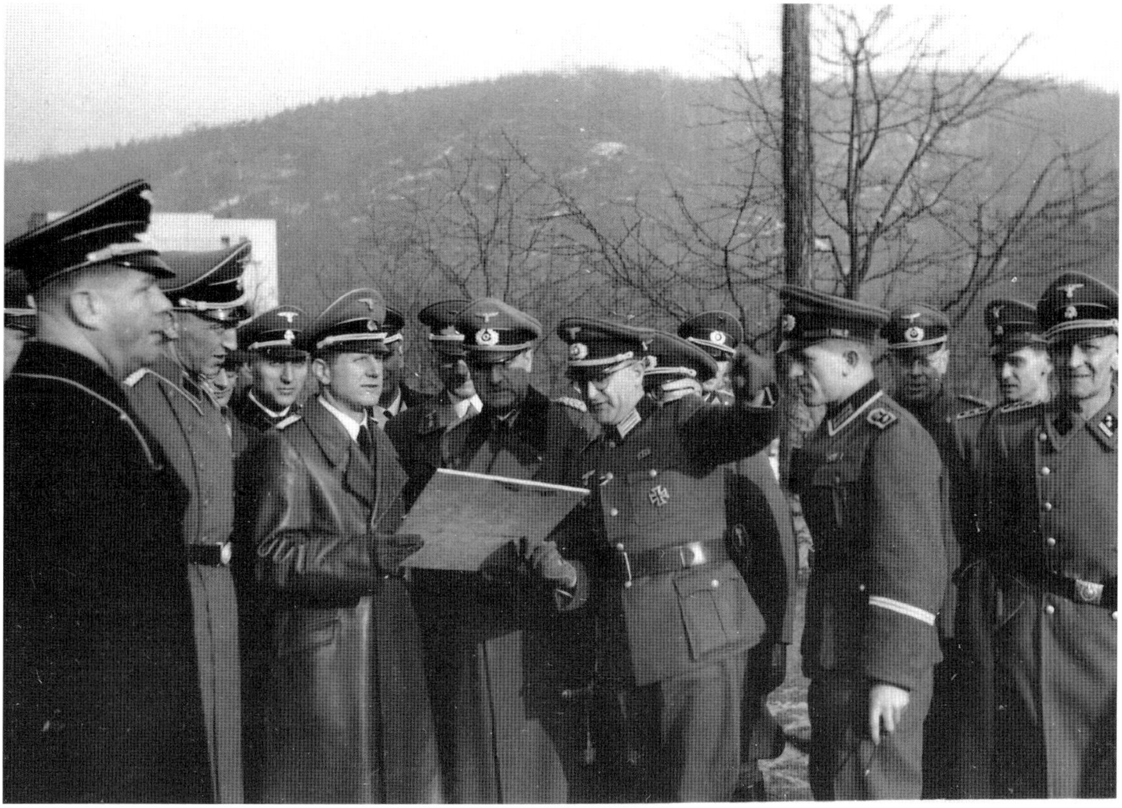

Conti meets peasants in traditional dress.

Prisoner of war Leonardo Conti.

KURT MAX FRANZ DALUEGE

K<small>URT</small> D<small>ALUEGE</small> was born on 15 September 1897 in Kreuzberg, Upper Silesia, the fourth son of agricultural inspector Paul Daluege and his wife Laura (born Ueker). Two days after his birth he was baptised in the Lutheran faith, but his family upbringing was not a strict, religious affair. Kurt's older brother, Joachim, died of an unknown cause when Kurt was very young, and the remaining three brothers—Artur, Erich, and Kurt—carried a strong sibling rivalry throughout their young lives. Erich (born 10 June 1895; NSDAP member 11 463) had a leg amputated in the First World War and was a later SS-Obersturmbannführer and local councillor. Kurt was always proud that in later life he had achieved more than both his older brothers. All three brothers suffered from inherited syphilis.

Before Kurt started school, the family moved from Kreuzburg to Breslau, where he began his formal education in 1903 at an elementary primary school. In 1907 Paul Daluege was promoted to chief agricultural inspector and transferred to Frankfurt-Oder, where Kurt attended a technical secondary school. He had his confirmation in the Lutheran Church on 7 March 1912. At school he studied modern languages and the sciences and excelled at athletics. His only recorded transgression of the school rules was on 23 December 1914, when he retaliated in the school gymnasium after being purposely tripped by another student, striking him in the face. For this he was rewarded with one-hour detention after school hours.

Whilst at school he joined the Wandervogel youth group and was a popular member, playing the lute, swimming, sailing and rowing competitively. With many other young men of his generation keen to fight for the Fatherland, Daluege took advantage of the emergency measures introduced during the war to sit his graduation examinations early, taking and passing his examinations in a single day on 21 June 1916. He graduated with high 'B' grades in maths, physics and technical drawing; standard 'B' grades in history, geography and handwriting; chemistry, religion, singing and languages were graded as 'sufficient' and Latin as 'insufficient'. His only 'A' grade was in athletics. Daluege was happy with these results, as his ambition was to become an engineer like his older brother, Artur. These subject grades qualified him for further education in the required disciplines.

Daluege reported for military service on 2 August 1916 at the recruit depot of the Reserve Battalion of 2nd Guards Regiment of Foot. After five weeks of initial training he was posted to the 4th company. He immediately volunteered for a machine-gun company. He went up the line after arriving by train on the Western Front on 11 November 1916 and found himself in the thick of the fighting in the vicinity of Louvremont, near Verdun, until 10 January 1917. His unit was transferred between 1 January and 24 March 1917 from Verdun to Aisne-Champagne in reserve. He fought at the second Battle of the Aisne River in April 1917, displaying exceptional courage under fire. He was recommended for promotion and the award of the Iron Cross First Class for his bravery by his commander, Leutnant Poppe. On 1 May 1917, he was awarded the Iron Cross 2nd Class, personally presented to him in the trenches by Crown Prince Wilhelm.

Daluege contracted a throat infection and was hospitalised in Carignau for two weeks from 10 May 1917. He returned to his unit for further training and was then transferred on 19 July 1917 to the Eastern Front, around Riga. He fought in the battle to take Riga until 5 September 1917 and was then granted three weeks' leave. With much encouragement from his commanding officer, he applied for a commission and attended the officer-training establishment at Döberitz for five months until 8 March 1918. On returning to his unit he was involved behind the lines, back on the Western Front, in preparation for the coming great German offensive, which started on 21 March 1918. Daluege participated in the area around St Quentin and on 1 April 1918 his upper-right thigh was seriously wounded by an artillery grenade. He could not be removed to a field hospital until 5 April 1918 and received emergency treatment at the front. He was hospitalised until 11 October 1918; the following day he reported to the 3rd Reserve Machine-gun Company of the Guards Corps in Frankfurt-Oder. He saw no further active service and was discharged from the Army on 9 January 1919 with a 23 per cent war disability pension.

During the war, Daluege engendered an ambition to become an engineer. Anticipating his military discharge, he obtained work in December 1918 at the J. Martens machine factory. Around the same time he was recruited by the 'Black Reichswehr', a secret paramilitary group of nationalistic war veterans. By March 1919 he had left J. Martens for an apprenticeship with Camin and Neumann, a firm making cast-iron parts for motors and other machinery. He lived at his parents' house from 1919 until 1920 and was determined to study engineering at the prestigious Charlottenburg Technical High School in Berlin. To obtain sufficient qualifications for Charlottenburg, he sat and passed further examinations on 23 April 1921. In May he joined the Upper Silesian Self Defence Organisation (SSOS), participating in fighting against Polish insurgents. Whilst with the SSOS he was approached by friends from the Freikorps Rossbach and asked to join their ranks.

Daluege studied constructional engineering at the Charlottenburg Technical High School from 1921 until 1924. He balanced his time between his studies, running the local Rossbach Freikorps unit (in which both his brothers joined him) and part-time work to pay for his studies. He also rowed for the Berlin Rowing Club in Wannsee.

In November 1922 he left his Freikorps unit and joined the anti-Semitic German Peoples' Protection and Defensive League. This led him to the Greater German Workers' Party (GAP), the Prussian equivalent of the NSDAP—which had been banned in Prussia—and in early 1923 he fell under the spell of Adolf Hitler. During the abortive Beer Hall Putsch of November 1923, Daluege was waiting in Potsdam, with about thirty men, for a telephone call from Munich which would order him to act in Berlin. With his tiny band of loyal supporters, he was prepared to try and seize control of the capital. It was doomed to failure.

The subsequent national ban on the NSDAP forced Daluege to found the Berlin Frontbann on 30 July 1924, a cover organisation in Berlin for the NSDAP storm troopers (*known in Bavaria as the SA*), but he was certainly involved in much street fighting before then. On one such occasion, on 9 July 1924, he was so seriously injured in a fight that the Saint Hedwig Hospital announced he had died and returned his mail as 'recipient deceased'.

During this politically volatile period, Daluege was heavily involved in street battles and beer-hall fights, some resulting in fatalities. The period became known as the 'period of struggle' by the NSDAP, and those who took part were proud to wear their battle scars. Daluege was arrested on several occasions, but was usually released either without charge or with a small fine. On 29 October 1925, he was arrested for being affiliated with secret organisations, but nothing came of it. With all this political unrest, Daluege amazingly found time to pass his examinations as a qualified civil engineer in 1924. He started work for an ironworks before working for the Prussian Ministry of Agrculture as a director of engineering for railways and canals.

Daluege was married on 16 October 1926 in Bad Liebenwerda to Käthe Schwarz (born on 23 November 1901 in Bad Liebenwerda, died 1974; NSDAP number 118363). Käthe's nickname for her new husband was 'Kutti'. By 1937 there had been no offspring from the marriage and the couple wished to adopt. However, to encourage natural procuration, Nazi regulations stipulated that Daluege—at forty years of age—was too young to adopt without sufficient health reasons. Therefore Daluege reluctantly contrived to declare himself impotent through inherited syphilis, and he obtained medical evidence in support. This remarkable false declaration enabled the Dalueges to adopt a baby boy on 14 March 1937—Helge Belbe (born on 6 March 1937). Käthe fell pregnant within a year, and a boy, Klaus, was born in August 1938, followed by a second son, Gunter, in 1940 and a daughter, Bärbel, on 11 May 1942. Heinrich Himmler agreed to be Godfather to Klaus.

On 12 March 1926, Daluege re-enrolled in the newly organised NSDAP and was allocated with membership number 31 981. Ten days later, he incorporated his Berlin section of Frontbann with the SA, but under the cover name Sportsabteilung (*sport section*). He was effectively the SA commander in Berlin until 21 June 1928, a position confirmed by Ernst Schlange—the then-Gauleiter of Berlin-Brandenburg and ally of Gregor Strasser. Daluege supported Dr Josef Goebbels in a fight for control of the Berlin Gau. Goebbels rewarded him on 9 November 1926 by appointing Daluege as his deputy Gauleiter, after succeeding in gaining control of the newly created Gau 'Gross-Berlin'.

Meanwhile, Daluege found a post in 1927 with the Berlin municipal sanitation department as a section head, responsible for construction of recycling and waste disposal plants. He remained in this position until January 1933.

During the re-organisation of the SA in 1928, Daluege failed to be nominated as one of the seven Reich SA-Gruppe Oberführer, even though he commanded the SA in the capital city. This was partly because his SA work suffered through his time-consuming full employment as an engineer, but also probably because of his lack of diplomacy and naïvety; for the latter, he gained the rather-derogatory nickname 'Dummi-Dummi'. Walter Stennes, the charismatic former Freikorps officer, was named as the new SA-Oberführer Ost, an area which included Berlin, much to the chagrin and anger of Daluege. In an effort to placate the overlooked Daluege, he was attached as SA-Führer for special assignments on the staff of the Reich SA leadership in July 1929.

Heinrich Himmler was appointed as Reichsführer-SS in January 1929 and the elitist nature of that organisation took seed. In Berlin, Hitler looked towards the ever-faithful Daluege and personally requested him to join the ranks of the SS. He acquiesced and on 25 July 1930, Daluege asked to be relieved from the SA in order to join the SS. He was allocated SS membership number 1 119, with the rank of SS-Oberführer Ost. Hitler wanted only the most loyal of men as his protection squad. In a letter to Daluege he wrote the words, '*SS-Mann, Deine Ehre heisst Treue*' ('*SS man, your honour is loyalty*'). Himmler seized upon this and chose the new SS motto, '*Meine Ehre heisst Treue*' ('*my honour is loyalty*').

Stennes instigated a dispute with the Party in August 1930, refusing to provide SA protection for Dr Goebbels at an important speech. Goebbels turned to Daluege and requested the deployment of SS men. The SA revolt escalated and was only diffused by the personal intervention of Hitler.

Daluege was rewarded with the leadership of SS-Abschnitt III Ost on 1 March 1931. He was placed in command of SS-Gruppe Ost on 15 March 1932, and effectively retained this post until 1 October 1933, when he transferred to the staff of the Reichsführer-SS, on special assignment. He was promoted to SS-Gruppenführer on 1 July 1932.

On 24 April 1932, he was elected as NSDAP member for Potsdam in the Prussian legislature. After the NSDAP came to power in January 1933, Daluege received a number of posts. He was appointed as an Under-Secretary in the Prussian Ministry of the Interior, a commissioner for special assignments, the leader of Special Bureau Daluege, chief of the Prussian police, and a Prussian State Councillor. These posts were at the behest of Hermann Göring. Daluege was now firmly in Göring's camp—much to the annoyance of Heinrich Himmler.

On 15 March 1933, Himmler dispatched his young deputy, Reinhard Heydrich, from Munich to Berlin to see Daluege, fearful of Daluege's fast-growing importance in Berlin. Himmler had not been elevated to any important role in the new Nazi government, but he had plans to control the various state-police authorities throughout the Reich. The old Party street-fighter Daluege considered Heydrich a young upstart and refused to receive him, keeping him waiting at the Savoy Hotel for an audience. Heydrich eventually gave up and returned, empty-handed, to his boss in Munich.

Daluege did, however, host the *SS-Appell Ost* mass parade in Berlin from 11 to 13 August 1933. Both Röhm and Himmler attended as guests of honour. Himmler removed Daluege as commander of SS-Gruppe Ost on 1 October 1933 and transferred him to his own staff.

Daluege was appointed the Ministerialdirektor for Police in the Prussian Interior Ministry on 11 May 1933. By 11 September 1933 he was able to report to Göring that all 'political undesirables' had been purged from the Prussian police. On 14 September 1933, Göring promoted him to General der Landespolizei and in doing so, Daluege—at thirty-six years of age—became the youngest General (non-political) on the European continent.

He was elected as a Reichstag member on 12 November 1933, representing Potsdam II. Later this would change to Berlin Ost.

As Berlin SS leader, Daluege held significant power within the SS. He considered the Bavarian Himmler and his right-hand man, Heydrich, as 'country bumpkin amateurs'. After all, it was Daluege who had experience in hand-to-hand fighting in the city streets—not the Bavarian chicken-farmer and his young upstart sidekick. He shunned attempts by Himmler to move his power base to the Reich capital and was favoured by Interior Minister Wilhelm Frick, Himmler's great rival. It was a serious miscalculation by Daluege, who did not reckon on the political cunning of Himmler; Himmler aligned himself with Frick against Göring and gained control of the Prussian Secret State Police (*Gestapo*) in April 1934. Daluege submitted and forever took second place behind the Himmler-Heydrich partnership.

Realising at last that gaining the enmity of Himmler was a dangerous business, he feared for his life during the events which became known as the Röhm purge from 30 June to 2 July 1934. Totally unaware of what had transpired at Bad Wiessee in the early hours of 30 June, Daluege was surprised by police and troop deployments in the capital city. He made his way to Göring's office in the sumptuous building he occupied as his home, at Leipziger Platz 11, only to find it cordoned-off by guards.

He gained admission and waited nervously in an ante-room, listening to raised voices interspersed with raucous laughter from those within. They were Göring, Himmler, Heydrich and Körner, who were in the process of drawing up lists for arrest and execution. For all he knew, Daluege's own name might have been on one of the lists. He was eventually admitted, and for a time he was witness to how revenge was meted out by the aforementioned. After taking his leave and now fully aware of the facts, he returned to his office on Unter den Linden and spent a very uncomfortable day and night, fearing to go home and listening for footsteps in the corridors outside. It was a lesson for him and he would never again challenge the authority of Himmler.

In the aftermath of the SA slaughter, Daluege was tasked with the command and reorganisation of the SA-Gruppen Berlin-Brandenburg, Pommern, Schlesien, Grenzmark, and Mitte, effective 1 July 1934. He had always been somewhat of a favourite of Hitler, who rewarded him with promotion to SS-Obergruppenführer on 9 September 1934.

On 1 November 1934, Daluege was appointed to head the newly combined departments in the Reich and Prussian Ministries of the Interior which dealt with all police matters, under the title Abteilung III. He was selected to lead the German delegation at the 11th assembly of Interpol in Copenhagen the following June, where he was elected as the vice-President. He was promoted to Generalleutnant der Landespolizei on 20 April 1935 and for his birthday, on 15 September, Himmler presented him with the coveted Damascus blade, the special birthday SS sword.

In early March 1936, Daluege suffered what was probably a mild heart attack and was admitted to the sanatorium of Dr Büdingen in Konstanz. The doctor would henceforth figure in Daluege's life for the rest of his days, carefully monitoring his health regime and carrying out twice-yearly examinations. Daluege was ordered to rest and alter his eating habits and lifestyle.

On 17 June 1936, Hitler announced a re-organisation of the Reich Police, with Himmler appointed as Chief of German Police and Daluege promoted to General der Polizei. By a Himmler decree on 26 June 1936, the ever-faithful Heydrich gratefully received his reward: control of the Security Police, the Secret State Police, the Criminal Police and the Frontier Police. Daluege, nominally Himmler's deputy, swept up the leftovers: the Ordnungspolizei (*ordinary uniformed police*), which included the Schutzpolizei, the Gendarmerie and the police administration, and eventually was also to include the fire service. Clearly, Heydrich emerged as the winner, with Daluege left to lick his wounded pride.

Daluege was appointed to the Olympic committee for the 1936 Berlin games and also the 1940 Helsinki games (*which did not take place*). He was included in Himmler's entourage for the diplomatic visit to Rome in October 1936.

The Dalueges withdrew from the Church on 30 November 1936 and declared themselves 'Gottgläubig' (*'God believers'*). The following year they moved to a larger house in the fashionable Berlin-Dahlem district and Daluege furnished it in the style befitting a senior member of the Nazi regime. There was a hunting room, adorned with mounted antlers, and his office was home to numerous framed and autographed photos of numerous high-profile Nazis. He had also started a collection of archaeological artefacts.

March 1938 witnessed the peaceful annexation of Austria and Daluege was soon in Vienna to reorganise the Austro-German police. He also accompanied Hitler into the Sudetenlands the following October and returned to Rome with Himmler on 18 October 1938.

Daluege agreed to the formation of the SS-Polizei Division from 15,000 members of his Ordnungspolizei in October 1939 and oversaw the development of the unit with great skill. Apparently he was very popular with the police troops. He was included in the planning of the invasion of Russia. He attended several strategic meetings in the first half of 1941 concerning the role of the police after the invasion on 22 June. He was also present at Wewelsburg Castle from 12–15 June 1941, when Himmler outlined the policy to eliminate the Slavic races and the Jews.

After the start of Operation Barbarossa (*the German invasion of the Soviet Union*), Daluege visited units behind the German lines and personally witnessed the shooting of Jews and Soviet prisoners. It was Daluege's signature on the directive, dated 24 October 1941, which approved the deportation of Jews from the Altreich (*Germany*) and the Protectorate. Many were subsequently murdered by Rudolf Lange's Einsatzkommando in the Rumboli forest outside Riga.

Kurt Daluege became one of only four men to hold the rank of SS-Oberst-Gruppenführer when he was promoted on 20 April 1942. He also became Generaloberst der Polizei.

On 27 May 1942, Reinhard Heydrich—by now the Acting Reich Protector of Bohemia-Moravia—was attacked in Prague by Czech Army exiles. Daluege immediately flew to Prague and visited the Bulovka hospital where Heydrich lay seriously wounded by grenade fragments. According to one source, Daluege upset Heydrich's wife by sending her back to the family home outside Prague. Hitler, looking for a temporary replacement for the stricken Heydrich, telephoned Daluege and delegated him with the duties of Acting Reich Protector until the former recovered. This was confirmed in writing on 29 May 1942. By then, Daluege had introduced new security methods in the Protectorate, having declared a state of emergency and issued an order on 28 May that all males over fifteen must register with the authorities; failure to do so would result in the death sentence. On 30 May, he directed that anyone making comments against the Reich or in support of the attack would be summarily shot.

Heydrich succumbed to his wounds on 4 June 1942 and Daluege's more permanent appointment was confirmed. He read the eulogy at Heydrich's memorial service in Prague on 7 June, before flying to Berlin for the funeral on 9 June. The

Czech parachutists responsible were captured and killed on 18 June, but reprisals continued for several weeks. By the time Karl Hermann Frank reported the outcome to Hitler, there had been 3,188 arrests, 1,357 executions, and the villages of Lidice and Lezhaky had been razed to the ground.

Who ordered the destruction of Lidice remains a a matter of conjecture to this day. Daluege's authority was gained retrospectively and it was almost certainly carried out on orders from the highest level, via Karl Hermann Frank. Daluege bears ultimate responsibility as the authority in the Protectorate. It is likely that he knew nothing of the directive until after the event.

Daluege and Karl Hermann Frank despised each other. The envious Frank recognised that Daluege was not politically astute and intrigued to have him removed—finding an ally in Himmler, whose patience with Daluege had also expired. When in the Protecorate, Daluege resided at the Hradcany Castle in Prague or at his country retreat, Schloss Doberschisch. His police duties kept Daluege in Berlin for the majority of his time and he was only in Prague for two days a week, allowing Frank the freedom to wield the real power as State Secretary. By March 1943, Frank had resolved to diminish the powers of the Reich Protector by new legislation. Himmler's wrath had been peaked by Daluege's refusal to carry out his orders to shoot the families of resistance fighters and arrest 500 Czechs as an example. He was also annoyed at Daluege's steadfast support of his police officers' autonomy against the SS and for his personal approach to the Reichsführer to gain an advantageous role for his brother Erich.

The conspirators' chance came in early June 1943, when Daluege suffered a second heart attack—this time more serious—one which would eventually lead to his final downfall. By 7 July 1943 he was back in Konstanz, under the care of Dr Rühl and Dr Koch. He took with him one of his secretaries, Fräulein Margareta Knoblauch, to whom he dictated letters in an attempt to retain his position. Himmler was furious and ordered him to refrain from work and to rest, at the same time informing the psychiatrist Professor Max de Crinis. Himmler was playing on Daluege's previous health history of inherited venereal disease causing mental illness and memory loss.

Adding to his health problems, a scandal involving art treasure stolen from the Protectorate by Einsatzstab II under Major Walter Jurk, an old friend of Daluege, was beginning to surface. By 10 August 1943, Daluege was so depressed he considered suicide, but on 17 August he accepted defeat and finally asked to be relieved from his posts. He was replaced in Prague by a new permanent Reich Protector, Wilhelm Frick, and he was succeeded as chief of the Ordnungspolizei by Alfred Wünnenberg.

Hitler was grateful for his past service and granted him an estate of his choice as a reward. Daluege chose Schloss Doberschisch, but he was thwarted by Frick, who insisted that the manor and the estate should be his own residence. Daluege was left to make another choice.

He was finally ordered to leave the Protectorate on 28 September 1943. He departed for Berlin on 7 October, taking with him a quantity of unauthorised art treasures from his former home—almost certainly the work of Major Jurk. Himmler was furious again and lost interest in assisting Daluege to find a new home. Although he insisted on a property near Berlin, Daluege's final choice fell upon the Ilsenau estate, near Posen, and it was to here that the Daluege family were to move.

In his speech to the Gruppenführer and Obergruppenführer at Posen on 4 October 1943, Himmler repeated his adamant order that Daluege must not return to duty in the near future:

> Our old friend Daluege has such a serious heart problem that he is taking a cure and must now withdraw from active service for 1 and a half to 2 years. I would like to send a teletype or telegram this evening to our two friends, namely Daluege and Kaltenbrunner, on behalf of us all. We hope that Daluege will be well again and able to go into action on the frontline again in, as I say, approximately 2 years.

In other words, he was gone.

Daluege remained a thorn in Himmler's side, refusing to co-operate and also refusing to reduce his staff numbers. By November 1943, Käthe Daluege suffered a nervous breakdown. Daluege refused Wünnenberg's request that he release his personal secretary, Margot Schiefelbein, in order that she could return to her duties at the Ordnungspolizei. For Himmler, this was the last straw. On 24 January 1944, he ordered that Käthe Daluege be admitted to a sanatorium and stopped all personal and friendly contact with Daluege, ordering him to Berlin for a showdown. The meeting never took place and Himmler was left bitterly complaining and admonishing his former colleague for his disobedience. Daluege replied on 17 February 1944, now resigned to his fate. It was the last personal contact between the two men.

The Dalueges stayed in Berlin from February to 25 September 1944, while renovations to the house at Ilsenau were carried out. They took up residence for barely five months, moving back to Berlin to avoid the Russian advance in February 1945. In April 1945 the family moved to Lübeck, where young Bärbel died of typhoid fever. Käthe never fully recovered from the loss of her daughter.

A sick man, Daluege was captured by the Allies in Lübeck and interned at Mondorf-Les-Bain, before being moved to Nuremberg to give evidence before the International Military Tribunal. Much to his surprise, he was handed over to the Czech authorities. He gave evidence at the trial of Karl Hermann Frank, before being put on trial for his own war crimes. In particular he was held responsible for the repressive measures carried out after the attack on Heydrich and for the destruction of the villages of Lidice and Lezhaky. After being found guilty, he was hanged at the Pancrac Prison, in Prague, at 1.03 p.m. on 23 October 1946, with death pronounced at 1.13 p.m. Just prior to execution he had cut his wrists in his cell with a piece from a broken bowl, in a forlorn attempt to commit suicide. He was discovered and his wounds were dressed before he was escorted to the scaffold. His words on hearing his sentence were:

> I die, not as a Christian, but as a State criminal. My work as chief of the Orpo is not acknowledged.

Kurt Daluege was more at home with the roughneck battles of the street fighters than within the political circles of diplomacy. As a result of his association with Himmler and the SS, he has been judged in the same vein, but it is clear his first loyalties were to Hitler and the policemen under his command—he was not the convinced SS man who is often portrayed. There is no doubt he was misguided and a strong anti-Semite—albeit somewhat naïve—which led him to commit major war crimes; this was a strange direction for a career policeman. A firm favourite of Hitler, he displayed leadership and organisational skills. He was rewarded with the German Cross in both Gold and Silver and the Knights Cross of the War Merit Cross with Swords. Popular with his colleagues and his subordinates, he was a family man. His children refused to speak against him; his adopted son, Helge, returned to his biological parents in 1946 and trained as an architect, but also refused to be drawn on his period with the Dalueges. Käthe Daluege returned to her hometown but later moved to West Germany, where she died in a nursing home in 1974.

Opposite below: SS-Gruppe Ost Appell in Berlin, August 1933. Grawitz sits on Daluege's right. Note the unceremonial hanging of caps on the tent poles.

The commander of SS-Gruppe Ost, SS-Gruppenführer Daluege.

SA-Oberführer Kurt Daluege (far left).

SS-Gruppenführer

SS-Obergruppenführer Kurt Daluege.

Shooting practice at the range.

The Daluege couple having fun at the beach.

Daluege realised that he was no match for the Himmler-Heydrich partnership.

Daluege had to be satisfied with the command of the uniform police.

Daluege saluting on the rostrum in Vienna. The SS men (left to right) are: Steinhäusl, Wolff, Heydrich, Himmler, Kaltenbrunner and Fitzthum.

In Austria with Sepp Dietrich and Josef Bürckel.

The Daluege family.

Daluege at the Berlin Reich Chancellery. Left to right: Himmler, Wolff, Meissner, Heydrich, Heissmeyer and Daluege.

Daluege was keen on hunting. He is seen here with Sepp Dietrich and Reinhard Heydrich.

General of Police Kurt Daluege.

Daluege in Riga—a study from a contemporary police magazine.

Daluege in conversation with Police General Müllverstedt in 1941. In the background is SS-Gruppenführer Hans Prützmann.

With Dr Hans Frank in the Generalgovernment.

Daluege aboard his Ju52 aircraft, used for visiting the front and commuting between towns.

At the front.

With Wilhelm Frick at a ski meeting.

The smiling police commander.

On leave with Josef Terboven.

Hitler chose Daluege to replace Heydrich in Prague. He is seen here on the 6 June 1942, when Heydrich's body was removed from the Bulovka hospital by torchlight. Behind him and Karl Hermann Frank are Streckenbach and Nebe.

Promoted to SS-Oberst-Gruppenführer, Daluege is here in Prague with Eigruber, Hacha and Jury.

The power in the Protectorate: Daluege and K. H. Frank.

Daluege gives the address at a memorial service for Heydrich. Note the bust.

A visit by SA-Stabschef Viktor Lutze (right). In the centre is SA-Gruppenführer Franz May.

SS-Oberst-Gruppenführer und Generaloberst der Polizei Daluege.

Anti-partisan action Operation Enzian in Yugoslavia, 1942. The personalities here are (left to right) Hermann, Knoblauch, Lang, Rainer, Rösener, Daluege and Dr Heierzegger.

Two police officers—Bernhard Griese and Rudolf Pannier—visit Himmler's Berlin office after being awarded the Knight's Cross.

Daluege visits Himmler at his Feldkommandostelle Hegewald, near Zhitomir in the Ukraine.

Daluege on trial.

Daluege playing chess in the condemned cell.

Daluege's execution at Pancrac Prison.

RICHARD WALTHER OSKAR DARRÉ

W ALTHER DARRÉ was born into a Protestant family on 14 July 1895 in Belgrano, a suburb of Buenos Aires, Argentina. His father, Richard Oskar Darré (born on 14 March 1854 in Berlin, died on 20 February 1929 in Wiesbaden) had emigrated to Argentina in 1876 and was a director of the import-export firm Engelbert Hardt and Company. Darré's mother, Emilia Berta Elenore (born Lagergren, died on 20 July 1936 in Bad Pyrmont), was half-Swedish and half-German. Walther had two sisters and one brother, Erich (born on 9 August 1902; NSDAP member 635 310), who became a SS-Sturmbannführer in the SS-RSHA (*SS-Rasse-und Siedlungshauptamt*)—of which Darré was in charge. One of his sisters later married SS-Obersturmbannführer Manfred von Knobelsdorf, the Burghauptmann of Wewelsburg Castle. Walther held dual Argentinian and German citizenship until 1933, when his Argentinian citizenship expired.

He attended the German School in Belgrano from 1902 until 1905. When he was nine years old, he was sent to live in Heidelberg, Germany, with Professor Elisabeth Gass. At first he attended the local elementary primary school, until moving later that same year to a high school in Heidelberg. He remained there until transferring to the Evangelical Padagogium School in Bad Godesberg for one year in 1910. As an exchange student, he then spent a year from 1911 to 1912 at King's College School in Wimbledon, south-west London, where he was strongly influenced by his science teacher. In 1912 he returned to Germany, to the evangelical high school in Gummersbach, and graduated from there at Easter 1914. He next attended the German Colonial School in Witzenhausen and intended to return to South America as a farmer, but this was cut short by the outbreak of war in August 1914.

Darré volunteered on 5 August 1914 with the 27th Field Artillery Regiment at Nassau. He was posted as a driver, observer and communications man with a field artillery ammunition column near Douchy, in France, from December 1914 until the following year. He was then assigned to the 111th Field Artillery Regiment until January 1917. He was promoted to Unteroffizier on 1 February 1916 and to

Leutnant on 11 January 1917, after attending a field artillery officers' course at Jüterborg. He was slightly wounded in July 1917, but remained at the front. In the spring of 1918 he transferred to the Field Artillery Regiment von Scharnhorst 10th Hannoverian Regiment, but reported sick with a fever on 19 October 1918. He was repatriated to Germany, where he was hospitalised until 1919. He was a participant at the battles of Champagne, Verdun, Marne, Somme, Aisne-Champagne, Soissons and Rheims.

The fever from which he suffered gave him long-term health problems, and he continued to receive treatment for a heart condition until 1923. On 3 May 1919, he returned to his studies at the Colonial School in Witzenhausen, following an unsuccessful attempt at bookkeeping. In 1920 he was successful in his diploma examination in estate management, but it was not actually awarded until May 1930, as a result of his expulsion from the school on 27 November 1920. This was enforced by a student court of honour, which accused him of lying. The verdict was quashed in 1929.

He became an apprentice farm manager in Hausleiten and then, in July 1921, he managed the estate farm Aumühle, near Wildeshausen, until December 1921. In April 1922 he attended the Friedrich-Witte University in Halle to study agriculture and animal breeding—in addition to racial hygiene, sociology and economics—receiving his diploma in farming in February 1925.

Darré was married on 29 April 1922 to Albertine 'Alma' Stadt (born on 16 July 1901 in Wiesbaden), but it ended in divorce in 1928. They had a daughter on 23 May 1923. His second marriage took place on 14 August 1931, in Neustrelitz, where he wedded Margarite Charlotte von Vietinghoff Scheel (born on 3 December 1900 in Timofejewka, Russia; NSDAP member 303 503). This marriage produced another daughter, Rajfa, on 30th August 1938. His second wife had been his secretary prior to their marriage.

Whilst in Halle he joined the Stahlhelm-Bund in 1923. The next year he joined the Artaman League, where he encountered fellow member Heinrich Himmler. He worked as a voluntary assistant to his old professor at the Friedrich-Witte University for four months until 1 June 1925. He then served as a volunteer at a horse-breeding establishment in Insterburg. In October 1925 he attended the university at Giessen for five months, studying animal breeding. He represented the Reich Ministry of Food at an animal show in Finland in June 1927. At that time he was living with his parents in Wiesbaden.

For one year from December 1928, Darré was appointed as the agricultural specialist at the German embassy in Riga, but he was suspended after a disagreement over seed-breeding exchanges between East Prussia and Finland. He returned to Germany on 1 January 1930 to stay with the sculptor Paul Schultze-Naumburg at his estate in Saaleck, and it was here that he first met Adolf Hitler on 10 May 1930.

He joined the NSDAP on 1 June 1930, with Party membership number 248 256.

Hitler immediately tasked him with assisting Konstantin Hierl to reorganise the German farmers. He moved to Munich on 1 August 1930 and was appointed as the advisor on agricultural matters in the NSDAP Reich leadership. He also became an agricultural specialist for the Reichsführer-SS.

Darré joined the SS on 16 April 1931, but was provided with an earlier effective date of 25 February 1931 and the SS number 6 882. He was given the rank of SS-Sturmbannführer and was promoted to SS-Standartenführer on 9 November 1931. On 10 December 1931 he was appointed leader of Abteilung V (Race) on the leadership staff of the Reichsführer-SS. Himmler saw in him an ideal candidate for his new office dealing with racial and settlement matters, appointing Darré as the chief on 1 January 1932. This later evolved into the SS-Rasse-und Siedlungshaupamt (*SS Race and Settlement Main Office*—RuSHA) in 1935, with Darré retaining control.

Darré was elected to the Reichstag on 6 November 1932 and soon held numerous posts on agricultural committees. He was appointed as Reich Farmers' Leader on 29 May 1933 and held this post until he was succeeded by Herbert Backe in 1943. He was also appointed as NSDAP Reichsleiter on 2 June 1933. On 29 June 1933, Darré was appointed as Reich Minister for Food and Agriculture. He retained the title until being replaced on 1 April 1944 by his more-astute deputy, Herbert Backe. He was suspended from the post on 23 May 1942, but he refused to recognise he no longer held the reins of power in the ministry.

Further SS promotions occurred—to SS-Oberführer on 24 December 1932, and to SS-Gruppenführer on 13 May 1933. His final SS promotion, to SS-Obergruppenführer, materialised on 9 November 1934. He was designated as a member of the staff of the Reichsführer-SS after being replaced as chief of RuSHA when he began to lose favour with Hitler and Himmler.

Highly thought of at first by Hitler, Darré's power began to wane from 1936 when it became obvious that his far-fetched ideas were not in keeping with NSDAP policies. In August of that year, he was incapacitated by an operation on his leg. Both Hitler and Himmler realised that he was incompetent and his influence plunged. Although retaining his executive powers as Reich Minister until 1942, the real power behind the throne was his State Secretary and one-time disciple, Herbert Backe. At first, even though their friendship had cooled, Backe refused to accept the post of Reich Minister. He later relented, and proved a most-able replacement. Darré spent the majority of the war years writing letters from his home, complaining about his treatment, and refusing to acknowledge his demotion.

Darré surrendered to US troops on 14 April 1945 in Thuringia. He was interned at Mondorf-Les-Bain until being sent to Nuremberg, where he flatly refused to give evidence against his former colleagues. He was put on trial in the 'Wilhelmstrasse Case' and found guilty of the confiscation of Polish and Jewish farms; he was sentenced to five years in prison on 13 April 1949. He was released in October 1950 and settled in Bad Harzburg, near Goslar, his Reich farmers' capital, an ill and embittered man. His health had very been poor since 1937, suffering from liver problems, asthma and eczema. He died of liver failure in a clinic in Leopoldstrasse, Munich, on 5 September 1953, having rekindled his friendship with his first wife. He has been described by some as the originator of the Green Party because of his innovative ideas on organic farming.

Clockwise from right:

Darré's father.

Baby Darré with his mother.

Born in Argentina in 1895, Darré did not live in Germany until 1905.

Left: The student.

Below: On the western front.

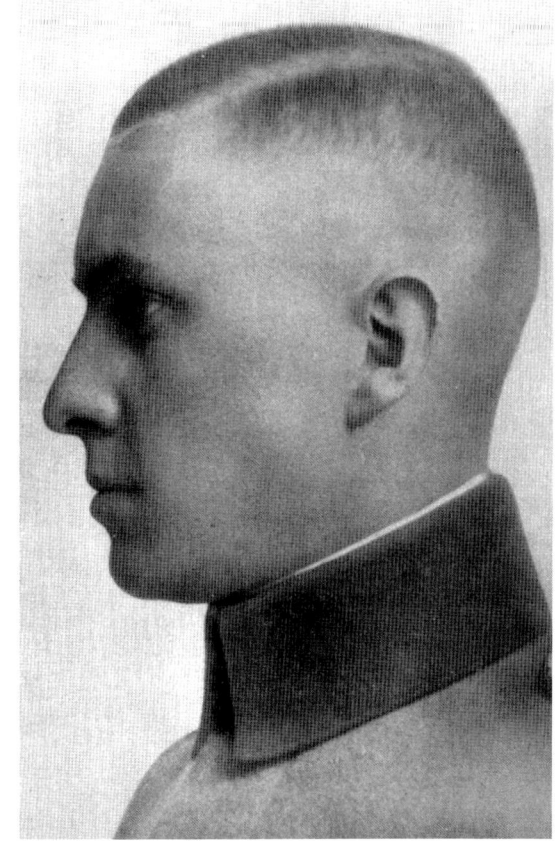

Clockwise from right:

Leutnant der Reserve Darré.

SS-Oberführer Darré.

The Reich farmers' leader and Reich Minister of Agriculture in 1935.

Left: Reichsleiter SS-Gruppenführer Darré.

Below: The Reich Minister during an official visit.

A formal painting of the Reichsminister.

Chief of the SS Race and Settlement Central Office, SS-Gruppenführer Darré.

SS-Obergruppenführer Darré greets his Führer.

Darré in his official car, with Gauleiter Sprenger in the rear seat. Note the car pennant.

A fine photographic study of SS-Obergruppenführer Darré.

Himmler and Wolff visit Darré and his RuSHA staff.

Darré entertains his fellow minister, Dr Goebbels.

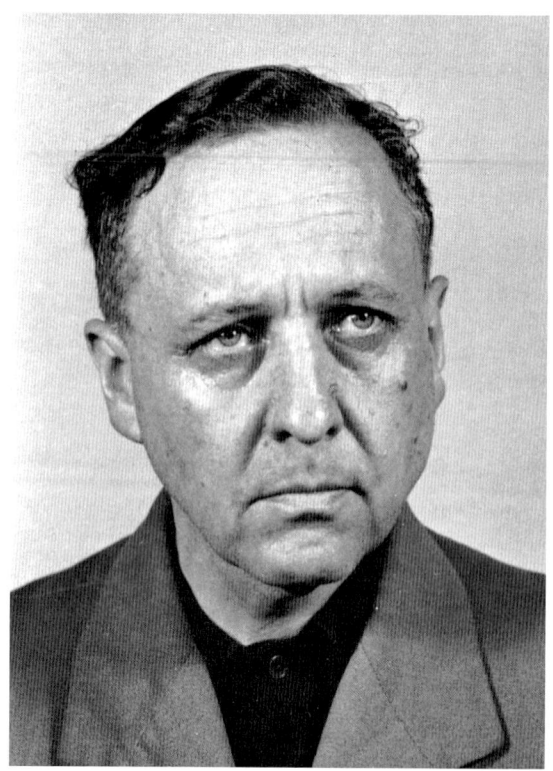

Prisoner of war.

The grave of Richard Walther Darré.

KARL-MARIA DEMELHUBER

KARL-MARIA DEMELHUBER was born the son of Catholic garrison administrator Karl Demelhuber (born on 20 May 1865 in Munich) and his wife Magdalena (born Pfaller, on 28 November 1867 in Breitenbrunn) on 27 May 1896 in Freising, Bavaria. He attended elementary school in Freising for four years until March 1906. Next was the Latin school in Landsberg am Lech from 1 April 1906, followed by the Wittelsbacher High School in Munich. Finally, he attended the Higher Business School in Munich where he gained a diploma in business studies in the summer of 1914.

On 2 August 1914, he volunteered with the Bavarian Field Artillery Regiment 'Prinz Regent Luitpold'. He went to the front on 25 January 1915 with the flak machine-gun detachment. He was wounded near Verdun on 4 June 1916 by grenade splinters in his right shoulder. He was hospitalised, followed by convalescent leave, before returning to the front late in the same year as an Unteroffizier. He received a commission as Leutnant on 24 October 1918 and was demobilised in Fürth in November 1918. He joined the Freikorps 'von Epp' in March 1919, and fought with that unit until May 1920. He was a member of the Reichswehr Artillery Regiment 21 until 1 March 1920, when he retired from active military service, having been promoted to Oberleutnant in 1919.

He studied at the Munich trade school and Munich University until 1921, when he received a further diploma in business studies. On 1 September 1921, he enlisted as a member of the Bavarian Land Police, with the rank of Oberleutnant der Polizei, backdated to an effective date of 1 January 1921.

On 19 May 1921, he was married to Isabella Hölzl (born in Munich on 8 November 1896). They had one son, Karl (born on 14 November 1923), who served later in the Waffen-SS as a NCO. Demelhuber was subsequently a widower, but the details of his wife's death are a mystery. He remarried in 1949 to the widow of another Waffen-SS officer, SS-Sturmbannführer Max Linn.

Demelhuber joined the NSDAP on 20 February 1922 and was allocated membership number 4 439. Following the abortive Beer Hall Putsch of November 1923, he was compelled to distance himself from the now-banned NSDAP because of his police membership. After 1925 the NSDAP leadership (in the person of Gregor Strasser) refused his readmission to the Party, but Demelhuber maintained his contacts at his own expense. Although actively participating in various NSDAP functions, he never rejoined the Party.

From 1 September 1927 until 1 October 1930, he was an instructor at the police academy in Eichsätt, but he was reassigned to Augburg as a result of his speeches in favour of the NSDAP. He remained in Augsburg until 10 March 1933, when he was appointed as adjutant to the Police President of Munich. In this capacity he was adjutant to Himmler, Schneidhuber and Bouhler, and was promoted to Polizei-Hauptmann on 1 June 1933. He was also involved in air defence and in training the staff guard of SA-Obergruppe VII in Munich.

He joined the SA on 1 May 1934 and was utilised as a trainer, with special responsibility for cross-country sports, based temporarily at Neustrelitz sport centre. He was assigned as Wehrgauführer VII in Munich and chief of SA training in the Munich area on 1 September 1934. On 31 January 1935, he left the police service.

Leaving the SA to join the SS, he was allocated SS membership number 252392 on 15 March 1935, with the rank of SS-Obersturmbannführer. He immediately took command of 2nd Sturmbann SS-Standarte 1 'Deutschland'. On 1 October 1936, on promotion to SS-Standartenführer, he was transferred to command SS-Standarte 2 (from 17 August 1938, SS-Standarte 'Germania') in Hamburg. Demelhuber commanded this unit during the Polish campaign of September 1939.

He was promoted on 30 January 1940 to SS-Oberführer. On 10 May 1940, he commanded Marschgruppe B of the SS-V-Division during the invasion of Holland. On 9 November 1940, he was promoted to SS-Brigadeführer und Generalmajor der Waffen-SS. He was posted as the commander of Waffen-SS Ost in Krakow on the staff of the HSSPF, SS-Obergruppenführer Friedrich-Wilhelm Krüger. From 1 April 1941 until 24 April 1941, he was appointed as Waffen-SS commander Südost in Breslau. From this command he transferred to take charge of the newly formed 1st SS-Brigade (Motorised) on 30 April 1941.

He transferred to the command of SS-Kampfgruppe Nord on 25 May 1941. The unit was upgraded to divisional status on 17 June 1941, with Demelhuber retaining command. For two short weeks in September 1941, he was simultaneously appointed as temporary Inspector of SS NCO schools. He was promoted to SS-Gruppenführer und Generalleutnant der Waffen-SS on 20 April 1942. He was placed in charge of the Waffen-SS in Holland on 11 June 1942, on the staff of HSSPF Nordwest (*Hanns Albin Rauter*).

His final promotion, to SS-Obergruppenführer and General of Waffen SS, came on 21 June 1944. He was appointed acting commander of the XII SS-Korps on 18 October 1944, for two days. He was posted to the command staff of the Baltic Sea coast in Fürstenberg on 9 November 1944. From 24 January 1945 he commanded the XVI SS-Armeekorps, and he was nominated as the standing deputy of the Reichsführer-SS in the operation zone of the Baltic Sea coast in February 1945 until 14 March 1945. With the situation rapidly deteriorating, his last post was as Inspector General of Waffen-SS and Army Reserves and Training in the SS-Führungshauptamt, from 21 March 1945.

Demelhuber was captured by the British in Schleswig-Holstein on 16 May 1945. He was initially held at Rendsburg prison, before being transferred to Neuengamme internment camp in June 1945. He was transported to London on 1 March 1946 for questioning about alleged crimes committed by SS-'Germania' in 1940. After interrogation he was transferred to Island Farm Special POW Camp 11 in Bridgend, South Wales. He was repatriated on 18 May 1948 and worked as a businessman in Fürstenfeldbruck from 1954, until finally settling in Seeshaupt, Bavaria. He died there on 18 March 1988. He had a fondness for men's cologne and was nicknamed 'Tosca', after his favourite fragrance. Himmler once told him, *'You may not be my best general, but you are certainly my sweetest!'*

Left to right: von Eberstein, Waldeck, Steiner and SS-Obersturmbannführer Demelhuber.

SS-Brigadeführer Demelhuber visiting Totenkopf in Lublin. Second left is Hermann Fegelein.

Demelhuber addresses the gathered troops.

The guard presents arms. Globocnik and Fegelein in the group, watching.

SS-Standartenführer Demelhuber.

Demelhuber and his dog in the snow.

Demelhuber on a street corner. Note the heavily damaged buildings in the background.

Demelhuber leaving the Andreas Bauriedl barracks, named after the Nazi martyr.

A signed portrait of Demelhuber.

Demelhuber chatting with his men.

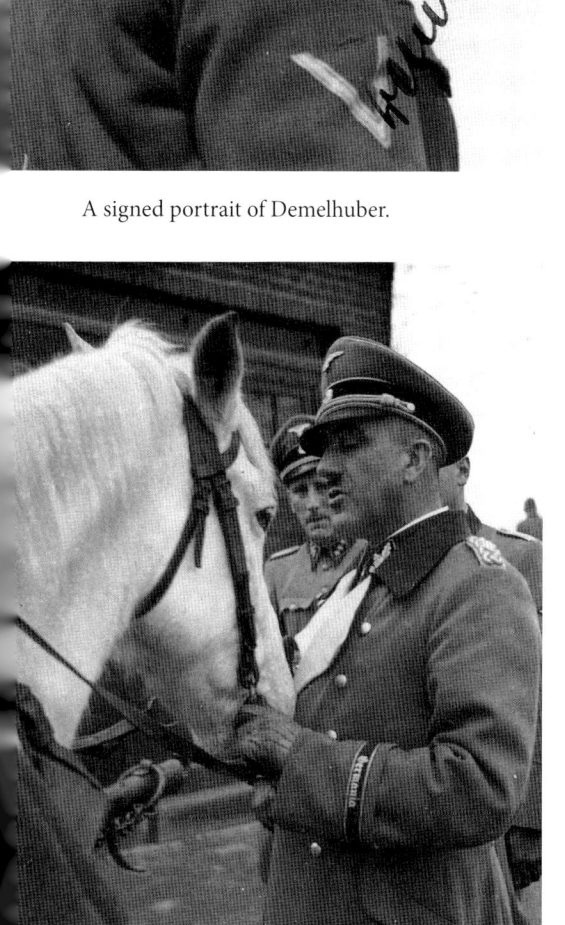

Left and right: The equestrian SS officer.

The commander of Waffen-SS troops in Holland gives his condolences to the widow of a SD man killed by Dutch resistance fighters. To the far left is Wilhelm Harster.

Demelhuber in a white summer tunic.

Demelhuber in the field.

A sun-tanned Demelhuber in white uniform.

SS-Gruppenführer Demelhuber.

A smiling Obergruppenführer poses for the camera.

SS-Obergruppenführer Karl-Maria 'Tosca' Demelhuber.

Demelhuber gained the nickname 'Tosca' due to his fondness for the eau de Cologne of the same name.

Demelhuber with his wife, after the war.

In his home after the war. Note the portrait of Frederick the Great.

The grave of Demelhuber.

JOSEF DIETRICH

Josef 'Sepp' Dietrich was born on 28 May 1892 in Hawangen, Schwabia. Some doubt exists around his parentage, but it appears that he may have been the illegitimate son of Kreszentia Dietrich (died 1948) and a man in service, Josef Högerle. His mother married a coachman, Pelagius Milz, and young Josef was raised as his son in a Catholic family of three boys and three girls—Josef being the oldest boy.

He attended the local primary school in Memmingen from 1898 until 1900, when his family moved to Kempten and he changed to a secondary school there. His first job was driving a farm tractor for one year from 1906, before he travelled to Austria, Italy and Holland, working as a waiter in various hotels. He opted for a career in the leisure industry and obtained an apprenticeship in a hotel in Zurich, Switzerland, only to change his mind in 1910, when he moved to Munich and started an apprenticeship as a butcher. Another change of direction found him enlisting in the military, when he joined the 4th Bavarian Artillery Regiment, based at Augsburg, on 18 October 1911. On 27 November 1911, after one month in training, he was medically discharged following a fall from a horse. He moved back to his family home and from December 1911 until 5 August 1914, he was a baker's errand boy in Kempten.

At the outbreak of war, Dietrich enlisted in the 7th Bavarian Field Artillery Regiment. In October 1914, he saw active service in Flanders with the 6th Bavarian Reserve Field Artillery Regiment. He was seriously wounded by shrapnel in his lower-right leg the following month. After a speedy recovery, he attended an artillery school in Sonthofen in January 1915, before returning to his original posting with the 7th Regiment 'Prinzregent Luitpold'. He was seriously wounded again in 1916, at the Somme, when he received shell splinters to his head and was buried alive. Upon discharge from hospital, he transferred to infantry gun battery 10 in November 1916, followed by Infantry Regiment 8 from 1917 until February 1918. He joined the Bavarian Tank Detachment 13 in Berlin on 19 February 1918. He was assigned as a gunner to a tank nicknamed 'Moritz' at the German Marne offensive in May 1918. His tank was destroyed on 31 May 1918. As a six-pounder tank gunner on a captured British Mark IV tank, he participated at Soissons in July and at Cambrai in October. After the armistice he returned to his old artillery unit, 'Prinzregent Luitpold'. He was discharged on 26 March 1919 as a Vize-Wachtmeister.

Dietrich returned to Munich in April 1919 and possibly took part in the uprising pacifying the communists. He joined the Bavarian Landespolizei on 1 October of that year and held the rank of Polizei-Wachtmeister. By 24 February 1920, he was given command of the reconnaissance platoon of Group I in Munich. At the same time he was assigned to Wehrregiment 1 Munich. In May 1921 he joined the Freikorps Oberland.

Dietrich was married twice, the first on 17 February 1921. His first wife, Barbara Seidl (born in Munich on 24 April 1896), held NSDAP membership number 233 700. They had no children and divorced on 17 January 1942. His second marriage, two days later, on 19 January 1942, was with Ursula Brenner (born Moninger on 26 March 1915, in Karlsruhe, died 1983). She was previously married to SS-Gruppenführer Karl-Heinrich Brenner in 1935. Dietrich had three sons by Ursula: one before they were married, Wolf-Dieter (born on 16 February 1939 in Karlsruhe), followed by Lutz (born on 20 March 1943 in Karlsruhe) and Götz-Hubertus (born on 23 November 1944 in Karlsruhe). Heinrich Himmler was the godfather of both younger boys.

He resigned from the police service in 1923 as a Polizei-Oberwachtmeister and joined the NSDAP and the SA. He had previously taken a leave of absence from his police duties in 1921 to serve with the Freikorps Oberland in Upper Silesia. He returned to this Freikorps unit to participate at the 'Beer Hall' Putsch in Munich on 8—9 November 1923.

From 1925 until 1927, he worked as the manager of the Blue Buck filling station in Munich, owned by Christian Weber. From 1927 until 1929 he was employed as a hat-maker, errand boy and warehouse manager in the tobacco factory of the Austria Tobacco Company.

Dietrich provided bodyguard services for Adolf Hitler from 1927 and joined the NSDAP on 1 May 1928, becoming member number 89 015. He then joined the SS on 5 May 1928, being allocated SS number 1 177. On 1 June that year, he was promoted to SS-Sturmführer, taking charge of the 1st SS-Sturm in Munich. This unit became the 1st SS-Standarte 'Munich' on 1 August 1928. Dietrich was promoted to SS-Sturmbannführer the same day. On 18 September 1929, he was appointed Leader of SS-Brigade Bayern, and was duly promoted to SS-Standartenführer on 18 November 1929. He was at that time employed as a packer and dispatch clerk with the Franz-Eher-Verlag publishing house. He was also a member of Hitler's personal bodyguard unit.

On 11 July 1930, Dietrich was promoted to SS-Oberführer and placed in command of SS-Gruppe Süd. On 14 September 1930, Dietrich took his seat as the elected Reichstag member for Lower Bavaria. On 14 August 1931 he took charge of SS-Abschnitt IV in Hildesheim, and he was promoted to SS-Gruppenführer on 18 December 1931. On 29 February 1932, he was entrusted with the command of the SS-Begleitkommando der Führer (*Hitler's personal bodyguard escort unit*). By order of the SA-Führerbefehl number 1 of 1 July 1932, Dietrich was appointed as commander of SS-Gruppe Süd. He was then appointed to the command of SS-Gruppe Nord in Hamburg on 1 October 1932, as the personal representative of the Führer.

On 17 March 1933, Hitler commissioned Dietrich with the formation of the SS-Stabswache 'Dietrich' in Berlin, later to become SS-Sonderkommando Berlin and the fledgling Leibstandarte-SS 'Adolf Hitler'. He was attached to the staff of the RFSS on special assignment on 20 March 1933. On 1 October 1933, he was placed in command of SS-Gruppe Ost in Berlin and the Adolf-Hitler-Standarte. From 16 November 1933 until 14 November 1939, Dietrich was the commander of SS-Oberabschnitt Ost. On 13 April 1934, he was appointed as commander of the prestigious Leibstandarte-SS 'Adolf Hitler', a post he retained until 15 July 1942.

During the events of 30 June 1934 and beyond, Dietrich played a major role in the suppression of the so-called Röhm Putsch. He accompanied Hitler to Bad Wiessee and then quickly arranged for the Berlin-Lichterfelde barracks of his Leibstandarte to be available for the ordered executions of SA leaders. He participated in the executions of the SA leaders at the Stadelheim prison in Munich, before flying to Berlin on 1 July to carry out similar duties there. He was duly promoted to SS-Obergruppenführer on the same day.

Before the war, Dietrich was regularly seen with Hitler and was counted among his close entourage. He placed his Leibstandarte at the will of the Führer, and it subsequently took active roles in the re-occupation of the Rhineland and the Austrian Anschluss. Before the war, its most famous duty was to provide the smart black, silver and white uniform which adorned sentries for the Reich Chancellery in Berlin, other residences of the Führer, and at special, important events.

In April 1938, Dietrich was elected as Reichstag deputy for Frankfurt-Oder. He retained this seat until the end of the war. He was also a member of the State Press Chamber, a Labour Front Supreme Disciplinary Court judge and a Berlin city councillor.

On 14 November 1939, Dietrich was appointed as commander of SS-Oberabschnitt Spree, a post that was effectively administered by his deputy, SS-Gruppenführer Max Schneller.

During the Second World War, the Leibstandarte-SS 'Adolf Hitler' saw distinguished action in nearly all theatres of battle, including Poland, Holland, France, the Balkans, Italy and the Soviet Union. Dietrich was in operational command throughout most of the war, only being replaced in the later stages as he gained extra responsibility. In May 1942, he was granted 100,000 Reichsmarks by Hitler as a reward for his 'special services'. On 4 June 1943, he was granted special leave, and returned on 23 June 1943 as the newly appointed Panzer General of Waffen-SS to organise the new 1st SS-Panzer Corps, of which he took command on 27 July 1943. On 6 June 1944, he was ordered to Normandy as part of the counter-invasion force. On 9 August 1944, he took command of the 5th Panzer Army. However, he transferred his command to the 6th Panzer Army on 14 September 1944 on Hitler's direct orders, leading this unit during the Ardennes offensive and the Hungarian action around Lake Balaton, before defending Vienna.

Dietrich was promoted to SS-Oberst-Gruppenführer and Panzer Generaloberst of Waffen-SS on 1 August 1944, made retrospectively effective from 20 April 1942. He was one of the most highly decorated German officers of the war. He could boast the award of the Knights Cross of the Iron Cross, Oakleaves of the Knights Cross of the Iron Cross (*the 41st recipient*), Swords to the Knights Cross of the Iron Cross (*the 26th recipient*) and Diamonds to the Knights Cross of the Iron Cross (*the 16th recipient*).

Dietrich surrendered with his wife to Master Sergeant Herbert Kraus of the US 36th Infantry Division at Krems in Austria on 9 May 1945. He was held at Kufstein until being transferred to an interrogation centre at Augsburg on 15 May 1945. He was held in various internment centres throughout Germany until 26 April 1946, when he was incarcerated in Dachau Internment Camp to stand trial as chief defendant in the Malmedy Process, losing his prisoner-of-war status. On 16 July 1946, he was sentenced to life in prison and was transported to Landsberg Prison the following day. On 10 August 1946, his sentence was reduced to twenty-five years. His fourth application for parole proved successful, and he was released on 22 October 1955 to live in Ludwigsburg.

Dietrich soon found himself in front of the courts again, this time on 6 May 1957 in Munich, as a defendant in the trial of the perpetrators of the murders on 30 June–1 July 1934. Defended by his ex-brother-in-law Alfred Seidl (*the defence attorney of Rudolf Hess*), he was found guilty and sentenced to eighteen months in prison by the Munich court on 13 May 1957. He started his sentence at Landsberg am Lech prison on 7 August 1958. Six months later, on 2 February 1959, he was released on medical grounds as a result of circulation problems and a heart condition. He returned to live in Ludwigsburg.

Sepp Dietrich was a popular man, both with his troops and the circle around Hitler. He was a personal favourite of Hitler—only falling out with him on one occasion, when the Leibstandarte was forced to retreat in the Hungarian campaign, during the final stages of the war. An angry Hitler declared the men to be cowards and ordered that they remove their cufftitles, which bore his name. Dietrich ignored the order. He was a particular favourite of Eva Braun and a welcome visitor at the Berghof. He had a somewhat strained relationship with the Reichsführer-SS, who found him frustrating; Dietrich ignored many orders which he deemed idiotic. Much to the chagrin of Himmler, he wore unauthorised versions of SS insignia on his uniform. In the post-war years, Dietrich was honoured as the senior ex-Waffen-SS officer by HIAG, the organisation formed to assist ex-Waffen-SS men. He took an active interest in the plight and welfare of his men, vehmently arguing in support of their military status. The great war leader died peacefully in his bed, suffering a massive heart attack, in Ludwigsburg on 21 April 1966.

SS-Gruppenführer Dietrich.

The commander of the Leibstandarte-SS Adolf Hitler.

Dietrich wearing the ceremonial dress of the LAH.

With Jürgen Stroop (left) and Rolf Humann-Hainhofen.

Left and right: Obergruppenführer Dietrich in the field-grey SS uniform.

Left and right: On the terrace at the Berghof.

A hand-signed and dedicated portrait of SS-Obergruppenführer Sepp Dietrich.

Dietrich in winter uniform, wearing the Knight's Cross with Oakleaves.

A formal portrait.

Dietrich with his staff.

A relaxed SS-Obergruppenführer.

A magnificent official portrait of SS-Obergruppenführer Sepp Dietrich.

Dietrich receiving awards with Hitler.

Dietrich in his lightweight tunic, wearing the Knight's Cross with Oakleaves and Swords.

SS-Oberst-Gruppenführer Sepp Dietrich.

Dietrich with his new bride, Ursula Moninger.

Prisoner of war.

Dietrich stands accused before a post-war court.

With old comrades.

The grave of Sepp Dietrich, before the headstone was removed by the authorities.

OTTO DIETRICH

O TTO DIETRICH was born on 31 August 1897 in Essen. He attended the local elementary school from 1903 until 1907, followed by high school in Essen, from where he matriculated in 1914.

He volunteered for military service on 10 August 1914 with Field Artillery Regiment 7. On 10 March 1915, he transferred to the 43rd Field Artillery Regiment and served with it until 5 May 1915. He saw action in France and Flanders with his original unit, the 7th Field Artillery Regiment, from May 1915 until the end of the war. He was commissioned as a Leutnant der Reserve on 12 November 1917. During a period of leave in 1917, he obtained his high school leaving diploma in Ghent. He was discharged from military service on 12 December 1918.

From 1918 until 1921, he studied political science, economics and philosophy at the universities of Munich, Frankfurt am Main and Freiburg. He gained his doctorate in 1921.

From 1922 until 1928, he was first a research assistant with the Essen chamber of commerce, before being subsequently appointed the trade editor and Munich correspondent of the *Tagezeitung*. He was then taken on as deputy editor of the *Essen Allgemeine Zeitung*. In 1928 he was appointed business manager and commercial editor of the *Munich-Augsburg Abendzeitung*, and also legal advisor and business agent of the Rheinische Steel Goods Syndicate.

Dietrich joined the NSDAP on 1 April 1929 and was allocated membership number 126 727. He was appointed as an assistant in the Reich leadership of the NSDAP, and subsequently became the NSDAP press chief on 1 August 1931. Hitler entrusted Dietrich with the organisation of his election campaign for the Chancellorship in 1932. He travelled the length and breadth of Germany as a member of Hitler's close entourage. Dietrich filled numerous posts on NSDAP committees as the press representative and spokesman. In 1933 he was appointed as Hitler's press advisor, and joined his personal staff as Reichsleiter for press matters. He remained in this post until March 1945, when he was sacked on Goebbels' insistence for defeatism. Among his assignments in 1933 were the Presidency of the

German Press Association and vice-presidency of the Reich Press Chamber. On 15 January 1938, he became a State Secretary in the Reich Propaganda Ministry under Dr Goebbels, who considered him to be an idiot. The appointment was a personal choice of Hitler, who was blind to Dietrich's shortcomings. Simultaneously, he was appointed President of the Reich Press Chamber and Press Chief of the Reich government. He was also a Reich culture senator and an elected Reichstag deputy.

Dr Dietrich joined the SS on 31 July 1933, with a retrospective effective date of 24 December 1932, as an honorary SS-Oberführer with SS-Gruppe Süd. His SS number was 101 349. He was promoted to SS-Brigadeführer on 1 January 1934 and to SS-Gruppenführer on 27 January 1934. On 23 January 1936, he was transferred to the staff of the Reichsführer-SS. He was promoted to SS-Obergruppenführer on 20 April 1941.

He suffered a nervous breakdown in the spring of 1943, following the German defeat at Stalingrad. He had been confident of an early German victory in 1941, announcing to the press in autumn of that year that the Soviet Army was finished and Hitler would dictate when the campaign finished. Eighteen months later, the realisation of defeat hit him hard and he was unable to handle the humiliation of the reversal.

Dietrich was married to Almut Reismann (born on 31 August 1900 in Essen; Party number 263 007). They had one daughter, who was born in 1934.

As a member of the Führer's personal staff, Dietrich was in regular attendance at all of Hitler's headquarters and can be seen in the background in many photographs of Hitler during the war. During the latter stages of the war, he was outspoken about Germany's precarious position—incurring the wrath of Goebbels, with his 'total war' philosophy. Dietrich was finally dismissed from all his posts by Hitler on 30 March 1945, at the request of Dr Goebbels. He was imprisoned in 1945 and stood trial in the Wilhelmstrasse Case at Nuremberg, where he received a seven-year prison term on 11 April 1949. He was released from Landsberg prison on 16 August 1950 for good behaviour, and then lived and worked in Düsseldorf for the German Motor Traffic Society. He died on 22 November 1952 in Düsseldorf.

A young Otto Dietrich during the First World War.

Hitler's press chief, SS-Gruppenführer Dietrich.

An official portrait.

A close-up of the SS-Gruppenführer.

Dietrich reports to Hitler.

Dietrich with Hitler and Goebbels. The Reich Minister of Propaganda considered Dietrich to be lacking in intelligence and original ideas.

The rank of SS-Obergruppenführer was considered suitable for Dietrich's position.

Dietrich in profile.

Dietrich joins Wagner and Hitler at an evening outdoor event. Note Eva Braun, seated directly behind Hitler.

Dietrich in his white summer tunic, on the terrace of the Berghof with Schaub.

Reichsleiter SS-Obergruppenführer Otto Dietrich at Hitler's field headquarters.

Dietrich in Reichsleiter uniform, greeting NSDAP officials.

Left and right: SS-Obergruppenführer Otto Dietrich.

Dietrich in France.

At the Führerhauptquartier.

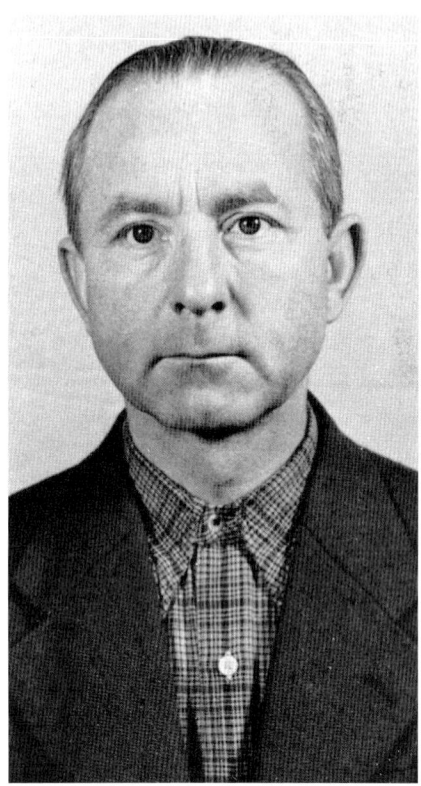

Prisoner of war.

Dietrich hears his sentence at Nuremberg.

FRIEDRICH KARL FREIHERR VON EBERSTEIN

T HE HALLE aristocratic von Eberstein family proudly announced the birth of a baby boy in their hometown on 14 January 1894. The baby's father was retired Army Major Ernst Freiherr von Eberstein (born in Schiepzig on 7 April 1847, died in Halle on 2 November 1907), and his mother was Elise Frieda Klara (born von Kotze in Trakehnen on 17 May 1859, died in Halle on 22 February 1935). In 1904, they became the godparents of Reinhard Heydrich. The couple lived at Heinrichstrasse 8/I and Karl was their only child.

After his initial private tutoring at home, Karl von Eberstein was sent in April 1904 to the Army officer cadet academies at Naumburg and then Lichterfelde in Berlin. He stayed there until March 1912, when he left on health grounds to study agriculture and economics at the University of Halle. He gained practical experience in estate administration by working at estates in Schkeuditz and Altenrode.

He volunteered for war service in Halle with Field Artillery Regiment 75 in August 1914, but he suffered a fall from a horse and did not go to the front until December 1914, with the newly formed Field Artillery Regiment 'General Government'. In January 1915 he was taken ill and repatriated to Germany; he was then posted to the Field Artillery Regiment 17 in July 1915, after attending an officer candidate's course in Jüterborg in April–May 1915. He was promoted to Leutnant der Reserve on 25 November 1915. He was at the airship school in Jüterborg in January 1916, for training as a secured balloon observer. He returned to the Western Front in February 1916, attached to Field Airship Section 14, but was returned to his original unit in September 1916 on health grounds. He stayed with it until the end of the war and was discharged from Army service on 28 November 1918.

From March until April 1919, von Eberstein was a volunteer member of General von Maercker's Freikorps. Throughout the remainder of that year and into 1920, he was an active member of the 1st company of Freikorps Regiment Halle—officially in the 16th Brigade until May 1920. He took part in the Kapp Putsch of March 1920 as commander of Battery 3 Field Artillery Regiment 16, under Hauptmann Mahraun.

Due to lack of funds, von Eberstein had to give up his agricultural studies. He found employment as a bank trainee—first with the Commerz-& Privat Bank AG in Delitzsch and Halle, and then with the Genossenschaftsbank GmbH. He was appointed as a volunteer Polizei-Oberwachtmeister with the Halle Schutzpolizei in April 1921. The following month, along with many students from Halle, he went to the area of Cosel and Ratibor, Upper Silesia, as adjutant of the Volunteer Regiment Martin of Freikorps Brigade Graf Magnis until July 1921.

To avoid arrest, he fled temporarily to the Tyrol and Salzkammergut mountain areas in Austria, at the beginning of September 1921. He returned to his bank employment later in September for one year, staying in Halle and joining the NSDAP in October 1922. He took part in a military exercise in April 1923 with the 4th Infantry Division at Königsbrück. On 10 September 1923, he started work as a commercial salesman for the Ammoniawerkes Merseburg GmbH. However, he left to work as a private secretary in asset administration for Wolf-Heinrich Graf von Helldorff at Schloss Wohlmirstedt on 17 August 1924.

Von Eberstein was married twice; the first marriage was in Halle, on 8 June 1923, to Margarete Putze, but it did not last—the couple divorced on 29 June 1926 without issue. He married again on 17 December 1927, in Erfurt, to the widow Helene Hopf (born Meinel-Scholer on 22 May 1892 in Klingentahl, died on 4 April 1969 in Tegernsee; NSDAP membership number 1 303 045). They had one son, Wolf-Dieter (born on 8 May 1930, died on 22 January 1975). The boy was baptised in the Lutheran faith on 9 August 1930—with Ernst Röhm as his Godfather.

Von Eberstein was appointed as adjutant of the Frontbann-Gruppe-Mitte command staff on 30 March 1925. He rejoined the NSDAP on 17 August 1925, being issued with Party membership number 15 067.

From 1 October 1926 until 1 July 1927, he worked as a civilian employee of the Army administration at Ohrdruf, but he was dismissed on political grounds. He next found employment, from 1 August to 1 October 1927, as a commercial employee of the Polte cartridge factory in Magdeburg-Wilhelmstadt. On 15 October 1927, he returned to banking with the Thüringer Bauernbank GmbH in Weimar. He lost this position on 31 January 1928 as the company ran into financial difficulties. From 1 August until 31 December 1928, von Eberstein formed a partnership with Carl Bollmann in a small art wool and cotton factory in Gotha, but the company was not successful. His next employment was from 1 April 1929 until 1 July 1930, with Nord-Lloyd Travel, at their office in Gotha.

Von Eberstein joined the SS on 12 April 1929 and was allocated number 1 386. The new Reichsführer-SS, Heinrich Himmler, was keen to attract members of the aristocracy to the order, which he was in the process of expanding and reorganising. The new recruit was given the rank of SS-Sturmführer and appointed as adjutant of SS-Staffel VIII, but was reassigned as adjutant of the SS-Oberführer Thüringen on 1 July 1930; he was simultaneously also adjutant of SA-Oberführer Thüringen, headquartered in Weimar. His main duties from July 1930 until February 1933, were as a member of the SA.

On 1 February 1931, he was promoted to SA-Standartenführer on the staff of the SA leadership in Munich. He was appointed as advisor and adjutant of Adolf Hühnlein. Von Eberstein was promoted to SA-Oberführer on 15 November 1931, and appointed as SA-Gausturmführer Munich and Upper Bavaria. On 1 July 1932 he was appointed as commander of SA-Gruppe Hochland, in Munich, and on 15 September 1932 he was promoted to SA-Gruppenführer.

From 20 February 1933, his SS membership took precedence over his SA membership and his remaining postings and promotions were with the SS. He was accorded the rank of SS-Gruppenführer on the same day, with an effective seniority from 1 September 1932. On 21 February 1933, he became the temporary commander of SS-Abschnitt XVIII in Weimar, before confirmation of the command on 6 March 1933. He was also an elected member of the Reichstag from 5 March 1933. He was appointed commander of SS-Oberabschnitt Mitte in Halle on 15 November 1933. Between 1 May 1934 and 15 June 1934, he was commander of SS-Oberabschnitt Elbe, in Dresden, before being appointed to the command of the newly reorganised SS-Oberabschnitt Mitte in Dresden on 15 June 1934. He retained this post until 1 April 1936.

Himmler ordered von Eberstein to Berlin on 22 June 1934 and informed him that Röhm was planning a coup. He directed that von Eberstein must place his troops on unobtrusive alert in local barracks, in order to deploy them when alerted. In the event, von Eberstein subsequently gave post-war evidence that eight men were ordered by Heydrich to be executed on 1 July 1934 in his area of responsibility, and these executions were duly carried out.

On 15 December 1934, von Eberstein was appointed as district governor of Dresden-Bautzen. He was placed in command of SS-Oberabschnitt Süd on 1 April 1936 and simultaneously, he was appointed as Police President of Munich, followed by promotion to SS-Obergruppenführer on 20 April 1936.

During a large part of 1937 von Eberstein was sick with angina, but he returned to duty in the latter quarter of the year. On 15 December, he took control of the police office in the Bavarian Ministry of the Interior.

On 12 March 1938, von Eberstein became HSSPF Süd and HSSPF Main. He retained the Munich posting until 20 April 1945, but was succeeded in Nuremberg by Dr Benno Martin—who effectively administered the post until von Eberstein held appropriate rank to take full control, on 17 December 1942. Von Eberstein attained the rank of Ministerialdirektor in the Bavarian Interior Ministry on 14 June 1939. On 8 April 1941, he was accorded the rank of General der Polizei. On 1 July 1944, he attained the rank of General der Waffen-SS und der Polizei.

At the instigation of Gauleiter Paul Giesler and Martin Bormann, von Eberstein was relieved of his all his posts for defeatism on 20 April 1945. Giesler had earlier ordered von Eberstein to arrange for the shooting of the remaining prisoners in Dachau on the approach of US troops, but von Eberstein flatly refused. They also had differences of opinion over the defence of the city of Munich.

Von Eberstein surrendered voluntarily to American authorities in Munich on 8 May 1945. He was held as a suspect for war crimes in various prisons and internment centres until it could be decided what to do with him. During this time, he protested his innocence of any crimes and his lack of visits by his family, writing numerous letters to the Allied authorities declaring his poor state of health. He contested that he had never served in a post outside Germany and that his treatment was exasperating his heart condition. He suffered two heart attacks in captivity—the first on 22 September 1946, and the second on 18 March 1947. It was finally decided not to put him on trial and he was released on 26 October 1948 to live in Tegernsee. He was subsequently given a suspended prison sentence by a Munich de-Nazification court, and subjected to a 30 per cent property asset confiscation. Further attempts to prosecute him came to nought and all proceedings were finally suspended in February 1953. He continued to be used as a witness in other legal proceedings, but retired to a quiet life on the shores of the Tegernsee—sometimes helping out at the casino in Bad Wiessee. His weak heart survived for more than thirty years, until finally giving up in Tegernsee on 10 February 1979.

The concentration camp at Dachau fell into von Eberstein's sphere of responsibility, and there is little doubt that he was aware of the conditions and treatment of inmates there. He escaped punishment by the post-war Allied authorities because he had only served in home postings. One of the earliest and most-senior SS officers, he was a personal family friend of Reinhard Heydrich from his early Halle days. In fact, von Eberstein introduced Heydrich to Himmler in 1931—a fateful meeting that would have dire consequences for many thousands of lives.

SA-Oberführer von Eberstein.

The SS-Abschnitt XVIII commander in Weimar, 1933. Behind him is SS-Standartenführer Paul Hennicke.

Above: von Eberstein with his son, Wolf-Dieter. Note the Mitte cuff title.

Left: SS-Gruppenführer von Eberstein at the Boxberg rally in May 1933.

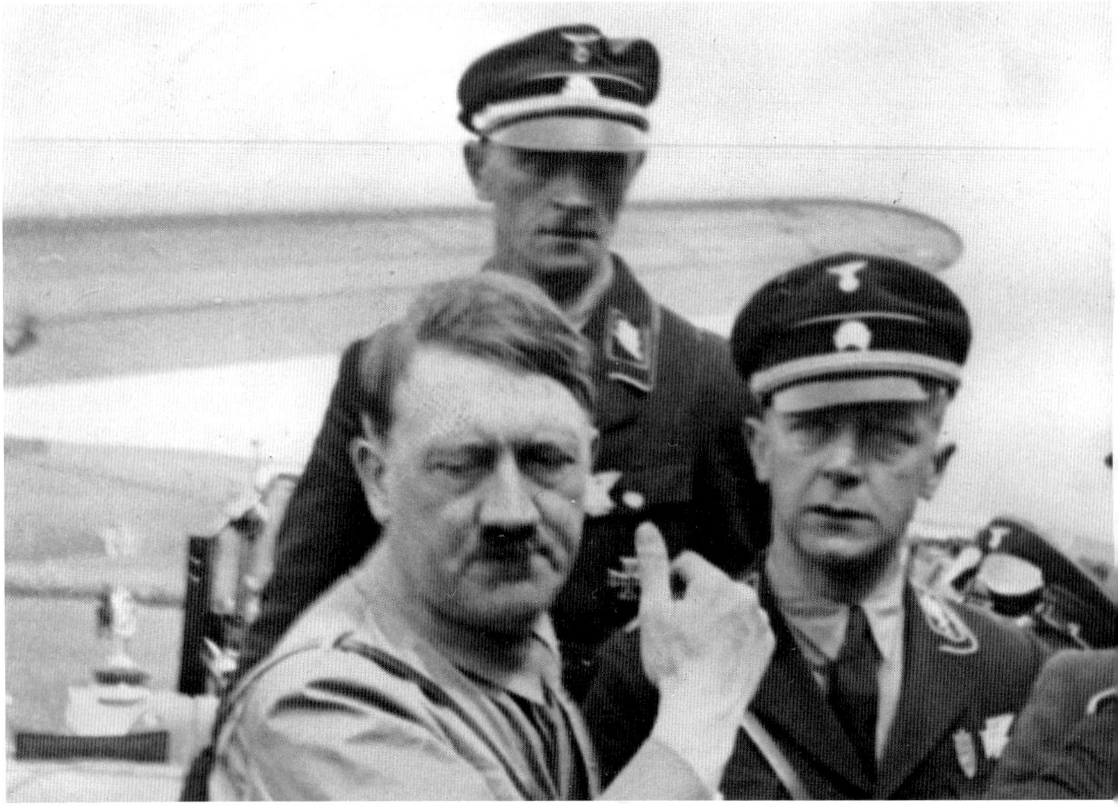

With Hitler and Hennicke at the Gauparteitag in Erfut, June 1933.

The SS-Gruppenführer and Abschnitt XVIII commander, 1933.

von Eberstein remained a favourite of Hitler.

The SS-Obergruppenführer and SS-Oberabschnitt Mitte commander inspecting the guard.

von Eberstein talking to a member of the local SA.

SS-Obergruppenführer Karl von Eberstein.

Wearing his SS sword.

von Eberstein transferred to the command of SS-Oberabschnitt Süd in Munich. He is seen here with Adolf Wagner.

von Eberstein talking to a SS man.

Chatting with actors during a visit to a film set in Munich.

SS-Obergruppenführer and Police President of Munich Karl von Eberstein.

Posing for official photographs.

The von Eberstein couple in traditional Bavarian clothing.

Left and right: SS-Obergruppenführer von Eberstein.

Friedrich Karl Freiherr von Eberstein.

The von Eberstein family coat of arms.

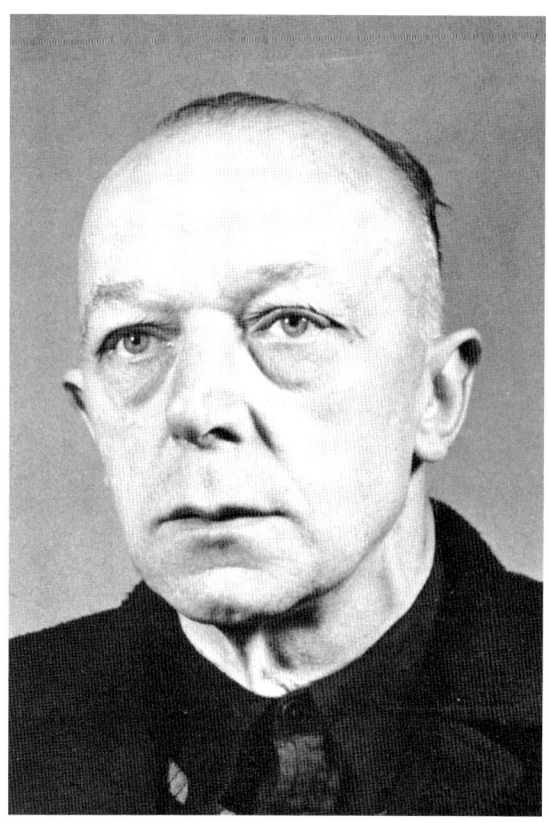

Prisoner of war Karl von Eberstein.

The family grave.

JOACHIM ALBRECHT LEO EGGELING

Joachim Eggeling was born on 30 November 1884 in Blankenburg-Harz, the son of farmer and retired Leutnant Max Friedrich Wilhelm Leo Eggeling and his wife, Marie (born Kricheldorff). His father came from an old farming family in Quedlinburg. Eggeling attended the Bürgerschule in Blankenburg from 1891, before moving to the local secondary school, where he stayed until 1898.

Following in his father's footsteps, he opted for a military career as an officer. He enrolled in the officer cadet school in Oranienstein in 1898, followed by the cadet academy at Berlin-Lichterfelde. On 10 March 1904, he received a commission as a Leutnant and joined the 10th Hannoverian Jäger Battalion, until being assigned on 1 March 1913 to machine-gun section 7. From 1 August 1914, he was deployed on the Western Front, where he was slightly wounded twice. This preceded a transfer to the Eastern Front where he sustained a serious wound on 20 November 1914, near Brzesiny. He was promoted to Hauptmann on 27 January 1915 and took command of machine-gun section 5 on 1 April 1915, until the end of the war.

He was married on 6 May 1911 to Nora Margarethe Braune (born on 1 June 1890 in Nieder-Rossloo, NSDAP membership number 2 050 309). They had a daughter on 28 January 1912, and a son on 29 January 1918.

After the war, from February 1919 until 1 October 1919, Eggeling remained with the 10th Jäger Battalion in Goslar, before retiring from military service. From October 1919 until November 1922, he attended agricultural college in Halle, gaining practical experience in farming in Jena from 1920 to 1921. In 1921 he took control of the state agricultural farm Domäne Frose, in Anhalt, from his father-in-law—who was unable to continue through ill health—and ran the concern on his behalf until 27 November 1922, when he was appointed as agricultural inspector of Domäne Frose.

He was a member of Stahlhelm from 1923 until 1926, when he was expelled for disagreements with the leadership. He first joined the NSDAP in September 1923 and re-enrolled on 20 July 1925, when he was recorded as member number 11 579. From 1926 until 1930 he was agricultural advisor to the NSDAP Gauleiter of

Gau Anhalt-Sachsen-Nord. He was leader of the agrarian political organisation in Gau Magdeburg-Anhalt from 1930 until 20 April 1937. From October 1932 until 1933, he was the agricultural advisor for the Gau Halle-Merseburg, Magdeburg-Anhalt and Kurmark. From 1933 until 10 February 1936, he was Deputy Gauleiter of Gau Magdeburg-Anhalt, controlling the Gau as temporary Gauleiter from 10 February 1936. He was appointed Gauleiter of Magdeburg-Anhalt on 23 October 1935, until he was appointed as Gauleiter for Halle-Merseburg on 20 April 1937, holding this post until his death.

He joined the SS on 9 June 1936 and was allocated membership number 186 515. With the rank of SS-Brigadeführer, he was attached to the staff of the Reichsführer-SS. He was promoted to SS-Gruppenführer on 20 April 1937, becoming a Prussian State Councillor on the same day. On 22 September 1939, he was appointed as Representative of the Reich Defence Commission for Wehrkreis IV (Halle-Merseburg). He was promoted to SS-Obergruppenführer on 21 June 1943 and on 18 August 1944, he became Oberpräsident of Merseburg Province.

Eggeling was also a Reichstag deputy, a member of the German Farmers' Council and the Reich Distribution Council, and the Peasants' Leader for the province of Saxon-Anhalt.

On 13 April 1945 he travelled to Berlin to meet with Hitler for the last time. They discussed the defence of Halle; Hitler ordered that the city be defended to the last man. On his return to Halle, Eggeling decided to personally take part in the fighting. An account dated 23 April 1946, which is now held at the Stadtarchiv Halle, gives a possible version of events leading up to the death of Gauleiter Eggeling:

On the morning of 14th April 1945, Eggeling left Halle in the company of the Kreisleiter Carl Julius Dohmgoergen. That afternoon, Generalleutnant Radke [*sic, Anton Rathke, Kampfkommandant of Halle*] and his adjutant arrived in the town looking for the Gauleiter. On discovering that Eggeling had gone, the young adjutant was heard to remark, '*The man gambles with his head*'. The following day, Eggeling and Dohmgoergen returned to Halle with the intention of going to the front with machine pistols. However, they took shelter in the cellars of the Moritzburg Church. During the night of 15th to 16th April, they both took poison from coffee cups and Dohmgoergen also shot himself in the head. Their bodies were loaded onto a refuse truck by locals and were taken away and cremated. The American military authority subsequently complained about this as they wished to view the bodies for confirmation of death.

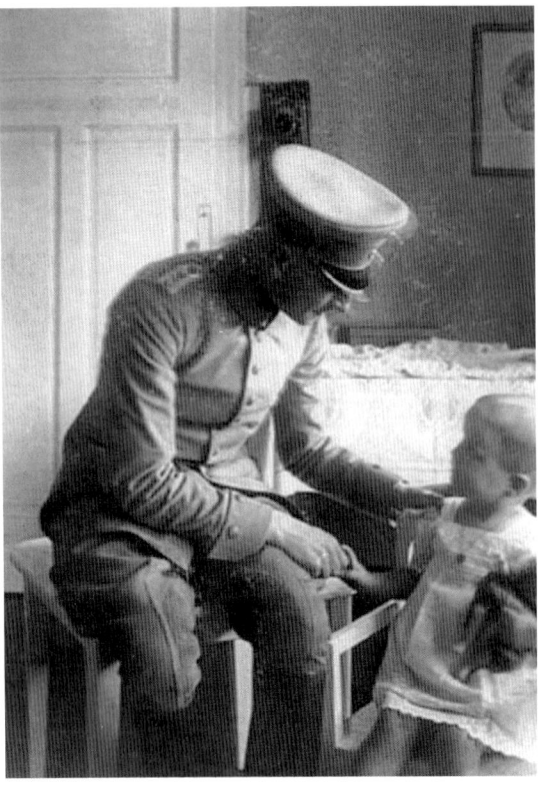

Joachim Eggeling with his young daughter.

Eggeling in NSDAP uniform.

Joachim Albrecht Eggeling
Landesbauernführer der Provinz Sachsen und Anhalt.

An early contemporary news photograph of
Eggeling.

Deputy Gauleiter Eggeling with Reichsleiter Buch.

Hitler between Hess and Deputy Gauleiter Eggeling at the funeral of Gauleiter Wilhelm Loeper 1935.

Gauleiter Eggeling taking an outside meal at a youth festival.

Gauleiter Eggeling (left) saluting a formation of local SA troopers.

An original newspaper photograph of Eggeling's home.

1937

Gauleiter Joachim Eggeling.

Left and right: Gauleiter Joachim Eggeling.

A signed photograph of Gauleiter Joachim Eggeling.

An original newspaper photograph of SS-Gruppenführer Eggeling.

SS-Gruppenführer Joachim Eggeling.

THEODOR EICKE

T HEODOR EICKE was the second son of a total of seven boys and four girls in a family whose male line originated from Gittelda, in the Harz Mountains. He was born on 17 October 1892 in the small village of Hampont, in Alsace. His father, Heinrich Eicke (died 13 June 1926) was a railroad stationmaster and was Protestant, unlike his French-born Catholic wife and mother of the young Theodor, Josefina (born Henning, died on 7 November 1935). Several of Theodor's nephews later joined the Waffen-SS. Theodor attended the local village primary and secondary combined school from 1899 until 1909, but he left to join the Army without achieving a school leaving diploma.

Without any qualifications, he enlisted as a volunteer in the 23rd Bavarian Infantry Regiment, based in Landau-Pfalz. He then served as a clerk and trainee paymaster with the 3rd Bavarian Chevalier Regiment from 1 October 1913 until 1 August 1914. His undistinguished Army career continued during the First World War, when he served with the 22nd Bavarian Infantry Regiment as a deputy paymaster until 1916. This was followed by service with the 2nd Bavarian Foot Artillery Regiment until 1917. He finished the war as a paymaster with the 6th replacement machine-gun company of the 2nd Army Corps.

Theodor Eicke married Bertha Schwebel (born in Riesthal-Hagenau on 16 April 1893) on 26 December 1914. They had two children: a daughter, Irma (born on 4 May 1916), and a son, Hermann (born on 5 April 1920). Irma was married to SS-Obersturmbannführer Karl Leiner. Hermann Eicke was killed in action on 2 December 1941, fighting as an Army Leutnant on the Eastern Front. Bertha exchanged several letters with Himmler after her husband's death regarding her late husband's gravesite. She continued to occupy the family home in Adolf-Hitler-Damm, Oranienburg—the location of the concentration camp inspectorate.

Eicke resigned from the Army on 1 March 1919 and moved to Ilmenau, where he began studies at the Technical High School. However, he was forced to give up in September 1919 as a result of his father-in-law refusing financial support. He was unemployed until December 1919, when he found work as a paid police informer, but his political activities against the Weimar Republic earned him an ignominious dismissal in July 1920. Determined to work for the police, he immediately obtained a position with the police service in Cottbus and attended the local police school, where he was successful in his examination for the post of Polizei-Kommissar. His old problem of political agitation led him into trouble again and he was dismissed in July 1921. He next moved on to Weimar, where he was engaged as a police officer candidate, but only lasted fourteen days before he was dismissed for his reactionary views. After a short period of unemployment and an unsuccessful application in autumn 1921 to become a criminal investigator for the police in Sorau, he was appointed as a police assistant in Ludwigshafen am Rhein. This lasted until January 1923, when he was again dismissed for political agitation. On 1 February 1923, he took up a position with I. G. Farben in Ludwigshafen. He first worked as a sales representative, but then transferred to their security department in 1925 as deputy head of security—retaining this employment until 6 March 1932.

He became active with the local SA in 1927, but did not officially join the SA until 28 August 1928, when he was assigned to SA-Sturm Frankenthal as SA-Truppführer. He joined NSDAP Ortsgruppe Ludwigshafen on 1 December 1928, gaining the membership number 114 901, and later helped to form NSDAP Ortsgruppe Eppstein in Gau Saarpfalz.

Eicke transferred to the SS on 29 July 1930 and was allocated SS number 2 921. He was promoted from SS-Mann to SS-Truppführer on 20 August. He was appointed leader of SS-Sturm 147 on 27 November 1930, with the rank of SS-Sturmführer.

His superiors were impressed with the new recruit and duly promoted him again, to SS-Sturmbannführer, on 30 January 1931. He also took command of the 2nd SS-Sturmbann of SS-Standarte 10 on 15 February 1931. Having taken over the responsibilities of the administrative officer for the 10th SS-Standarte on 7 November 1931, he was promoted again on 15 November to SS-Standartenführer. Five weeks later, on 21 December 1931, he was appointed commander of SS-Standarte 10.

During his tenure at SS-Standarte 10 in Pfalz, Eicke had a major disagreement with Gauleiter Bürckel, which festered over a few years. It began because Bürckel considered himself as responsible for all SA and SS matters in his area. Eicke refused to obey orders issued by the Gauleiter, and the two men locked horns.

On 6 March 1932, Eicke was arrested for illegal possession of explosives and conspiring to cause explosions. His illegal activities with the SS drew the unapproving attention of his employers at I. G. Farben, and he lost his job. He was held in custody at Pirmasens prison until 7 July 1932, when he was given a two-year prison term. He was granted a temporary parole to regain his health and was released on 16 July 1932. Eicke returned to Ludwigshafen and resumed his political career of agitation. He attracted the attention of the local police, who noted his return and forced him into hiding in Landau.

Himmler was embarrassed by the episode and ordered Eicke to report to him in Munich. Eicke was immediately dispatched to Italy, out of harm's way. With false identity documents, he left Germany on 18 September 1932 and travelled through Austria to a SS fugitives' camp in Malcesine, on Lake Garda. Given command of the camp, he was appointed as commander of SS-Standarte J and also promoted to SS-Oberführer on 21 October 1932.

Eicke continued his bad behaviour in Italy, further embarrassing Himmler and enraging the Austrian press over the control of the South Tyrol. The old quarrel with Gauleiter Josef Bürckel ignited once again when Eicke heard that Bürckel was saying that the SS man had been dismissed from the NSDAP. Eicke made several threats to '...*get even, using the old ways*' when he returned. His return was not long in coming. With the NSDAP seizure of power in January 1933, Eicke was free to come home. He did so the following month, but to Thuringia, not Ludwigshafen, where he was still a wanted man. He was assigned to command SS-Standarte 46 in Dresden. On 10 March 1933, he was amnestied in Ludwigshafen and granted permission to return to his family—on condition he avoided Gauleiter Bürckel.

He continued to plot against his old enemy and was arrested on 21 March 1933 for participating in a rebellion against the local NSDAP leadership. Eicke stormed the Gau headquarters in Neustadt with a band of his men. He successfully captured Bürckel in the headquarters and locked him in a janitor's cupboard. Enraged, Himmler ordered Eicke to be struck off the SS membership roll on 3 April 1933, and he was committed to a mental institution in Würzburg. There, Eicke made friends with his psychiatrist, Dr Werner Heyde. The doctor wrote to Himmler that Eicke did not appear mentally disturbed and had conducted himself honourably. The patient also wrote lengthy letters to Himmler, pleading for his release.

Himmler finally agreed, and Eicke was released on 26 June 1933. Restored to his old rank of SS-Oberführer, he was attached to SS-Gruppe Süd on special duties. Himmler had been looking for a replacement for the commander at the new Dachau concentration camp. He sent Eicke there on 9 March 1934, with instructions to get the place into shape. Eicke immediately set about reorganising the camp guard and formulated a new 'code of conduct' for the prisoners. This introduced strict regulations into the camp, which were later to form the basis of rules for the entire concentration camp system.

Eicke was promoted to SS-Brigadeführer on 30 January 1934, and was subsequently transferred to the staff of the Reichsführer-SS on 20 June 1934. For the time being, he retained command of Konzentrationslager (KZ) Dachau. He personally participated in the round-up of senior SA men during the Röhm Purge. On 1 July 1934, Eicke, SS-Sturmbannführer Michael Lippert (*Eicke's adjutant*), and SS-Gruppenführer Ernst-Heinrich Schmauser were despatched to Stadelheim Prison in Munich to carry out the Führer's direct order that Röhm was to die. In disbelief, Röhm refused to accept the offer of a pistol to take his own life, prompting both Eicke and Lippert to enter cell 474 and shoot the SA chief.

On 4 July 1934, Eicke was appointed Inspector of Concentration Camps. He was promoted to SS-Gruppenführer on 11 July 1934, assigned to the command of all concentration camps and SS guard formations. This was the embryo of the Totenkopf Standarten, the subsequent Totenkopfverbände and later the Totenkopf Division.

On 29 March 1936, Eicke was elected as the Reichstag Deputy for Wahlkreis 30, Chemnitz-Zwickau.

He introduced stringent guidelines on who would be accepted as candidates for his formations, and ruled with an iron fist; his discipline code was the strictest in all of the SS units. His popularity with his men did not suffer and his tough regime resulted in utmost respect, with his men affectionately nicknaming him 'Papa Eicke'.

At the outbreak of war in September 1939, Eicke led the Totenkopf regiments in the Polish campaign. For a short time in the first month of war, from 10 September 1939, he was appointed HSSPF for the VIII and X Army Corps areas. This was the nucleus of HSSPF Ost, soon to be commanded by Friedrich-Wilhelm Krüger, in Krakow. On 30 October 1939, Eicke was officially assigned to command the new Totenkopf Division. He was succeeded in his other posts by SS-Obergruppenführer August Heissmeyer (SS-Totenkopfstandarten) and SS-Brigadeführer Richard Glücks (Inspector of Concentration Camps). He gained military ranking on 14 November 1939, when he was appointed as Generalleutnant der Verfügungstruppen (*the equivalent of reserve troops*).

Eicke took his Division to both France and Russia. His right foot was seriously injured on 6 July 1941 at Sasitino, when his vehicle hit a mine. He was hospitalised in Berlin from 7 July until 12 September and then recovered at his home, until returning to his unit on 19 September 1941. He was promoted to SS-Obergruppenführer and General der Waffen-SS on 20 April 1942. The same year, he was awarded a dotation by Hitler, who held a great respect for him. Poor health forced him to take leave during the summer, until he was fit enough to resume his command in October 1942.

During the campaign in the Ukraine on the afternoon of 26 February 1943, Eicke lost radio contact with an element of his armoured unit. He ordered up his single-engine Fieseler Storch, piloted by Oberfeldwebel Michael Werner. Eicke and his adjutant, SS-Hauptsturmführer Otto Friedrich, took off to find the missing unit. At about 4.30 p.m., they spotted some of their men in the village of Michelouka, near Orelka. As the aircraft manoeuvred to land, it dropped to an altitude of about 300 feet over the village of Artelnoye. Unseen Russian troops in the village opened up with anti-aircraft fire and small arms. Badly damaged in mid-air, the aircraft crashed between the two villages, killing all three on board.

The SS troops immediately attempted to recover the bodies, but were driven back by heavy Russian fire. The following day, an assault group successfully drove the

Russians from their positions and recovered the bodies. All three were buried with full military honours on 1 March in Otdochnina. When the Russians pushed the German Army back six months later, Himmler ordered that Eicke's body should be moved to the Hegewald cemetery, south of Zhitomir. This was sited directly across the road from the RFSS field headquarters. In the spring of 1944 the Russians overran the Ukraine, but this time Eicke's body was abandoned—his remains are still interred in the soil of the Ukraine.

Eicke was a highly decorated soldier. His awards and decorations included the Knights Cross of the Iron Cross and the Oakleaves to the Knights Cross (*the 88th recipient*). Hitler held Eicke in great esteem and personally presented him with his Oakleaves at the Wolfsschanze, near Rastenburg, in June 1942. On 2 March 1943, Hitler ordered that SS-Totenkopf-Panzer-Grenadier-Regiment 3 be henceforth known by the honour title 'Theodor Eicke'. Although not a brilliant tactician, Eicke was a more-than-competent Waffen-SS General who was much admired by his men with his down-to-earth approach, sharing the hardships of his troops.

Eicke in Italy, where his behaviour embarrassed Himmler.

Eicke wearing the cuff title of SS-Standarte 10.

Inspector of Concencentration Camps.

Guards at Sachsenburg concentration camp put on a heavy machine-gun display for Himmler and Eicke.

Eicke (in the light greatcoat) in front of the gatehouse at Sachsenhausen.

Inspecting the zoo at Buchenwald concentration camp. Left to right: Hennicke, Himmler, von Alvensleben, Eicke and camp commandant Koch.

At Dachau concentration camp.

SS-Gruppenführer Eicke.

Above: Eicke with Michael Lippert—the two executioners of Ernst Röhm.

Right: Eicke with Richard Glücks (centre), his deputy and eventual successor as Inspector of Concentration Camps.

Left and right: Theodor Eicke.

Eicke in conversation with Karl Hermann Frank.

The commander of SS-Totenkopf.

A signed photograph of Eicke.

A visit to Totenkopf by Leo von Jena.

The commander of the SS-Totenkopf armoured division.

A portrait of Eicke taken at the Führer Headquarters.

The pipe-smoking 'Papa' Eicke is presented with a SS candle by his men.

Eicke had a lump removed from his left cheek, leaving a small scar.

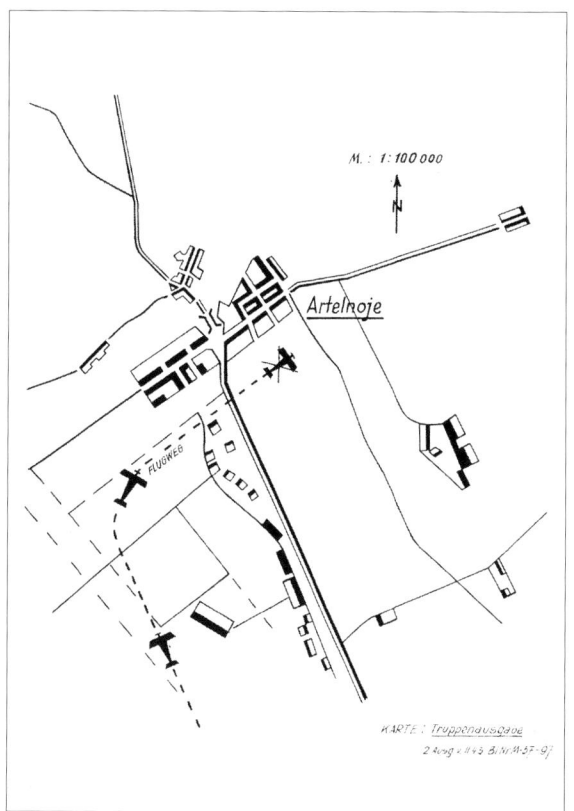

A diagram of Eicke's fatal flight over Artelnoje.

Eicke's first grave, between that of his adjutant and pilot.

The original three graves by the road in Otdochnina.

GUSTAV AUGUST EIGRUBER

AUGUST EIGRUBER was born on 16 April 1907 in Steyr, Austria, the son of Augustin Eigruber and Aloisia Eigruber. After attending elementary primary and middle schools from 1913 until 1921, he studied to be a technician and precision engineer at a trade school for the iron and steel industry.

On 16 November 1922, he joined the Austrian National Socialist Workers' Youth Group in Steyr. From 1925 until August 1927, he was the youth leader for Austria in that organisation, joining the Hitler Youth in April 1927. From 1925 until 1929, he had various jobs, including working as a mechanic in a Steyr parts factory and on calculating machines for the Reithofer rubber factory. He also held a labouring job in a crane factory and worked in the Steyr district survey office. From 21 August 1927 until April 1930, he was appointed as Gauführer for the Upper Austrian Hitler Youth.

He was married to Johanna Maria Spatzenegger (born in Steyr on 18 May 1905) on 25 September 1930. They had six children; Adolf on 28 January 1929, Hermann on 10 October 1930, Alfred on 22 December 1932, Ingeborg on 15 September 1933, Gertraud on 23 November 1934, and another daughter on 8 August 1939.

He joined the Austrian NSDAP on 18 April 1928 and was issued with membership number 83 432. He worked as a warehouse assistant in a Steyr parts factory from 1929 until 1934, but was dismissed as a result of his right-wing political activities. From 1930 until 1931, he was the district NSDAP leader for Steyr-Land, the district leader for the town of Steyr from 1931 to 1933, and from 1933 until May 1935, he was Kreisleiter of Steyr. Suspected of involvement in the assassination of Chancellor Engelbert Dollfuss in July 1934, he was arrested and interned at the Anhaltelager Wöllersdorf for several months. Recognised by the Austrian authorities as a high-profile Nazi, Eigruber was targeted by the police during 1934, when he experienced several arrests and numerous house searches.

From May 1935 until March 1936, he was the regional business manager for the illegal NSDAP in Upper Austria. He was appointed NSDAP Gauleiter of Upper Austria on 1 August 1935. On 21 February 1938, Eigruber carried out the duties of acting regional governor for Upper Austria. On 12 March 1938, he was authorised by Wilhelm Keppler,

Hitler's representative in Austria, to seize control as official regional governor, a post in which he was confirmed on 14 March 1938. From 10 April 1938, he was a Reichstag deputy for Upper Austria. On 25 May 1938, Eigruber's Gau was redesignated NSDAP Gau Oberdonau and he remained as Gauleiter until the end of the war.

Eigruber joined the SA on 12 March 1938 with the rank of SA-Oberführer. He then joined the SS on 25 July 1938—with a seniority date of 12 March 1938—and was allocated membership number 292 778. He was given the rank of SS-Standartenführer. He was promoted to SS-Oberführer from 25 July 1938, and on 9 November 1938 he was promoted to SA-Gruppenführer. From 3 December 1938, he was posted to the staff of the Reichsführer-SS. He was promoted to SS-Brigadeführer on 1 January 1939, and to SS-Gruppenführer, attached to SS-Oberabschnitt Donau, on 9 November 1940. He returned to the staff of the Reichsführer-SS on 1 January 1942. On 21 June 1943, Eigruber was promoted to SS-Obergruppenführer. His final promotion occurred on 9 November 1943, when he was elevated to SA-Obergruppenführer.

August Eigruber took flight from Krems on 8 May 1945, in possession of fake identity papers in the name of a farmer, Bernhard Gruber. He managed to evade capture until 11 August 1945, when he was betrayed by ex-Hitler Youth leaders. He was stopped in a vehicle with Stefan Schachermayr, at a road block near the Vogel Inn at Steyrling. The two Germans put up a brief resistance, but were quickly overpowered and arrested. Eigruber was unable to use the cyanide capsule he was carrying. He was first detained in Kirchdorf and then Linz, where, on 18 August, he was initially questioned about his involvement with Mauthausen concentration camp. On 22 October 1945, he was transferred from Gemünden to Nuremberg, where he admitted knowledge of the euthanasia murders at Schloss Hartheim and confirmed he had inspected KZ Mauthausen and witnessed executions.

He was tried in the Mauthausen Case between 29 March and 13 May 1946, when he was sentenced to death. Although he had little influence in the running of the camp, it was found that he had re-directed food destined for the camp to the local inhabitants, who were short of rations. Eigruber was executed at Landsberg am Lech War Criminals Prison 1 at 9 a.m. on 28 May 1947, by Master-Sergeant John Clarence Woods of the US Army. Upon leaving his cell for the scaffold, Eigruber shouted, "*Long live Germany!*" On the gallows, he said:

> God protect Germany; God protect my family; God protect my children. I consider it an honour to be hanged by this, the most brutal victor.

As Woods pulled the trapdoor lever, Eigruber shouted, "*Will of God, preacher!*" The inept Woods had miscalculated the drop and the prisoner's weight, resulting in the unfortunate Eigruber choking at the end of the rope. Woods stuffed cotton up his nostrils and in his mouth and he consequently suffocated.

Gauleiter August Eigruber.

The Eigruber family.

Eigruber next to Hitler, studying plans for Linz. Brandt, Hoffmann, Speer, Bormann and Giesler are also present.

Eigruber wore his black Allgemeine-SS uniform during Himmler's visit to Mauthausen concentration camp in April 1941.

In the quarry, Eigruber peers over Himmler's arm, with Wolff behind and camp commandant Franz Ziereis beside Himmler.

The group in the quarry. From far left: Kaltenbrunner, Wolff, Eigruber, Himmler and Pohl behind.

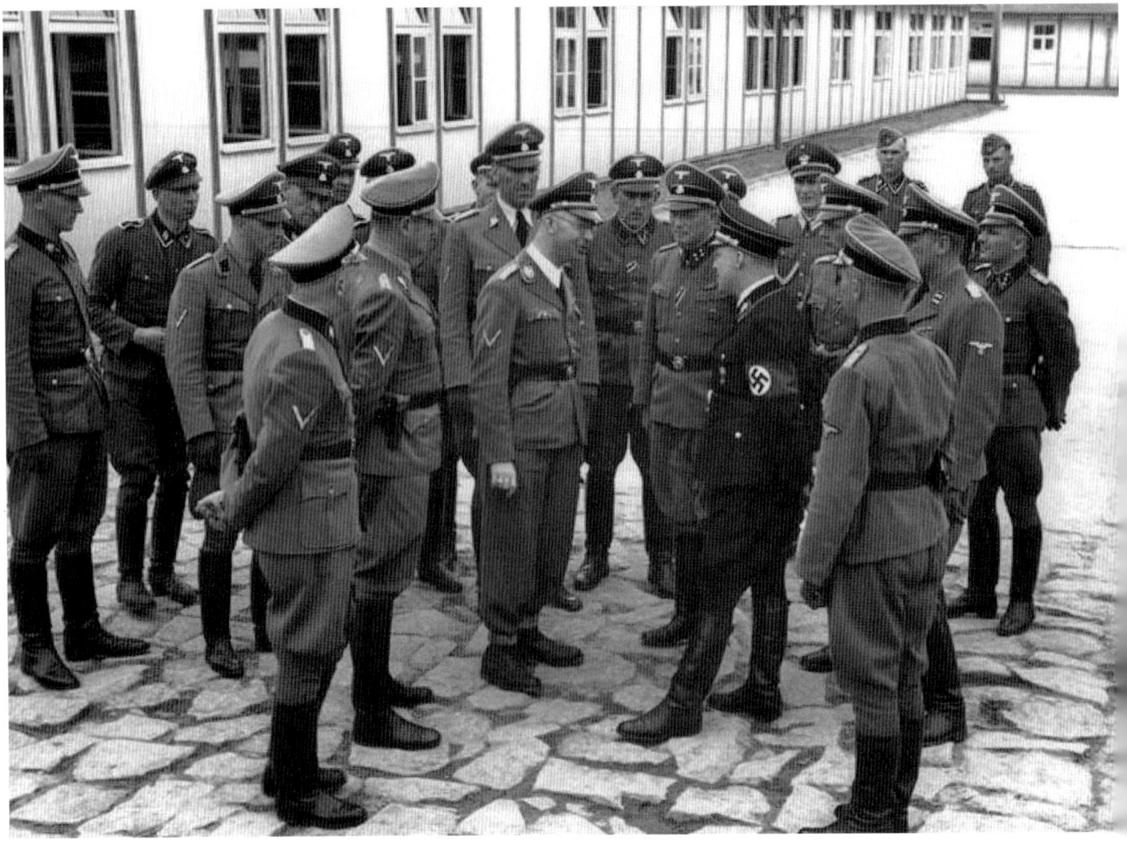

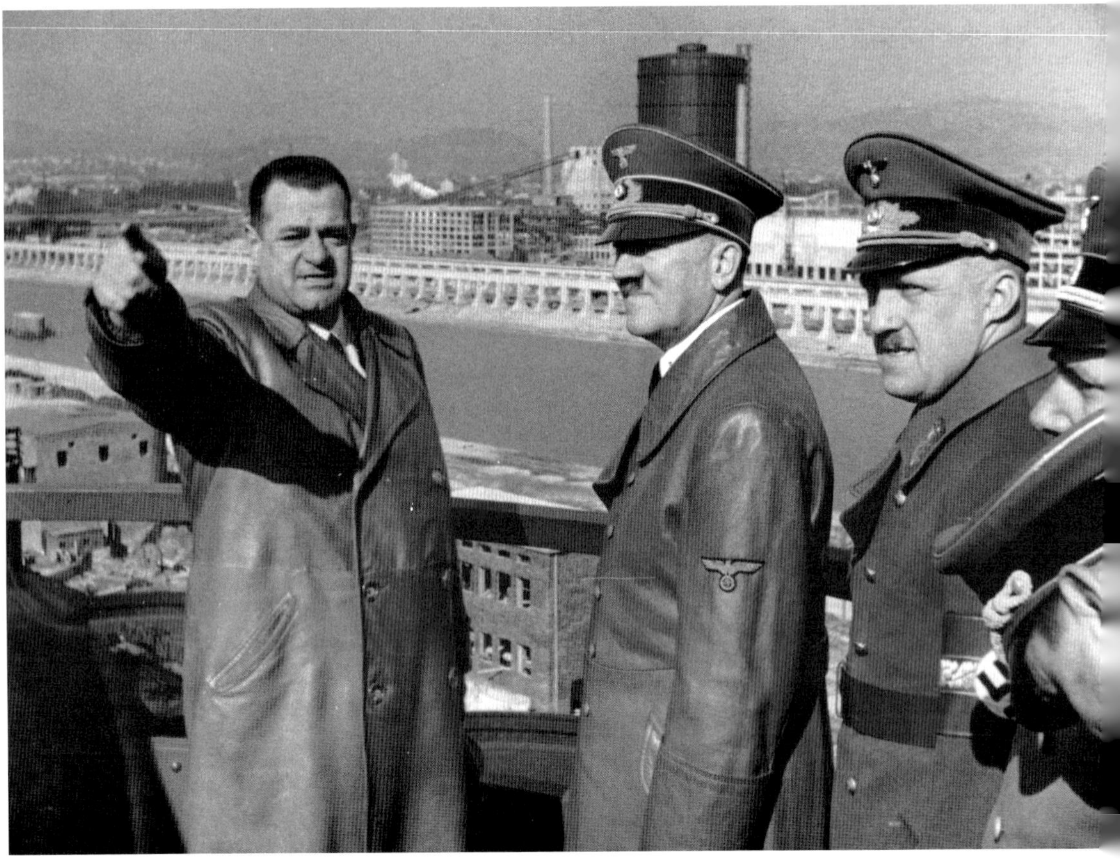

Above: Henlein and Eigruber look on as Daluege examines Bohemian glass. In the background is Karl Hermann Frank.

Opposite page:

Above: In the camp compound; standing behind Himmler are Wolff and Kaltenbrunner, with Ziereis between Himmler and Eigruber.

Below: Eigruber accompanies Hitler, overlooking an industrial complex.

Himmler and Eigruber.

Right: Eigruber prepares to die on the scaffold at Landsberg Prison.

Below: Eigruber dead.

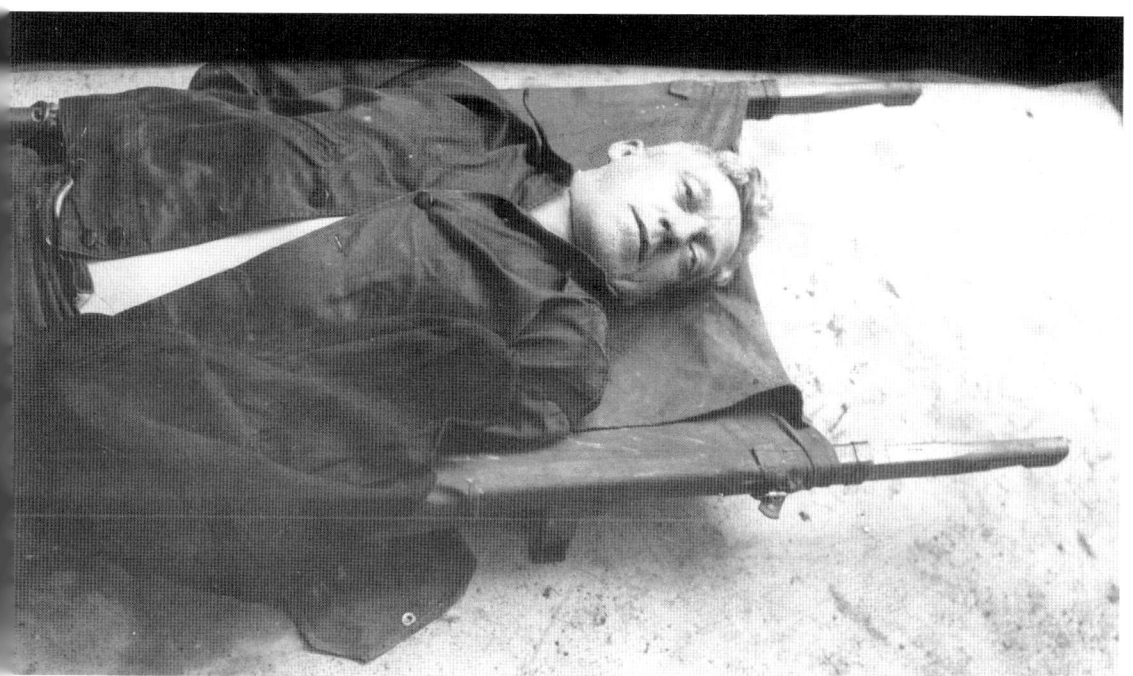

KARL FIEHLER

KARL FIEHLER was born in Braunschweig on 31 August 1895, the youngest son of an evangelist preacher, Heinrich Fiehler, and his wife, Emma Fiehler (born Wulff). He had four brothers and two sisters. It is unclear when the family moved to Munich, but Karl attended an elementary primary school for four years, followed by six years at a secondary school in the Bavarian city. Graduating from there, he studied at a Munich school for business and administration—as part of a commercial apprenticeship with Diamalt AG—from 1 August 1912 until 31 July 1914.

On 2 August 1914, Fiehler volunteered for the Navy in Kiel, but he was rejected on health grounds. He worked in Schleswig-Holstein until 13 May the following year, when his application to join the Replacement Battalion of the 84th Infantry Regiment as a rifleman was accepted. From September 1915 until June 1918, he saw active service on the Western Front with Reserve Infantry Regiment 215. On 3 May 1917 he was commissioned as a Leutnant der Reserve. Fiehler was seriously wounded in the leg in June 1918 and played no further part in the hostilities. He was hospitalized, but remained in the Army until December 1918, when he left to become a businessman. He was then a civil servant for the Munich city administration from 19 March 1919. He passed his civil service examination in 1922 and was confirmed as an established civil servant on 1 February 1922.

Fiehler was married on 25 September 1918 to Regina Rosina Kiendl (born in Munich on 29 September 1896, NSDAP number 25 915). The couple had three daughters, born between June 1919 and November 1932.

Fiehler joined the Thule-Gesellschaft in 1919, and was an early supporter of Hitler's NSDAP. He was a founder member of the 'Stosstrupp Hitler', joining the same day as the start of his membership of the Party on 5 November 1923. He was sentenced to fifteen months' imprisonment on 28 April 1924 for his part in the failed November Putsch, and was incarcerated in Landsberg Prison with Hitler.

Released early in November 1924, he joined the National Socialist Freedom Movement (NSFB), the cover organisation for the now-illegal NSDAP. The Munich city council dismissed him from his civil service post, but after a complaint to the government of Upper Bavaria, he was reinstated and returned to his work with the Munich city administration. From 8 December of that year he was a town councillor. His membership of the newly formed NSDAP dates from February 1925, when he was allocated membership number 37. He became the chairman of the NSDAP faction on the Munich city council.

From July 1926 until June 1930, Fiehler was the NSDAP Ortsgruppenleiter for Munich-Schwabing, and from September 1927 he was a member of the Reich supreme leadership of the NSDAP. From 1927 he was the Party specialist on municipal politics. He was appointed secretary of the Party from 31 August 1928, retaining this post until 1935. He headed the various offices dealing with municipal political questions from 1930. When they were all accumulated under one national department on 15 December 1933, Fiehler retained the leadership. He was the NSDAP Mayor of Munich from 23 May 1933, effectively taking up the duties from 3 October, and he remained in post until 29 April 1945. Fiehler was appointed a NSDAP Reichsleiter in June 1933. He was an elected deputy to the Reichstag for Wehrkreis 24 (Upper Bavaria-Schwabia) from 12 November 1933.

Fiehler joined the SS as a member of SS-Gruppe Süd on 31 July 1933. He was accorded the rank of SS-Standartenführer with SS number 91 724. He was promoted to SS-Oberführer on 24 December 1933, SS-Gruppenführer on 27 January 1934 and finally to SS-Obergruppenführer on 30 January 1942. He was assigned to the staff of the Reichsführer-SS from 1 April 1936.

In a typewritten CV dated 4 March 1944, Fiehler listed his positions (in addition to those previously mentioned) as:

Honorary Senator of the Academy for German Law;
President of the International Community Association;
President of the European Chess Federation and
Senator of the Kaiser Wilhelm Society.

He also listed his writing and publishing positions:

Author of a booklet entitled '*Nationalsozialistische Gemeindepolitik*';
Publisher of '*NS-Gemeinde*';
Publisher of '*Handbuches für Kommunalpolitik*';
Author of '*Deutsches Gemeinderecht*' in the handbook '*Die Verwaltungsakademie*';
Writer in the National Socialist press specialising in communal journals.

Karl Fiehler handed over the administration of the city of Munich to the Americans on 30 April 1945 and was interned by the US authorities. He remained in captivity until 16 January 1949, when he stood trial before a German court for his part in the NSDAP regime. He was sentenced the same month to two years of detention in a labour camp and twelve years of prohibition from practising his profession as a civil servant. He was released very soon after, deemed to have served his term whilst in American captivity. He found employment as a commercial manager with a construction company and died on 8 December 1969 at Diessen am Ammersee.

Fiehler (far right) with his parents and siblings.

Fiehler was a member of the Stosstrupp Adolf Hitler in 1923, seen here in their truck. The man directly above the double 'S' in Stosstrupp strongly resembles Fiehler.

A young Fiehler, without his trademark spectacles.

The early NSDAP member.

Fiehler in SA-Gruppenführer uniform, but wearing a black tie to denote membership of the SS.

Fiehler wearing Gruppenführer rank insignia.

Fiehler stands to Hitler's left, examining a large book in Hitler's private apartment.

Reichsleiter Fiehler wearing his Blood Order.

The Oberbürgermeister of Munich, the capital of the movement.

Reichsleiter Karl Fiehler.

SS-Standartenführer Fiehler (right) in conversation with Adolf Wagner.

SS-Gruppenführer Fiehler in the Munich city hall.

Fiehler reads from his speech notes.

SS-Gruppenführer Karl Fiehler.

Fiehler (right).

SS-Obergruppenführer Fiehler (right) and Artur Axmann salute the grave of Heydrich, Berlin, 9 June 1942.

SS-Obergruppenführer Karl Fiehler.

Fiehler in his leather SS greatcoat.

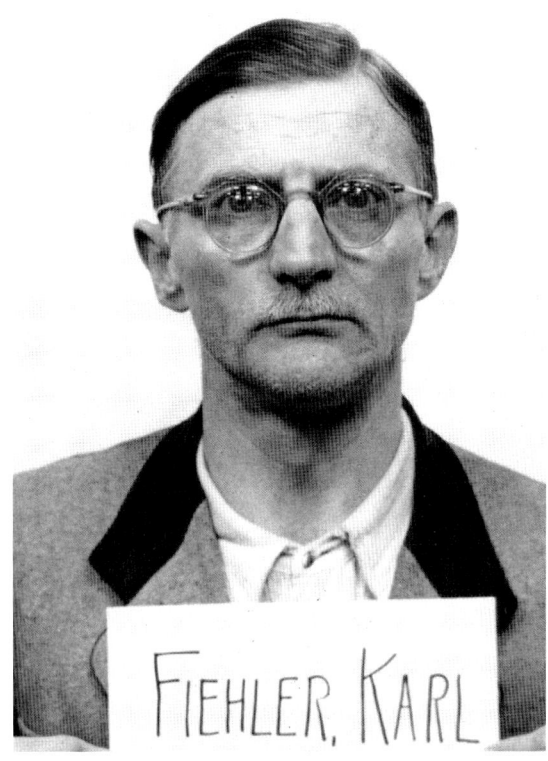

Prisoner of war Karl Fiehler.

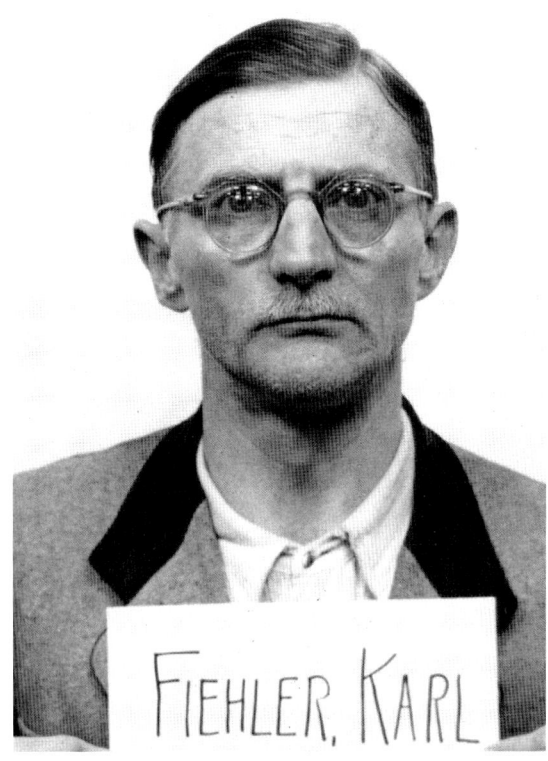

Post-war interrogation.

ALBERT MARIA FORSTER

Albert Forster was the only son out of a total of six children of the senior prison administrator in Fürth, Christoph Forster (born on 20 March 1855 in Herzheim), and his wife, Kreszenz (born Bruckmeyer on 30 November 1860 in Ingolstadt, died 29 December 1932 in Ingolstadt). They were practising Roman Catholics and had a family of five girls before little Albert arrived on 26 July 1902.

He attended the local elementary school in Fürth from 1908 until 1912, followed by the humanistic high school on Kaiserstrasse in Fürth, graduating in 1920. He was a trainee bank clerk from 1920 until 1922, when he was employed by the Bankhaus Brückner in Fürth, but was asked to leave on 30 May 1924 as a result of his strong anti-Jewish beliefs.

Forster joined the new NSDAP Ortsgruppe Fürth in September 1923, followed by the SA on 7 November 1923. (*Confusion exists over his NSDAP entry date. Some sources state he joined the Party on the same day he joined the SA, but Forster himself writes in his Lebenslauf that he first joined the NSDAP in September 1923*). During the forbidden period for the NSDAP, he continued to lead the Grossdeutsche Volksgemeinschaft (a cover organisation for the NSDAP) in Fürth, through a connection with Julius Streicher. He subsequently worked as a part-time journalist on Streicher's newspaper Der Stürmer.

Forster met Hitler in Munich in February 1925 and, following the lift of the prohibition on the NSDAP, he rejoined the Party on 5 April 1925. He was allocated membership card number 1 924. He was the Ortsgruppenleiter for the NSDAP in Fürth until December 1929. During 1926 he was appointed as temporary editor of the newspaper *Wau-Wau*.

Forster joined the SS on 12 May 1926 and received SS number 158. He was the founder member (and appointed leader) of SS-Gruppe Nuremberg-Fürth on 14 July 1926.

In 1928 he became the NSDAP district leader for Mid-Franconia. Forster was employed as an accounts officer for the Deutschnationalen

Handlungsgehilfen-Verbandes (DHV—*German National Commercial Employees Association*) in Nuremberg from 22 February 1928 until 1930. He was appointed the DHV district business manager for Lower Elbe in April 1930, based in Hamburg-Harburg. He used this time as an opportunity to tour the area giving speeches. He was eventually dismissed from his post with the DHV on 5 March 1932 for an article he had written in *Der Vorposten*.

On 14 September 1930, Forster was elected to the Reichstag as NSDAP representative for Wahlkreis 26 (Franconia). From 1930 until 1933, he was the Advisor for Labour Service and Clerical Workers in the NSDAP faction of the Reichstag. He was also appointed to the Reichstag Foreign Committee.

On 15 October 1930, with retrospective effect from 1 October 1930, Hitler appointed Forster as Gauleiter for Danzig; from 26 October 1939 this incorporated West Prussia. He retained this post until 1945. This appointment was unpopular with a large number of the NSDAP members in Danzig, as Forster was viewed as an outsider. Their choice would have been Forster's appointed deputy, Artur Greiser, who was a native of the city. The conflict resulted in two opposing factions and the disagreements continued until 1939, when Greiser was appointed as Gauleiter for the Wartheland.

Forster was appointed as SS-Standartenführer on 1 October 1932 and assigned to SS-Standarte 36, based in Danzig.

Following the Nazi seizure of power in 1933, Forster was bestowed with numerous honours and appointments, many of which had connections to the Labour Front. He was nominated as a commissioner on the administrative council of the DHV. In May 1933 he gained an absolute majority for the NSDAP in the Danzig Senate. On 10 May he was nominated as Leader of the General Association of German Clerical Employees, a post which gave him total control over all national office employee organisations. On 14 July 1933, Forster was appointed as an honorary citizen of the Free City of Danzig. He also joined the board of directors of the Bank der Deutschen Arbeit. From August 1933 until October 1939, he was in charge of the courts of the City of Danzig. His hometown city of Fürth nominated him as an honorary citizen on 26 April 1934.

On 15 August 1933, Forster was promoted to SS-Oberführer and on 15 September 1933 he was appointed as a Prussian State Councillor. He was further promoted to SS-Gruppenführer on 27 January 1934 and was eventually posted to the staff of the Reichsführer-SS on 23 January 1936.

Albert Forster was married to Gertrud Deetz (born 11 May 1910 in Posen; NSDAP number 465 488) on 9 May 1934. Hitler and Hess acted as witnesses at the ceremony. There were no children of the marriage.

Forster had military training as a Kanonier der Reserve with a Luftwaffe flak regiment during March-April 1937. He announced in April 1937 that the Nuremberg race laws would be formally recognised and enacted in the Free City of Danzig, affecting around 7,500 Jewish inhabitants. In March and April 1939, Forster was hospitalised with a lung embolism and varicose veins in his left leg. He underwent successful surgery which was followed by a period of rest throughout May.

In his capacity as Gauleiter for Danzig, Forster was at the forefront of Hitler's expansion policy. On the first day of war, Hitler appointed him head of civil administration for the Danzig area. As a war zone, his authority was transferred to the command of the military commander for West Prussia. He was also under the area of responsibility of the Higher SS and Police Leader Danzig-West Prussia (until 26 October 1939). In 1940 he was appointed as Reich Defence Commissioner for Danzig, and this was followed throughout the war with various civil and administrative posts associated with the defence and reconstruction of the city. His final promotion, to SS-Obergruppenführer, was on 31 December 1941.

From 25 September 1944, Forster was the leader of the Deutschen Volkssturm in Danzig West Prussia. He finally left the city on 27 March 1945, aboard the steamship Zoppot, accompanied by SS-Brigadeführer Wilhelm Huth and SS-Oberführer Prof. Dr Erich Grossmann. They arrived in eastern Holstein on 30 March and evaded capture until 27 May 1945, when Forster was arrested by the 53rd (Welsh) Division in Hamburg. He was then interned at the British internment camp at Fallingbostel. His true identity went undetected until July 1946, when he was transferred to the British internment camp at Neuengamme, on the outskirts of Hamburg. Forster was handed over to the Polish authorities by the British Military Government on 10 August 1946.

He was held at the Central Prison in Warsaw before being charged by the Polish National Supreme Court with mass murder on 25 August 1946. Forster was transferred to a prison in Gdansk (*Danzig*) on 14 September 1946. He stood trial there from 4 April until 29 April 1948, when he was convicted and sentenced to death by hanging. He remained in prison awaiting execution, but was turned over to the Polish security service in June 1951. Following his transfer, all trace of Forster disappeared, prompting speculation that his death sentence was commuted to life imprisonment. Repeated enquiries by his wife and the German authorities were met with a wall of silence. Further speculation surrounded the death sentence being carried out. There were three versions of Forster's death—the International Red Cross maintained he was executed at Christmas 1955 and another source stated he died in March 1954; the Polish authorities informed Frau Forster that he was executed in 1952.

The true circumstances surrounding Forster's demise were not revealed until 1999, when his biographer, Dieter Schenk, presented final proof that he was hanged on 28 February 1952 in Mokotow Prison Warsaw. This was after the Polish President had declined a petition for clemency a week earlier.

Albert Forster was an old NSDAP member from the time of struggle and was popular with certain sections of the Party. Importantly, this included Hitler. He

Hitler solved the problem of rivalry between Greiser and Forster by transferring Greiser to Posen and appointing him as Gauleiter for the Wartheland.

Greiser divorced his first wife and remarried in 1935. Himmler attended the wedding.

Greiser with his second wife.

The couple relax at home.

Deputy Gauleiter Greiser (far left) next to von dem Bach-Zelewski and Forster. Koppe is at the far right.

The two rivals for power in Danzig on the right, Forster and Greiser.

Deputy Gauleiter Greiser.

SS-Brigadeführer Greiser.

Greiser wearing his field-grey SS greatcoat.

Greiser in the field-grey SS uniform of a Brigadeführer.

SS-Oberführer Arthur Greiser.

Gauleiter of Danzig Albert Forster.

Forster (left) carrying out his official duties at a function.

Forster's residence in Danzig.

Studio images of SS-Gruppenführer Albert Forster.

Forster leaving his civil marriage ceremony.

Exiting the church after the wedding.

Gauleiter Forster speaks.

Forster, wearing his white summer Gauleiter tunic in the Danzig sunshine.

The Gauleiter in his Reserve Luftwaffe uniform.

Forster (right) during a visit by Hitler, Göring and
senior Luftwaffe figures.

Prisoner Albert Forster enters captivity.

AUGUST FRANZ FRANK

Augustus Frank was born a Catholic on 5 April 1898 in Augsburg, the son of railway worker Wenzel Frank (died of stomach cancer aged fifty-four) and his wife Elisabeth (born Amann). He attended elementary primary school from 1904 until 1909, followed by high school until 1912. Upon leaving school, August found employment as a business apprentice with the Augsburg firm of Klunk and Gerber from 16 July 1912 until 30 June 1915. He then worked as a warehouseman from 1 July 1915 until 18 August 1916.

On 19 August 1916, Frank volunteered for the Army. He was enlisted two days later in the 9th Bavarian Field Artillery Regiment in Landsberg. He also served with the 4th Bavarian Field Artillery Regiment in Augsburg from 26 October 1916. He transferred to the 1st Bavarian Reserve Field Artillery Regiment on 26 January 1917 as an Unteroffizier, and served at the front. He remained with that unit until 13 December 1918, when he transferred back to the 4th Field Artillery Regiment as a paymaster—remaining with it until 30 June 1919, when he was discharged.

From 1 July 1919 until 13 October 1920, Frank worked for Weissenhorn & Company, a local transport and removals firm. Frank applied to join the Bavarian Landespolizei on 14 October 1920, and was accepted six days later on 20 October. He used this period to study and gain qualifications as a paymaster and in administration. He became a paymaster with the police, and was posted to the auditing office of the Bavarian State Ministry of the Interior on 1 June 1923.

He was married on 22 October 1923 to Rosa Hofmann (born on 26 February 1901 in Dorfern). They had two daughters—one in 1929 and the other in 1935.

On 1 July 1927, Frank qualified as a government administration official within the police service. He subsequently resigned from the police on 30 April 1930, in order to become a self-employed forwarding agent.

He joined the SS on 8 April 1932 as a member of the 4th Sturm, 2nd Sturmbann of SS-Standarte 1. His SS number was 56 169. From 25 March to 29 August 1933, he served on the administrative staff of Dachau concentration camp. On 1 July 1933, he was promoted to SS-Scharführer and then to SS-Truppführer on 29

August 1933, simultaneously moving to the staff of the Reichsführer-SS. On 9 November 1933, he was promoted to SS-Sturmführer and transferred to the RFSS administration department.

August Frank's actual date of joining the NSDAP is confusing, as his SS file records three different dates. Frank himself notes the date as 12 March 1932, on a questionnaire dated 24 March 1933. A short report prepared for Himmler by the Chief of the SS Personnel Office, Walter Schmitt, records the date as 8 April 1932, but his orange service card shows 11 February 1933. Frank became a member of NSDAP Ortsgruppe Neuhausen and was allocated card number 1471185.

He was further promoted on 20 April 1934 to SS-Obersturmführer. He took charge of Abteilung IV (Administration) on 1 January 1935 with another promotion, to SS-Hauptsturmführer. Frank was also attached to Ortsgruppe 'Braun Haus' in Munich. On 15 September 1935 he was promoted to SS-Sturmbannführer in the administration section of the SS-Hauptamt. Transferring again on 1 April 1936, he was appointed to the SS-VT Inspectorate. He was promoted to SS-Obersturmbannführer on 20 April 1936 and to SS-Standartenführer on 20 April 1937. Another promotion, to SS-Oberführer, on 20 April 1938, saw him transfer to become the Staff Officer of the SS-Hauptamt and deputy to the chief of administration, Oswald Pohl.

Frank's next posting, on 20 April 1939, was as chief of the SS-Verwaltungsamt (*Administration Office*) in the SS-Hauptamt. Promoted again on 20 April 1940—to SS-Brigadeführer and Generalmajor der SS-VT—he moved to the office of budget and construction. His next promotion was on 30 January 1943, to SS-Gruppenführer und Generalleutnant der Waffen-SS in the SS-Wirtschafts-Verwaltungshauptamtes (SS-WVHA—*Economic and Administration Central Office*). He was chief of Department A and the deputy to the central office chief, SS-Obergruppenführer Oswald Pohl. Yet another transfer occurred on 16 September 1943, when he became chief of the economic and administrative department in the Ordnungspolizei Hauptamt. Frank was also accorded the right to wear the uniform of a Generalleutnant der Polizei from 27 September 1943. He was transferred again on 18 August 1944, this time to the command staff of SS-Obergruppenführer Jüttner, under the commander-in-chief of the Reserve Army, Reichsführer-SS Heinrich Himmler. His final promotion, to SS-Obergruppenführer und General der Waffen-SS und Polizei, came on 9 October 1944. Frank was appointed chief of the Army Administration Department on 1 November 1944, as the replacement for General Osterkamp.

In May 1945, Frank adopted the false identity of one 'Franz Müller', and avoided capture for several months, working in a cement factory. He was finally arrested on 17 December 1945.

On 13 July 1946, August Frank stated in an affidavit for the International Military Tribunal in Nuremberg that his Department A in the SS-WVHA had

little knowledge of the concentration camps. The camps came under Department D in the same Hauptamt. As he was deputy to the chief of the SS-WVHA, Frank's story is hard to believe. Frank himself stood trial in Case 4 of the US Military Tribunals. He was sentenced to life imprisonment on 3 November 1947. This was subsequently reduced to fifteen years and he was released in 1954.

In later years, Frank replied to letters from historians and collectors. In one, he mentions that all his possessions, other than a few items, were stolen when he was captured. He was forced to sell what things he had left to supplement his income. He died on 21 March 1984 in Karlsruhe.

August Frank (right) accompanies Himmler as he inspects SS men in sports kit.

Left and right: SS-Standartenführer August Frank.

SS-Brigadeführer August Frank.

The SS-WVHA file photograph of SS-Brigadeführer August Frank.

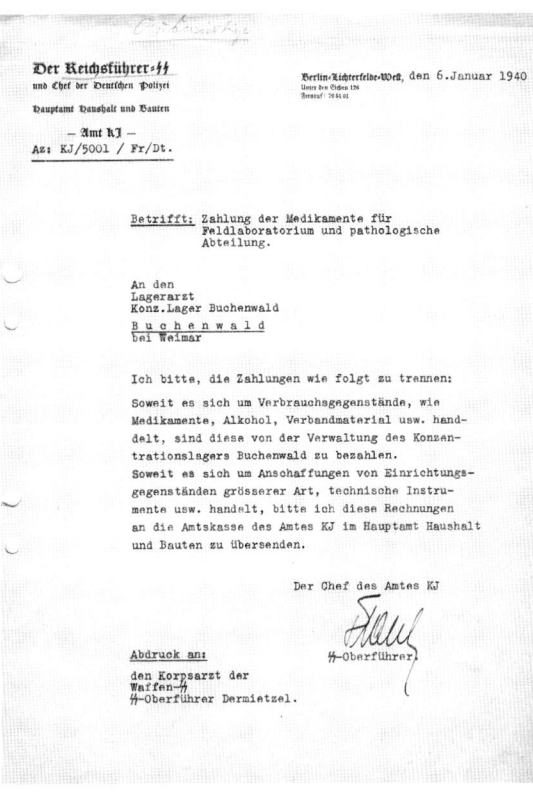

Two department chiefs in the SS-WVHA, Richard Glücks (left) and August Frank (right).

Frank forwards an invoice for medication to the camp doctor at Buchenwald concentration camp.

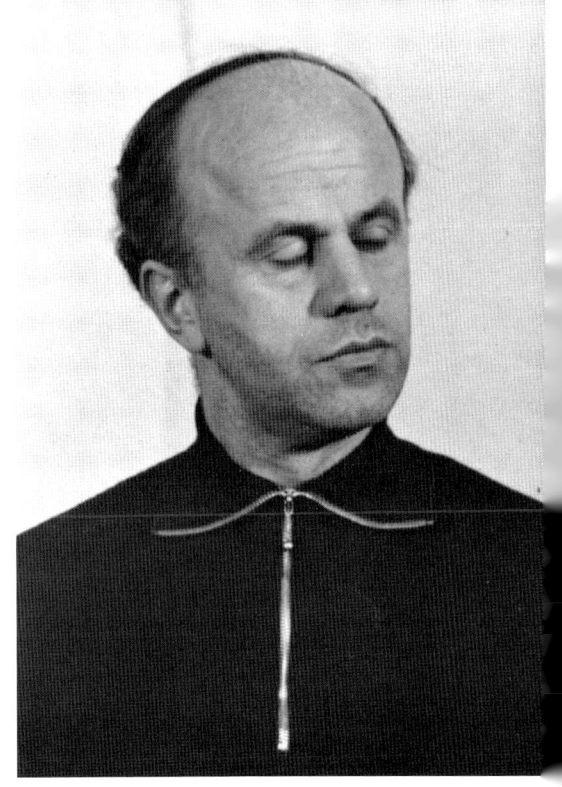

Left and right: August Frank, prisoner of war.

Frank in the dock at Nuremberg.

The grave of August Frank.

KARL HERMANN FRANK

K ARL HERMANN FRANK was born on 24 January 1898, in Karlsbad (*today Karlovy Vary*). He was the son of teacher Heinrich Frank (born on 15 September 1859 in Karlsbad, died 29 October 1928 in Karlsbad) and his wife, Paula Frank (born Eberhardt in Karlsbad on 16 February 1869, died 15 May 1940 in Karlsbad). The family were of good Germanic stock and Frank's paternal grandparents, Josef Frank and Rosina Frank (born Scherzer), were proud of their Germanic roots in the Habsburg Empire.

Frank spent five years at elementary school from 1903, before eventually matriculating from a Karlsbad high school in 1916. From 1912 until 1916, Frank was an active member of the youth movement 'Wandervogel'. It was here that his interest in politics was nurtured—something which was not unusual for one so young in the politically volatile period of the early twentieth century. He also participated (as leader) in the first Land Work Service in Egerland from 1914 to 1915.

In 1916, at the first opportunity, Frank volunteered for active service with the Austrian Army, applying to the 73rd Infantry Regiment in Prague. His application was rejected on medical grounds. As a result of an accident in his childhood, he had lost his right eye and he wore a glass substitute in its place.

From 1916 to 1918, Frank studied jurisprudence for four terms at the German University in Prague and then he learnt bookkeeping. He served for a short time in 1919–1920 with the Silesian Frontier Police as a volunteer, but his main employment at this time was as a civil servant.

Frank worked as a bookkeeper with the Dux-Bodenbacher Railway from 1921 until 1923, but his main interest had already manifested itself in politics. He joined the Sudeten National Socialist Party from its early days in 1919, and remained active until it was banned in 1923. During 1922, he was an official with the first Volunteer Work Service in Karlsbad. From 1923 until 1925, Frank was employed by the Erich Matthes Publishing House, first as an apprentice in Hartenstein, and then as an assistant in Leipzig.

On 21 January 1925, Frank married Anna Müller (born in Karlsbad on 5 January

1899), the daughter of a master cutter. They had two sons: Harald, born 20 January 1926, and Gerhard, born 22 April 1931. Harald later served with the SS-Leibstandarte 'Adolf Hitler' and was seriously wounded in Hungary in March 1945.

From 1925 until 1932, Frank was a self-employed book dealer in Elbogen, near Karlsbad. His business was called the 'Egerlandhaus für Buch und Kunst', but he also simultaneously ran his own publishing house for National Socialist agitation and propaganda.

In 1930, Frank joined the German National Party (DNP) in Czechoslovakia. Wishing to move closer to the centre of politics, he moved his book business into Karlsbad in 1932. On 1 October 1933, he founded the Karlsbad group of the Sudeten German Homefront (SHF). He rose rapidly in the ranks of this movement, and from February 1932 he published the weekly magazine *Rundschau*.

In 1934 a woman named Mitze Kleisner, from Děčín, alleged that Frank had fathered a baby with her, but Frank hushed up the circumstance and nothing further was heard of the matter.

On 19 April 1935, Frank joined the Sudeten German Party (SDP), an offspring of the banned Czechoslovakian National Socialist Party. He was allocated membership number 18 and served as a senior member of the Party. In May 1935 he was elected as the SDP Karlsbad delegate of the Czech national assembly. Frank held various senior posts within the SDP, with responsibilities for propaganda, labour, political committees and the leadership council. On 15 January 1937 he was appointed deputy to the SDP leader, Konrad Henlein. From 17 September 1938 until 10 October 1938, he was deputy leader of the Sudeten German Freikorps.

On 9 October 1938, Frank joined the NSDAP and was allocated Party card 6 600 002 (*there is an alternative date recorded in his SSO file as 1 November 1938*). He was appointed Deputy Reich Commissar for the Sudeten German Zone on 10 October 1938. He became Deputy Gauleiter for the Sudetenland on 4 November 1938.

Frank joined the SS on 1 November 1938, gaining the rank of SS-Brigadeführer on the staff of the RFSS, with membership number 310 466. On 4 December 1938, he was elected as a member of the Reichstag, representing the Sudetenland. After the creation of the Protectorate of Bohemia Moravia, Frank was appointed on 18 March 1939 as State Secretary representing the Reichsprotektor (Reich Protector), Constantin von Neurath. He was designated HSSPF Böhmen-Mähren (*Bohemia-Moravia*) and Deputy Reichsprotektor on 28 April 1939. He served as a judge on the People's Court from 1939 until 1945. Frank was promoted to SS-Gruppenführer on 9 November 1939, following his ruthless suppression of student demonstrations in the Protectorate.

The marriage between Frank and Anna Frank had been unhappy for a number of years, culminating in divorce on 17 February 1940. Later the same year, she married Frank's successor as Deputy Gauleiter in the Sudetenland, SA-Brigadeführer Dr Fritz Köllner. Frank had begun a relationship with the beautiful doctor Karola

Blaschek (born 13 August 1913 in Brüx, and a member of the SDP) and on 14 April 1940 the couple were married. They produced three children: Edda on 16 August 1941, Wolf-Dietrich on 20 August 1942 and Holle on 8 March 1944. It appears that Wolf-Dietrich was baptised in the Catholic faith at the Prague hospital where he was born, without the knowledge of his father. Frank then began a process to remove him from the Catholic Church, succeeding on 3 November 1942. The Gestapo were tasked with investigating the circumstances.

Frank served for four weeks of reserve duty with SS-Standarte 'Germania' in Hamburg-Langenhorn from 20 May 1940. He was hopeful of gaining the Reich Protectorship when Hitler replaced von Neurath on engineered grounds of ill health in September 1941, only to be outdone by the more cunning Reinhard Heydrich. Frank was designated as deputy to Heydrich, the new Acting Reichsprotektor. Frank was again passed over when Heydrich was assassinated in 1942, remaining as deputy to Heydrich's replacement, Kurt Daluege. On 21 June 1943, he was promoted to SS-Obergruppenführer and General der Polizei and on 1 July 1944 he was given the rank of General der Waffen-SS und Polizei.

Frank was appointed German Minister for Bohemia-Moravia on 20 August 1943. His last meeting with Hitler occurred on 4 April 1945, when he flew to Berlin. Following Hitler's suicide, Frank flew to Flensburg to meet with Dönitz, but the Grossadmiral had no use for Frank in his new government. He returned to Prague, a dejected and beaten man.

On 9 May 1945, Frank left Prague and headed in the direction of Bavaria, via Pilsen. He was captured by American forces near Rokitzan and transported to Wiesbaden, and thence to London on 21 June. In early 1946 he was handed over to the Czech authorities. He stood trial in Prague from 22 March to 28 April 1946, when the death sentence was passed.

On 22 May 1946, Frank was led into the courtyard of the State Prison at Pancrac. A scaffold had been set up at the side of the cellblock and the courtyard was packed with invited guests. Frank was asked if he wished to say anything. He nodded, and was helped into a position where everyone could hear his voice. He shouted, '*As I die, my people will live!*' As the rope was placed around his neck, he called out, '*Long live the German people! Long live the German spirit!*' He died at 1.37 p.m. in front of an audience of approximately 4,000 people. He was pronounced dead by Dr Navarra, whose wife, Marie Navarrová, had ironically assisted the stricken Reinhard Heydrich to be transported to the Bulovka hospital on 27 May 1942. For her help she had been rewarded with 10,000 crowns, which she donated to the German Red Cross. In 1948 she received a lengthy prison term for her actions.

In another ironic twist, Frank's corpse was examined for autopsy on on the same anatomy table, in same building (in Studničkova Street, in Prague), as the seven Czechoslovak paratroopers killed in the Church of St Cyril and St Methodious. These included the Heydrich assassins, Josef Gabčík and Jan Kubiš. Frank was

buried in a collective grave at the cemetery at Prague-Ďáblice, the same site as the seven paratroopers.

Frank's children were apparently raised after the war by his oldest brother, Ernst Frank, who died on 20 September 1982. Their mother, Dr Karola Frank, was arrested in May 1945 and sent to the Lubyanka prison in Moscow, where she was held for a year before being imprisoned in a gulag in Kazakhstan for ten years. After her repatriation to Germany in 1956, she spent four years unsuccessfully searching for her children in various foster families. An unconfirmed report states she died in 1982.

Karl Hermann Frank was a Sudeten German whose hatred for the Czechs stemmed from the treatment they handed out to the Sudeten German minority. He was an intelligent, cultured and politically astute man, who is portrayed today as uncouth and vicious. There is little doubt that he was brutal towards those he saw as enemies of the German people. However, it was also Frank who convinced Hitler not to execute thousands in retribution for the attack on Heydrich. In contrast, it was also Frank who issued the orders by telephone to SS-Standartenführer Horst Böhme, the SD chief in Prague, for reprisal actions against the villages of Lidice and Lezhaky:

1. All adult male inhabitants are to be shot;
2. All females are to be evacuated to a concentration camp;
3. The children are to be collected together; if capable of Germanization, they are to be delivered to SS-families in the Reich and the rest are to undergo a different education;
4. The place is to be burnt down and razed to the ground.

Today the name of Lidice is remembered throughout the world as a symbol of aggression against innocence. The former inhabitants are immortalised in memorials and museums, and the sites of both the former villages are visited by thousands annually.

Frank's father.

Frank's mother.

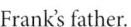

Frank (arrowed) in Elbogen in June 1921, during Bohemia Week.

A young Karl Hermann Frank.

The Frank family; his first wife, Anna, and their son.

The deputy leader of the Sudeten German Party.

A smiling Frank wears his SDP lapel pin.

The SDP became affiliated to the NSDAP and Frank joined the Nazi Party.

The new NSDAP member joined the SS and was accorded the rank of SS-Brigadeführer.

A formal portrait of SS-Brigadeführer Frank in his SS greatcoat and cap.

Frank wearing his field-grey SS uniform.

Frank was appointed as NSDAP Deputy Gauleiter for the Sudetenland.

Soon promoted to SS-Gruppenführer, Frank wears the RFSS cuff title.

Frank divorced his first wife and married the beautiful Dr Karola Blaschek.

State Secretary and SS-Gruppenführer Karl Hermann Frank.

Frank poses in his office at the Czernin Palace in Prague.

Heydrich frustrated Frank's attempt to gain the appointment of Reichsprotektor.

Even after Heydrich's assassination, Frank was passed over and Daluege was appointed as his replacement. Here, Frank was part of the escort for Heydrich's body.

Frank during a visit to the SS training facility at Beneschau.

SS-Gruppenführer Karl Hermann Frank.

SS-Obergruppenführer Karl Hermann Frank.

SS-Obergruppenführer Frank relaxes for the photographer.

A superb study of Frank in a leather greatcoat.

SS-Obergruppenführer Frank displays his awards.

Opposite page:

Above left: Frank strikes a pose.

Above right: Heydrich's replacement in Prague was Kurt Daluege, who carried out the duties of Deputy Reichsprotektor from May 1942 until August 1943.

At his post-war trial, Frank is confronted with Daluege. Frank unsuccessfully attempted to place the blame for the brutality of the revenge actions over Heydrich's assassination upon Daluege's shoulders.

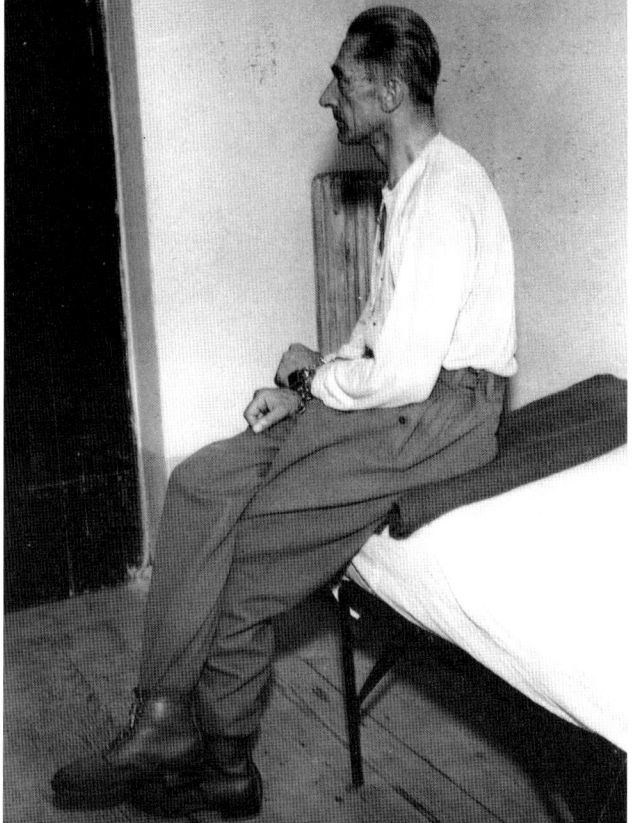

Above: Condemned to death, Frank awaits his fate in his Panrac prison cell.

Left: Frank was photographed in his cell before his execution.

Right: Frank was hanged publicly in the prison yard at Pancrac.

Below: Karl Hermann Frank lies dead following his execution and autopsy.

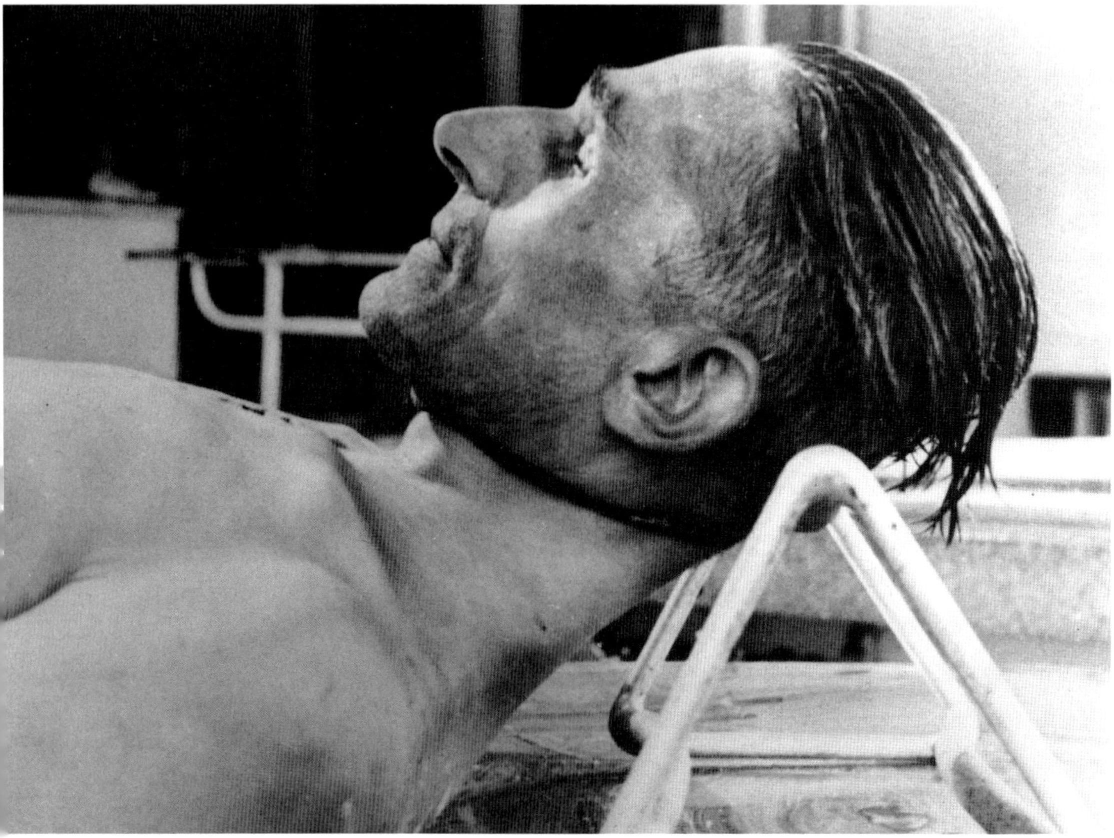

HERBERT OTTO WILHELM HERMANN GILLE

ERBERT GILLE was born on 8 March 1897, one of four sons of factory manager Hermann Gille, in Gandersheim am Harz. He attended the local elementary school and high school until March 1909, before joining the cadet corps in April 1909 at Bensberg. He then finished his military training at the Berlin-Lichterfelde cadet officer academy in August 1914.

From 2 August 1914, he was assigned to the 30th Field Artillery Regiment. On 29 December 1914, he was assigned to the 55th Reserve Field Artillery Regiment, an element of the 75th Infantry Division. Gille served as a platoon leader and battery officer, attaining the rank of Leutnant on 27 January 1915, and was a battery commander from January 1917 until January 1919. On 31 March 1919, he was promoted to Oberleutnant and he left military service.

From 1 April 1919, Gille studied agriculture administration whilst gaining practical experience on estates at Bätzigerode, Bamhof and Abbesbüttel until 1923. From 1923 until 1929, he was an inspector of estates at Immendorf, Bährdorf (near Oebisfelde), Stemmen and Poggenhagen. In 1929 he found employment as a commercial traveller for a car factory in Braunschweig. From 1931 until 1933, he was a self-employed car salesman.

From 1922 until 1926, Gille was a member of Stahlhelm. He joined the NSDAP on 1 May 1931 and was allocated membership number 537 337. He joined the SS in December 1931 with SS number 39 854, signing on the roll of the 5th Sturm, 1st Sturmbann of the 49th SS-Standarte. He was promoted to SS-Scharführer on 25 September 1932 and on 27 January 1933, Gille assumed command of the Motorstaffel of the 49th Standarte, with the rank of SS-Truppführer. He was promoted on 20 April 1933 to SS-Sturmführer, and was appointed as Staff Officer of SS-Abschnitt IV in Braunschweig.

As a supporter of Reichstag vice-President Ernst Zörner, Gille became involved in an intrigue against the Braunschweig Minister President Dietrich Klagges. For his part in the plot, Gille was degraded, released from the SS and his membership of the Party was suspended. From 20 July until 27 October 1933, he was held in

the Braunschweig Prison. Gille insisted he was innocent of any conspiracy for the downfall of Klagges. He appealed, requesting a hearing by the Party. On 14 February 1934 he was exonerated, readmitted to the Party and reinstated in the SS with his old rank of SS-Sturmführer.

From 9 April until 29 May 1934, he was a special duties officer with the 2nd Sturmbann 49th SS-Standarte. On 29 May 1934, Gille transferred to the 2nd Sturm 3rd Sturmbann of SS-Standarte I (*later entitled SS-Standarte 'Deutschland'*) in the SS-Verfügungstruppe. From 7 June until 14 August 1934, Gille had command of the 1st Sturmbann of the 2nd SS-VT-Standarte.

Gille was married on 3 January 1935 to Sophie Charlotte Mennecke (born on 31 December 1903 in Stemmen-Hannover). They had one daughter, Ingeborg, born on 9 October 1935.

Gille was promoted to SS-Obersturmführer on 20 April 1935. He moved to command the 12th Sturm 3rd Sturmbann of SS-Standarte 1 on 9 November 1935, with a further promotion to SS-Hauptsturmführer. With the expansion of the Standarte, Gille became the commander of the 19th Sturm, 4th Sturmbann of SS-Standarte 1 'Deutschland'. He transferred on 1 October 1936 to be the Staff Officer of SS-Standarte 2 'Germania'. He took over command of the 2nd Sturmbann on 1 February 1937, and was promoted to SS-Sturmbannführer on 20 April 1937. He attended numerous courses at military schools including Doberitz, Jüterborg and Wünsdorf.

In April 1939, Gille was reminded that he had to submit details of his heritage stretching back to 1750—a requirement of all SS officers. There is no record of his compliance with this request in his files. Therefore it is not clear whether the necessary paperwork has gone missing or whether or not Gille just ignored this order.

He took charge of the 1st Battalion SS Artillery Regiment on 1 June 1939. He served in the Polish and western campaigns, and was promoted to SS-Obersturmbannführer on 19 October 1939. Gille was given command of the 5th SS Artillery Regiment on 15 November 1940 (*this became part of SS-Division 'Wiking'*).

Gille was promoted to SS-Standartenführer on 30 January 1941, and to SS-Oberführer on 1 October 1941. On 1 February 1942, he was assigned temporary command of SS-Regiment 'Westland'. He was the first commander of the SS Artillery Corps from 20 June 1942 until 31 July 1942, when he was posted back to the SS 'Wiking' Division.

On 9 November 1942 (*his orange file card shows 1 December 1942*), Gille was promoted to SS-Brigadeführer und Generalmajor der Waffen-SS. He was given command of SS-Division 'Wiking' on 1 May 1943. On 9 November 1943, Gille was promoted to SS-Gruppenführer und Generalleutnant der Waffen-SS. He took over command of IV SS-Panzer-Korps on 6 August 1944, and was finally promoted to SS-Obergruppenführer und General der Waffen-SS on 9 November 1944.

Gille was one of the most highly decorated officers of the SS; his awards include the Knights Cross of the Iron Cross, Oakleaves to the Knights Cross of the Iron Cross (*315th recipient*), Swords to the Knights Cross of the Iron Cross (*47th recipient*), and Diamonds to the Oakleaves and Swords of the Knights Cross of the Iron Cross (*12th recipient*).

Gille was captured at Radstadt, outside Vienna, on 8 May 1945. He was detained at various centres—including Dachau—until 21 May 1948. He subsequently opened a bookstore in Stemmen and founded the Waffen-SS veteran's magazine *Wiking Ruf*, which later changed its name to *Der Freiwillige*. Gille was an active member of HIAG. He died of a heart attack on 26 December 1966 in Stemmen-Hannover.

Left and right: SS-Untersturmführer Herbert Gille.

SS-Obersturmführer Gille.

SS-Sturmbannführer Gille.

SS-Sturmbannführer Gille with SS-Standarte Germania.

Gille accompanies a NSDAP official who is inspecting the guard provided by Germania.

Gille with Gauleiter Mutschmann.

SS-Brigadeführer Gille wearing his Knight's Cross and German Cross in Gold.

Gille with a wounded Hans Dorr, the adjutant of 'Germania'.

SS-Gruppenführer Herbert Otto Gille.

Gille at the front.

A popular, highly decorated soldier.

Gille with SS-Standartenführer Mühlenkamp.

Hitler presents Gille with the Swords to the Knight's Cross. To the left is Degrelle, with Fegelein and Himmler looking on.

Gille at his desk.

SS-Obergruppenführer Gille in his black panzer tunic.

A post-war photograph of Gille wearing his decorations.

The grave marker for Herbert Gille.

CURT VON GOTTBERG

URT VON GOTTBERG was born on 11 February 1896 in Wilten, East Prussia. His father, the Protestant Rittmeister der Reserve Walter von Gottberg (born on 7 January 1870), was an estate owner. His mother, Agnes (born on 16 August 1869, died on 25 May 1923), was a member of the aristocratic von der Goltz family.

The young Curt attended elementary school from 1902 to 1906 and then the Wilhelms-Gymnasium (*high school*) in Königsberg from 1906 to 1914. He volunteered for active service on 2 August 1914 and was posted to the Reconnaissance Cavalry Regiment 'Graf Wrangel'. He served with this unit until 20 September 1914, when he was commissioned as a Leutnant. He was transferred to the 1st Guard Foot Regiment in 1916 and remained with that unit until April 1919, having been promoted to Oberleutnant. In April 1917, von Gottberg was seriously wounded on the Western Front and spent weeks in hospital. He was discharged from the Army on 1 April 1920.

From 1919 until 1924, he was a member of the Freikorps Brigade 'Erhardt', and was a section commander during the failed Hitler Putsch of 9 November 1923. In 1924, disillusioned with politics for the time being, von Gottberg took up farming and estate management, travelling to Sweden and Italy.

Curt von Gottberg was married in February 1919. The couple produced three daughters from 1920 until 1923, but the oldest daughter died in 1942. The marriage ended in divorce on 20 April 1928 (*some sources state that the marriage ended with the death of his wife*). He remarried on 21 December 1928 to Charlotte Kniep (born on 1 August 1903 in Budzuhnen; NSDAP member number 842 230). They had four sons, including twin boys, between 1930 and 1937. One son died in 1941 after a prolonged illness.

Von Gottberg joined the SA on 15 November 1931 and the NSDAP on 1 February 1932. He held Party membership number 948 753.

He transferred to the SS and was assigned to SS-Standarte 18 on 20 July 1932, with SS number 45 923. He was promoted to SS-Scharführer on 1 April 1933 and to

SS-Truppführer on 25 April 1933. Six months passed and he was rapidly promoted again: to SS-Obertruppführer on 20 October 1933 and to SS-Sturmführer on 6 November 1933. He then served as a special duties officer with SS-Oberabschnitt West from 6 November 1933, and then with the SS-Totenkopf-Verbände on 13 November 1933. He was subsequently attached to SS-Oberabschnitt Südwest.

He was promoted to SS-Sturmhauptführer on 15 December 1933, and to SS-Sturmbannführer on 30 January 1934. On 25 March 1934, he transferred to the leadership of the Political Readiness Squad in Ellwangen, with the rank of SS-Obersturmbannführer. This unit was redesignated as the 3rd Sturmbann of SS-Standarte I in October 1934 and he retained command.

On 13 March until 28 May 1935, von Gottberg attended a combat instruction course at Doberitz. He took charge of SS-Standarte 49 on 1 June 1935. During a car journey between Braunschweig and Goslar on 5 January 1936, he was seriously injured in an accident, resulting in the amputation of his lower-left leg. (*There is some suggestion that von Gottberg was drunk behind the wheel of his car at the time of his accident*). He was placed on extended convalescent leave, officially unfit for duty, until 3 August 1936—but during this period he was appointed as Inspekteur der SS-Stammabteilung Mitte (*Inspector of Reserve Auxiliary Formations SS-Oberabschnitt Mitte*) on 15 April 1936. Shortly after his return to full duty, with a false leg fitted, Reichsführer-SS Himmler issued him with a personal order to abstain from the use of alcohol.

From 1 July 1937 until 7 November 1939, von Gottberg was also assigned as Chief of the Settlement Office and the Central Land Office in the SS-Rasse-und Siedlungs-Hauptamt (*SS-Race and Settlement Main Office—RuSHA*). He was promoted to SS-Standartenführer on 9 November 1937, and to SS-Oberführer on 30 January 1939. He was also appointed as an arbitrator in the Senior Court of the Reichsführer-SS.

From 18th April 1939, von Gottberg headed the Land Department in the Agricultural Section of the Protectorate of Bohemia-Moravia. This appointment was at the instigation of Karl Hermann Frank and was opposed by Reichsprotektor von Neurath. Von Gottberg was also given responsibility for forest economy as State Minister in this department. Von Neurath's reservations were subsequently well-founded, as von Gottberg was removed from all his SS appointments on 7 November 1939 for exceeding his authority and for corruption whilst in his post in Prague. He was not found another posting until 27 July 1940, when he was given command of Amt III (Requisitioning) in the SS-Hauptamt. This department was later re-designated as Amt VI.

During the Polish campaign of September–October 1939, von Gottberg was responsible for the co-ordination of RuSHA elements attached to the Einsatzgruppen.

On 1 December 1940, he was appointed as a reserve officer in the Waffen-SS, with the Waffen-SS rank of SS-Obersturmbannführer. From 17 September 1941 until 1 October 1941, von Gottberg attended a training course in police duties,

and he relinquished his Waffen-SS rank on 20 April 1942 with his promotion to SS-Brigadeführer und Generalmajor der Polizei.

He was appointed as honorary member of the Peoples' Court on 10 July 1942 for the duration of the war.

Von Gottberg was transferred to the east and was appointed to the staff of HSSPF Ostland on 1 October 1942. He formed and commanded Kampfgruppe 'von Gottberg' on anti-partisan operations in Weissruthenien (*east Belarus*) from 16 November 1942. This groupparticipated in numerous actions.

He was appointed SS-und Polizei Führer (SSPF—*SS and Police Leader*) in Minsk on 1 December 1942, with seniority from 21 July 1942. Von Gottberg was promoted to SS-Gruppenführer und Generalleutnant der Polizei on 15 July 1943.

When Wilhelm Kube was assassinated by Yelena Gregoyevna Mazanik, by placing an explosive device under his bed on 22 September 1943, von Gottberg replaced him as Generalkommissar Weissruthenien. In retaliation, von Gottberg ordered the summary execution of approximately 2,000 Minsk citizens. In December 1943, von Gottberg himself was the target of an unsuccessful assassination attempt. His Kampgruppe 'von Gottberg' continued its activities under his command through-out the summer of 1944.

Von Gottberg assumed full responsibilities for the post of HSSPF Russland-Mitte und Weissruthenien on 21 June 1944, having been deputy to Erich von dem Bach from 5 July 1943. This post was abolished in August 1944. Von Gottberg fled from Minsk to Bielitz during the night of 2–3 July 1944.

He was promoted to SS-Obergruppenführer and General of Waffen-SS and Police on 21 July 1944, with seniority from 30 June 1944, and he was given command of XII SS Armee Korps on 7 August. Realising that he did not possess the necessary military skills for such a command, von Gottberg protested—without success. From 1 September until 18 October 1944, he held the title of Chef der Bandenkampfung (*chief of anti-partisan operations*) in France, but he never actually took command. On 18 October 1944, he reported sick with thrombosis and was hospitalised until December of that year.

In December 1944 he was assigned as Deputy Commander of the Replacement Army under Himmler. Von Gottberg was given responsibility for identifying and rounding up those soldiers in Berlin who had lost their units, in order to return them to the front. On 29 April 1945, he was posted to Army Group Nordwest, where he commanded Special Staff 'von Gottberg', a unit commissioned with rounding up straggling soldiers to strengthen that Army Group.

Curt von Gottberg was arrested by the Allies in May 1945, and was held in captivity until his suicide on 31 May 1945, at Lutzhöft in Schleswig-Holstein (*some sources give his date of death as 9 May 1945*).

Von Gottberg has been described as crude and greedy. However, even after alienating himself from many SS leaders, he retained a great amount of respect.

Gottlob Berger discussed Heydrich's views on von Gottberg in a letter to Himmler, written just after the death of the RSHA chief in Prague. Heydrich had mentioned to Berger that although von Gottberg had to be replaced, his many talents would be missed. He was also a more-than-competent military leader, winning the Knights Cross of the Iron Cross in 1944.

Top: Curt von Gottberg's portrait from his SS file.

Above: von Gottberg in civilian clothes.

Right: Curt von Gottberg wears the rare Württemberg cuff title.

Heydrich, Prützmann, Himmler and von Gottberg.

Gauleiter Murr in discussion with Prützmann. At the right rear is von Malsen-Ponickau and at the far right is von Gottberg.

von Gottberg is saluted by a member of Polizei. A contemporary magazine photograph.

Above: The photograph from von Gottberg's SS Soldbuch.

Right: Curt von Gottberg entertains.

von Gottberg addresses members of the Russian Church in Minsk.

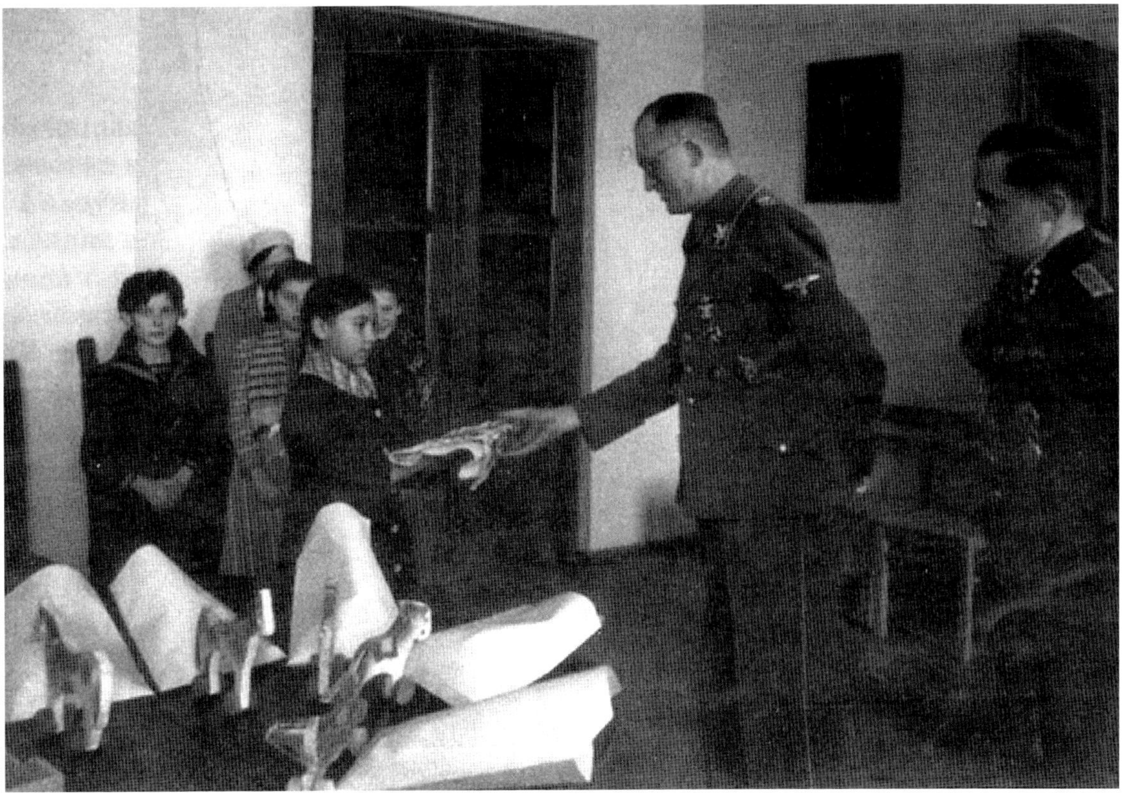

von Gottberg accepts a gift from local Minsk children.

von Gottberg speaking during a break in the music.

During an event in Minsk attended by Erich von dem Bach.

SS-Obergruppenführer Curt von Gottberg.

ERNST-ROBERT GRAWITZ

Ernst-Robert Grawitz was born on 8 June 1899 in Berlin-Charlottenburg, the son of Professor Dr Ernst Grawitz (born on 18 March 1860, died on 11 July 1911 in Berlin) and his wife, Helene (born Liebau in Magdeburg on 14 October 1869). His father was a Protestant and a leading physician at the City Hospital in Berlin-Charlottenburg. From the age of six to nine years old, Ernst-Robert attended a private school in Charlottenburg, and from June 1908 until 1917 he attended the Mommsen und Fichte High School in Berlin.

On 4 June 1917, he enlisted in the 10th Jäger Replacement Battalion in Goslar as an officer candidate. From 13 August 1917 until 20 October 1917, he trained with the X Army Corps. He then joined the 10th Jäger Battalion on the Italian Front on 8 November 1917. From 4 April until 4 July 1918, he attended the military school at Döberitz on a cadet course, and on 29 July 1918 he rejoined his unit on the Western Front. He was captured by the British at Epehy on 18 September and was posted as missing. He was released from captivity in Holzminden on 5 November 1919 and was discharged from the Army. Grawitz appeared in Verordnungsblatt Nr. 58, dated 4 May 1920, as being promoted to Leutnant.

From 1919 to 1920, he was a member of the civil militia in Berlin-Charlottenburg, during which period he began his medical studies at the Friedrich-Wilhelm University in Berlin. In March 1920 he participated in the Kapp Putsch and from 1920 until 1924, he commanded a machine-gun company in Freikorps Olympia. On 24 May 1924, he was successful in his state medical examinations. He qualified as a medical practioner on 1 July 1925, when he took up an appointment as an assistant doctor to Professor Umber at the Berlin-Westend Hospital. He received his medical doctorate on 13 July 1925, and remained on the staff of the same hospital until 30 September 1933, specialising in internal medicine. He became the director of internal medicine at the Berlin-Charlottenburg Hospital from 1933 until 1936.

On 14 October 1926, Grawitz married the daughter of later SS-Obergruppenführer Siegfried Taubert, Ilse Taubert (born on 8 February 1905 in Wesel am Rhein, died

in Potsdam April 1945; NSDAP number 1 102 843). The Grawitz couple had five children—three boys and two girls—between 1927 and 1943.

Grawitz joined the NSDAP on 1 November 1931 and was allocated membership number 1 102 844. He joined the SS on 29 March 1932 with SS number 27 483. He was immediately given the rank of SS-Truppführer with SS-Abschnitt III and appointed as SS-Sturmbannarzt. He was promoted to SS-Sturmbannführer on 1 July 1933 and was a member of the medical team for SS-Gruppe Ost. On 16 August 1933, Grawitz was promoted to SS-Obersturmbannführer.

He was appointed as the chief physician for SS-Oberabschnitt Ost on 10 May 1934, and was promoted to SS-Standartenführer on 13 June 1934—with seniority from 10 May 1934. On 20 April 1935, he was promoted to SS-Oberführer and transferred to the leadership of the Medical Office (Amt V) at the SS-Hauptamt eleven days later. On 1 June 1935, Grawitz transferred to the staff of the Reichsführer-SS; he was assigned as Chief Medical Officer for the entire SS.

Grawitz was appointed as Deputy President of the German Red Cross in December 1936 (with effect from 1 January 1937), and simultaneously became the First Deputy to the Commissioners for Auxiliary Nurses.

He was promoted to SS-Brigadeführer on 20 April 1937. On 15 December 1937, he was appointed as President of the German Red Cross. From 14 December 1938 until 11 January 1940, Grawitz was the Health Inspector and Group Doctor for all SS and Police Hospitals, simultaneously holding the post of Medical Inspector for Concentration Camps.

From 13 November 1939 until 10 May 1940, Grawitz was the Health Inspector to the SS-VT Divisions and the SS-Leibstandarte 'Adolf Hitler'. From 28 December 1939 until 24 April 1940, he was Medical Supervisor to the Lebensborn Society. On 1 April 1940, he was appointed as SS Reich Physician and Health Inspector for the Waffen-SS.

Grawitz served three periods of duty as a reserve medical officer with the Waffen-SS. From 10 May until 19 June 1940, he served on the staff of SS-Totenkopf Division in France. On 30 March 1941, he was appointed Generalmajor der Waffen-SS, and was further promoted on 1 October 1941 to SS-Gruppenführer und Generalleutnant der Waffen-SS. In July and August 1941 he saw active service with SS-Division 'Wiking'.

Grawitz was presented with an Honorary Professorship in the Medical Faculty of the University of Berlin on 22 December 1941.

He was promoted to SS-Obergruppenführer und General der Waffen-SS on 20 April 1944.

The role played by Grawitz in war crimes cannot be denied. As chief doctor of the SS, he was consulted on many questions regarding the use of experiments on prisoners in concentration camps. There is also some conjecture that Himmler approached Grawitz with the problem of how to quickly liquidate large numbers

of Polish Jews. Grawitz is said to have referred Himmler to Christian Wirth, who had supervised the gassing procedures in the euthanasia programme.

In August 1942, Grawitz insisted on the testing of real bullet wounds on inmates at Ravensbrück during experimental research into wound infection. The following month, Grawitz visited Auschwitz and discussed research into the treatment of typhus. This resulted in the deliberate infection of prisoners and their subsequent deaths.

The authorization of Grawitz to carry out medical experiments on concentration camp inmates would therefore have been sufficient for him to have been a prime candidate for a death sentence at the Doctors' Tribunal held by the Americans in Nuremberg. Grawitz, however, had other ideas.

Surviving records of the German Red Cross show that Grawitz ate lunch at his office at noon on 22 April 1945. The Soviet Army occupied Babelsberg on 24 April and requisitioned the Grawitz villa, which was searched and ransacked. Inside, they discovered the remains of several bodies. On 30 April, two female Red Cross workers were ordered to remove the bodies from the house and identify them. The notes of Lina Hauchecorne, who witnessed the final days of the German Red Cross in Babelsberg, states that they only took a quick look at the bodies in the cellar, as it was too harrowing for them. The following day, the bodies were buried without any formalities. It is probable that the family was buried in the Babelsberger Goethe cemetery under the name of 'Lambrecht', as shown in the German Red Cross file on the Grawitz villa. The grave no longer exists.

There are two versions of the method used by the Grawitz family to commit suicide. The first and most probable is that Grawitz detonated two grenades in a room where his family had gathered, killing them all. It is likely that this occurred in the basement, where the bodies were discovered by the Russians and left for subsequent removal. Grawitz would also have been aware that the effects of the explosion would have been more catastrophic in the confined area of the cellar, rather than in one of the upper rooms. The second is that Grawitz administered potassium cyanide to his family by the cherry tree in the garden, and then used a Panzerfaust to blow up their corpses and kill himself.

On 26 May 1945 a Dr Röggla appeared at the offices of the German Red Cross and demanded the return of his house (the Grawitz villa). He stated that the extensive damage to the house—caused by the explosions and subsequent fires initiated by Grawitz—was the responsibility of the Red Cross, and that they should provide the costs of the necessary repairs. His request was rejected and he left, bemoaning the failure of the German Red Cross. This incident is significant, however, as it indicates that the house damage was caused by an explosion inside the premises and not in the garden.

The date of the Grawitz family suicide is also open to conjecture. Three dates have been suggested: 20 April, 22 April and 24 April 1945. Clearly, the first is not

possible, as Grawitz took lunch at his office on 22 April. The Russians occupied Babelsberg on 24 April and immediately searched the Grawitz villa, discovering the corpses. The records of the German Red Cross indicate that Grawitz was dead by the morning of 23 April, and that he probably killed himself and his family during the evening of 22 April 1945.

Ernst Robert Grawitz in his army uniform.

The young SS applicant.

Left and right: SS-Oberführer Grawitz.

Grawitz with the President of the German Red Cross, SA-Obergruppenführer Charles Edward, Duke of Saxe-Coburg and Gotha.

SS-Brigadeführer Grawitz greets the head of the Red Cross in Berlin-Steglitz. To the far left is Julius Lippert.

Grawitz outside the Reich Chancellery in Wilhelmstrasse.

Grawitz in his German Red Cross uniform.

SS-Brigadeführer Ernst Robert Grawitz.

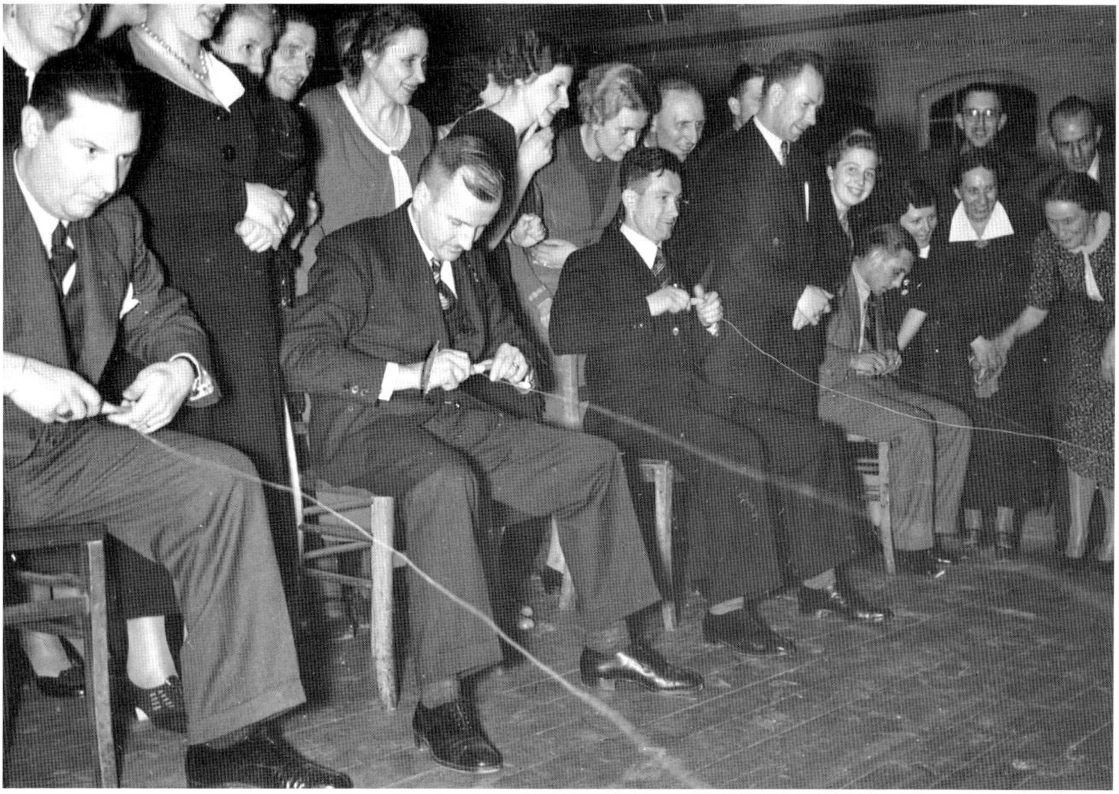

Grawitz (centre) playing a game at a Red Cross function in Steglitz.

Grawitz in Berlin. Lippert is second from the left.

Grawitz laying a foundation stone.

Grawitz at the front, on active service with Theodor Eicke.

Grawitz practising rifle accuracy at a function.

SS-Gruppenführer Grawitz, the head SS physician.

Grawitz at Wewelsburg with the castle housekeeper.

Above: SS-Obergruppenführer Ernst Robert Grawitz.

Right: The Grawitz villa in Berlin, scene of the family suicide.

ULRICH HEINRICH EMIL GREIFELT

ULRICH GREIFELT was born on 8 December 1896 in Berlin. His parents were Richard Greifelt, a pharmacist (who died aged thirty-nine of heart defects), and his wife Elisabeth (born Krach), who died of an embolism brought on by Basedow disease (otherwise known as Graves' disease). A sister of Greifelt also suffered from the same condition. He was an excellent student, first attending the local elementary primary school and then graduating from his high school in Berlin-Lichterfelde with top honours in 1914.

He enlisted in the 48th Infantry Regiment in August 1914 and saw active service with his unit at the front. In August 1916, he was assigned to the flying corps. He attended the observers' flying school at Gotha from August to September of that year. He next went to the advanced observers' school at Königsberg, until joining the new 249th Flying Detachment of Captain Sperrle on the Western Front. In November 1916, this unit was posted to the area near Verdun, between Maas and Argonne. The following year he attended two training courses before being appointed in December as deputy adjutant of the VII Army Corps Flying Group, under Captain Seraphim. From April to September 1918, he was posted to the Ukraine as adjutant to the Jekaterinoslav Region Flight Group, under Captain Spehr. His final wartime posting was in October 1918, as adjutant to the Flight Group Posen. He finished the war as an Oberleutnant and was finally discharged from military service on 31 March 1920. This was after having served in the Baltic area and in Magdeburg with the 4th (later the 25th) Reichswehr Infantry Brigade, and then the German Protection Division, formerly the 31st Infantry Division. This was a Freikorps unit and he stayed with it until his discharge.

He was married on 4 May 1921 to Anne-Marie Kühn (born on 22 September 1899 in Berlin), the daughter of a pharmacist acquaintance of Greifelt's father. They had no children.

Greifelt was a member of the Johannis Lodge of the Prussian Grand Lodge of Freemasons from 1921 until 1927. In 1922 he began employment with the manufacturing firm of Israel Brothers AG. He steadily worked his way up to become

a factory manager, and was the company secretary by the time the firm went into liquidation in 1932. Greifelt was unemployed from June 1932.

He joined the NSDAP on 1 April 1933 as NSDAP member number 1 667 407. He then enrolled in the SS on 18 June 1933 and was issued with SS number 72 909. This was at the suggestion of one of his former commanders, SS-Gruppenführer Siegfried Seidel-Dittmarsch. He was promoted to SS-Sturmführer, on the staff of the Reichsführer-SS, on 6 July 1933. Greifelt was further promoted to SS-Obersturmführer on 31 July 1933. He was assigned as consultant advisor on the staff of the Reichsführer-SS on 10 August 1933. He was then selected as adjutant to the Chief of Staff of the SS (*Seidel-Dittmarsch*) on 15 September. Greifelt remained in this post until 30 January 1934. Further promotion—to SS-Sturmhauptführer—occurred on 9 November 1933.

On 30 January 1934, Greifelt was promoted again, to SS-Sturmbannführer on the staff of the Reichsführer-SS. He transferred to SS-Oberabschnitt Elbe on 1 March 1934, with the post of Oberabschnitt Staff Officer. Another move took place on 15 June 1934, when he transferred to be the new Staff Officer of SS-Oberabschnitt Rhein. He remained there until he transferred to the staff of the SS-Hauptamt on 25 May 1935. In the meantime, he had attempted to resign from the SS as a result of the anti-clerical attitude in the SS, coupled with a desire to return to Berlin. Himmler refused the resignation, but compromised by transferring Greifelt to Berlin. He was appointed as chief of the Central Chancellery of the SS-Hauptamt on 12 June 1935 and was simultaneously promoted to SS-Obersturmbannführer, with seniority from 1 June 1935.

More rapid promotion to SS-Standartenführer occurred on 30 January 1936. Greifelt moved again, this time on 24 February 1937, back to the staff of the Reichsführer-SS. Yet another transfer took place on 20 April 1937, this time to the Reichsführer-SS Personal Staff. This accompanied promotion to SS-Oberführer. In this post, he was a special advisor on economic affairs and Himmler's representative for the Four Year Plan.

On 30 March 1938, Greifelt was once again appointed as chief of the Central Chancellery of the SS-Hauptamt. He held this appointment until 1 June 1940, when the post was dissolved. In June 1938, Greifelt was assigned to the head office for immigration on the Reichsführer-SS staff, and one year later he was appointed chief of the office dealing with immigration and emigration matters. He was selected as an associate judge in the Reich Court of Honour on 22 February 1939.

On 7 October 1939, he became Chief of Staff to the Reich Commissioner for the Strengthening of German Nationhood (RKFDV). He was promoted to SS-Brigadeführer on 9 November 1939, and was appointed as Chief of the SS Main Office for the Strengthening of German Nationhood on 11 June 1941. This position afforded him the rank of SS-Gruppenführer and he was duly promoted on 1 August 1941. He also attained police rank on 15 August 1942, when he was granted the rank of Generalleutnant der Polizei.

On 30 December 1942, Greifelt suffered a heart attack and a nervous breakdown following a severe disagreement with Himmler. He was admitted to a sanatorium in Weisser-Hirsch, near Dresden, where he remained until May the following year. His health never fully recovered.

Greifelt was promoted to SS-Obergruppenführer and General of Police on 30 January 1944.

Ulrich Greifelt stood trial at Nuremberg in Case 8, the Race and Resettlement Case, from 20 October 1947 until 10 March 1948. He maintained that his department had no dealings with organising the SS rule of occupied territories. Nevertheless, he was found guilty and sentenced to life imprisonment. He died of another heart attack on 6 February 1949, whilst serving that sentence in Landsberg am Lech prison.

SS-Sturmbannführer Ulrich Greifelt on the staff of SS-Oberabschnitt Rhein.

Greifelt behind SS-Standartenführer Freiherr von Schade.

The Greifelt couple.

SS-Brigadeführer Greifelt addresses a group of BDM girls.

With Gauleiter Hofer.

France, 1940, during an inspection tour of the Reichsführer-SS. Greifelt is far right and Berger is on the left.

France, 1940. Greifelt is second right, between Himmler and Wolff, studying a route map.

France, 1940. Who knows the way?

France, 1940, on the French Maginot Line.

France, 1940. Descending from a French defensive embankment on the Maginot Line.

Greifelt behind Himmler at a resettlement exhibition. Also present are Meyer, Bouhler, Hess and Daluege.

Gleiwitz, 1 March 1941, with Gauleiter Bracht and Himmler.

SS-Gruppenführer Greifelt and Berger.

SS-Gruppenführer Greifelt and SS-Oberführer Meyer.

Greifelt pleads not guilty at Nuremberg.

Prisoner of war.

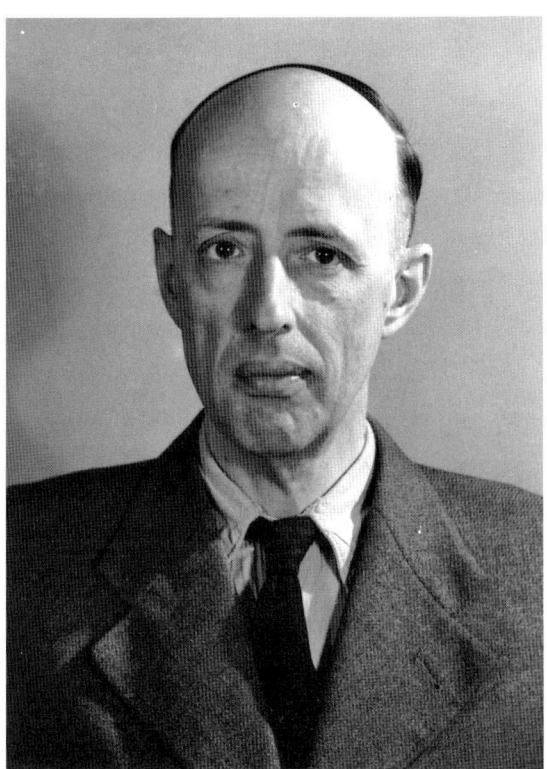

The change in Greifelt's appearance after his weight loss as a prisoner is remarkable.

Greifelt died of natural causes in Landsberg Prison in 1949. The authorities misspelled his name on the grave marker.

ARTHUR KARL GREISER

Arthur Greiser was the son of Protestant court bailiff August Gustav Friedrich Greiser (born in Gdingen in 1861, died on 29 March 1935 in Berlin) and his wife Ida (born Siegmund in Kempen in 1870, died in 1951). His parents were married in 1888 and Arthur was born on 22 January 1897 at house number 1 of the Market Square in Schroda-Posen—the youngest of a total of four children, consisting of three boys and one girl. His father was a glazier by trade, but a hand injury forced him to seek another career. Arthur's brother Otto was killed in January 1945, his oldest brother Willy died in 1951, and his sister Käthe died in 1966 in the USA.

The young Arthur attended elementary school and the classical Royal Humanistic High School in Hohensalza, where his father had been transferred in 1900. In 1941 the school was renamed the Arthur-Greiser-School, but the young man left in 1914 without taking his school examination in order to volunteer for the armed forces.

He reported for naval service on 4 August 1914 and was posted to the naval artillery training unit at Friedrichsort, near Kiel, before transferring to the battery unit at Laboe as an artillery observer. He left for Flanders and the front on 25 September 1915 with the Marine Corps Flanders. He was soon actively involved as a wire layer on the front line, and was stationed near Ostend, assigned to the 2nd Sailor Artillery Regiment. He was recommended for the Reserve Officers' course in February 1916. He was promoted to Vizefeuenwerker der Reserve (*Reserve Petty Officer*) on 24 November 1916, and to Leutnant der Reserve on 20 August 1917.

In April 1917 he volunteered as a marine flight observer at Zeebrugge, seeing active service over the front, the Channel and the North Sea with Friedrich Christiansen's squadron. In January 1918 he began training as a pilot; however, when the training took him away from the front, he became depressed. For a while he was diagnosed with clinical depression and he was unable to fly until the end of the summer of 1918. On 3 September 1918, he was shot down and seriously injured, ending his war. He was still in hospital when the armistice was signed. He was granted a 50 per cent disability war pension after he was discharged from naval service on 30 September 1919.

Arthur Greiser was married on 25 June 1919 to Ruth Tripler (born in Zopport, died in Hamburg in 1984). They were divorced on 15 October 1934, having produced two girls—Ingrid (born 1920, died in Munich in February 1946) and Rotraut (born in 1930)—and one son—Erhardt (born in 1925, died in a car accident outside Posen on 20 December 1939). Ruth never remarried. Greiser was then married on 9 April 1935 to Maria Theodora Koerfer (born on 30 March 1908 in Cologne). Koerfer was an accomplished concert pianist. They had no children. Following her husband's death, she lived with the support of her family and never remarried.

From 1919 until 1921, he was a member of Freikorps 'Grenzschutz Ost'. The loss of the war and the consequent loss of the Prussian provinces to Poland had a major effect on the young Greiser. He joined the German Socialist Party in Danzig in 1922, and two years later he helped found the Danzig branch of Stahlhelm.

During this period he was also a member of the Johannis Freemasons Lodge in Danzig. His membership was the subject of an investigation by the Reichssicherheitshauptamt in 1942, on the orders of Heydrich. The results, after the death of the instigator, found that Greiser had been a member from 1921 until 1929, and that he had failed to declare his membership on SS questionnaires.

Greiser found various employment during the twenties—first as an export clerk, then as an agent for the Stettin Oil Company in Danzig. From 1928 until 1930, he worked as a pleasure boat captain in Danzig harbour.

Greiser joined the NSDAP on 1 November 1929 and was given membership number 166 635. He joined the SA at the same time and remained until subsequently transferring to the SS. From 1 September 1930 until 19 June 1933, Greiser was the business manager in the NSDAP Danzig Gauleitung. On 3 October 1930, Hermann Göring appointed Greiser as temporary Gauleiter of Danzig, only to be supplanted on 15 October 1930 by his permanent replacement, Albert Forster. He was appointed the NSDAP leader for the Danzig Free State Senate on 15 October 1930. He retained this post until 20 June 1933.

Greiser joined the SS on 30 June 1931, with SS membership number 10 795. He was promoted to SS-Sturmführer on 29 September 1931 with SS-Abschnitt VII. He was next promoted to SS-Sturmhauptführer on 4 September 1932, and then to SS-Standartenführer on 20 June 1933—bypassing the rank of SS-Sturmbannführer.

Greiser was sentenced to one week in prison and fined 200 RM on 5 October 1932 for anti-government activities, but this was quashed by a government amnesty.

On 20 June 1933 he was elected as vice-President of the Danzig Senate. He was appointed Deputy Gauleiter of Danzig on 18 October 1933, holding this appointment until 7 October 1939. Greiser was finally elected as Danzig Senate President on 28 November 1934.

On promotion to SS-Oberführer on 12 March 1934, he was posted to SS-Oberabschnitt Nordost, assigned to special duties. Another promotion (on 1 January 1935, to SS-Brigadeführer) saw him transfer to the staff of the

Reichsführer-SS, designated special duties. He became an official member of the Reichsführer-SS staff on 1 April 1936.

In the summer of 1939, Greiser played an important role in the formation of the SS-Heimwehr Danzig, a unit which eventually numbered some 4,000 men and was subsequently incorporated into the SS-Totenkopf Division.

Following the invasion of Poland, on 8th September 1939 Greiser was assigned chief of the civil administration in Posen, under the direction of the local military commander. On 21 October 1939, he was appointed Gauleiter and Reich Governor of the Warthegau, and from 2 November 1939 he was Reichsstatthalter. In this capacity, Greiser appointed SS-Gruppenführer Wilhelm Koppe as responsible for all resettlement measures on 4 December 1939.

From 8 April 1940, Greiser was the Representative for the Reich Commission for Strengthening of the German People in the Warthegau. From 7 July 1940, he was elected as the Reichstag deputy for Wahlkreis Warthegau. He was appointed Reich Defence Commissioner for the Warthegau on 16 November 1942.

From 6 April 1940, Greiser also held the senior rank of Gruppenführer in the NSFK. He was promoted to SS-Gruppenführer on 24 October 1939, and then to SS-Obergruppenführer on 30 January 1942.

On 24 November 1943, Greiser was involved in a freak hunting accident. A shot fired by his brother-in-law, Hubert Koerfer, ricocheted off the ground and splinters hit Greiser's left eye, blinding him. Subsequent operations to save the eye were unsuccessful and he received a false eye in spring 1944.

Arthur Greiser experienced a long fued with Danzig Gauleiter Albert Forster. Greiser was not such an avid supporter of SS policy as Forster, and this eventually resulted in the formation of the Warthegau. Nevertheless, he gained the reputation of a severe ruler. He was highly thought of by Hitler, who even considered him as a replacement for Dr Hans Frank as Governor General in occupied Poland.

At the end of hostilities in 1945, Greiser fled to the Bavarian Alps, where he was captured by American troops on 25 May 1945 in civilian attire with SS-Gruppenführer Heinz Reinefarth. He was promptly handed over the Poles, who tried him for crimes committed during his tenure in the Warthegau. He was found guilty and publicly hanged in front of his former office in Posen (*today Poznan*) on 14 July 1946.

The building in which Greiser was born, adorned with decorations and flags.

Greiser (right) with his father and brothers.

Greiser's mother.

Greiser and his first wife and children.

SS-Sturmführer Greiser on the staff of
SS-Abschnitt VII.

SS-Standartenführer Greiser.

Left and right: SS-Standartenführer Forster.

SS-Brigadeführer Forster.

SS-Gruppenführer Forster.

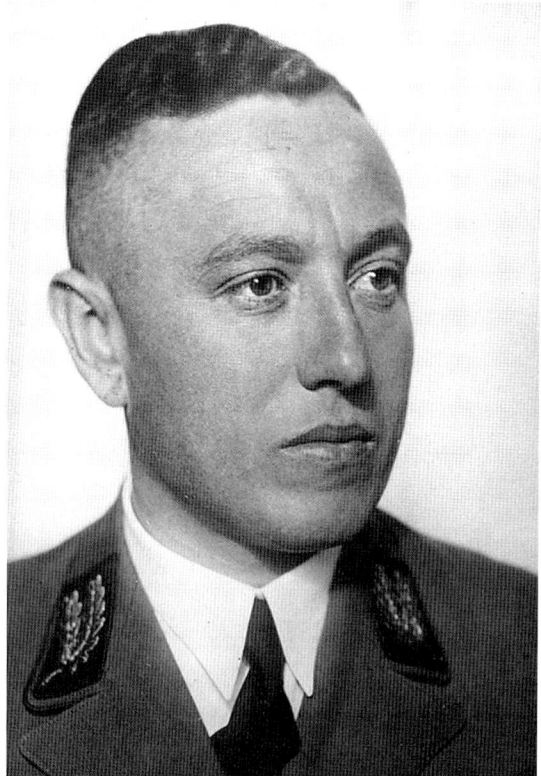

Left and right: Gauleiter Forster—a favourite of Hitler.

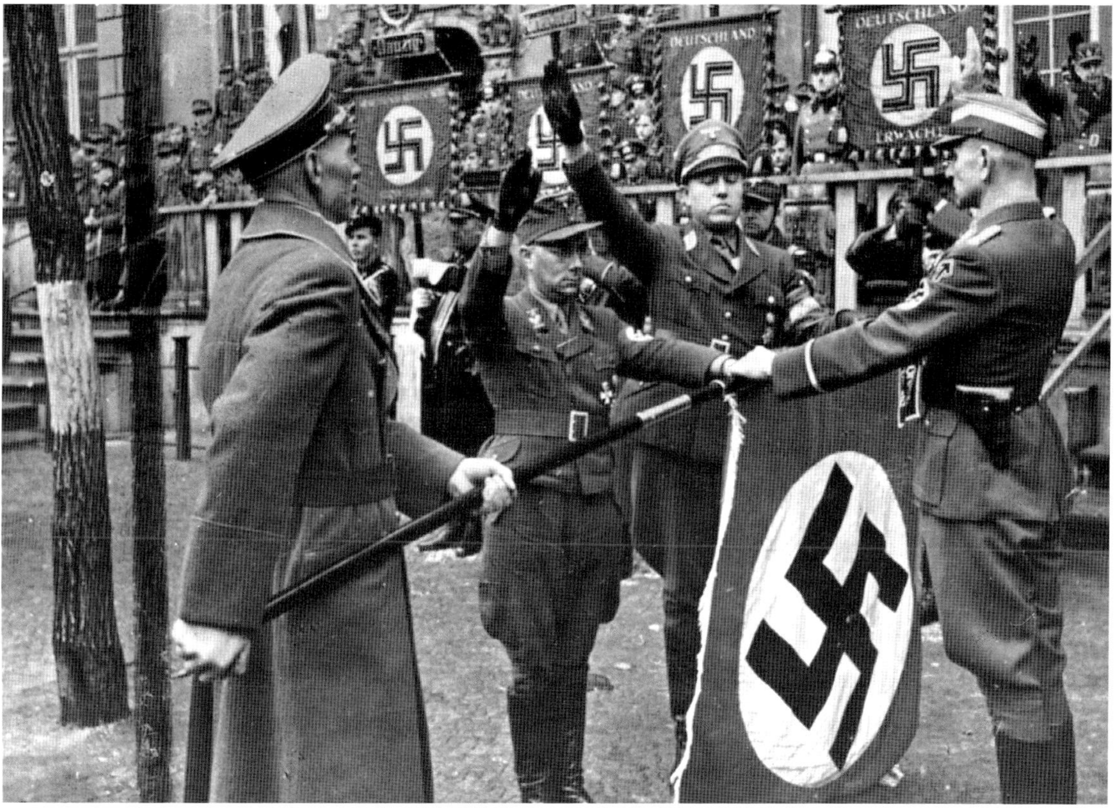

Forster dedicates a NSDAP flag.

Left and right: The young NSDAP leader.

Forster with Hitler at Haus Wachenfeld, on the Obersalzberg.

The new Gauleiter of Danzig.

Albert Forster und seine Fürther SS.

An early image from a contemporary book on Albert Forster, showing him with his first SS men from Nuremberg-Fürth.

Forster, in a light windsheeter, marches beside Julius Streicher.

was admired by Dr Goebbels, who wrote positively of him in his diaries. Some who had day-to-day dealings with him, however, looked upon him as unreliable. He was described as such by the local Higher SS and Police Leader, Richard Hildebrandt. Himmler viewed him as somebody who was prone to exaggeration. In return, although a confirmed anti-Semite, Forster opposed many of Himmler's racial policies, some of which he saw as extreme. He is quoted as saying of the Reichsführer-SS: '*If I looked like him, I would not speak of race at all.*' He was also a strong opponent of the resettlement of ethnic Germans in his Gau. A frequent visitor to the Berghof as Hitler's personal guest, Forster remained a loyal Party man to the end. Born within prison walls, his life was also destined to end within them.

Clockwise from right:

A signed and dedicated portrait of the Gauleiter, 1942.

Greiser lived like a feudal lord in his kingdom.

Here, Greiser plays host to a visit by Dr Goebbels, who is seen signing the guest book in the Posen City Hall.

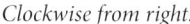

Clockwise from left:

Greiser at his desk. On the left is Gauleiter Bracht.

Two SS-Gruppenführer, Koppe and Greiser.

A visit by State Secretary Wilhelm Stuckart.

SS-Obergruppenführer Arthur Greiser.

A fine study of the Gauleiter and Reichsstatthalter.

Greiser congratulates the one millionth ethnic German settler in his Gau. Heinz Reinefarth is centre.

Greiser was publicly hanged before a large crowd in Posen.

KARL MICHAEL GUTENBERGER

K̲ARL G̲UTENBERGER was born in Essen on 18 April 1905. His father, Michael
Gutenberger (born in Rheinböllen on 12 September 1865), worked as
a stores administrator for the Krupp steel firm. From 1911 the young
Karl attended elementary primary school in Essen, before moving to the Krupp-
Oberrealschule (Krupp High School). He finally transferred to the Realgymnasium
(*high school*) in Altenessen. After leaving school in 1921, Gutenberger trained in
banking and found employment as a bank clerk until 1923, when he started work
as a clerk in a business firm.

Gutenberger joined the NSDAP and the SA in 1923, but left after the failed Beer
Hall Putsch in November of the same year. His NSDAP membership dates from 15
December 1925, when he rejoined the Party and immediately became the leader
of Essen-Siegeroth Ortsgruppe and also the speaker for Gau Essen. His NSDAP
membership number was 25 249.

After working for several firms, Gutenberger became a finance clerk for the
Essen and Rhein Steelworks in 1928 and 1929.

In December 1929 he was appointed as commander of SA-Standarte 159 in
Essen-Mülheim. On 1 January 1932, he transferred to the command of the 60th
SA-Standarte in Essen. In April 1932 Gutenberger stood unsuccessfully as a NSDAP
candidate for Düsseldorf-West in the elections for the Preussischen Landtag
(*Prussian parliament*), but on 24 November of the same year he was successful. He
was also elected to the Reichstag on 31 July 1932 for Wahlkreis 23 (Düsseldorf-West).

As a newly promoted SA-Standartenführer, Gutenberger transferred to the
leadership of SA-Standarte 138 in Wesel on 1 July 1933. From 15 August 1933 to
1 May 1934, he was commander of SA-Brigade 74 in Duisburg, realising a further
promotion, to SA-Oberführer, on 9 November 1933. Another move occurred on 1
May 1934, when he gained command of the new SA-Brigade 173. This lasted until
1 March 1935, when Gutenberger took control of SA-Brigade 73 in Essen. He was
promoted to SA-Brigadeführer on 20 April 1936, and returned to the command
of SA-Brigade 74 in Wesel on 1 January 1937.

Gutenberger was married on 27 December 1934 to Herta Martha Schulz (born in Dessau on 31 December 1900, died on 24 November 1983 in Essen). They had no children.

On 1 May 1937, Gutenberger was appointed Police Commissioner of Duisburg. One year later, on 7 May 1938, he became Police President of Duisburg. From 14 November 1939, he was Police President of Essen, remaining in post until 1 May 1941.

At the request of SS-Obergruppenführer Fritz Weitzel, Gutenberger applied to leave the SA and transfer to the SS. Without permission from SA-Stabschef Viktor Lutze, Gutenberger left the SA on 9 April 1940 and joined the SS on 1 June. He held comparative SS rank (SS-Brigadeführer) and was attached to SS-Oberabschnitt West, with SS membership number 372 303.

On 1 May 1941, Gutenberger took charge of SS-Oberabschnitt West and on 29 June 1941 he was appointed as HSSPF. He was accorded the police rank of Generalmajor der Polizei on 1 March 1942, and was promoted to SS-Gruppenführer und Generalleutnant der Polizei on 9 November 1942. On 1 August 1944 he was promoted to SS-Obergruppenführer und General der Polizei und Waffen-SS.

Gutenberger was also the Reich Commissioner for Public Safety in North Limburg from August until November 1944, and was then appointed Inspector for Passive Resistance and Special Defence West. This post encompassed the formation and training of Werewolf units in the area and Gutenberger ruthlessly dealt with any sign of defeatism—sentencing the mayor of Aachen to death.

Gutenberger was captured on 10 May 1945 at Schloss Lopshorn, Lippe. He was tried as a war criminal by a British military court in Hamburg and on 22 October 1949, he was sentenced to twelve years' imprisonment. Four years of his sentence were for his part in the Werewolf execution of the US-appointed mayor of Aachen, Franz Oppenhoff. He received another term, of five years' imprisonment, on 16 March 1950, for his part in the murder of Allied airmen who had been shot down. Following his release on 11 December 1953, he set up a wholesale business in Essen. He died in Essen on 8 July 1961 and was buried four days later in the Ostfriedhof. His grave no longer exists.

SA-Oberführer Gutenberger; a newspaper photograph.

SA-Brigadeführer Gutenberger.

SS-Brigadeführer Gutenberger.

Gutenberger stands behind Himmler during the visit of the Reichsführer.

Gutenberger on Himmler's left, viewing unexploded ordnance.

SS-Brigadeführer Gutenberger (third from right) at Fritz Weitzel's grave in Düsseldorf, on the occasion of a visit by Himmler.

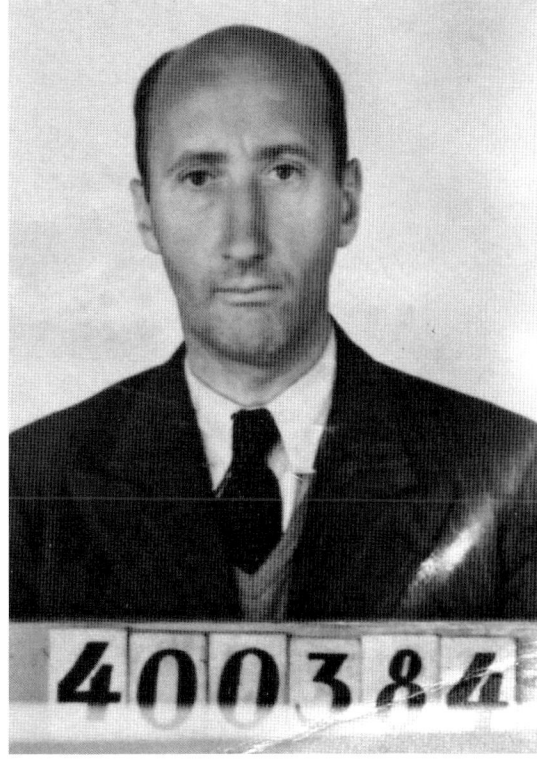

Gutenberger during the visit of the Reichsführer-SS.   Prisoner of the British.

KARL AUGUST HANKE

Karl Hanke was born on 24 August 1903 in Lauban, Silesia, one of two sons of train driver Robert Hanke. Karl's elder brother was killed in the First World War. He attended the local elementary primary school from 1910, and high school from 1914 until 1920. On 7 August 1920, he reported as a one-year volunteer for military service with Infantry Regiment 19 in Frankfurt-Oder.

After his discharge he trained as a miller, attending the German Miller School in Dippoldiswade and also worked in the textile trade. As a supplement to his income, he helped out in the railway workshop in Lauban. During the early 1920s, he took on practical experience of unpaid work in mills in Silesia, Bavaria and in Austria. This was before undergoing a course at a vocational training college in Berlin and qualifying as an instructor for the milling trade. From 1928 until April 1931, he was employed in Berlin-Steglitz as a master miller; he also taught the trade.

He joined the NSDAP on 1 November 1928 and held Party card number 102 606. He immediately began to promote NSDAP politics as a speaker and factory-floor organiser. From 1929 until 1931, he attended local SA meetings and demonstrations. In 1930 he became a street leader (*Blockleiter*) for the NSDAP. The following year he was appointed as 1st Section Leader for the NSDAP in Berlin and Kreisleiter West. As a result of his political activities, he was dismissed from his employment as an instructor in the milling business in April 1931.

By 1932 he had been appointed as personal adjutant to Dr Josef Goebbels, and was Gau Organisation Leader of Gau Gross-Berlin. He was elected to the Prussian parliament on 24 April 1932 and as a Reichstag deputy on 6 November 1932. He also became department head of the propaganda office of the NSDAP on the same day. From 13 March 1933 until August 1939, Hanke was personal advisor and head of the private secretariat of the Reich Minister for Propaganda. He held the rank of Ministerialrat from 27 June 1933.

He joined the SS on 15 February 1934, with membership number 202 013. He was posted to SS-Abschnitt XXIII as leader with special duties in the Reich Propaganda Ministry. He was promoted to SS-Sturmbannführer on 1 July 1934, and was transferred to the staff of the Reichsführer-SS on 23 January 1935. On 20 April 1935, he was promoted to SS-Obersturmbannführer, followed by another promotion, to SS-Standartenführer, on 15 September 1935. He was transferred to the SS-Hauptamt staff on 1 April 1936. He transferred again, to the staff of the Reichsführer-SS, on 20 April 1937, with promotion to SS-Oberführer.

From January 1937 until January 1941, Hanke was the second vice-President of the Reich Culture Chamber. He became State Secretary in the Reich Propaganda Ministry on 26 November 1937.

Hanke spent one month of reserve military training, attached to the Army, in November 1937. From 14 August 1939 until February 1940, he was attached to the Panzer Lehr Regiment and saw active service in the Polish campaign. In February 1940 he was posted as an ordnance officer to Erwin Rommel in the 7th Panzer Division. From May that year, he was a company commander in Panzer Regiment 25, taking part in the western offensive. He led an abortive attack at Saint Valéry on 11 June 1940 and had to be rescued by his regimental commander. He was a courageous officer and was recommended for the Knight's Cross of the Iron Cross by Rommel—who subsequently withdrew the recommendation after an unpleasant exchange of words. Hanke left military service on 24 January 1941, with the rank of Oberleutnant der Reserve.

On 28 January 1941, he was appointed as Gauleiter of Lower Silesia and President of the Provincial Council. From 16 November 1942 until 1943, he was Reich Defence Commissioner for Lower Silesia. In 1943 he became head of the Central Office for Armaments and War Production. He held this position until 21 June 1944. He was also responsible for labour allocation in his Gau.

Hanke was promoted to SS-Brigadeführer on 30 January 1941, to SS-Gruppenführer on 20 April 1941, and to SS-Obergruppenführer on 30 January 1944. He was present during the second speech by Himmler on 6 October 1943 in Posen, when the Reichsführer spoke openly about the solution of the Jewish problem. Hanke apparently visited Auschwitz at some point in 1944 and was allegedly horrified at what he found.

On 25 September 1944, he was appointed as commander of the Volkssturm units in his Gau. In January 1945 he issued a number of proclamations in the press and on the radio concerning the defence of 'Fortress Breslau'. He ordered that no man must leave his post and that the city must be defended 'until death'. On 22 January 1945, he ordered that all men aged 16–60 were to report to their local Volkssturm unit under military law. He continued to rant in the press about defence of the city to stop the Soviet Army, which encircled Breslau on 13 February 1945. Hanke's orders had little regard for the welfare of the populace or the city buildings, and his ruthless methods of executing anyone displaying a defeatist attitude greatly impressed Hitler. Breslau finally fell to the Soviet Army on 6 May 1945.

Hanke was married on 25 November 1944 to Freda Freiin von Fircks, the daughter of a wealthy landowner and Berlin university lecturer. She was a former employee of the Berlin NSDAP Gauleitung from November 1931. She bore Hanke one daughter, born 1943, and a son. She was at the Obersalzberg when it was bombed by the RAF on 25 April 1945, but escaped by bus to the Tyrol with Gerda Bormann and her children. After the war, the widowed Freiin von Fircks-Hanke remarried and took the name Rössler. Hanke was romantically involved with Magda Goebbels, the wife of the Reich Propaganda Minister. When the Goebbels' marriage appeared to be over, as a result of the Reich Minister's liaisons with other women, Hanke asked Magda to marry him. Having become aware of the marriage difficulties between Goebbels and his wife, Hitler stepped in to save the Goebbels' marriage and Hanke was abandoned.

At the end of April 1945, Hitler discovered that Himmler had been secretly making preparations to negotiate peace with the Americans. Enraged at Himmler's treachery, he dismissed Himmler from all his NSDAP and government posts. In his political testament dated 29 April 1945, Hitler appointed Karl Hanke as Reichsführer-SS and Chief of the German Police:

> Before my death I expel the former Reichsführer-SS and Minister of the Interior Heinrich Himmler from the Party and all offices of State. In his place I appoint Gauleiter Karl Hanke as Reichsführer-SS and Chief of the German Police and Gauleiter Paul Giesler as Reich Minister of the Interior…

During the night of 5–6 May 1945, Hanke fled from Breslau in the Fieseler Storch light aircraft of General Niehoff. He had learnt earlier that day that the General was about to surrender the city. He also learnt that he had been appointed as the new Reichsführer-SS and Chief of the German Police before Hitler's suicide. Niehoff discovered that his aircraft was missing the next morning, when attempts were made to locate the Gauleiter. Reichsführer-SS Hanke arrived in Hirschberg and had a short meeting with Generalfeldmarschall Schörner before leaving for Prague, where he arrived on 7 May. Realising the situation was hopeless, he decided to attempt to make his way up to Flensburg, where the new administration of Grossadmiral Karl Dönitz was based. Dressed in SS uniform with no rank insignia, he encountered Czech partisans at the airfield and joined some stragglers from the SS-Panzer-Grenadier-Division 18 making their way towards Chomutov. He was captured by Czech partisans at a farm near Chomutov and was held prisoner in a cellar with other Germans at Jirkov. The Czechs, still unaware of the identity of one of their captives, decided to move the prisoners by foot, and on 8 June 1945 Hanke and two other prisoners made a run for it to a passing train. They clung to the train, but the guards opened fire and all three were hit. The guards then finished them off by beating them with their rifle butts until there was no sign of life. They had no idea that they had just killed the Reichsführer-SS and returned to the rest of the prisoners laughing and joking.

Hanke, personal assistant to Dr Josef Goebbels.   NSDAP member Karl Hanke.

Karl Hanke (third from right) was a member of the German delegation at the disarmament conference in Geneva. Seated at the front (second and third from left) are Constantin von Neurath and Josef Goebbels. Behind Hanke is Josias Erbprinz zu Waldeck und Pyrmont.

SS-Oberführer Hanke.

Hanke served with an armoured unit during his military service.

Gauleiter Hanke with Gauleiter Bracht. Behind him are Greifelt and Gutterer.

SS-Gruppenführer and future Reichsführer-SS Karl Hanke.

Hanke as the guest of Heydrich in Prague. To the bottom right is Horst Böhme.

Above left: Hanke stands behind Streckenbach as part of the guard of honour beside Heydrich's grave, Berlin, 9 June 1942.

Above right: Invaliden cemetery, Berlin, 9 June 1942.

Opposite page:

Above: SS-Gruppenführer Hanke, a guest of von Neurath in Prague.

Below: SS-Gruppenführer Hanke enjoying after-dinner drinks and a smoke with Karl Hermann Frank, Rudolf Toussaint and August Eigruber.

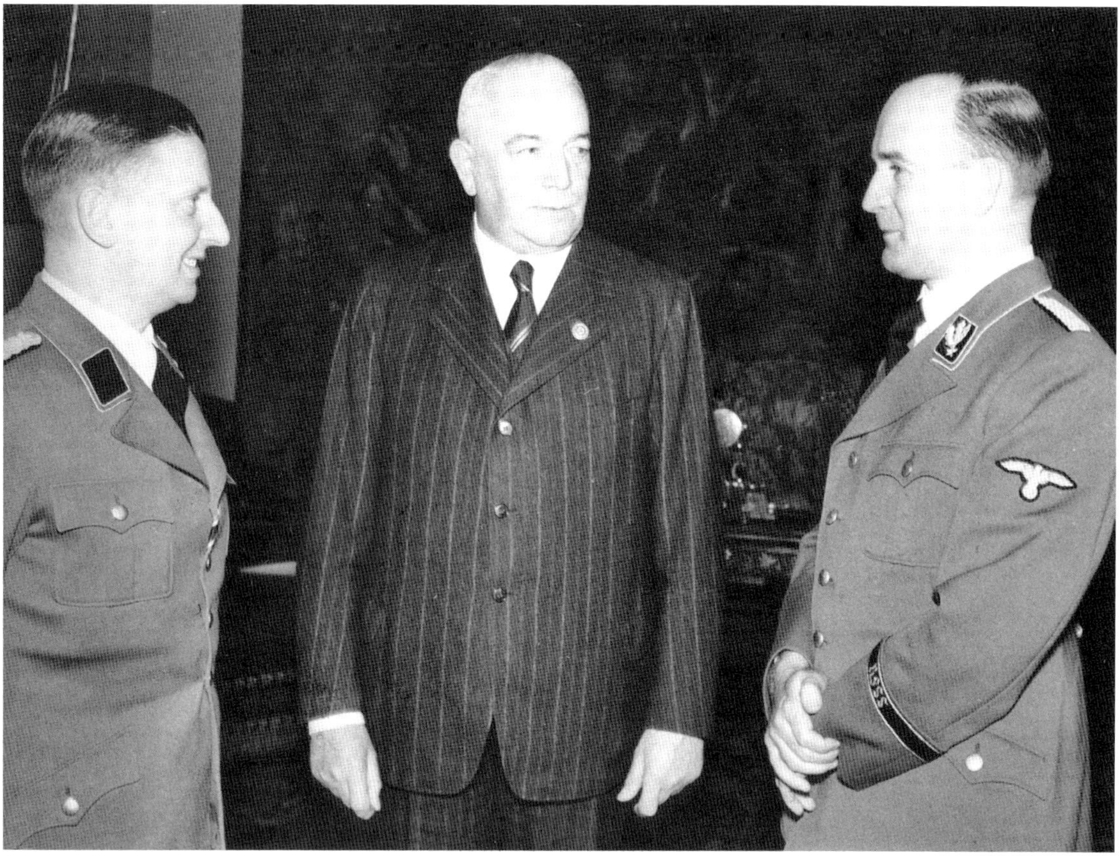

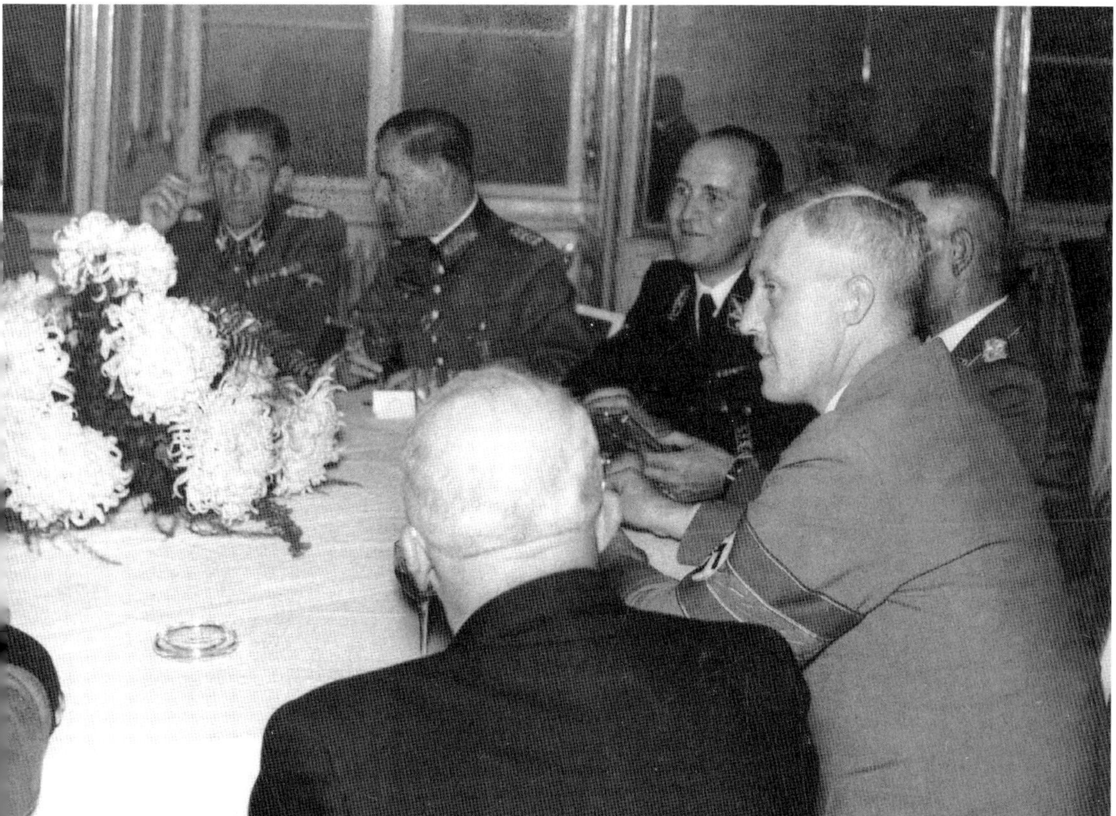

PAUL HAUSSER

Paul Hausser was was born on 7 October 1880 in Brandenburg an der Havel, the son of Kurt Hausser, a Leutnant and later Major in the Kaiser's Army, and his wife, Anna (born Otto). He attended primary school between 1887 and 1890 in Brandenburg, where his father was serving with Fusilier Regiment 35. Following his father's transfer to Stettin in 1890, the family moved there, and Paul attended a local high school.

Echoing his father's choice of career, the twelve-year-old Paul joined the Prussian cadet corps in 1892. He attended the cadet school in Köslin until 1896, and then the military academy at Berlin-Lichterfelde until March 1899. He graduated and was commissioned as a Leutnant with the 155th Infantry Regiment on 20 March 1899. On 1 October 1903 he was assigned as adjutant of the 2 Battalion. From 1906 he was the regimental adjutant in Ostrowo.

In early 1908, in Posen, he passed the entrance examination for the Berlin War Academy and he reported there on 1 October 1908 for training as a General Staff Officer. He remained there until 21 July 1911. He was promoted to Oberleutnant on 19 August 1909 and then had various attachments. First, to a field artillery unit in Stettin during autumn 1909; then to a hussar regiment in Ulm in autumn 1910; finally to the battleship Schlesien from 22 August until 15 September 1911. He returned to his parent unit in October 1911. He transferred to the Army General Staff topography section on 22 March 1912—this involved training as an aerial observer with a flying battalion at Döberitz in 1913.

Hausser was married on 9 November 1912 to Elizabeth Gerard (born on 18 July 1891 in Brandenburg, died on 16 October 1978 in Munich). They had one daughter (born on 28 December 1913).

He was promoted to Hauptmann on 1 October 1913. On 22 March 1914, he was posted to the photography section of the Greater General Staff mapping division. From 2 August 1914, he was assigned to the the General Staff of the 6th Army, under the command of Crown Prince Rupprecht of Bavaria. He saw active service as an aircraft observer on the Western Front. In 1915 he fought as a company commander with Infantry Regiment 28, and from October 1915 until the end of the war, he was a staff executive officer of the General Staff of the 109th Infantry Division on the Eastern Front. This involved various attachments: he was an executive officer with a marine unit in Libbau; then an executive officer of the General Staff of the 1st Reserve Corps; then with the General Staff of General Commando 59; and finally an executive officer of the General Staff of a Rumanian Corps. He gained promotion to Major on 22 March 1918, and returned to his family in Eisenach in November 1918.

January 1919 found Hausser attached to the General Staff of the 5th Army Corps. For the next three years he served with the Border Protection Unit East, the Reichswehr-Brigade 5, the military command in Stettin, and then on the staff of the 2nd Division in Stettin. From 1922 until March 1923, he was a company commander in Infantry Regiment 5 and was promoted to Oberleutnant on 1 April 1923 (with effective seniority from 15 November 1922). From 1 April 1923 until 1 March 1925, he was commander of the 3rd battalion of the 4th Infantry Regiment, leaving that unit to take up a post as Chief of Staff of the 2nd Division. Promoted to Oberst on 1 November 1927 (effective 1 July 1927), he transferred to the staff of the 10th Infantry Regiment in Dresden, taking over command of the regiment one year later. Hausser was promoted to Generalmajor on 1 February 1931 and retired from the Army on 31 January 1932, when he was promoted to the rank of Generalleutnant.

On 5 February 1933, he joined the Berlin-Brandenburg Stahlhelm in Teltow as the local commander. He remained with that organisation until 1 March 1934, when he was appointed to the command of SA-Reserve Brigade 25 as SA-Standartenführer. He retained that post until 29 October 1934. During this period he met an old regimental colleague, Paul Scharfe, who introduced him to Heinrich Himmler. Himmler immediately recognised the potential in Hausser and commissioned him to set up a SS officer cadet school in Braunschweig. Hausser resigned from the SA on 1 November 1934 and joined the SS on 15 November 1934. He was immediately promoted to SS-Standartenführer, with membership number 239 795. His seniority in the rank was backdated to 1 November 1934.

Hausser officially became the first commandant of the Braunschweig SS cadet school on 1 July 1935, with promotion to SS-Oberführer. He directed that instruction at the school would be conducted along the lines of the old Reichswehr. On 1 August 1935, he was appointed Inspector of the SS cadet schools at Braunschweig and Bad Tölz. He was promoted to SS-Brigadeführer on 22 May 1936 and was simultaneously assigned to the leadership office in the SS-Hauptamt.

For some time, Reichsführer-SS Himmler had envisaged an elite SS fighting force. He had encouraged the formation of SS units designed, not only as protection squads, but also as fully equipped fighting units. This was the nucleus of the future Waffen-SS. He recognised the value of Hausser's contribution to the SS officer cadet schools, and appointed him as Inspector of the SS-Verfügungstruppe on 1 October 1936. Hausser joined the NSDAP on 1 May 1937 as member number 4 158 779.

Hausser was promoted to SS-Gruppenführer on 1 June 1938. He saw active service in the Polish campaign with his SS-VT units, as part of Panzer Division 'Kempf'. On 19 October 1939, the three pre-war SS-Regiments—'Deutschland', 'Germania', and 'Der Führer'—were formed into the SS-Verfügungstruppen Division, with Hausser as the commander. His command became operational on 1 November 1939. He was promoted to Generalleutnant der Waffen-SS on 19 November 1939.

For approximately two months from June 1940, Hausser was chief of the command office of the Waffen-SS in the SS-Hauptamt. On 18 August 1940, this office was absorbed into the SS-Führungshauptamt (SS *Leadership Central Office*) under Hans Jüttner. Hausser subsequently transferred to the command of SS-Divisions 'Deutschland' in Holland and 'Reich' in the Balkans and later the Eastern Front. He was promoted to SS-Obergruppenführer and General der Waffen-SS on 1 October 1941.

He was seriously wounded, losing his right eye and part of his upper jaw, on 14 October 1941, and was hospitalised until the following May. On his recovery, he was posted to the staff of the SS General Command. On 14 September 1942, he was appointed as commanding General of the SS-Panzer Corps on the Eastern Front. His unit was transferred to the Italian theatre on 23 July 1943. Hausser was assigned to the temporary command of the 7th Army in France on 28 June 1944. He was promoted to SS-Oberst-Gruppenführer und Generaloberst der Waffen-SS on 1 August 1944, when his command of the 7th Army was confirmed. On 16 August, he was appointed acting commander of Army Group B, but he was wounded by shrapnel to the face on 20 August.

He returned to duty on 23 January 1945 as deputy commander of Army Group Upper Rhine, replacing Himmler as commander of Army Group G (Upper Rhine) on 28 January. Following a heated argument with Hitler, Hausser was dismissed from this post on 3 April 1945. For the remainder of the war, he was designated as General on the staff of commander-in-chief Süd.

Hausser was a more than capable military leader and he was highly decorated. His awards included the Knights Cross of the Iron Cross, Oakleaves to the Knights Cross of the Iron Cross (*as 261st recipient*), and Swords to the Knights Cross of the Iron Cross (*as 90th recipient*). He was captured on 9 May 1945 near Zell am See and was interned in approximately twenty detention centres—including Dachau. He gave evidence on the role of the Waffen-SS in August 1946 before the IMT in Nuremberg. He was sentenced to two years in a labour camp in 1948 by a de-Nazification court. Hausser continued to lead his men after the war, defending their wartime role and writing articles to correct the misunderstanding of the function of the Waffen-SS. He can certainly be described as the 'Father of the Waffen-SS', and gained the nickname 'Papa Hausser'. He was revered by the former members of the Waffen-SS and was the senior figure of HIAG, the organisation set up to assist such men and their families. He died on 21 December 1972 in Ludwigsburg. His funeral was attended by a large number of former Waffen-SS men.

A First World War photograph, with Hausser at the front right with a swagger stick.

Himmler inspecting the Braunschweig Junkerschule. Left to right: SS-Standartenführer Hausser, SS-Gruppenführer Jeckeln, SS-Gruppenführer Klagges and Himmler.

Braunschweig Junkerschule commander Hausser, in a steel helmet, reports to Himmler.

SS-Oberführer Hausser during a military exercise.

Left and right: SS-Gruppenführer Hausser.

Hausser at an awards ceremony. To the left is Ludwig Kepplinger; to the right are Georg Keppler and Otto Kumm.

Hausser presents Kepplinger with his decoration; to the right foreground is Georg Keppler.

Hausser at the front (left, in sunglasses) with Georg Keppler.

Hausser with Demelhuber during an inspection.

Hausser (left) and Demelhuber (right, in steel helmet).

Hausser (centre) watching troops on the move.

SS-Obergruppenführer Hausser in the turret of a tank.

Above: Himmler stands between
SS-Gruppenführer Krüger (left) and
SS-Obergruppenführer Hausser (right).

Left: Hausser, Krüger and Himmler discuss the
troop exercise. To the far left is Vincenz Kaiser.

Hausser attends the funeral of Sepp Dietrich.

The grave of Paul 'Papa' Hausser.

ERHARD HEIDEN

ERHARD HEIDEN was one of the more-obscure leaders of the SS and very little is known of him. He was born on 23 February 1901 in Solln, south of Munich. He was too young to serve in the First World War, but he apparently did join a Freikorps unit afterwards. He worked as a salesman and was an agent for the Bavarian police for a short time. He was an early member of the NSDAP, first joining in about 1921. He was allocated the early NSDAP membership number 74. He was also an early member of the 'Stosstrupp Adolf Hitler', participating in the Beer Hall Putsch of November 1923 and appearing in court as a result the following year. He re-enrolled in the reorganised NSDAP in 1925 and was appointed as deputy leader of the SS, succeeding Josef Berchtold as Reichsführer-SS on 1 March 1927. In these early days, his official title was also known as Reich-SS-Führer or RSSF.

His tenure as Reichsführer-SS was not an easy one, since he competed for independent control of the SS with the chief of the expanding SA, Franz Pfeffer von Salomon. Heiden introduced and maintained strict regulations for the SS. In SS Order No. 1, dated 13 September 1927, Heiden ordered:

> The SS will never participate in discussions at members' meetings. SS men will attend discussion evenings for the purpose of political instruction only. No SS man will smoke during the address and nobody will be allowed to leave the room. The SS man and SS commander will remain silent and will never become involved in matters (concerning the local political leadership and SA) which do not concern him.

At the end of 1928 Heiden became involved in a scandal with another SS member, Franz Rottenberger, who ran a firm which supplied clothing to the SS and in which Heiden also had some control. Another company (in Kaiserstrasse, Munich) supplied Rottenberger and Heiden with the black trousers which formed an integral part of the SS uniform. It transpired that this firm was owned by a Jew. Rottenberger and Heiden were alleged to have made large profits from the purchase and subsequent sales to the SS. Heiden had advance notice that the scandal was about to break and he approached Hitler on 1 December 1928 with his intention to resign as RFSS. This materialised on 6 January 1929 with his written resignation—it was accepted by Hitler, who announced on 20 January that he had appointed Heiden's deputy, Heinrich Himmler, as the new Reichsführer-SS, with effect from 6 January 1929. The internal memorandum stated:

Decree

(For the SS only, not for the press)

The Reichsführer of the Schutzstaffel, Party Comrade Erhard Heiden, had already requested me on 1 December 1928 to relieve him from his assignment as the Reichsführer of the Schutzstaffel because of family-related and economic reasons.

On 6 January 1929, I have relieved Party Comrade Heiden of his post as the Reichsführer of the SS and want to express to him my gratefulness that he had faithfully and honestly served the movement in the Schutzstaffel, ever since he had founded the first Schutzstaffel unit in München together with some comrades.

I wish to stress that Party Comrade Heiden's dismissal was undertaken at his own request and that it has no connection whatsoever to the social democratic press' wrongful accusations. I appoint the former Deputy SS Führer, Party Comrade Heinrich Himmler, as the new Reichsführer-SS.

München, 20 January 1929
Signed Adolf Hitler

The scandal broke on 16 January 1929 with a newspaper article headlined *'Jews as Hitler Suppliers!'* Himmler promptly suspended Heiden from all SS duties, culminating in his resignation from the SS and the NSDAP on 22 January 1929. Rottenberger also resigned from the SS, declaring complete innocence. The ensuing hearings within the Party lasted for many months.

A NSDAP membership file card shows Heiden as re-entering the NSDAP on 5 July 1932 and leaving on 18 March 1933. The grounds for his leaving the Party are simply recorded as *'reported missing'*. According to post-war testimony of former SS-Sturmbannführer Josef Gerum, Heiden was arrested in April 1933 in the Orlando Coffee House in Munich, on the orders of Himmler and Heydrich; he was then murdered at some unknown place at an unknown time. His body lay undiscovered until September 1933, when it was buried on the 15th of that month in Munich. His grave no longer exists.

Left: Erhard Heiden, Reichsführer-SS.

Below: Members of the Stosstrupp Adolf Hitler outside the Munich courthouse, awaiting their sentencing for their part in the failed Hitler Putsch. Heiden is eleventh from the right, in front of Karl Fiehler. Walther Hewel is at the rear centre in a light-coloured suit; Maurer is in military uniform to the left, and Fobke is in front of him to his left.

AUGUST FRIEDRICH HEISSMEYER

UGUST HEISSMEYER was born in Gellersen-Hameln on 11 January 1897, the son of Lutheran farmer Heinrich Friedrich Wilhelm Heissmeyer (born 28 November 1841, died 1927) and his second wife, Minna Anna Sophie Wilhelmine Heissmeyer (born Stukenbrok on 5 March 1859, died 1947). The new arrival had eleven brothers and sisters, two of whom were boys from his father's first marriage. August was named after his paternal grandfather, August Christian Wilhelm Heissmeyer, who had married Sophie Karoline Luise Rehse. His maternal grandparents were Wilhelm Ludwig Stukenbrok and Hanne Friederike Poock.

The young Heissmeyer attended the local elementary school in Gellersen from 1903 until 1907, when he came under the private tutelage of Pastor Morgenstern of Hämelschenburg. The Protestant parson prepared his pupils for the Gymnasium school in his house. Heissmeyer succeeded in his primary education studies and from 1910 until the summer of 1914, he attended the Gymnasium in Hameln.

On 2 August 1914, Heissmeyer volunteered for the Army. He was posted to a reserve battalion of Infantry Regiment 164 until 9 October the same year, when he joined the first transport of war volunteers sent to the Western Front. He was posted on 15 October to the 11th Company of his infantry regiment, near Reims.

Heissmeyer attended an eight-week officer training course at Pomacle in February 1915, and returned to his unit on its completion. He was promoted to Leutnant der Reserve on 18 August 1916 and transferred to command a platoon in the 2nd company of his regiment. Soon afterwards, he was appointed as Ordnance Officer for his brigade, and then as Ordnance Officer for the 111th Infantry Division.

He volunteered for the command of the division assault company and took part in numerous patrols in 'No Man's Land'. On one of these patrols—when he was sent out to find a unit which had been cut off on 9 April 1917 in the village of Pavrelle—Heissmeyer was wounded by shrapnel in his upper left arm. This resulted in his hospitalisation for several weeks at Wilhelmshöhe, near Kassel.

By June 1917 he was fit enough to return to the Reserve Battalion in Hameln.

He was soon ordered to join the 79th Reserve Division of the Reserve Infantry Regiment 269 and was given command of the 1st company.

On 18 August 1917, Heissmeyer was ordered to report to the Army Flying Corps. He underwent training at two airfields (one of which was Altenburg). He was subsequently posted on 21 March 1918 to Flying Detachment 260 at Douai, on the Western Front. He saw action over Reims, Cambrai, Arras and Lille, finally ending the war in the area above Valenciennes-Mons. His unit returned to Hannover, where it was disbanded. Heissmeyer returned to his parent regiment and was ordered to set up a volunteer unit for defence of the eastern borders. This took him fourteen days to complete. He requested an appointment with his commanding General in Berlin and drove there to personally resign from the Army, as there was no possibility of his remaining as a reserve officer on active service. He was released from his regiment on 11 February 1919. (*Note: this is the date provided by August Heissmeyer in his Lebenslauf dated 1933. Another date, 16 February 1919, is recorded in a typed note in his file*).

Heissmeyer found employment for the next few months as a labourer in the wool products factory 'Marienthal' in Hameln. In the summer of 1919, he studied to complete his arbiter (*graduation*) at the Kaiser Wilhelm II Oberrealschule in Göttingen. He passed in October 1920, having broken off his studies temporarily as a result of the Kapp Putsch.

In March 1920 he volunteered for the Freikorps Battalion Hanstein in the Südharz. His company joined with the Brigade Löwenfeld in Sennelager, Westphalia, where the fighting ended the following August.

From October 1920 until February 1922, Heissmeyer studied Jurisprudence and Political Economics at the Universities of Kiel and Göttingen, but he was compelled to terminate his studies early through lack of funds caused by rocketing inflation. He found work as a tractor operator in the mines Viktor I and Viktor II at Castrop-Rauxel. This episode made a profound impression on the twenty-five-year-old Heissmeyer, who had nothing but respect for his fellow workers, struggling to provide for their families in these difficult times. It was during this period that he turned towards National Socialist politics.

In the autumn of 1922 Heissmeyer worked for Hoechster Farbwerken. The following February he became the leader of the section for pest control. It was here in 1925 that he formed the first National Socialist factory cell, but on 1 April 1925 the factory management terminated his employment as a result of his political work. His attempts to return to flying came to nought, as the Allied Control Commission had banned flying associations.

Heissmeyer married Red Cross nurse Marie Lode (born 12 November 1894 in Neumünster, died in Berlin in 1939) in Hameln on 4 August 1923. The couple moved in with Heissmeyer's in-laws after the birth of their first child. In all, they had six children: Eckfried (20 October 1924), Frohild (20 October 1930), Ute

(19 December 1931), Jens (2 May 1934), Almut (10 March 1936) and Helke (1 October 1937). Marie Heissmeyer died in childbirth on 23 November 1939, and the baby was stillborn.

Heissmeyer joined the SA in Göttingen in May 1925, and then the NSDAP on 30 October 1925. He was allocated NSDAP membership card number 21 573 and was the SA Leader for Göttingen from 1925 until 1928. During this time he administered the duties of Gauleiter for the incumbent Dr Ludolf Haase, who suffered from continuous ill health following a head injury. Heissmeyer officially took over the post of Deputy Gauleiter of Hannover-Süd in 1927 and retained the appointment until April 1928.

He returned to Göttingen University, with the financial support of his father-in-law, to resume his studies from 1925 until 1927, but when his father-in-law discovered the extent of his political activities, he withdrew his support—forcing Heissmeyer once again to terminate his studies and find employment.

He withdrew from political work in order to spend all his energy on finding suitable employment to support his family—which he moved to Göttingen, having lived mostly apart for several years. He took over an agency for selling fruit trees, and when this market was exhausted after eighteen months, he transferred to an agency of the Siemens Schuckertwerke. Due to the economic situation, the business did not go well. In February 1930 Heissmeyer began working as a driving instructor for the Schmehl driving school in Göttingen, owned by an engineer, R. J. Schmidt. He remained in his employ until November 1931.

In his Lebenslauf of 1933, Heissmeyer notes: *'In November 1930 I had joined the Göttinger 1 Staffel. I succeeded in bringing the 18 men strength of the Staffel up to 600 men by November 1931.'* Just to what he refers here is open to conjecture, as Heissmeyer's SS file shows him officially joining the SS on 17 December 1930, when he was allocated membership number 4 370 and assigned to SS-Sturm 61 in Göttingen.

His first promotion, to SS-Truppführer, is shown as 9 January 1931, with seniority from 5 January 1931. He was further promoted to SS-Sturmführer on 31 March 1931 and given command of I/III SS-Standarte 12 in Braunschweig the following day. This resulted in his move to that town and another enforced separation from his family—they remained in Göttingen.

Heissmeyer was given command of SS-Sturmbann III/12 on 25 August 1931, with promotion to SS-Sturmbannführer. He was placed on the staff of SS-Standarte 12 as acting administration officer on 21 December 1931. He was promoted to SS-Standartenführer on 18 March 1932, taking charge of the 12th SS-Standarte the same day. Promoted to SS-Oberführer on 6 October 1932, he transferred to the command of SS-Abschnitt XVII. On 9 November 1933, he was promoted to SS-Brigadeführer. He was given command of SS-Oberabschnitt Elbe in Dresden one week later, on 16 November. Heissmeyer was quickly promoted again, this time to SS-Gruppenführer, on 28 February 1934. He transferred to the leadership of SS-Oberabschnitt Rhein in Wiesbaden on 5 April 1934.

From 14 May 1935 until 11 January 1941, Heissmeyer was chief of the SS-Hauptamt. From February 1936 until the end of the war, he was Inspector of SS and Hitler Youth Schools. On 9 November 1936, he was promoted to SS-Obergruppenführer. He was selected by Himmler as HSSPF Gross-Berlin on 2 September 1939, retaining this post under various titles until 20 February 1944. From 9 November 1939 until 31 July 1940, Heissmeyer was Acting Inspector General of the SS-Totenkopf Standarten.

He was appointed as a Ministerialdirektor in the Reich Ministry for Science and Education in 1940.

On 6 December 1940, Heissmeyer married the Reich Women's Leader Gertrud Scholtz-Klink. Gertrud Treusch was born in Adelsheim-Baden on 9 February 1902. She joined the NSDAP on 1 September 1929 and held membership number 157 007. In 1921 she married a teacher, Friedrich Klink, who was a later NSDAP activist and member of the SA. The Klink marriage produced five children: Isolde (1921), Gertrud (29 October 1922), Ernst (5 December 1923), Hans (7 August 1925—later posted as missing in action as SS-Untersturmführer with Panzer-Abteilung 102) and finally Kurt (1926—died tragically in an accident in 1928). Friedrich Klink died of a heart attack in Gutach in March 1930. A friend of the family, Dr Günther Scholtz, became close to the widow Gertrud Klink and they subsequently agreed to marry. The ceremony took place in Ellmendingen on 20 August 1932, but the union produced no offspring. Gertrud took the name Scholtz-Klink, and this is the name she made famous as the NSDAP Reich Women's Leader. The Scholtz marriage ended in divorce in December 1938. The marriage between August Heissmeyer and Gertrud Scholtz-Klink produced one further child—a son, Hartmut (born on 16 June 1944).

On 11 January 1941, Heissmeyer was given his own Main Office, which bore his name: SS-Hauptamt Dienststelle Obergruppenführer Heissmeyer. It was responsible for National Socialist education. On 1 July 1944, he was appointed General der Polizei and on 19 November 1944, he gained the rank of General der Waffen-SS, backdated to 1 July 1944.

During April 1945, Heissmeyer commanded battle group 'Heissmeyer' at Potsdam, consisting of members of his department, Volkssturm and Hitler Youth, in the struggle for Berlin. His wife Gertrud, dressed in a camouflage uniform and armed with a sub-machine gun, was with him, although she did not play an active part in the fighting. Heissmeyer was wounded in the latter stages of the battle.

Heissmeyer and his wife could not return to their house at Rothenburgstrasse in Berlin-Steglitz, as they were encircled in Potsdam. They eventually managed to break out and link up with other units, joining a motor convoy heading west, but it was intercepted by a Russian combat unit and the Heissmeyers fell into captivity. The SS-Obergruppenführer had previously removed his badges of rank and destroyed them, along with his true identity papers. He wore an unmarked camouflage uniform. The couple were briefly separated, but met up in a Russian internment camp, where they were able to convince their captors that they were refugees from the East who had lost their identity papers—they were both released.

They worked for about eight weeks on farms near Leitzkau, where they applied to the local mayor's office for replacement identity papers with photos under the false names of Heinrich and Maria Stukenbrok, the surname being Heissmeyer's mother's maiden name. Before the end of the war, they had sent their children south to Schloss Bronnen, near Beuron, in the Danube valley. The Heissmeyers convinced the local mayor that they required new papers to travel south to recover their children and he duly obliged, issuing identity papers in their new names. They made their way across the River Elbe and south, via Magdeburg and Coburg, towards Beuron, where the children had been placed in the care of the prior of the monastery. Reunited with their family, the Heissmeyers then travelled to Tübingen-Bebenhausen, where they found work as domestic servants.

By this time, the condition of Heissmeyer's wound, sustained in the last days of the battle in Berlin, was deteriorating and he was suffering from complete physical exhaustion. He was hospitalised for four weeks. In the meantime, Gertrud contacted and visited Princess Pauline zu Wied, an old acquaintance from the Third Reich period and the holder of a NSDAP Golden Party Badge. She arranged for the family to move into two rooms in the monastery mill at Bebenhausen, where they presented themselves as refugees from East Prussia. Heissmeyer and his wife supplemented their family income as domestics by also working in the local forest. They underwent a de-Nazification process in their false identities and were judged to be non-Nazis.

In October 1946, the press reported that Gertrud Scholtz-Klink had committed suicide, and the pair felt more secure. They settled in Bebenhausen and looked forward to a future in freedom. On 9 February 1948, at 11.30 p.m., the Stukenbroks were detained by an officer of the French security service during a joint action by French and American troops. They were found to be in possession of false papers and arrested. They appeared before the French Military Court in Reutlingen, charged with being in possession of false papers and providing false identities. On 14 April 1948, Gertrud Heissmeyer and the former SS-Obergruppenführer August Heissmeyer were sentenced to eighteen months in prison. Heissmeyer served his term of imprisonment in the State prison at Rottenburg and was released on 13 August 1948.

He found work as a labourer in the Zanker factory in Tübingen for an average weekly wage of 50 DM. There was no other income and Heissmeyer struggled to support his family. Proceedings against him were instigated by the State Spruchkammer, with the court announcing its decision on 4 May 1950:

Decision of the de-Nazification hearing against August Heissmeyer of Böblingerstrasse 73, Bebenhausen:

August Heissmeyer is a major offender;

He is forbidden to hold public office;

He forfeits any right to a pension or remuneration paid from public funds;

He forfeits the right to vote, to participate in political activities and to belong to a political party;

He is forbidden to be a member of a trade union or any similar economic or vocational organisation;

For ten years—until 31st December 1958—he is forbidden to:

Administer his own business or finance or control in any way such business;

Hold a managerial post in a dependant occupation;

Work as a teacher, educator, preacher, publisher, editor, journalist or radio commentator.

He is fined 1,500 Deutschmarks.

The costs of this case are awarded against him.

The costs have been set at 18,000 Deutschmarks.

The Heissmeyers made money by selling handmade straw stars, made from moss and branches and covered in flowers. They also sold bouquets of flowers on the local sports field. August Heissmeyer found work in a Coca Cola factory, eventually working his way up on the business side. He became an agent for the soft drinks firm Canada Dry, and for many years after he was able to provide a good living for his family. His son describes him as a broken, reserved, and retired man after the war, who never spoke of his former life in the SS, but who enjoyed his special interests of nature and culture. Heissmeyer died in Schwäbisch-Hall on 16 January 1979; his wife lived into advanced old age, dying on 24 March 1999.

August Heissmeyer wearing his First World War uniform.

A young Heissmeyer.

Marie Heissmeyer. The couple married in 1923 and had six children, but Marie died in childbirth in 1939.

SS-Standartenführer Heissmeyer.

Heissmeyer began climbing the promotion ladder early and was soon a SS-Gruppenführer.

Heissmeyer was promoted to SS-Gruppenführer in February 1934.

Initially the commander of SS-Oberabschnitt Rhein, he soon took charge of the SS-Hauptamt.

In 1936, August Heissmeyer was promoted to SS-Obergruppenführer.

With Gauleiter Sprenger.

As chief of the SS-Hauptamt, Heissmeyer attended many functions in his official capacity.

Here, Heissmeyer inspects SS-Totenkopf.

In Austria, Heissmeyer tries the unit's canteen food. On the left is Ernst Kaltenbrunner.

Heissmeyer salutes the grave of Hitler's parents in Leonding with Otto Jungkunz.

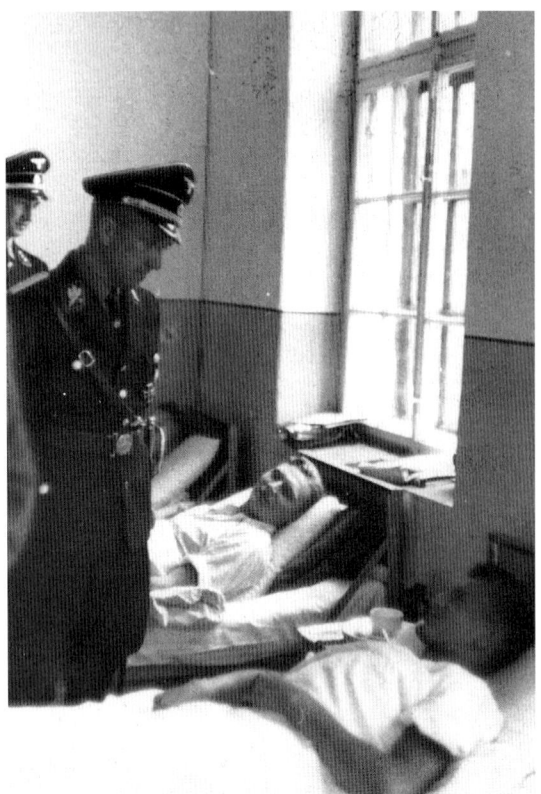

Not the tallest of men, Heissmeyer uses a stool to boost his height.

A hospital visit by the Obergruppenführer.

Heissmeyer delivering a speech.

SS-Obergruppenführer August Heissmeyer.

A file photograph of Heissmeyer.

Heissmeyer was considered by Himmler to be a weak SS leader.

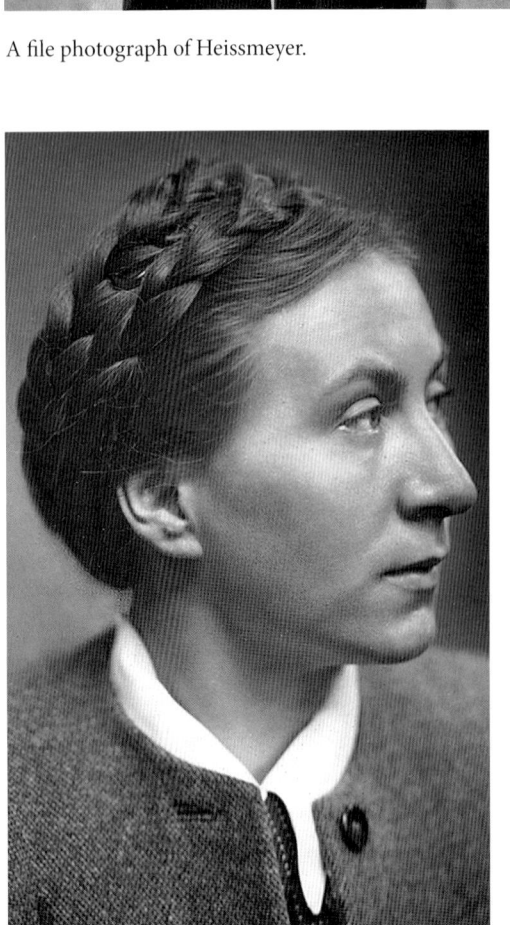

Left: Gertrud Scholz-Klink, the Reich Women's Leader and Heissmeyer's second wife.

Above: The marriage provided a stable home for the numerous children of both Heissmeyer and his new wife.

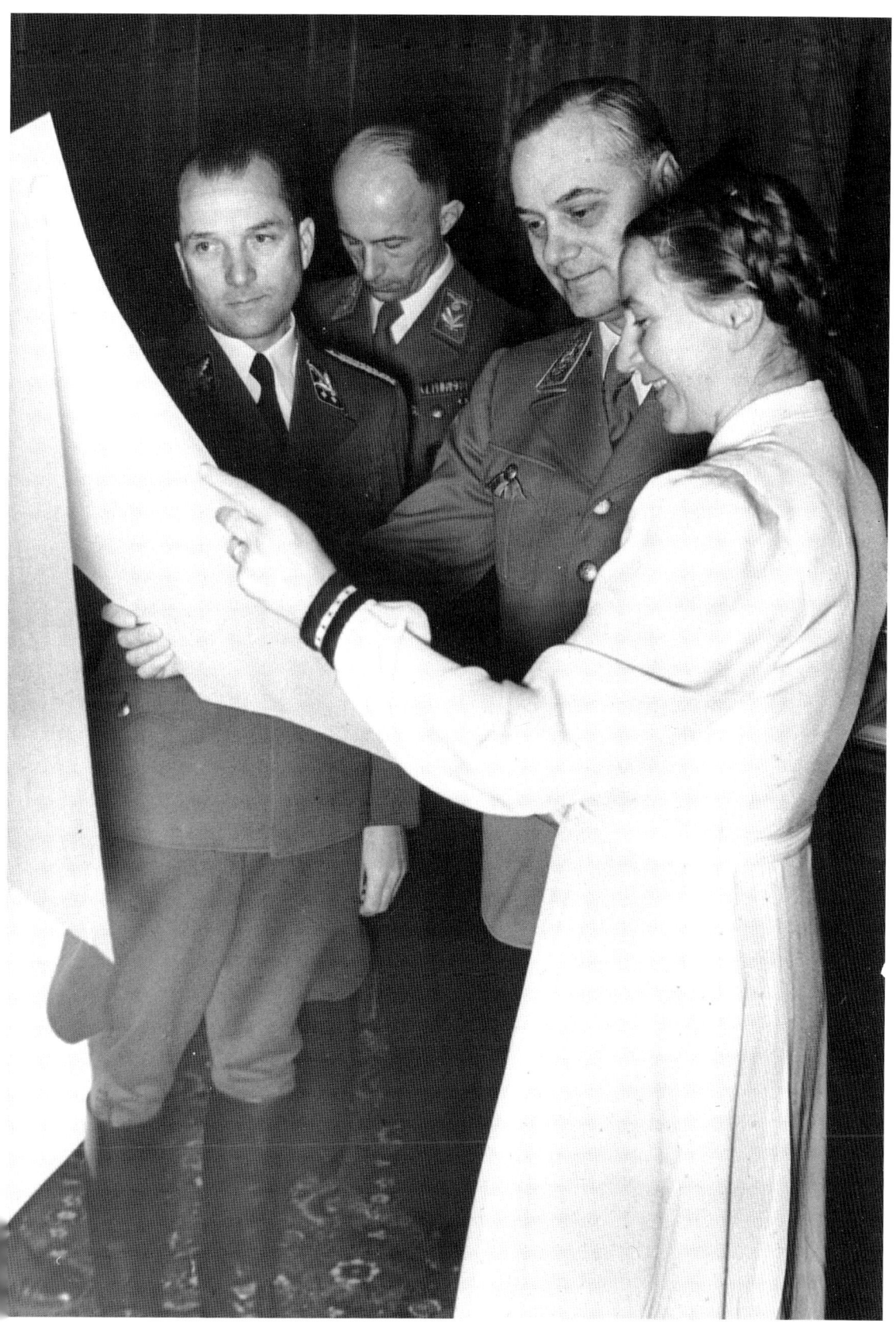

Heissmeyer with his wife and Alfred Rosenberg. Heissmeyer is wearing late pattern rank insignia for SS-Obergruppenführer.

Der Höhere SS- und Pol.-Führer
der Reichshauptstadt Berlin
und beim Oberpräsidenten der Provinz Mark
Brandenburg im Wehrkreis III
S - IV - Ru./Ra.S.B.-Nr. 71

Bitte in der Antwort vorstehendes Geschäftszeichen und Datum anzugeben.

Berlin-Grunewald, den 12. November 1942
Königsallee 11a
Fernsprecher 97 78 41

Einschreiben!

Reichskommissar für die Festigung deutschen Volkstums
Stabshauptamt
P
Eing. 18. NOV. 1942
Akt.-Zch.: 166190/12

Z.d.A.

An die
Geheime Staatspolizei
Staatspolizeistelle Frankfurt/Oder
Frankfurt/Oder

Betr.: Polnischen Zivilarbeiter Jan Dabrowski geb. am 24.6.1923 in Liziny.
Vorg.: Bericht vom 21.10.42. - II E(P) 4 - 2196/42 a

Mit der vorgeschlagenen Exekution bin ich einverstanden.

SS-Obergruppenführer

An den
Reichskommissar für die
Festigung deutschen Volkstums
- Stabshauptamt -
Berlin-Halensee
Kurfürstendamm 140
mit der Bitte um Kenntnisnahme zugesandt.

Im Auftrage:

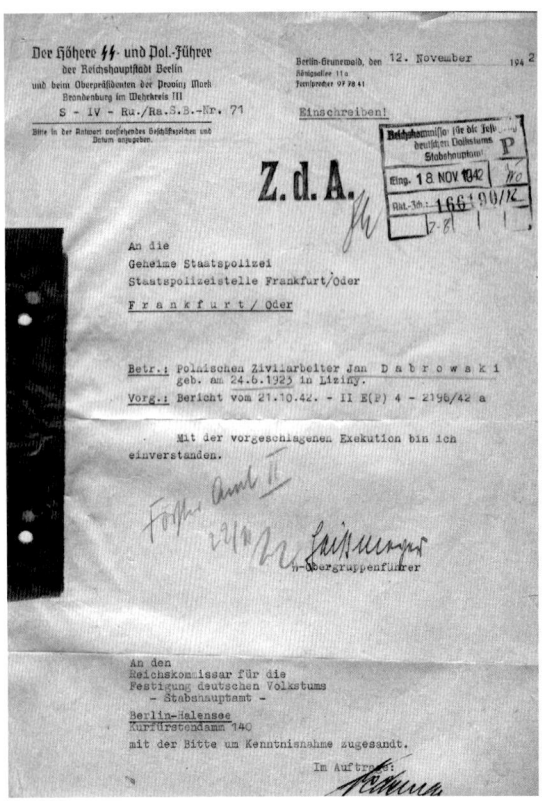

An interesting document, in which Heissmeyer gives authority for an execution in his capacity as HSSPF Berlin.

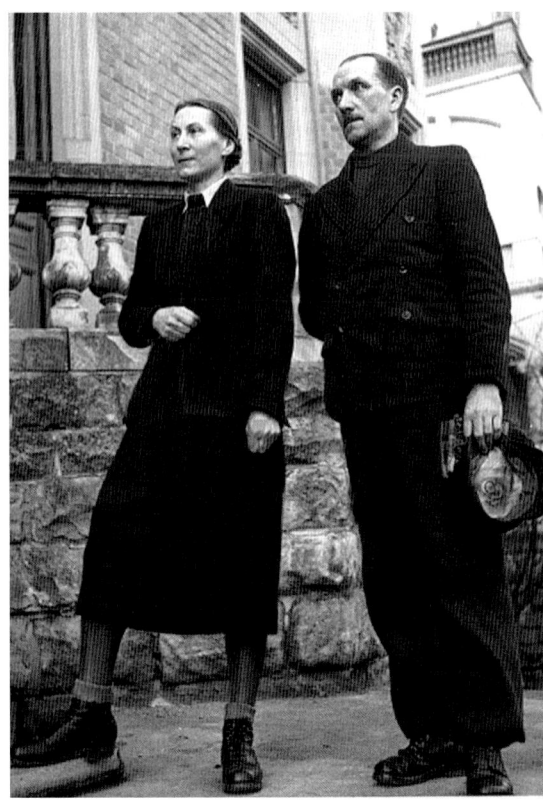

The Heissmeyer couple hid under false names after the war, but they were finally arrested by the French in 1948.

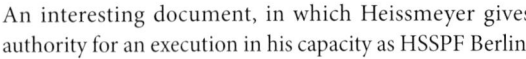

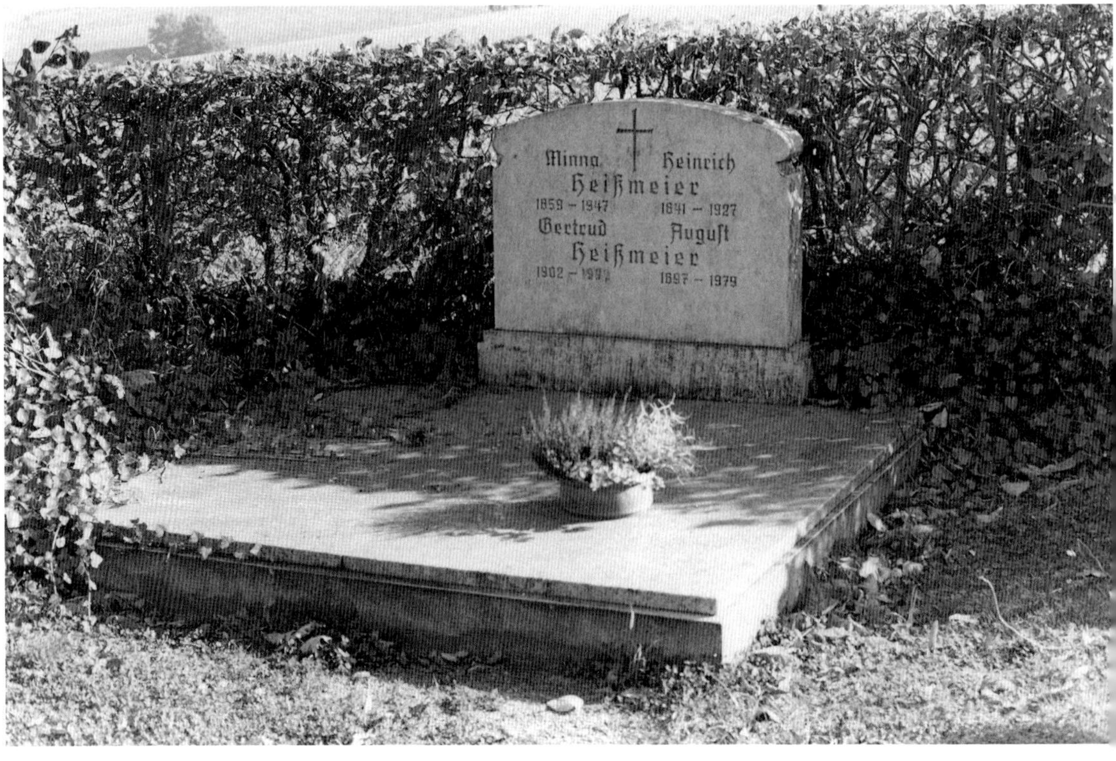

The Heissmeyer grave.

KONRAD ERNST EDUARD HENLEIN

K onrad Henlein was born into a Protestant family in Maffersdorf-Reichenberg, Bohemia, on 6 May 1898. His father, Konrad Henlein (born in Reichenau), was a civil servant, and his mother, Hedvika Anna Augusta (born Dvoakova in Maffersdorf), was of Czech descent on her father's side. In 1938 Konrad arranged to have her maiden name changed to Hedwig Dvoraschek, which was considered to be more Germanic.

The young Henlein attended elementary school and Bürgerschule in Znaim and Berlin, before returning to the Sudetenland to study business practice at the Handelsakademie in Gablonz. In early 1916 he left the academy before graduating in order to volunteer for the Austro-Hungarian Imperial Army. He was posted to the Tiroler Kaiser-Jäger Regiment no. 3.

Henlein subsequently saw active service in the Dolomites theatre of war, after transferring to the 27th Infantry Regiment. He was captured by the Italians on 17 November 1917 and was held as a prisoner of war on the Italian island of Asinara, off Sardinia. Released in April 1919, he returned to Gablonz.

He then found work as a clerk in a branch of Kreditanstalt der Deutschen Bank. He stayed in this employment until 1925, when he was appointed as a gymnastics instructor for the Sudeten German Sports Club in Asch. In 1931 he became the leader of the German Gymnastic Union for Czechoslovakia.

On 1 October 1933, Henlein founded and led the Sudeten German Home Front, with membership number 1. This organisation had the support of Adolf Hitler and financial support was forthcoming from the NSDAP. It changed its name on 19 April 1935 to the Sudeten German Party or SDP. Henlein wished to remain independent from the NSDAP, stating in 1934 that his party had *fundamental differences'* from Hitler's party. He had even banned and absorbed the Sudeten Nazi Party. Henlein survived an assassination attempt without injury on 28 April 1934.

Henlein travelled to Britain in December 1935 and delivered a highly-charged speech at the Royal Institute for International Affairs in London. He outlined the problems and demands of the German majority in the Sudetenland. The following year, he received honorary doctorates in law and political science from the University of Breslau. In November 1936, Henlein was appointed to the Administrative Council of the Association of German Ethnic Groups in Europe.

From 23 to 24 April 1938, the SDP held a party rally in Karlsbad where Henlein outlined the policy of the SDP:

1. Restoration of complete equality of the Sudeten German national group with the Czech people;
2. Recognition of the Sudeten German national group as a legal entity for the safe-guarding of this position of equality within the State;
3. Confirmation and recognition of the Sudeten German settlement area;
4. Development of Sudeten German self-government in the Sudeten German settle-ment area in all branches of public life regarding questions affecting the interests and affairs of the German national group;
5. Introduction of legal provisions for the protection of those Sudeten German citizens living outside the defined settlement area of their national group;
6. Eradication of injustice committed against the Sudeten German element since 1918 and restitution for damage suffered;
7. Recognition and enforcement of principle: German public servants in the German area;
8. Complete freedom to profess adherence to the German element and German ideology.

Heydrich's SD viewed Henlein with suspicion and attempted to usurp him during the summer of 1938. However, Henlein was too shrewd for the NSDAP security service, and came to an agreement with Hitler at the Breslau German Gymnastic Festival in July 1938. Hitler ordered Heydrich to desist, but Henlein paid a heavy price in the loss of independence.

Henlein visited Hitler in September 1938, and later that month President Benes imposed martial law following a revolt by Sudeten Germans. Henlein then demanded the ceding of the Sudetenland to Germany, resulting in President Benes declaring the SDP an illegal organisation on 16 September. Henlein fled to Germany to avoid certain arrest. Once there, he formed the Sudeten German Freikorps. Its members were involved in numerous border skirmishes and eventually assisted the German occupying forces the following month.

On 29 and 30 September 1938, Hitler hosted the infamous Munich Conference, where he obtained agreement from Chamberlain, Mussolini and Daladier that the Czech Government must cede the Sudetenland to Germany by 10 October. President Benes was not invited.

Henlein was appointed Reich Commissioner for the Sudeten German Region, directly responsible to Hitler, on 1 October 1938. Henlein's SDP was absorbed into the NSDAP and its leader became a member of the latter on 9 October 1938. His Party card number was 6 600 001. Simultaneously, Himmler accepted him into the SS with the rank of SS-Gruppenführer. His allocated SS number was 310 307 and he was attached to the staff of the RFSS.

On 21 October Henlein assumed full authority in the Sudetenland. On 30 October Hitler rewarded Henlein by appointing him Gauleiter and Reich Governor of the Sudetenland. He was elected as a deputy to the Reichstag on 4 December 1938. On 16 March 1939, he was commissioned as head of the civil administration for Bohemia and Moravia, but this post only lasted until 1 May 1939. On 16 November 1942, Hitler nominated Henlein as Reich Commissioner for Defence for Gau Sudetenland. In March 1943 he was considered as a replacement for the deceased Reichssportführer von Tschammer und Osten. He was promoted to SS-Obergruppenführer on 21 June 1943.

Henlein was married to Emma Geyer (born in Asch on 22 August 1904). She was imprisoned by the post-war Czech authorities and died in 1995. They had three children.

Henlein's influence diminished after the creation of the Protectorate of Bohemia and Moravia, and during the war years. He was captured by the Americans and was interned in the former flak barracks at Rotzikau, near Pilsen. During the night of 9–10 May 1945, he used a razor blade he had secreted in a cigarette case to slash his wrists and end his own life.

The leaders of the Sudeten German Party, Karl Hermann Frank and Konrad Henlein.

Henlein was courted by Hitler, who convinced the Sudeten leader to disband his SDP and join the NSDAP.

Henlein and Frank realised that their path to power lay with an alliance of the Sudeten Germans with the military might of Germany.

Hitler rewarded Henlein by appointing him as Gauleiter of the Sudetenlands.

A swastika-franked postcard portrait of the Sudeten leader.

Above and right: Gauleiter Henlein.

Gauleiter Konrad Henlein.

Henlein displays total loyalty to the NSDAP by handing over the banner of his SDP to Rudolf Hess.

Henlein looks on as Hess plants a tree; a magazine photograph.

Henlein became the deputy for the Sudetenlands in the Reichstag. He is in the front row to the right, between Seyss-Inquart and Mutschmann.

A formal portrait painting, later produced as a postcard.

Opposite page, clockwise from top left:

Henlein joined the SS and was given the rank of SS-Gruppenführer. He is seen here on the left, with Seyss-Inquart and Gütt.

SS-Gruppenführer Henlein.

Henlein with SS-Gruppenführer Frank.

Henlein entertains visitors. Left to right: Krebs, Henlein, Frank, Rust, (unidentified), and Heissmeyer.

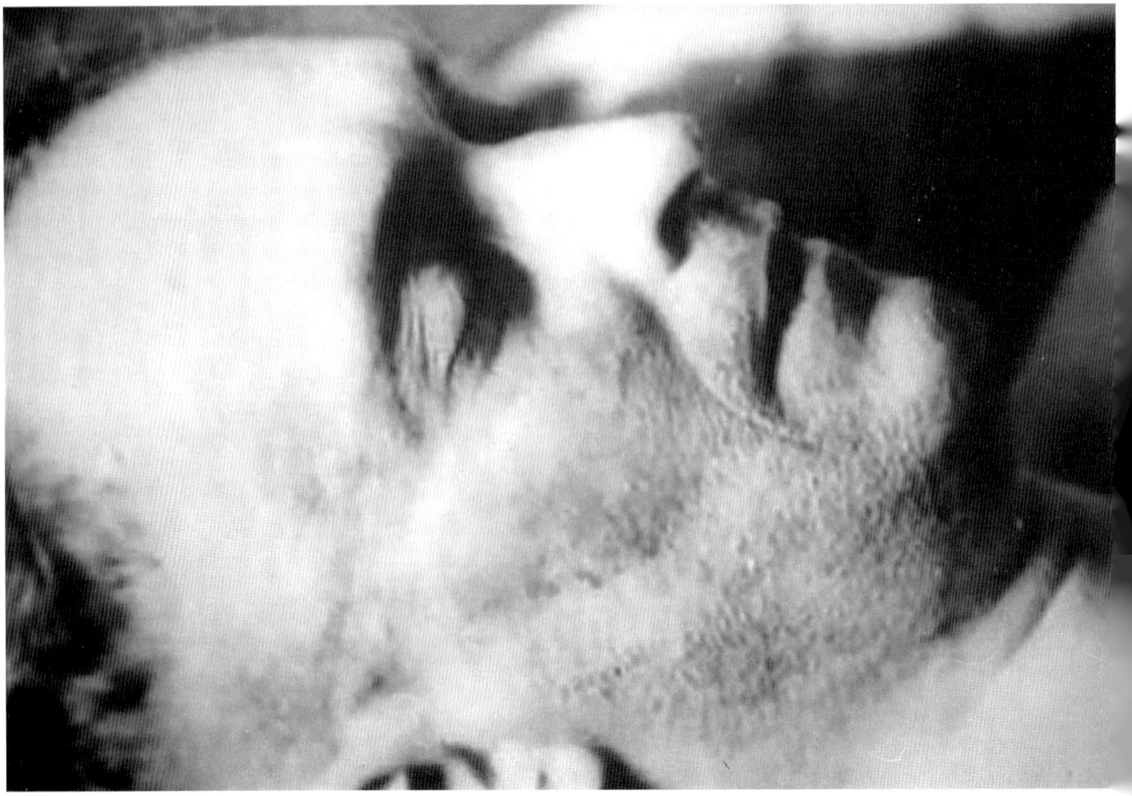

Henlein's influence diminished during the war. He was captured by the Americans and committed suicide in May 1945.

MAXIMILIAN VON HERFF

MAXIMILIAN VON HERFF was born in Hannover on 17 April 1893, the son of physician and member of the Prussian Medical Council in the Prussian health service Ferdinand von Herff (born on 4 August 1864) and his wife, Olga (born on 4 July 1869 in Annenburg). His family was attributed with the aristocratic 'von' title in 1814. After attending elementary school from 1899 for about three years, Maximilian matriculated from the local Gymnasium in 1911.

On 4 August 1914, von Herff joined the Lifeguard Infantry Regiment 115 in Darmstadt. He was commissioned as a Leutnant on 11 February 1915 and at some point was transferred to the 154th Infantry Regiment, where he finished the war. He was promoted to the rank of Oberleutnant on 18 October 1918 and joined the Hannoverian Freikorps Zeitfreiwilligen-Regiment on 1 March 1919. On 4 August 1919, von Herff joined the Hanichun Freikorps until 1 October 1919.

He married Hedwig von Grolman (born on 28 June 1896 in Emmerich) on 14 August 1920. They had three daughters, who were born between 1921 and 1927.

Von Herff continued to serve with the Reichswehr and was posted to various infantry units, in addition to the 18th Cavalry Regiment in 1926. He returned to 15th Infantry Regiment on 1 February 1928. He was promoted to Major on 1 October 1934 and was posted to the staff of the VIII Army Corps in Breslau on 16 March 1935. Another promotion, to Oberstleutnant, followed on 1 August 1937. He was appointed adjutant to the XVII Army Corps in Vienna on 3 January 1939.

On 11 November 1940, von Herff was appointed commander of Schützen-Regiment 115, part of the 15th Panzer Division. His division transferred to the North African front as part of the Afrika-Korps. From May until 8 June 1941, he commanded 'Kampfgruppe Herff' in the area of Bardia-Capuzzo-Sollum.

During his command of this unit, von Herff was awarded the Knights Cross of the Iron Cross for bravery and leadership skills whilst leading an attack on the Halfaya Pass on 26 May 1941. In his own words:

> We rolled into action at 4.30 a.m. on 27th May and by 6.15 a.m. the pass was in our hands. The British took to their heels along the coastal plain towards Sidi Barrani. We picked up a lot of booty, above all artillery (nine guns) tanks (seven Matildas, including three in working order) and the trucks we needed so badly.

On 1 November 1941, von Herff was promoted to Oberst. However, he apparently fell out with Rommel and was transferred from the North African arena to the Führerreserve des Oberkommando des Heeres (Standort Berlin).

At a meeting with Himmler on 17 November 1941, the Reichsführer-SS was quick to seize his opportunity and convinced von Herff to transfer to the Waffen-SS. He had already spent some time attached to the SS Personnel Central Office in 1939. Hitler and von Brauchitsch reached agreement on 21 November 1941 and von Herff was retired from the Army on 30 November 1941. He was placed at the disposal of the Reichsführer-SS on 1 December 1941 and was allocated SS membership number 405 894. His SS seniority was backdated to 1 October 1939 with the rank of SS-Oberführer. For the month of December he was attached to the Reichssicherheitshauptamt.

In January 1942, von Herff was assigned to the SS-Führungshauptamt for the purpose of instruction. This was followed by instructional periods with the other main offices of the SS, before being attached to the SS-Personalhauptamt. He joined the NSDAP on 8 April 1942 (backdated to 1 April 1942) and was allocated membership number 8 858 661.

He was promoted to SS-Brigadeführer and Generalmajor der Waffen-SS on 20 April 1942. He was posted to the SS-Personalhauptamt, as acting head of department, on 30 July 1942 as a result of SS-Obergruppenführer Schmitt's illness. He was confirmed as chief of SS personnel on 1 October 1942. Von Herff was promoted to SS-Gruppenführer und Generalleutnant der Waffen-SS on 30 January 1943.

His record shows that he gave up his evangelical faith on 4 March 1943 and withdrew from the Church, declaring himself a 'God believer'. From 4 May until 16 May 1943, von Herff undertook an inspection tour of the Generalgovernment to assess the calibre of SS and police officers. On 12 May, he visited Odilo Globocnik in Lublin and was taken on a tour of both Majdanek concentration camp and Trawniki work camp. Two days later he was in Warsaw to witness the liquidation of the Warsaw Ghetto by Jürgen Stroop's forces. His final promotion—to SS-Obergruppenführer and General der Waffen-SS—occurred on 20 April 1944.

As chief of the SS-Personalhauptamt, Max von Herff played an important role in the administration of SS records. His signature appears on many promotion file documents. He was captured by the Allies and eventually imprisoned at the British Prisoner of War facility at Grizedale Hall, Lake Windermere, north-west England, as prisoner number 967204. He suffered a stroke there and subsequently died of cerebral haemorrhage and arterio sclerosis in Conishead Priory emergency hospital, at Ulverston, on 6 September 1945. His death was certified by Dr H. P. Cook. He was initially buried at the priory, before his body was finally transferred to the German War Cemetery at Cannock. Along with Generalfeldmarschall Busch, von Herff is one of the most senior German officers buried in the United Kingdom.

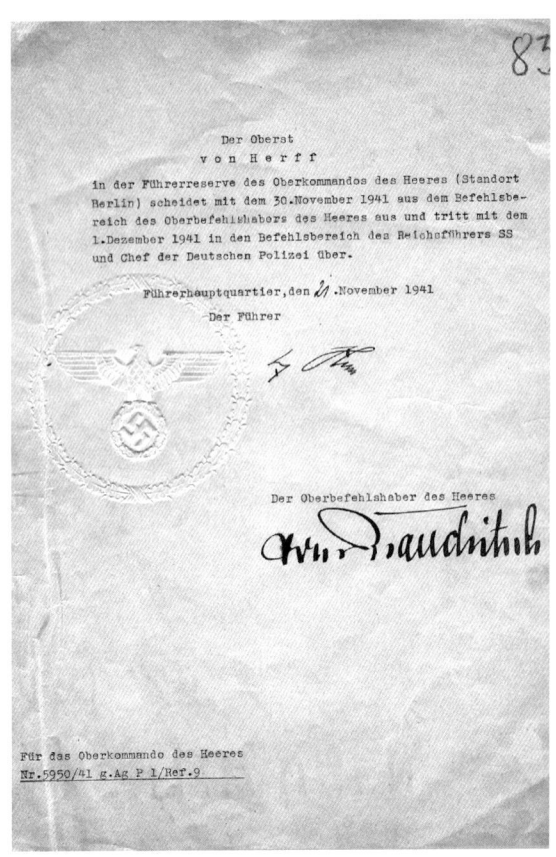

Clockwise from top left:

Max von Herff was awarded the Knight's Cross whilst serving with the Afrikakorps.

Recognising von Herff's administrative abilities, Himmler set his sights on capturing his skills for the SS. Hitler and von Brauchitsch signed the document transferring him from the army to the SS.

von Herff was placed in temporary command of the SS personnel office, before being confirmed as the new head of the SS-Personalhauptamt.

Clockwise from top left:

SS-Oberführer von Herff.

The von Herff family coat of arms.

von Herff at Himmler's field headquarters, Hegewald, near Zhitomir.

Left and right: SS-Brigadeführer Max von Herff.

von Herff with his family.

SS-Gruppenführer Max von Herff beside Himmler's Sonderzug Steiermark in the rail spur at the Reichsführer-SS Feldkommandostelle Hochwald in East Prussia.

von Herff at Hochwald.

In 1943 von Herff conducted a major inspection of SS and Wehrmacht units. Here he is with SS-Brigadeführer Harnys.

von Herff in Kassel during his tour.

Kassel.

![von Herff (centre) visiting Infantry Ersatz Battalion 15 in Kassel.](image above)

von Herff (centre) visiting Infantry Ersatz Battalion 15 in Kassel.

von Herff at the Möhne Dam, inspecting the bomb damage inflicted by RAF 617 Squadron.

von Herff with SS-Brigadeführer Hoffmann at the Möhne Dam.

von Herff greeting SS-Brigadeführer Hoffmann.

von Herff accompanied by SS-Brigadeführer Ullmann.

On 22 November 1943 von Herff (far left) carried out an inspection of the 13th SS Division. Next to him is SS-Brigadeführer Karl Sauberzweig, with an eye patch. Note the young age of the troops on the right.

The troops go through their paces with a mortar display.

Sauberzweig explains technicalities to von Herff.

von Herff is greeted by a junior SS officer.

The horses do not escape von Herff's attention.

von Herff covers all areas.

Left: von Herff questions the men.

Below: Left to right: Berger, von Herff, Göring, Müller, Himmler, and Grothmann.

SS-Obergruppenführer Maximilian von Herff.

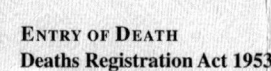
HC 691916

CERTIFIED COPY of an   **ENTRY OF DEATH**
Pursuant to the Births and   Deaths Registration Act 1953

	Registration District			Ulverston				
1945 .	Death in the Sub-district of			Ulverston		in the County of Lancaster		

Columns:

1	2	3	4	5	6	7	8	9
No.	When and where died	Name and surname	Sex	Age	Occupation	Cause of death	Signature, description, and residence of informant	When registered	Signature of registrar
158	Sixth September 1945 Conishead Priory Emergency Hospital U.D.	Max VON HERFF	Male	52 years	8 Grizedale Hall Hawkshead Ulverston R.D General in German Army (967204 Prisoner of War)	I (a) Cerebral Haemorrhage (b) Arterio Sclerosis certified by H.P. Cook F.R.C.S.	D.A. Buckler causing the body to be buried. Conishead Priory Ulverston	Seventh September 1945	William Dickinson Registrar.

Certified to be a true copy of an entry in a register in my custody.

Aleighton   Deputy   Superintendent Registrar

10ᵗʰ May 2000.   Date

Above: A copy of von Herff's death certificate.

Left: The grave of von Herff.

RUDOLF WALTER RICHARD HESS

Reflecting upon the whole of the story, I am glad not to be responsible for the way in which Hess has been and is being treated. Whatever may be the moral guilt of a German who stood near to Hitler, Hess had, in my view, atoned for this by his completely devoted and fanatic deed of lunatic benevolence. He came to us of his own free will and, though without authority, had something of the quality of an envoy. He was a medical and not a criminal case and should be so regarded.

Winston Churchill

Rudolf Hess was born on 26 April 1894 in Alexandria, Egypt. His father, Fritz Hess, was a wealthy businessman who ran the family import-export firm, Hess & Co. His mother, Clara, appears to have played a background role in the family, which was completely dominated by her husband. Rudolf's younger brother, Alfred (born in 1897), subsequently rose to become Deputy Gauleiter of the Auslandsorganisation.

At first, the young Rudolf Hess attended a small, one-room school which served the German community in Alexandria. From the age of twelve years he was taught at home. Fritz ensured his family never lost contact with the Fatherland, taking them home on annual trips to a house he had built at Reicholdsgrün, near the family roots at Wunsiedel. In August 1908, at the age of fourteen, Rudolf was despatched to an evangelical boarding school in Bad Godesberg. He spent three years there until moving to the École Supérieur de Commerce at Neuchâtel in Switzerland. This was an unhappy time for Hess, who left after one year and was then apprenticed to an import-export firm in Hamburg.

Along with his brother, Hess enlisted in Munich in the 7th Bavarian Field Artillery Regiment on 20 August 1914. His first choice, a cavalry regiment, was oversubscribed, so he settled for an artillery regiment. One month later, he transferred to the elite 1st Bavarian Foot Regiment. He first saw action on 4 November 1914 at Ypres and was promoted to Gefreiter on 21 April 1915. One month later, he was further promoted to Unteroffizier.

At the end of August 1915, he returned to Germany when posted to the Army Training School at Münster, on a course designed for officer applicants. Hess fell ill in February 1916 and was hospitalised with an acute throat infection. He returned to his unit at Verdun in May 1916, but within days of his return, during a barrage near Fort Douaumont on 12 May, he was wounded by shrapnel striking his left arm and hand. He was again hospitalized in Bad Homburg; he was here for just over a month, before being transferred to the reserve hospital at Ilsenburg. Whilst in hospital, Hess unsuccessfully applied for transfer to the Flying Corps.

On 4 December 1916, Hess was discharged from hospital and promoted to Vizefeldwebel. He was posted to the south-eastern front in Rumania with the 18th Bavarian Reserve Infantry Regiment, and was appointed Zugführer of the 10th Company on 25 December 1916.

At the Ditoz Pass in July 1917, he was again wounded in the left arm, but he did not report for medical leave and continued to fight with his men. During an assault on Ungureana on 29 August 1917, Hess was shot by a Rumanian infantryman from a distance of ten paces. The bullet entered his chest below the left shoulder, and exited cleanly at the back without damaging any bone structure. In September he was repatriated to a hospital in Germany. Whilst recovering in hospital, he was commissioned as a Leutnant, effective 8 October 1917.

On 10 December 1917, Hess was re-assigned to the Regiment List as an escort officer and immediately placed on leave. He returned to the family home at Reicholdsgrün and once again applied for transfer to the Flying Corps, travelling to Munich for medical tests. The following March he attended a flying aptitude course, followed by flying school at Lager Lechfeld, near Augsburg. He completed his flight training in October and transferred to the Fighter Squadron School at Nivelles in Belgium. On 1 November 1918, Hess was posted to Fighter Squadron 35 at Valenciennes. Although he saw action on the Western Front, he scored no aerial victories before the armistice and was discharged on 31 December 1918.

Hess once again returned to Reicholdsgrün, where he spent several frustrating weeks feeling at a loss, with time on his hands. On 18 February 1919, having travelled to Munich, he joined the Thule Society as head of its sabotage troops, and on 25 April Hess joined the Freikorps Regensburg. He participated in the Bavarian uprising and was lightly wounded in the leg on 1 May 1919. A week later, he joined the Freikorps von Epp.

In order to provide an income, Hess found employment as a clerk and part-time painter and decorator. In February 1920, he enrolled at the University of Munich, studying geopolitics, history and economic science. Here, he came under the strong influence of one of his tutors, Professor Karl Haushofer.

Hess rejoined the Freikorps von Epp on 29 March 1920 and was assigned to the Police Flying Staff at Schleissheim under Konrad Hafner. He remained with this unit until 30 April 1920.

Around this time, Hess first encountered Adolf Hitler; he joined the NSDAP on 1 July 1920, with membership number 1 600. He was assigned as press advisor to the Party leadership and in February 1921, he was Speaker of the National Socialist Group in Munich University. Hess was very active in politics during this year. Whilst balancing his studies with his new role as scientific assistant to Professor Haushofer, Hess joined the SA. He was badly cut in the face when a glass aimed at Hitler struck him instead. In November 1922, Hess was the leader of the 2nd SA-Kompanie in Munich, and the following year he was a founder member of the Stosstrupp Hitler.

Hess participated in the Putsch of November 1923, playing a leading role. He accompanied Hitler into the Bürgerbräukeller and arrested Minister President Gustav von Kahr, along with his associates. Hess then marched through Munich to the Feldherrnhalle, where the revolution came to an abrupt end, with the Bavarian Police opening fire on the ranks of National Socialists. Surprisingly—given his previous record with wounds—Hess escaped uninjured and he fled to a safe house where he made good his escape to Austria.

On hearing that Hitler had been imprisoned, Hess returned voluntarily to Germany and in April 1924, he was also convicted and imprisoned for eight months in Landsberg prison. He acted as personal secretary to Hitler and the first manuscript of *Mein Kampf* was typed by Hess whilst still in prison. He was released in December 1924.

Hess rejoined the NSDAP on 27 February 1925 and was allocated the new membership number 16. He was appointed as private secretary and personal adjutant to Hitler on 1 April 1925.

On 1 November 1925, Hess joined the SS as a Staffelführer. From 1927 until 1928, he was the SS commander for Upper Bavaria. In 1929, his responsibilities also took in Franconia and Lower Bavaria, with the area subsequently becoming known as Oberbereich Süd. As personal adjutant to Hitler, on 20 July 1929 Hess also became Personal SS Adjutant to the Führer. He was accorded the rank of SS-Oberführer on 18 December 1931.

Hess married Ilse Pröhl (born on 22 April 1900 in Hannover, died 1995) on 27 December 1927. They had one son, Wolf-Rüdiger (born on 18 November 1937, died 24 October 2001).

A SA-Führerbefehl shows that Hess was promoted to SS-Gruppenführer on 5 December 1932, although his SS file gives the date as 24 December 1932.

On 15 December 1932, he became the Chief of the NSDAP Liaison Staff in the Reich Leadership and Chairman of the NSDAP Central Political Commission. He was elected to the Reichstag on 4 March 1933, representing Leipzig.

On 21 April 1933, Hitler appointed Hess as Deputy Reich Leader and chief of the Party Office. The same day, Hitler promoted him to SS-Obergruppenführer. Also in 1933, he was designated leader of the People's Association for Germans Abroad and Chief of the NSDAP Foreign Organisation. He was named as Reichsleiter der NSDAP on 2 June 1933, but surrendered this rank on 20 September 1933, in favour of the title of 'Deputy Führer'.

Hess also relinquished his SS rank of Obergruppenführer on 26 September 1933, but he retained the right to wear the rank insignia on SS uniform by order of the Führer. He continued to appear in SS uniform until 1936, when he severed all connections with the organisation—not wishing to appear subordinate to the Reichsführer-SS.

From 3 October until December 1933, when he was succeeded by Ernst Bohle, Hess was head of the NSDAP Foreign Organization (AO), but the AO remained answerable to the Office of the Deputy Führer. He was also a member of the Academy of German Law. Hitler appointed Hess a Reich Minister Without Portfolio on 2 December 1933. In May 1934, Hess became the leader of the NS German Students' League and on 7 December 1934, he was officially recognized as Deputy Reich Chancellor.

In March 1935, Hess established conscription for the armed forces and the following September he ordered that all Party departments must report any criticism of the Party or State to the Gestapo. He was a signatory to the Nuremberg Race Laws on 15 September that year.

From 4 February 1938, he was a member of the Secret Cabinet Council. He was commissioned as Member of the Ministerial Council for Defence of the Reich on 30 August 1939. On 1 September 1939, Hess was officially recognised as the second in line to succeed Hitler, after Hermann Göring.

With the outbreak of war, the influence of Hess was on the wane. On 10 May 1941, in a forlorn attempt to recover his prestige and with a genuine intention to terminate hostilities between Great Britain and Germany, Hess piloted a Messerschmitt bf110 from Augsburg to Scotland. He hoped to gain a meeting with the Duke of Hamilton—whom he had met at the 1936 Berlin Olympics.

At just after 11 p.m., Hess parachuted out of his aircraft and landed in a field at Floors Farm, near Eaglesham, injuring his ankle. He was challenged by the ploughman, David McLean. Hess gave his name as Captain Alfred Horn, a name he always used when wishing to travel incognito. He declared he was German, but that he had an important message for the Duke of Hamilton. He was arrested by a somewhat-drunk Lieutenant Clarke of the local Home Guard. Hess was to spend the rest of his life in captivity.

Rudolf Hess was imprisoned throughout the war in various high-security establishments, including the Tower of London. When the realisation dawned upon him that his mission had failed, he became increasingly depressed and attempted to take his life. On 16th June 1941, at an interrogation centre, codenamed 'Camp Z'—Mytchett Place, near Aldershot—Hess jumped from a first-floor landing to the hallway below, fracturing his leg. He feigned loss of memory and his captors were uncertain of his mental condition for the next few years. Consequently, he spent most of his captive time at Maindiff Court Hospital, Abergavenny, South Wales.

On 8 October 1945, he was transferred to Nuremberg to face trial before the International Military Tribunal. He occupied seat number 2 in the dock, next to Göring. Throughout the proceedings, Hess displayed an acute lack of interest, even as the IMT sentenced him to life imprisonment.

He was incarcerated, along with the other defendants who had been lucky to escape the hangman's noose, in the military prison at Spandau-Berlin. After 1966 he was the sole inmate and he became a political pawn in the Cold War. Numerous campaigns to free him from his solitary confinement failed, along with his health. At first he refused all visits from his family; finally relenting after many years.

Ultimately, on 17 August 1987, the ninety-three-year-old Rudolf Hess was found in an outbuilding in the Spandau prison garden with an electric flex about his neck. The official version was suicide, but questions remain unanswered; the official post-mortem was scant in detail and unconvincing. How could a frail old man, too weak to carry out even the lightest of tasks and under constant supervision, succeed in hanging himself unnoticed? The Hess family commissioned a second autopsy and the report only fuelled the discussion. Various suggestions have been made as to the true events of that August day—some bizarre and some feasible. Whatever the truth, it does not detract from the inhuman treatment handed out to an old sick man, long after many contested that he had paid his debt to society.

Rudolf Hess with his mother.

Hess the student.

Leergewicht-700 kg.
Nutzlast— 180
Gesamtgew:-880 kg.

A pilot in the First World War.

In his Freikorps days, Hess sits atop the wagon.

A young Rudolf Hess.

Hess had a love of flying from his early days. Here he is holding the rear of his aircraft.

Hess (far right) on his release from Landsberg Prison. Next to him are Julius Schaub and Walther Hewel.

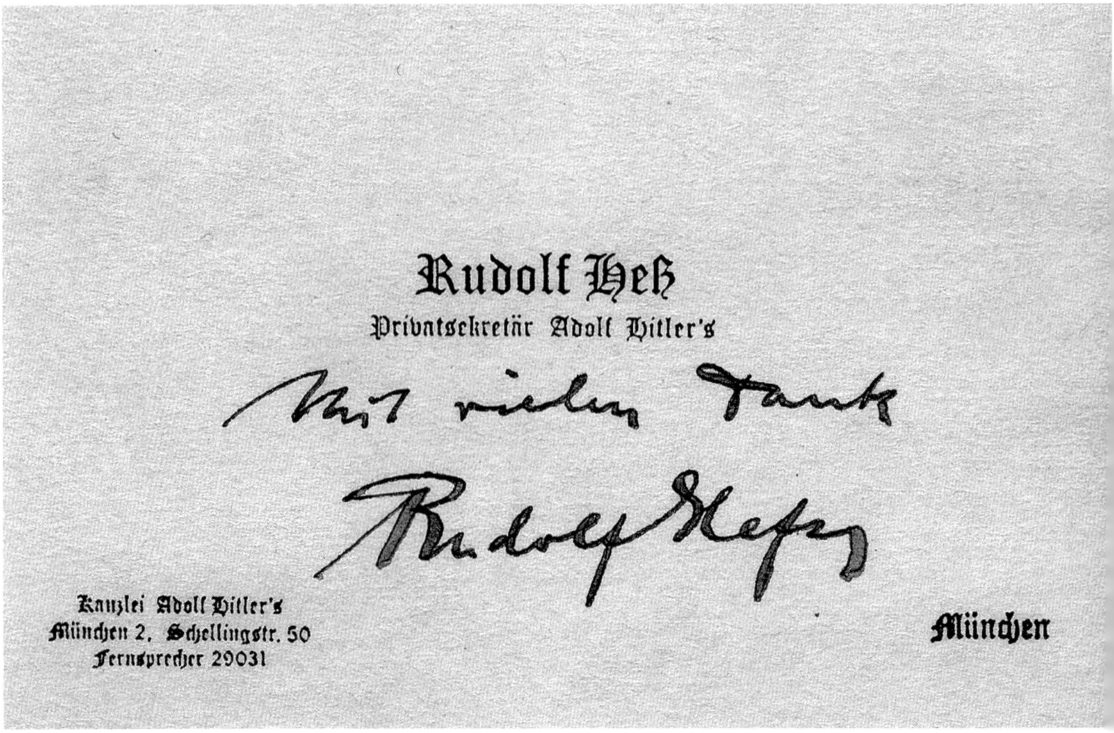

Rudolf Heß
Privatsekretär Adolf Hitler's

Mit vielen Dank

Rudolf Heß

Kanzlei Adolf Hitler's
München 2, Schellingstr. 50
Fernsprecher 29031

München

After his release from Landsberg, Hitler appointed Hess as his private secretary, as shown on this signed calling card from the period.

Hess (far right) in early SS uniform.

Left and right: Hess wears the rank insignia of a SS-Gruppenführer.

SS-Obergruppenführer Rudolf Hess.

The Deputy Führer in SS uniform.

A personal gift to Himmler at Christmas 1934, signed and dedicated by Hess.

Hess with Ernst Röhm.

Hess in the corridor outside his office door.

Hess in discussion with Julius Streicher.

Rudolf Hess.

A formal portrait of Rudolf Hess in SS-Obergruppenführer uniform.

Clockwise from top left:

Hess at a new housing project.

The proud father.

Hess in NSDAP uniform.

A visit to Vienna. Left to right: Globocnik, Klausner and Bürckel (obscured by Hess).

A captured Rudolf Hess is interrogated.

A part of the fuselage from Hess's crashed aircraft, now on display at the London Imperial War Museum.

Hess at Nuremberg with von Ribbentrop. In the background are Funk, Göring, and Dönitz.

An ageing Hess in Spandau Prison, inspecting his flying gear.

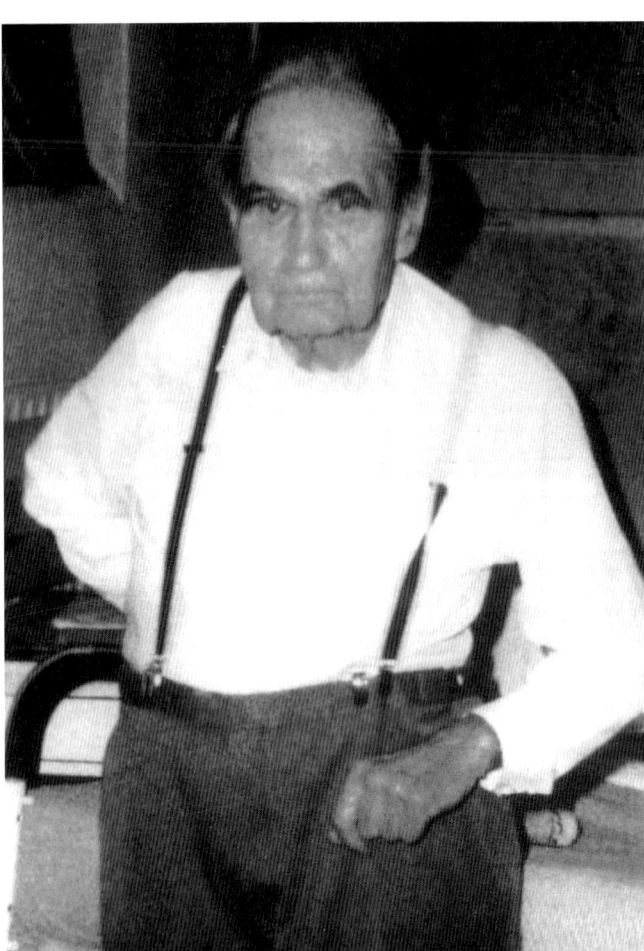

Left: A rare photograph of Hess in his Spandau prison cell; it was smuggled out.

Below: The summer house in the garden of Spandau Prison where Hess is alleged to have hanged himself with a length of flex. After his death, the summer house was destroyed and the prison was demolished and the site bulldozed.

REINHARD TRISTAN
EUGEN HEYDRICH

R EINHARD HEYDRICH was the son of the composer and music teacher Richard Bruno Heydrich (born 23 February 1863 in Leuben, died August 1938 in Halle) and his Catholic wife, Elisabeth Maria Anna Amalie (born Krantz on 19 June 1871 in Dresden). Reinhard was born on 7 March 1904 in Halle an der Saale, the second child of the family. He had an older sister, Maria (born in 1901), and a younger brother, Heinz (born in September 1905). The baby Reinhard was christened in the Catholic faith within days of his birth; his godparents were no less than the aristocratic Ernst Freiherr von Eberstein and his wife, Elise, who were well-acquainted with the Heydrich family.

Reinhard, affectionately known as 'Reini' within the family circle, attended the local elementary school, followed by the Reformrealgymnasium from 1910 until March 1922. As a young pupil he hoped to become a chemist, but world events transpired to change his ideas.

With the onset of war, Reinhard's nationalist and militaristic beliefs were nurtured and encouraged by the exciting seafaring tales of Admiral Graf von Luckner, resolving the young Heydrich to follow a military career. From 1918 until 1920, he was a member of the German National Youth Association and in March 1919, he joined the Halle Freikorps and served as a bicycle messenger with the Freikorps of General Maercker.

From 1920 until 1922, Heydrich was a member of the Deutschvölkischen Schutz- und Trutzbund (*German Peoples' Defensive and Offensive League*), serving in an auxiliary emergency capacity. There is some evidence that he participated in the suppression of a Polish rebellion in Silesia in May 1921.

The wartime stories regaled by Admiral von Luckner to the boys of Halle finally manifested in Heydrich applying for a commission in the Navy. On 30 March 1922, he reported for duty as a cadet in Kiel-Holtenau. Following his basic training at Kiel and the Marineschule Mürwick as a member of Crew 22, he was posted to the warship *Braunschweig* on 1 October 1922. He transferred to the training ship *Niobe* on 1 April 1923 as an Officer Candidate. His next posting was the light cruiser *Berlin* on 1 July 1923, where the first officer was Wilhelm Canaris. During January, February and March 1924, Heydrich was a member of the crew when the *Berlin* toured the Canary Islands.

On 1 April 1924, he was commissioned as a Fähnrich zur See and for one year, Heydrich attended an officers' course at the Marineschule Mürwick. He then supplemented this with further instruction courses in navigation, torpedo warfare, artillery, infantry and signals at the Reichsmarine Torpedo and Communications School. With his training complete in January 1926, as a new Oberfähnrich zur See, he spent one month aboard the flagship *Braunschweig* before being assigned to the new flagship, the battleship *Schleswig-Holstein*, on 1 February 1926. Aboard the *Schleswig-Holstein*, he was the second radio officer. He was promoted to Leutnant zur See on 1 October 1926.

Heydrich remained with the *Schleswig-Holstein* until he was re-assigned to Marine Communications School in October 1928. He was promoted to Oberleutnant on 1 July 1928. The following year he transferred to the Admirals Staff Office, at the Baltic Naval Station in Kiel, as a radio and communications officer.

During his naval service, Heydrich displayed great skill at fencing (he represented the Navy in sabre and foil), horsemanship, sailing (he gained his sea master's certificate for the Baltic and North Seas in the 12-foot dinghy class) and music, reaching an extremely high standard in the violin and guitar.

On 6 December 1930, Heydrich attended a ball at the Schleswig-Holstein Sailing and Rowing Club in Kiel, where his attention was drawn to a group of young women from the local Mädchenberufsschule. He noticed one young lady in particular and formally introduced himself rather stiffly, clicking his heels together. She gave her name as Lina von Osten, from Fehmarn, and the mutual attraction was obvious. Lina Mathilde von Osten was the daughter of the schoolmaster, Jürgen von Osten. At the time, he was the teacher in the tiny village of Lütjenbrode and the family lived in the schoolhouse. (Lina was born on 14 June 1911 in Avendorf-Fehmarn).

Heydrich impetuously proposed marriage on 9 December 1930. They became secretly engaged on 18 December, just twelve days after their first encounter. After informing her somewhat-reluctant parents, the young naval officer was invited to the von Osten home, where he impressed his prospective wife and her parents with his violin skills. In keeping with naval regulations, Heydrich wrote to his commanding officer, informing him of his intention to marry. Now accepted by Lina's parents, the couple became officially engaged on 26 December 1930 and their engagement was announced publicly.

The announcement came to the notice of another young lady, who had high hopes of marriage with the young naval officer herself. A former pupil of the Colonial Girls' School in Rendsburg, she had become acquainted with Oberleutnant Heydrich in the summer of 1930. The young lady visited him in Kiel and he had invited her to stay the night at his lodgings. Although nothing had transpired sexually, she expected an offer of marriage and she was distraught to discover that he intended to marry another. The tale would have ended there had her father (a senior naval civil servant) not held some influence with Admiral Raeder. Heydrich was portrayed as a dishonourable man and hauled before a naval court of honour, chaired by Vice-Admiral Gottfried Hansen. The court was made up by Gustav Kleikamp, Kurt Freiwald and Karl-Jesko von Puttkamer. Heydrich's demeanour during the proceedings was arrogant, and the court's recommendations were sent to Admiral Raeder. On 30 April 1931, Heydrich was promptly dismissed from the service.

Heydrich's plans for a glittering naval career were now in tatters; he was unemployed and without any prospects. A written appeal to Reich President von Hindenburg was unsuccessful and the future looked bleak. It appeared that the only positions open to him were as an instructor at the Hanseatic Yachting School, or an administrative post with the Rural District Council, but Heydrich still yearned for a military career.

Frau Elisabeth Heydrich suggested that her son should approach the son of his godparents, as she believed he held a senior post with a semi-military organisation connected to a political party. Karl von Eberstein was a SA-Oberführer and leader of the Upper Bavarian SA. He suggested joining the NSDAP and writing to SA-Stabschef Ernst Röhm in Munich. Heydrich obliged and joined the NSDAP on 1 June 1931, obtaining membership number 544 916. The introductory letter duly arrived on the desk of Röhm and he passed it on to Heinrich Himmler, who agreed to see the new applicant on 16 June after consulting with von Eberstein. Himmler at once recognised the potential in the young applicant and accepted him into the SS.

Heydrich enrolled in the SS in Hamburg on 14 July 1931 and SS-Mann Heydrich was allocated SS number 10 120. He was quickly promoted to SS-Sturmführer on 10 August 1931 and placed in charge of Section 1c of the Senior Staff Leadership of the Reichsführer-SS. On 1 December 1931, he was promoted to SS-Sturmhauptführer and on 25 December 1931, he was promoted to SS-Sturmbannführer.

On 26 December 1931, Heydrich married Lina von Osten at Grossenbrode. Her NSDAP membership number was 1 201 380. They had four children: Klaus (born on 17 June 1933), Heider (born on 28 December 1934), Silke (born on 9 April 1939), and Marte (born on 23 July 1942). Klaus was tragically killed by a lorry on 24 October 1943, and Lina died of lung cancer on 14 August 1985.

On 6 June 1932, Gauleiter Rudolf Jordan wrote to Gregor Strasser at the Brown House in Munich. He pointed out that a certain new member of the NSDAP, called Heydrich, had Jewish ancestry. An investigation was launched immediately, which resulted in Heydrich being found to be free from any Jewish blood.

Himmler formed the SS-Sicherheitsdienst (SD—*Security Service of the SS*) and placed Heydrich in command on 19 July 1932. Ten days later, he was promoted to SS-Standartenführer. He was transferred to the RFSS staff, with special assignment, on 27 January 1933.

He was appointed chief of the Munich Political Police on 16 March 1933, and was then promoted again to SS-Oberführer on 21 March 1933. On 1 April, he gained control of the whole of the Bavarian Political Police as deputy to its chief, Heinrich Himmler. Regaining the leadership of the SD on 9 November 1933, he was also promoted to SS-Brigadeführer.

Heydrich was appointed Preussischer Staatsrat (*Prussian State Councillor*) on 5 April 1934 and on 20 April, he was appointed deputy chief of the Prussian Secret Police. With this appointment, his sphere of operations moved him from Munich to Berlin, where he took up residence at Prinz-Albrecht-Strasse 8 on 22 April. He was then assigned the post of chief of the Criminal Police Office, under the Police President of Berlin, and Head of the Office of Prussian Secret Police (*Gestapa*). This was soon to change the title to Secret State Police (*Gestapo*). Heydrich eventually moved his seat of operations around the corner, from Prinz-Albrecht-Strasse to Wilhelmstrasse 102, the Prinz Albrecht Palace.

Heydrich played a key role in the 'Röhm Purge', also known as the '*Night of Long Knives*', on 30 June 1934. He personally ordered the execution of Catholic leader and politician, Hubert Klausner. Heydrich was promoted the same day to SS-Gruppenführer.

On 25 January 1935, Heydrich was placed in command of the Sicherheitshauptamtes der RFSS (SD-Hauptamt). This office was reorganized on 1 October 1939 as the Reichssicherheitshauptamt (RSHA). He also left the church in 1935 and declared himself 'Gottgläubig'. On 29 March 1936 Heydrich was elected to the Reichstag, representing Düsseldorf-Ost.

A keen sportsman, Heydrich was a member of the Olympic Committee for the 1936 Berlin Games. He was appointed by Himmler to the post of SS Inspector for Physical Training on 6 September 1939. On 1 January 1941, he was named as Head of Fencing under the Reich Association for Physical Training. In June of that year he manoeuvred the Presidency of the International Fencing Federation to Berlin, with himself at the helm.

After Himmler was appointed as Chief of German Police in 1936, Heydrich gained most of the spoils over his arch-rival, Kurt Daluege. Daluege was left with command of the Ordnungspolizei (*Order Police*), whilst Heydrich took Security, the Gestapo, Frontier Police and Criminal Police.

The Himmler-Heydrich partnership looked unassailable, but storm clouds were gathering. In May 1936, evidence was presented to Heydrich that Generaloberst von Fritsch, the chief of the Army, had been caught performing a sexual act with another man. Hitler was informed, but he ordered that the file be destroyed and no further action be taken against von Fritsch. For now, the affair was hushed up, but Heydrich had made copies of the more-important elements of the file in anticipation of possible future use.

On 12 January 1938, the Reichsminister for War, Generaloberst von Blomberg (a widower with five children), married a typist, Erna Gruhn. Both Hitler and Göring were witnesses. Shortly after, a number of pornographic postcard photos were discovered in the Reich Criminal Police HQ of the new Frau von Blomberg. Arthur Nebe exclaimed, *'Good God … this woman has kissed the Führer's hand!'* The photos ended up with Reichsmarschall Hermann Göring, von Blomberg's greatest rival.

Göring saw this as the opportunity to rid himself and Hitler of the two senior Army chiefs and he convinced Hitler to order the re-opening of the Fritsch case. When faced with the evidence of his wife's previous life, to his credit, von Blomberg stood by her and resigned. Although von Fritsch was replaced, he vehemently professed his innocence and demanded his say in a court of honour hearing. The subsequent investigation discovered that the Gestapo had long before uncovered the true identity of the parties involved in the homosexual act. Generaloberst von Fritsch was entirely innocent, having been mistaken for a Captain with a similar name. The Gestapo had suppressed this information in the hope it would never be discovered. On 18 March 1938, von Fritsch was declared innocent of all charges and he was rehabilitated by Hitler to the command of the 12th Artillery Regiment. He was killed in action on 22 September 1939, during the Polish campaign.

Both Himmler and Heydrich were now vulnerable, and there was a group of senior military personnel who demanded that senior Gestapo officers, plus Himmler and Heydrich, should be dismissed. General Beck decided not to forward the demands to Hitler and consequently, the Himmler-Heydrich partnership survived.

On 24 January 1939, as part of his commission as Representative for the Regulation of the Jewish Question, Hermann Göring appointed Heydrich as head of the Reich Central Office for Jewish Emigration.

By summer 1939, the situation in Europe had deteriorated to such an extent that Hitler was determined to use an armed offensive in order to regain territory lost to Poland by the Versailles Treaty. Great Britain and France had given Poland assurances that, if attacked, they would come to her aid. Hitler desired not to be viewed as the aggressor. Therefore, Heydrich was tasked with arranging clandestine operations that would appear to make Poland the provoker of hostilities if diplomatic measures failed.

Heydrich joined Himmler at two clandestine, high-level military meetings at the Berghof in August 1939, where it became clear what Hitler's intentions amounted to. Heinrich Müller received orders direct from Heydrich to provide what was euphemistically termed 'canned goods'—in fact, a dead body dressed in Polish military garb which was to be left at the scene of a staged attack at the German radio station at Gleiwitz. The fake incident went ahead and Hitler responded by ordering a strike against Poland. On 1 September 1939, the German war machine rolled across the frontier and Heydrich's old ship, the *Schleswig-Holstein*, opened fire on the Polish base at Westerplatte, Danzig.

Heydrich had learned to fly and had obtained a pilot's licence, using a small aircraft to fly between Berlin and the family summer home on the Baltic island of Fehmarn. After the outbreak of war, he took part in flying combat missions over the North Sea and France. He flew as an observer with Kampfgeschwader 55, and then as a fighter pilot with Jagdgeschwader 1. Following the invasion of Russia, Heydrich flew sorties with Jagdgeschwader 77 on the Eastern Front, against the orders of Himmler. During one of these missions in July 1941, to the east of the River Beresina, near Mogilew Podolsk, he had to ground his Bf109 with an emergency landing. He was missing behind enemy lines for two days, before coming across a detachment from Sonderkommando 10a, led by Heinz Seetzen (Einsatzgruppe D). When he turned up in Berlin with injuries, Himmler ordered him to cease flying sorties with immediate effect.

Prior to the war and for the purpose of combating anti-Nazi elements in annexed territories, Heydrich had created Einsatzgruppen *(Special Action Groups)*. For the annexation of Austria, the Sudetenland and then Bohemia-Moravia, they were static and to be based in the main cities. After the invasion of Poland and Russia, they became mobile, with the purpose of carrying out security 'sweeping-up' operations behind enemy lines. An integral part of their orders was to execute partisans, communists, political leaders and Jews.

Heydrich was appointed President of the International Criminal Police Commission, more commonly known as *Interpol*, in 1940. He moved the headquarters to Wannsee, a suburb of Berlin.

In July 1941, Göring tasked Heydrich with finding a 'final solution' to the Jewish question in Europe. As part of this strategy, Heydrich chaired a meeting for representatives of affected government departments on 20 January 1942, in order to discuss the method of solution. This meeting later became infamous as the Wannsee Conference, named after the suburb where it was held. The building was located at Am Grossen Wannsee 56–58, Berlin-Wannsee.

The security situation in the Protectorate of Bohemia-Moravia had become precarious, mainly due to the success of the underground resistance elements, supported by the exiled government in London. Protectorate State Secretary Karl Hermann Frank saw this as an opportunity to usurp the Reichsprotektor, Constantin von Neurath, whom he blamed for weak leadership. Heydrich's chief of Sipo and SD in Prague, Horst Böhme, kept Heydrich informed of the situation. When Frank flew to Rastenburg on the morning of 21 September 1941, in order to report direct to Hitler and Himmler, Heydrich joined the meeting at the Wolfsschanze in the afternoon. Where Frank had given an outline briefing in the morning, Heydrich presented a comprehensive report on the causes, organisation and consequences of the resistance movement in the Protectorate. The discussions continued the following day and von Neurath was summoned by Hitler.

Delayed by bad weather, von Neurath did not arrive until 23 September, but by then his fate had been decided. Hitler ordered von Neurath to take immediate sick leave and appointed Heydrich as Acting Reichsprotektor, effective as soon as he could arrange his affairs. Heydrich was also promoted to SS-Obergruppenführer und General der Polizei from 24 September 1941.

Heydrich assumed his new post officially on 27 September 1941. He made a success of his tenure as Acting Reichsprotektor, increasing war production and seriously undermining the efforts of the Czech underground movement. He became a serious threat to the Czech government-in-exile, based in London, under Eduard Benes. It consequently ordered steps to be taken to show that the German overlords were vulnerable.

An assassination team of Czech parachutists was selected, trained and despatched from England to be dropped into the Protectorate. After several months of preparation, they struck at their target during his last days in Prague. By May 1942, Heydrich had visited Paris and had formulated a concise plan with SS-Brigadeführer Carl-Albrecht Oberg to suppress the French resistance movement. His intention was to suggest himself as Reich Governor and then carry out a similar policy in France, which had proved so successful in the Protectorate.

On 27 May 1942, Sergeants Jan Kubis, Josef Gabcik and two other assassins waited along the route that Heydrich's Mercedes 320 car took every morning on his way into his office. When the car slowed to take a sharp bend, Gabcik stepped forward and aimed a sten machine gun at the startled occupants. The gun jammed, but Kubis tossed a handmade grenade at the vehicle. The resulting explosion tore a hole in the coachwork and punched a piece of shrapnel through the rear of Heydrich's leather upholstered seat. It carried with it a substantial amount of debris and horsehair from the seat, deep into a wound in Heydrich's back. The assassins made good their escape, but were discovered hiding in a church on 18 June 1942, and they were killed in the ensuing battle.

Himmler's 1942 service diary shows him holding four telephone conversations between 11.30 a.m. and 12.00 midday on 27 May. Dr Achim Ploetz, Heydrich's adjutant, was the first to report the assassination attempt. Himmler then spoke to Karl Hermann Frank, followed by Paul Baumert on his personal staff and Karl Wolff, his chief adjutant and head of the RFSS personal staff. The latter two were ordered to direct Professor Dr Karl Gebhardt to fly to Prague and treat Heydrich's wounds.

Back in Prague, Heydrich had been removed to the nearby Bulovka Hospital, where he lingered for several days. After rallying briefly, he finally succumbed to his wound early on 4 June 1942. Himmler's diary records him being informed of the death by telephone at 9.24 a.m. In the Reichsführer's own handwriting, he notes the simple entry: '*Heydrich*', followed by the death rune. He was buried as one of Germany's bravest soldiers, amid great pomp and ceremony, in Berlin on 9 June.

After his death, the 6th SS Infantry Standarte was awarded the honour title '*Reinhard Heydrich*', as was the Reichsarbeitsdienst unit 1/385 Schreibwald.

Left: Heydrich's childhood home in Halle.

Above: Elisabeth Heydrich with her three children in front of the music conservatoire; Reinhard is the middle child. Note the name over the archway entrance.

The Heydrich siblings playing a board game in their living room. To the left is Reinhard, with Maria and Heinz to the right.

A young Heydrich with his uncle Hans.

The young naval officer.

Heydrich (centre), a member of Crew 22 at the Flensburg-Mürwick Naval Academy.

Clockwise from left:

Heydrich (foreground) with friends aboard a yacht.

Oberleutnant zur See Reinhard Heydrich.

A young lady friend with the dashing naval officer.

Kiel, d. 20.12.30.

Hochzuverehrender
Herr Vizeadmiral!

Euer Hochwohlgeboren bitte ich gehorsamst, meine Verlobung mit Fräulein Lina von Osten, Tochter des Herrn Jürgen von Osten und seiner Frau Mathilde, geb. Hiss, melden zu dürfen.

Mit dem Ausdruck der vorzüglichsten Hochachtung bin ich
Euer Hochwohlgeboren
gehorsamer

Reinhard Heydrich
Oberleutnant zur See

Heydrich's handwritten letter informing his commanding officer of his engagement to marry Lina von Osten.

SS-Oberführer Reinhard Heydrich.

SS-Brigadeführer Heydrich at his desk in Munich.

At home with Lina (next to him) and his new son, Klaus. To the far left is Heydrich's mother.

SS-Gruppenführer Heydrich wearing his SS dagger.

The Heydrich couple in the doorway of their summer home on the Baltic island of Fehmarn.

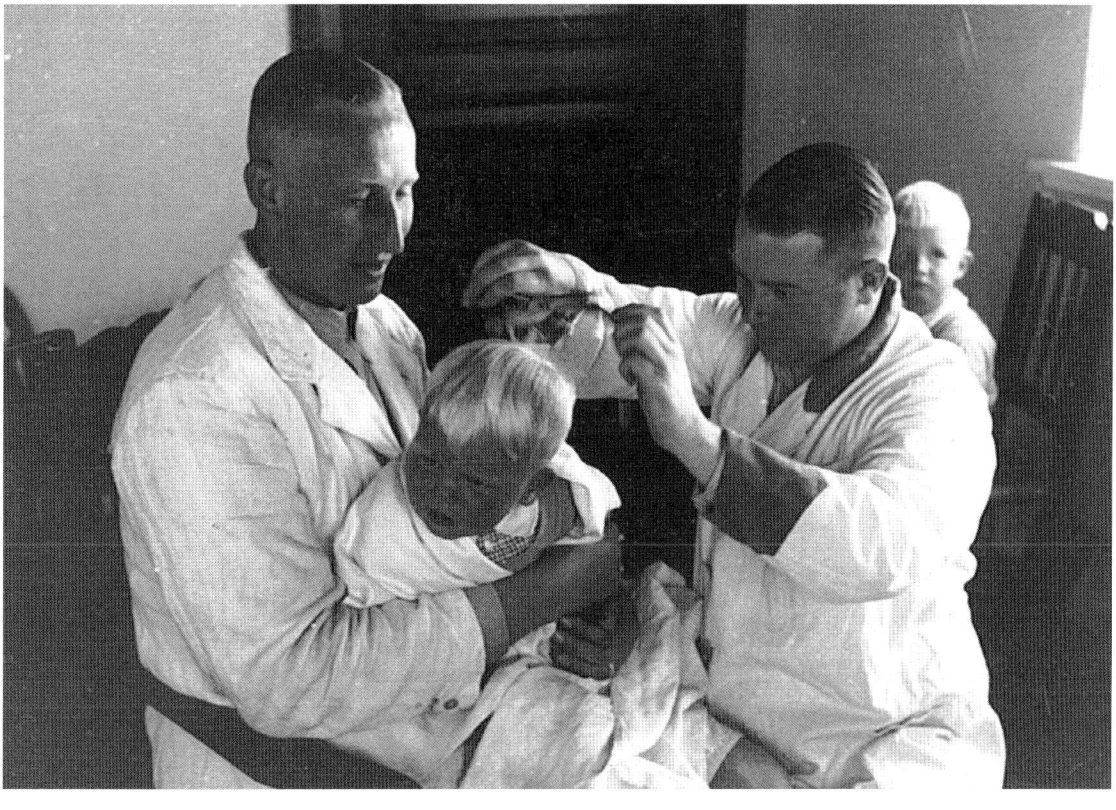

Heydrich holds his youngest son, Heider, for a haircut.

Clockwise from top left:

Lina Heydrich.

Reinhard Heydrich.

The Heydrichs and their three children, Klaus, Heider and Silke.

Right: The proud father.

Below: Finding time for the family on the beach.

This post-war photograph of Heydrich's house on Fehmarn illustrates the close proximity to the beach. After the war, Lina extended the original building (the section with thatched roofing) and opened it as a pension. It was destroyed by fire in 1969.

Heydrich and Himmler, in Bavarian dress, look into the sun, whilst Wolff (right) is in uniform.

Like many SS men, Heydrich enjoyed the hunt. Daluege is to the left, Sepp Dietrich is in the centre, and Heydrich is to the right.

Left and right: Heydrich was a keen and skilled fencer.

SS-Gruppenführer Reinhard Heydrich.

Above: Left to right: Heissmeyer, Daluege, Heydrich, Wolff, and Pancke.

Right: Himmler, Heydrich and Best formed a formidable partnership in the policing system of the Third Reich.

Left: Heydrich and Daluege greet a Spanish official.

Below: Waiting to cross the frontier into the Sudetenland. Left to right: Himmler, Lukas, Wolff, Lorenz, Daluege, von Woyrsch, Heydrich, Humann-Hainhofen and Peiper. It appears that Daluege has been delegated to hold the flowers and swords.

Above: A pre-war meeting of senior SS officers, probably in 1936. Those who are recognisable, left to right, are: Darré, Bouhler, Buch, Holzschuher, Heissmeyer, Daluege, Körner, von Woyrsch, Heydrich and Weitzel.

Right: Schaub, Heydrich, and Hewel on the terrace at the Berghof on the occasion of a secret military meeting, days before the outbreak of hostilities with Poland. All attendees wore civilian clothes.

von Reichenau in conversation with Heydrich.

Heydrich in the cockpit of his fighter aircraft during his military service at the front.

Left and right: Heydrich visiting Norway.

A wartime portrait of Heydrich.

Left and right: Heydrich photographed in Prague.

Himmler visiting Heydrich in Prague, October 1941. Left to right: Wolff, Heydrich, Himmler and Frank.

SS-Obergruppenführer Reinhard Heydrich, Acting Reichsprotektor of Bohemia-Moravia.

Reinhard Heydrich weeks before his death.

Professor Diek recommended an immediate operation, but considered the wound to be non-life-threatening.

Professor Holbaum carried out the operation to clean and suture the wound.

Professor Weyrich. A forensic scientist who assisted at the autopsy of Heydrich.

Professor Hamperl conducted the autopsy.

Himmler delivered the funeral address in the Berlin Reich Chancellery, 9 June 1942.

Heydrich's grave.

FRIEDRICH KARL HEINRICH AUGUST HILDEBRANDT

F RIEDRICH HILDEBRANDT was born on 19 September 1898 in Kiekindermark-Porchim, Mecklenburg, the son of a Protestant agricultural labourer. He attended the elementary school in Benzin in 1905, and then left his last school in Legde in 1913, without any qualifications. Following in his father's footsteps, he found employment on a farm, but he soon became a railway worker.

On 19 April 1916, Hildebrandt volunteered for the Army and was posted to Reserve Infantry Regiment 24. He saw active service on the Western Front, was gassed in Flanders in 1917 and wounded a further two times before the end of the war.

From January 1919 until March 1920, he was a member of Freikorps von Brandis in Upper Silesia and the Baltic area, where he was captured by the Red Army in Riga on 6 July 1919. Hildebrandt was repatriated to Germany and left the Army in 1920 as a Vizefeldwebel.

He joined the German National People's Party in 1919 and served for three months as an auxiliary security policeman in Halle during the Kapp Putsch. Accused of brutality, he was expelled from police service and returned to the land, again working as an agricultural labourer.

He was a member of the Brandenburger Agricultural Workers Federation from 1921 until 1922. In 1921, Hildebrandt joined the German Peoples' Freedom Movement. In 1924, he was elected to the Mecklenburg State Parliament as the leading candidate for his party.

On 19 October 1923, Hildebrandt was married to Elise Krüger (born on 7 December 1900 in Gross Breesen-Zenna; NSDAP number 25 806). They had three daughters and two sons, who were born between 1925 and 1941.

He joined the NSDAP on 1 February 1925 and held membership card number 3 653. He was appointed as Gauleiter for Mecklenburg-Lübeck on 27 March 1925, with Hitler confirming his appointment on 15 July 1925.

In 1927, Hildebrandt founded the *Niederdeutscher Beobachter* newspaper and became its first editor. He was a member of the Mecklenburg-Schwerin local parliament from 1929 until 1930.

In July 1930, Hildebrandt was suspended as Gauleiter by Rudolf Hess, as he criticised Hitler's involvement with industrialists and the investigation of his involvement in the Stennes Revolt. He resumed his post on 31 January 1931, after making a declaration of loyalty to Hitler.

He was elected as a Reichstag Deputy on 14 September 1930, representing Mecklenburg. Hitler appointed Hildebrandt as Reich Commissioner of Mecklenburg-Schwerin and Mecklenburg-Strelitz on 24 March 1933. On 26 May 1933, he was appointed Reichsstatthalter, with Lübeck also added to his area of responsibility.

Hildebrandt was appointed as head of the Nordic Society on 12 September 1933 and he also became editor of a number of local newspapers.

Hildebrandt joined the SS on 5 December 1933 as a Honorary SS Leader. He was attached to SS-Standarte 22 in Schwerin, with the rank of SS-Oberführer, holding SS number 128 802. He was promoted to SS-Gruppenführer on 27 January 1934 and was transferred to the RFSS staff on 23 January 1936. He was promoted to SS-Obergruppenführer on 30 January 1942.

Hildebrandt was selected as Reich Commissioner for the Defence of Mecklenburg on 22 September 1939 and, in September 1944, he took control of the Volkssturm in Mecklenbrug.

The US Army arrested Hildebrandt on 1 June 1945. He was tried at Dachau for the execution of shot-down US airmen and found guilty. Sentenced to death on 2 April 1947, he was not hanged until 5 November 1948 in the prison at Landsberg am Lech.

Friedrich Hildebrandt.

Hildebrandt wearing his NSDAP membership badge on his lapel.

Hildebrandt in early Party uniform.

A magazine portrait of the Gauleiter.

Hildebrandt (far right) at the funeral of Friedrich Loeper. To the far left is Bohle.

Three Gauleiter (left to right): Hinrich Lohse, Karl Kaufmann and Friedrich Hildebrandt.

Parchim, den 6. Okt. 1928.

Herrn

Himmler

München.

Sehr geehrter Herr Himmler!

Ich möchte Sie bitten, mit mitzuteilen, wann Sie im Laufe dieses Winters hier in Mecklenburg ein oder auch mehrere Male sprechen können, die Angabe der Zeit, Monat usw. wäre mir sehr lieb.

Im Voraus für Ihre Zusge bestens dankend

Mit deutschem Gruß!

A 1928 communication from Hildebrandt to Himmler. Note the official stamp (top left) and the poor standard of typing.

Foto: F. F. Bauer, München-Berlin

Nur treuer
Einsatz aller
Deutschen für
Führer und Volk
gewährleistet
Großdeutschlands
Zukunft.

Gauleiter und Reichsstatthalter Friedrich Hildebrandt

Above: A page from a NSDAP calendar.

Right: A stern-looking Hildebrandt.

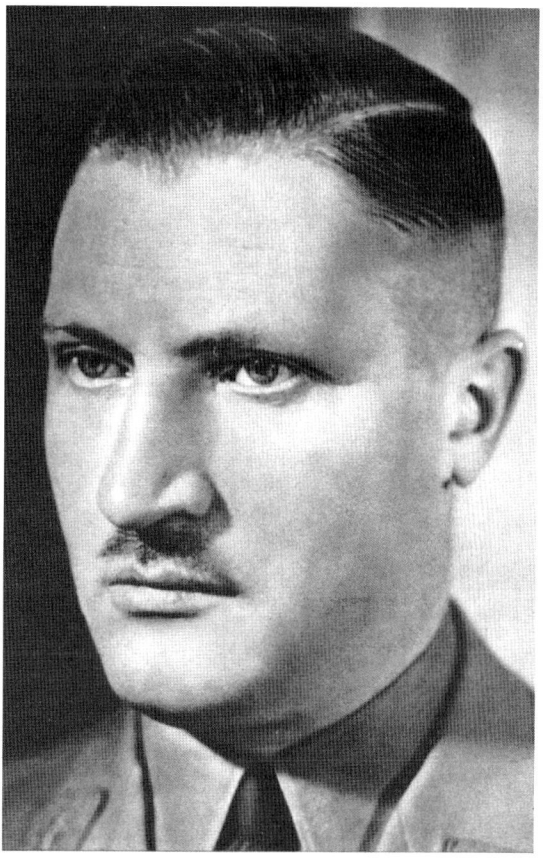

Friedrich Hildebrandt prepares to hang at Landsberg Prison.

The grave marker of Hildebrandt.

RICHARD HERMANN HILDEBRANDT

RICHARD HILDEBRANDT was born in Worms am Rhein on 13 March 1897, the fourth of six sons of the ceramic factory director and retired Bürgermeister Johann Karl Albert Hildebrandt (born on 4 December 1866 in St George, died on 23 September 1939) and his wife, Margareta Christiana (born Dost on 19 September 1867 in Warmensteinach, died on 7 November 1927 in Windsheim). Two of Richard Hildebrandt's brothers served in the SS and reached senior rank. They were SS-Oberführer Ernst Hildebrandt (born on 31 May 1895 in Offstein-Worms; NSDAP number 1 664 468; SS number 25 517) and SS-Standartenführer Fritz Hildebrandt (born on 2 November 1892; NSDAP number 2 176 645; SS number 181 214). Another brother, Karl, was a NSDAP leader who headed the Gemeinschaftslager 'Hanns Kerrl.'

The young Richard Hildebrandt attended the local elementary school in Worms, followed by the Gymnasium schools in Frankfurt-Main and Dorsten, from where he graduated in May 1915. He immediately volunteered for the Army and was posted to the Western Front in November 1915 as an artillery observer with the 22nd Field Artillery Regiment. He also saw active service on the Russian front with Foot Artillery Regiment 18. In February 1918, Hildebrandt was commissioned as a Leutnant der Reserve. He finished the war as a battery commander, being discharged in November 1918.

After the war, he was briefly employed in his father's factory before studying economics and business at the universities of Köln and Munich. Discovering he was not suited to commerce, Hildebrandt changed to languages, history and the history of art, but again he was unsettled and terminated his studies prematurely in 1921, without graduating. He found employment as a news correspondent for business and industry, followed by jobs in banking in Trier, Köln, Münster, Augsburg, Worms, Frankfurt-Main and Hannover. These positions were usually interspersed with periods of unemployment.

In August 1922, Hildebrandt joined the NSDAP in Windsheim and the Bund Oberland the following May. He also joined the Windsheim SA in June 1923 and led this unit on a march through Nuremberg during the abortive Hitler Putsch of November 1923.

In March 1928, Hildebrandt emigrated to the USA. He was married in New York City on 24 March 1928 to a high school principal's daughter, Johanna Fischer (born on 26 June 1903 in Bamberg) who was an Ortsgruppenleiter in the NS-Frauenschaft. They had two sons (born on 14 March 1932 and 6 July 1936) and one daughter (born on 7 September 1934).

In the USA, Hildebrandt worked on a farm as a garden labourer and as a clerk, first in a New York construction company and then in a book-export business. Whilst there, he rejoined the NSDAP on 1 June 1928, becoming a member of Ortsgruppe New York. His membership number was 89 221. By May 1930, the Hildebrandts decided that their future lay back in Germany and so they returned that month to his adopted family hometown of Windsheim.

There, Hildebrandt became the local NSDAP leader. He re-joined the SA in January 1931, but soon moved to Munich. In February 1931, he transferred to the SS and was allocated SS number 7 088. The following 24 June, he was appointed to the HQ staff of SS-Abschnitt I in Munich as SS-Sturmführer.

On 14 August 1931, Hildebrandt was promoted to SS-Sturmbannführer and posted as adjutant and staff officer of SS-Abschnitt I. This assignment meant that he was transferred to the staff of the Oberst SA Leadership, with an office in the Brown House, which he shared with another young aspiring SS officer by the name of Heydrich. The two became close friends.

On 18 October 1931, Hildebrandt was promoted to SS-Standartenführer and that same day he participated in the SA march in Braunschweig. He was again promoted on 1 January 1932, to SS-Oberführer in the Reich Leadership Office of the NSDAP. During 1932 Hildebrandt was assigned as one of Hitler's personal security officers for the election campaigns. He accompanied Hitler around the country, often by air.

On 1 July 1932, Hildebrandt was appointed adjutant and staff officer of SS-Gruppe Süd. He took command of the region on 1 October 1932. He was promoted again, to SS-Brigadeführer, on 9 November 1933.

From 12 November 1933 until 28 March 1936, Hildebrandt was the Reichstag representative for Breslau, and from 29 March 1936 he represented Hessen-Nassau.

He took command of SS-Abschnitt XXI in Görlitz on 13 November 1933 and in 1934, he was appointed as a Prussian Provincial Councillor. On 15 April 1935, Hildebrandt transferred to the command of SS-Abschnitt XI in Wiesbaden. He was promoted to SS-Gruppenführer on 13 September 1936. He was subsequently appointed as commander of SS-Oberabschnitt Rhein on 1 January 1937.

On 19 April 1938, Hildebrandt was placed on sick leave following an appendectomy, and the Oberabschnitt was run in his absence by his staff officer,

SS-Obersturmbannführer Hans Hoffmann. From 1 April 1939, Hildebrandt was designated as HSSPF Rhein.

With the invasion of Poland and the outbreak of war in September 1939, Hildebrandt was high on Himmler's list of candidates for senior SS posts in occupied territories. Himmler appointed him as HSSPF in Danzig-West Prussia on 21 September 1939, initially as a temporary measure. This was made permanent on 26 October 1939 and he adopted the title HSSPF Weichsel.

In October, November and December 1939, a special action squad, under the command of Kurt Eimann, carried out liquidations of several thousand mentally handicapped patients. Hildebrandt ordered Georg Ebrecht to carry out these actions in his area of responsibility, under the authority of the euthanasia directive signed by Hitler in September 1939.

On 9 November 1939, Hildebrandt was nominated as joint leader for Peoples' Medical Care and Housing Assistance, and concurrently Deputy Reich Commissioner for the Strengthening of the German Nationhood in Danzig and West Prussia. On 23 April 1940, he was appointed to the Peoples' Court.

For one week, from 20 May 1940, he trained with the 1st Reserve Battalion SS Artillery Regiment, and from 14–25 June 1940, he served as a battery officer with the SS Artillery Regiment, SS-V-Division. On 10 April 1941, he attained the rank of Generalleutnant der Polizei. He was promoted to SS-Obergruppenführer and General of Police on 30 January 1942. He was also given the rank of General der Waffen-SS und Polizei on 1 December 1944.

Hildebrandt held several high-profile SS posts simultaneously. He was appointed chief of the SS Race and Settlement Main Office (RuSHA) on 20 April 1943, retaining this post until the end of the war by virtue of his deputies carrying out his duties. From 25 December 1943, he was also Representative of the HSSPF in Army Group A and SS and Police Leader of the Crimea. Assigned to be HSSPF on 5 September 1944, the post was cancelled the same day. On 23 February 1945, he was appointed as HSSPF and Oberabschnitt Leader of Südost, in Breslau, under the command of Army Group Centre. His final posting was as HSSPF Böhmen-Mähren in April 1945.

Hildebrandt was captured by the Americans in Wiesbaden using a false identity and he was held in an internment camp in Regensburg. His true identity revealed, he was included in a transport to Poland where he remained in captivity, being ill-treated by his captors. He was sent back to the American sector in Germany in July 1947. He was placed on trial in Nuremberg in Case Number 7 (the RuSHA Case) from 20 October 1947 until 10 March 1948, when he was sentenced to twenty-five years in prison.

He was extradited by the Polish authorities and stood trial with former SS-Brigadeführer Max Henze from 8 October to 4 November 1949, for crimes committed during his tenure as HSSPF Weichsel. He was sentenced to death on

4 November 1949 by the court in Bydgoszcz (*the former Bromberg*). The sentence was upheld by the Polish High Court in Warsaw on 25 November 1950. Polish President Boleslaw Bierut confirmed the sentence on 3 December. Hildebrandt and Henze were both hanged in the prison at Bydgoszcz on 10 March 1951.

SS-Oberführer Richard Hildebrandt (centre) between Daluege and Himmler. To the top left is August Heissmeyer.

SS-Brigadeführer Richard Hildebrandt, 1934.

A Das Schwarze Korps newspaper image from 1935.

Another early news image of Hildebrandt.

SS-Brigadeführer Hildebrandt (front, second right) attends the opera. The fourth right is Wilhelm Rediess.

Hildebrandt in the foreground, with von Eberstein and Waldeck in the rear seat.

SS-Gruppenführer Richard Hildebrandt.

Hildebrandt (left) reviewing SA stormtroopers.

Hildebrandt (left centre) visiting a concentration camp with August Heissmeyer.

SS-Obergruppenführer Hildebrandt with Walter Krüger.   Hildebrandt and Werner Lorenz (right).

Hildebrandt (left foreground) saluting the interred coffin of Heydrich, 9 June 1942. Next to him is Wilhelm Reinhard, with Koppe and von Eberstein on the left and Grawitz on the right, with moustache and wearing his medical sleeve diamond.

SS-Obergruppenführer Richard Hildebrandt.

Hildebrandt and von Eberstein.

The first anniversary of Heydrich's death, 1943. Left to right: Hacha, Frank, Hildebrandt and von Eberstein. To the far left is the former adjutant of Heydrich, Hermann Kluckhohn.

Hildebrandt (right) and von Eberstein escort Lina Heydrich, 1943.

Hildebrandt with Dr Erhard Kröger.

Hildebrandt and Kröger enjoy drinks with Russian defectors.

Hildebrandt (right) with Ferdinand Schörner (centre) and a foreign General.

Hildebrandt sits with Sepp Dietrich. Behind them is Erich von dem Bach.

Hildebrandt visiting a German police active unit involved in anti-partisan operations.

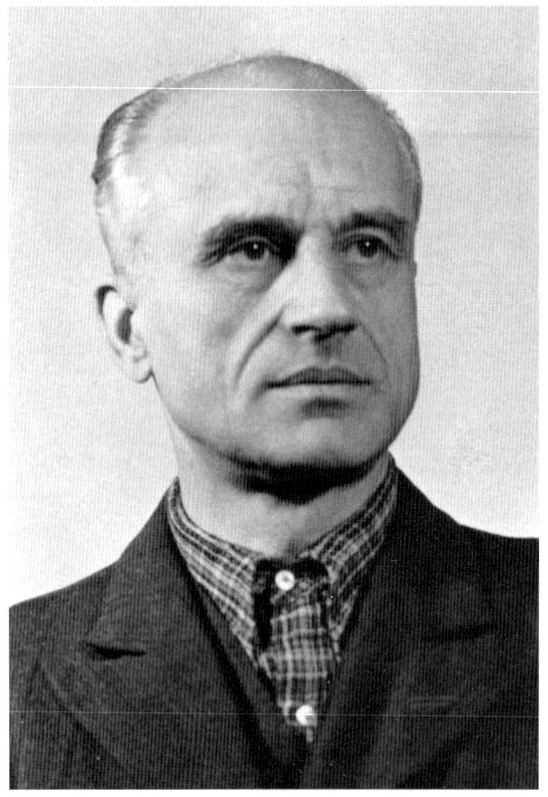

Prisoner of war.

Hildebrandt in the dock at Nuremberg.

Hildebrandt (far right) prepares his defence at Nuremberg, sat next to Otto Hofmann.

Following conviction and sentencing at Nuremberg, Hildebrandt was handed over to Polish authorities for further trial. A dejected Hildebrandt is resigned to his fate in Polish hands.

HEINRICH LUITPOLD HIMMLER

A STRICT CATHOLIC, Gebhard Himmler (born Josef Gebhard Himmler on 17 May 1865 in Lindau, died 29 October 1936 in Munich) was tutor to Prince Heinrich of the Bavarian Wittelsbacher royal family. When Gebhard's wife, Anna Maria Auguste (born Heyder on 19 January 1866 in Munich, died on 10 September 1941 in Munich) gave birth to their second son at Hildegardstrasse 2, in Munich, on 7 October 1900, he respectfully requested that the royal prince give permission for his name to be given to the new arrival, and also that he might act as godfather. Prince Heinrich readily agreed. The young Heinrich, affectionately known as 'Heini' in the family circle, had an older brother, Gebhard (born 29 July 1898). A third boy, Ernst, arrived on 23 December 1905 (died 1945).

Heinrich attended the cathedral school in Munich from 4 September 1906 until August 1908, followed by the Amalien School in Munich from September 1908 until August 1910, but his poor health kept him away so much that his father hired a tutor to supplement his education. The tactics were successful, as he obtained excellent results. In September 1910, Heinrich entered the Royal Wilhelm High School in Munich. Academically, he continued to excel, but he failed miserably at sport. In September 1913, the family moved to Landshut, where the professor had obtained a post as deputy head teacher at the local high school. Both Heinrich and his brother Gebhard attended their father's school as students. There they became acquainted with another student in Gebhard's year group, the later SS-Gruppenführer Professor Dr Karl Gebhardt.

Heinrich Himmler was not dissimilar to many of Germany's proud youth, and he persuaded his father to let him enlist in 1917. His father agreed upon condition that he become an officer. He wrote to the royal Bavarian household requesting that his son be allowed to join Bavarian Infantry Regiment 1 as an officer candidate. However, the unit was oversubscribed and Himmler's application was rejected. On 6 October 1917, he began working for the War Welfare Office, probably in an attempt to forestall being called up as an ordinary infantryman. Heinrich forwarded numerous unsuccessful applications for a commission to various Bavarian units, until he was finally accepted by the 11th Bavarian Infantry Regiment Number 9 for initial training as an officer. He joyfully reported for duty at Regensburg on 1 January 1918, but although he was keen to get into action, he was too young and untrained, and had to attend various courses before being sent to the front as a combat officer. The Germans capitulated before his chance came and young Himmler was discharged on 17 December 1918 as Officer Cadet Retired, before he had experienced active service.

Himmler joined the Bavarian People's Party in December 1918. He returned to school in Landshut from January to June 1919, to complete his education. He joined the Freikorps Landshut and the Reserve Company of the Freikorps Oberland in April 1919, the latter as the commanding officer's adjutant from May. Again he failed to see active service and, without further hope of an Army career, he turned to agriculture.

The Himmler family moved to Ingolstadt and on 1 August 1919, Heinrich found employment on a farm nearby as the first practical year of a course in agriculture. On 2 September 1919, he fell ill and was diagnosed as having a Paratyphus infection. He was hospitalised in Ingolstadt from 4 September for three weeks and was ordered by his doctor to defer the practical year. He therefore started with his academic studies. He enrolled in the Technical High School and the university in Munich on 28 October 1919, to study agricultural science, with an emphasis on chicken farming.

In November 1919, Heinrich, his brother Gebhard and a cousin, Ludwig, joined the 11th Alarm Company of the 21st Munich Protection Brigade. As a student he joined numerous student-based political organisations. On 1 September 1920, he began his deferred year of practical work on a farm and mill at Fridolfing, where he was heavily influenced by the owner, Alois Rehrl. He also took part in a course of instruction for agricultural machines in March 1921 as part of his praktikum. On 5 August 1922, he left the Technical High school with a diploma in agriculture. The following month he started work as an assistant at Stickstoff-Land GmbH, an agricultural-fertiliser company in Munich-Schleissheim, where he stayed for one year.

Himmler was politically active around this time and joined several paramilitary groups, one of which was the Reichsflagge in January 1922. He found a parallel political view with one of its leaders, Captain Ernst Röhm. When this organisation split, he followed Röhm into the Reichskriegsflagge. He joined the NSDAP on 1 August 1923 and was allocated membership number 42 404. He is to be seen in a photograph, carrying the banner of the Reichskriegsflagge, whilst manning a barrier at the War Ministry in Munich during the failed Hitler Putsch of 9 November 1923.

With the resultant outlawing of the NSDAP, Himmler became active in the National Socialist Freedom Movement (NSFB). Now unemployed, he was a speaker during the election campaign for the National Socialist Freedom Movement and travelled around the countryside on a motorcycle. He was appointed secretary and deputy to the local regional leader, Gregor Strasser, from July 1924, and was deputy leader of the Lower Bavarian Frontbann from September 1924. He also joined the Artamis League in 1925, where he developed his interest in the 'blood and soil' ideology of farming politics.

With the ban against the NSDAP lifted, Himmler once again enrolled in the re-formed Party on 2 August 1925. This time he was assigned number 14 303. He joined the newly formed Schutzstaffel under Julius Schreck and was given SS number 168, almost certainly on the same day as rejoining the Party. He was appointed as a national speaker for the NSDAP, the leader of NSDAP propaganda in Lower Bavaria and secretary of the NSDAP Gau leadership staff for Lower Bavaria.

In Bad Reichenhall in December 1926, Himmler first met Margarete Boden (born on 9 September 1893 in Gonzercewo; NSDAP number 87 252), the daughter of a German landowner in West Prussia. A qualified nurse, she had been divorced following a short, disastrous marriage to a man named Siegroth. Marga Boden ran a small clinic in Berlin, which she had opened with her father's money. Himmler and Marga continued their relationship, mainly by correspondence, and on 3 July 1928 the couple married in Berlin-Schöneberg. She shared her husband's interest in the land and in herbal remedies. They moved to a smallholding in Waldtrudering, near Munich, and on 8 August 1929, Marga gave birth to a baby girl, Gudrun. The Himmlers added a young boy, Gerhard—the son of SS-Scharführer Kurt von der Ahe—to their family by the adoption process, but he developed into a rather unruly boy, who later joined the Waffen-SS as a young recruit in 1945. Himmler mainly ignored him and he became estranged to the family.

In 1926, Himmler was appointed as Deputy Gauleiter and Business Manager for NSDAP Gau Lower Bavaria-Upper Pfalz. He held these posts until 1 October 1928. Simultaneously, Himmler became Deputy Gauleiter of Upper Bavaria-Schwabia for one year in 1926. He was appointed as deputy Reich propaganda leader from 12 September 1926 until 27 April 1930. On 1 October 1928, he was assigned as Deputy Gauleiter and Gau Business Manager of NSDAP Gau Lower Bavaria.

Himmler also held the post of Gau-SS-Führer for Lower Bavaria from 1926 until 1927. Josef Berchtold replaced Schreck as leader of the SS, and was himself succeeded in 1927 by Erhard Heiden. On 1 March 1927, Himmler was designated Deputy Reichsführer-SS, a grandiose title which had little meaning at that time as the SS were still subordinate to the parent SA. It was during this period that many of the strict guidelines for SS members and uniform regulations were laid down, under the direction of Heiden and his deputy, Himmler. It is more likely that the perfectionist Himmler had an influential hand in their creation. SS Order No. 4, circulated on 17 January 1928, stated:

> ...all practical duties of the SS will be arranged by Party Member Himmler ... all orders will be signed by either Heiden or Himmler.

At the end of December 1928, Heiden became embroiled in a scandal which resulted in his resignation in the following January. Hitler looked to his deputy to fill the vacancy, and Heinrich Himmler was appointed Reichsführer-SS on 20 January 1929, effective from 6 January 1929.

At that time, the SS numbered less than 300 men. Himmler immediately began a reorganisation, which resulted in the massive black order that we now associate with the core of National Socialist policies. Himmler's first SS adjutant was SS-Mann Hustert.

Himmler was elected as a Reichstag deputy for Upper Bavaria-Schwabia on 14 September 1930. By a Hitler order of 7 November 1930, the SS were subordinated to the larger SA and the Reichsführer-SS was subordinate to the SA-Stabschef. On 10 August 1931, Himmler delegated Heydrich with the responsibility of building a SS security service and the embryonic Sicherheitsdienst (SD) was born. On 25 January 1932, Himmler was appointed head of security for the Brown House in Munich.

By order of the Führer on 15 December 1932, Himmler was authorized to wear the rank insignia of an Obergruppenführer, effective 1 January 1933.

After Hitler seized power in January 1933, Himmler exploited the opportunity to use the economy experts in the Keppler Circle for the benefit of the SS. This group subsequently transformed into the Freundeskreis Reichsführer-SS (*Circle of Friends of the RFSS*). The members annually donated approximately 1 million Reichsmarks to the Reichsführer-SS from 1935 to 1944.

When the NSDAP came to power, Himmler did not gain any major government posts. On 10 March 1933, he was appointed as Police Director in Munich. Five days later he became Political Advisor for police questions in Bavaria in the State Interior Ministry. On 22 March 1933, Himmler opened the concentration camp in Dachau to 5,000 inmates who were considered as a political threat to the State. On 26 March, he became Police President of Nuremberg, and by 1 April he had been appointed as the Political Police Commander in Bavaria. On 10 April, Adolf Wagner made Himmler responsible for all protective custody matters.

Himmler was appointed a NSDAP Reichsleiter in June 1933 and on 10 July 1933, he was selected as a Prussian State Councillor. During the remainder of 1933 and 1934, he took control of numerous state political police organizations, including Lübeck, Hamburg, Württemberg, Baden, Anhalt, Hessen-Darmstadt, Weimar, Thuringia, Bremen, Saxony, Oldenburg and Brunswick. The Himmler-Heydrich partnership eventually controlled all the political police authorities in the Reich—but not in Prussia, where it was controlled by Prussian Minister President Hermann Göring. On 20 April 1934, Prussia also fell to Himmler, when he was created Inspector of the Prussian Secret State Police (*Geheime Staatspolizei—Gestapo*).

Himmler and Heydrich took the opportunity to settle old scores and to obliterate any rivals. During the events which became known as the Röhm Purge, on 30 June–1 July 1934, the two men joined Göring and Körner at Göring's official residence in Berlin to draw up a death list. Himmler was rewarded for his loyalty by Hitler on 20 July 1934, when he made the SS independent of the SA. The Reichsführer-SS was also henceforth authorised to wear his own uniform rank insignia.

In late 1933, at the village of Wewelsburg in Westphalia, Himmler visited the triangular-shaped castle. He was so impressed that he leased the castle for the SS in early 1934. The location was centred in an area of historical and archeological interest. Himmler installed a Burghauptmann (*castle commander*) and created a SS school within the castle walls. It would later be considered by Himmler as the centre of the 'New World'. Around this time he was heavily influenced by Germanic ancestry, and in particular by Karl Wiligut-Weisthor—who many considered as a crank. Himmler founded the Ahnenerbe Society on 1 July 1935, with a brief to research the archaeological and cultural background of the Aryan race. This period also witnessed the introduction of the Nuremberg Race Laws at the Reichsparteitage from 10–16 September 1935, severely restricting the freedom of non-Aryan Germans.

Hedwig Potthast was born in Cologne on 6 February 1912, the daughter of a merchant. In January 1936, she was offered a position as one of Himmler's secretaries. She soon became his principal private secretary and subsequently his lover. Himmler provided her with an apartment in Berlin-Steglitz and also obtained a cash advance from Bormann to build a house near the Königsee, in Bavaria. Hedwig bore Himmler two children: Helge, on 5 February 1942, and Nanette Dorothea, on 3 June 1944. He legalised his paternity of the two illegitimate children on 12 September 1944. After the war, Hedwig shunned publicity and died in 1997.

On 17 June 1936, Himmler was appointed Reichsführer-SS and Chief of the German Police, as a State Secretary in the Reich Ministry of the Interior.

The one-thousandth anniversary of the death by cerebral stroke of the Germanic King Heinrich I, in AD 936, fell on 2 July 1936. Himmler became extremely interested in the dead king. He held a remarkable SS ceremony to mark the anniversary at the site of his vacant tomb, in the castle church at Quedlinburg. Himmler's beliefs in pagan rituals encouraged him to leave the Catholic Church on 9 October 1936, henceforth declaring himself a 'God believer'.

On 29 October 1936, Gebhard Himmler senior died of pancreatic cancer in Munich. Himmler was very close to his parents and the loss of his father hit him quite badly. At the father's funeral in Munich, the SS was very much in evidence.

On 13 November 1937, Himmler created the role of Higher SS and Police Leader (*Höher SS-und Polizei Führer*—HSSPF), based upon existing military districts (Wehrkreise). His HSSPF were answerable to him directly. By this single move he administered total control over the various police districts throughout the Reich and later-occupied territories. It also created potential conflict with the local political commanders, when police and political policy were at odds.

At the beginning of 1938, Himmler's position became very tenuous. His criminal police and SS had uncovered a scandal involving the Reich Minister of War, Werner von Blomberg. His new wife was discovered to have been photographed in pornographic images and von Blomberg resigned as a result. Himmler had also been heavily implicated in the failed plot to discredit the head of the Army, Generaloberst von Fritsch, when accusations of homosexuality were revealed to be false and contrived. For a while, Himmler feared for his relationship with Hitler, but he survived. Hitler's reshuffle appointed von Ribbentrop as Foreign Minister and Hitler himself as supreme commander of the Wehrmacht. The post of Reich War Minister, coveted by Göring, was abolished.

Hitler seized control of Austria in March 1938. Himmler arrived in Vienna on 13 March, ahead of the Führer, to secure the Austrian police and security services. On 17 August, Hitler formally recognized the role of the SS-Verfügungstruppe and the juggernaut which later evolved into the vast Waffen-SS, began its unstoppable journey.

Events on the world stage began to gain momentum and British Prime Minister Neville Chamberlain attended a meeting with Hitler in Bad Godesberg on 22 September 1938. Hitler demanded the annexation of the German Sudetenland from Czechoslovakia. A further meeting was held in the Führerbau in Munich between Germany, France, Great Britain and Italy. Czechoslovakia was not invited. Agreement was reached in the early hours of 30 September 1938 and German troops crossed the frontier and occupied the Sudeten territory on 1 October. Hitler annexed the Sudetenland after the Munich Agreement and immediately toured his new province, accompanied by Himmler.

On 26 October 1938, Himmler ordered the Gestapo to arrest all Jews of Polish origin and to expel them from German territory immediately. The young Jew Herschel Grynszpan was angry at the plight of his parents and on the morning of 7 November, he entered the German embassy in Paris with a revolver, fatally shooting the Third Secretary, Ernst vom Rath. This action was used as an excuse for Krystallnacht (*the night of broken glass*) throughout Germany, during the night of 9–10 November, when hundreds of Jews were detained, abused and assaulted— some fatally—and many Jewish-owned businesses and synagogues were destroyed.

In March 1939, Hitler occupied the remainder of Czechoslovakia and once again visited his conquered territory. Himmler and Heydrich accompanied him to Prague.

On 21 August 1939, Himmler flew south to visit Hitler again at the Berghof. Karl Wolff testified at Nuremberg after the war that he was present with Himmler at the Berghof on 22 August 1939, when Hitler made his famous speech to his Wehrmacht commanders. However, Himmler's diary records that he returned to Berlin on 21 August. (*Wolff may have confused this meeting with another meeting at the Berghof on 16 August 1939*). Civilian attire was ordered by Hitler for both meetings, to maintain an air of secrecy. Molotov and von Ribbentrop signed the non-aggression pact on 23 August 1939, which made war inevitable.

Germany invaded Poland on 1 September 1939 and the subsequent world-changing events are well-documented. As for Himmler, he was initially attached to Army Group North under Generaloberst von Bock. He toured the areas behind the front line (sometimes in the company of Hitler) until returning to Berlin on 26 September.

On 12 September 1939, Himmler was assigned as the permanent deputy and special representative of Wilhelm Frick in matters of Reich administration. On 7 October, he was appointed as Reich Commissioner for the Strengthening of German Nationality (RKF). The same month, he also took on the role of Reich Commissioner for Resettlement. From 24–28 October 1939, Himmler toured the occupied areas of Poland with Friedrich-Wilhelm Krüger. On 30 October, Himmler ordered the deportation of Poles and Jews to the territory of the General Government, an enforced movement of nearly one million people, which set the precedent of Himmler's policy towards minority and Slavic races.

Himmler's war consisted mainly of meetings with his subordinates and with Hitler, countless inspection tours, and the administration of a policy of mass annihilation, initially through his mobile Einstatzgruppen (*special action murder squads*) and then through his concentration-camp and death-camp system.

He met with his senior SS police commanders at Wewelsburg, from 12–15 June 1941, and informed them of their roles in the coming invasion of the Soviet Union. On 12 March 1942, he was appointed as the chief of all Volkssturm (German Home Army) questions. After Heydrich died on 4 June 1942 from wounds received in an assassination attack in Prague, Himmler himself took over the control of the Reichssicherheitshauptamt (RSHA—*Reich Security Main Office*) on 8 June 1942. He remained in this position until appointing Dr Ernst Kaltenbrunner as Heydrich's permanent replacement on 30 January 1943.

A similar situation arose in July 1943, when the chief of the Ordnungspolizei (uniformed police), Kurt Daluege, suffered a heart attack. Himmler took over personal control of the Ordnungspolizei on 30 July 1943, until finding a replacement on 31 August 1943.

Hitler appointed Himmler as head of the A4 rocket project (V1 and V2 rockets) on 21 August 1943. Himmler delegated the responsibility to Dr Hans Kammler.

On 25 August 1943, Hitler removed Wilhelm Frick as Reich Interior Minister and replaced him with Himmler. As Reichs-und Preussischer Minister des Innern, Reichsführer-SS und Chef der Deutschen Polizei, Heinrich Himmler was at the pinnacle of his power.

Himmler gave two important speeches in the Golden Room of the Posen Town Hall on 4 and 6 October 1943. The first was before ninety-two of his gathered SS-Obergruppenführer and SS-Gruppenführer; the second before a conference of Reichsminister, Reichsleiter and Gauleiter. During both speeches, he spoke openly about the tasks allotted to his SS in killing the Jews and other 'inferior' races.

When Claus Graf von Stauffenberg's bomb failed to kill Hitler at the Wolfsschanze on 20 July 1944, Hitler selected his trusted 'Reichsheini' as commander-in-chief of the Replacement Army. He gained his first field command when Hitler tasked him with the command of Army Group Rhine on 2 December 1944, followed by his appointment as commander-in-chief Army Group Vistula on 25 January 1945. Both commands proved to be disasterous, much to the amusement of Martin Bormann.

Not averse to ingratiating himself with the Allies, Himmler attempted to negotiate a separate peace with the western Allies via Count Folke Bernadotte. Himmler negotiated the possible exchange of concentration camp inmates for trucks. He held the mistaken belief that he was important to the Allied occupation force as the man to maintain order after the surrender. The radio announced his independent 'peace feelers' to the world, and Hitler was beside himself with rage. He dismissed Himmler from all his Government and Party posts, and replaced him as Reichsführer-SS with Gauleiter Karl Hanke on 29 April 1945, before killing himself the following day.

Grossadmiral Karl Dönitz was at Himmler's headquarters in Lübeck when he discovered that Himmler had been dismissed by Hitler and that he had himself been appointed as the new Reich President. Himmler ignored his dismissal by Hitler and considered himself of use to the Dönitz administration. Dönitz summoned Himmler to his headquarters at Flensburg and told him directly that his services were no longer required. Not sure of what to do next, Himmler continued to hang around the Dönitz headquarters for several days. On 6 May 1945, Dönitz officially dismissed Himmler from all his former offices as Minister of the Interior, commander-in-chief of the Reserve Army, Reichsführer-SS and Chief of the German Police.

Finally, Himmler left Flensburg and set out with his entourage on their way south to Bavaria by car. At Marne, just north of the Elbe, they abandoned their four cars and proceeded on foot. Himmler shaved off his moustache, donned civilian clothes and wore a patch over his right eye. His two adjutants, Werner Grothmann and Heinz Macher, also wore a mixture of uniform and civilian clothes. He travelled under the false name of Heinrich Hitzinger of the Secret Field Police. Unfortunately for him, the choice of identity Himmler chose was to be his downfall. The Secret Field Police was known to be affiliated to the SD, and this meant automatic arrest.

The group of fifteen arrived at Bremervörde and spent the nights of 18 and 19 May in a farmhouse. On 20 May, two of the group went into town to obtain permits, and Himmler and the others were left behind. Himmler became nervous when the two had not returned by midday and decided that he would leave with Grothmann and Macher and head south. An hour after they left, a British Army lorry pulled up outside the houses and the remainder of the party were all detained.

Himmler (dressed in civilian clothing and a blue raincoat), with Grothmann and Macher (both dressed in civilian trousers with military tunics and rubberised greatcoats without insignia), trudged down lanes and across fields, towards the village of Meinstedt. There, at about 7 p.m. on 21 May, they emerged from a hedge-row and encountered two Russian soldiers, Vasilij Gubarev and Ivan Sidorov. They were both liberated POWs, who were attached to a British security patrol under Corporal Morris of 73rd Assault Regiment. The British were brewing up tea when the Russians stopped the three men and demanded their papers for examination. The papers of one were found to be defective and all three were detained and put into an Army vehicle. They were taken to the camp at Seedorf, where they spent the night in the guardhouse. The next morning, they were taken under escort to the bridge-control point in Bremervörde, where arrest reports were created and initial interrogations carried out.

Himmler's arrest report, dated 22 May and signed by Staff-Sergeant John Hogg, of 1003 Field Security Detachment, based at Westertimke Cage, indicates that 'Hizinger' (*sic., correct Hitzinger*) was formally arrested at 5 p.m. and had been interrogated by Sergeant Arthur Britton of 45 Field Security Section. They spent that night in a mill.

At 7 a.m. on 23 May 1945, the three prisoners left by an Army truck driven by Sergeant Britton and an escort of two guards; the intended destination was the civil internment camp at Westertimke. At around 2 p.m. that day, the three prisoners and their escort made their way to Civilian Interrogation Camp 031 at Kolkhagen, near Barnstedt, finally arriving, after several stops to collect other prisoners, at approximately 6.40 p.m.

At the camp, Himmler removed his eye patch and put on his spectacles, admitting his true identity. He was searched and two small, brass cases were discovered, one containing a glass phial of clear liquid. The other was empty. Himmler then underwent an unsuccessful thorough body search, and was offered a mug of tea and a cheese sandwich in the hope that he would remove the missing phial from his mouth, where it was suspected of being secreted. It remained undiscovered.

Himmler was then taken by car, dressed only in shirt, underpants and socks, wrapped in an Army blanket, to 31a Uelzenerstrasse, in Lüneburg. The house had been requisitioned for the purpose of interrogating high-ranking Germans. Himmler arrived at 10.45 p.m. and was taken into the front-downstairs room, where he was examined by the medical officer, Captain C. J. Wells. He thoroughly searched Himmler's body orifices and between his fingers and toes. He then asked Himmler to open his mouth. Himmler opened his mouth, pulling his head slightly back. Dr. Wells commented later that his teeth were in good condition, with some gold and amalgam fillings. He noticed a small, blue-tit-like object sticking out of the lower inside of his left cheek. The doctor reached into the mouth to sweep out the object. Himmler immediately clamped his jaws on the doctor's fingers and wrenched his hand out of his mouth. He then looked directly at the doctor and crushed the glass phial between his teeth, inhaling deeply. His face immediately blushed and became contorted with pain. His head dropped forward and his body crashed to the wooden floorboards. Desperate attempts lasting about fifteen minutes to extricate the poison, these failed and Himmler was pronounced dead at 11.14 p.m. on 23 May 1945. His body was left *in situ* and various senior officers of the US, British and Russian armies came to view it. An autopsy was performed in the room on the 25 May and a plaster cast was taken of Himmler's facial features. The body was then taken out onto the Lüneburg Heath and unceremoniously buried in an unmarked, secret grave.

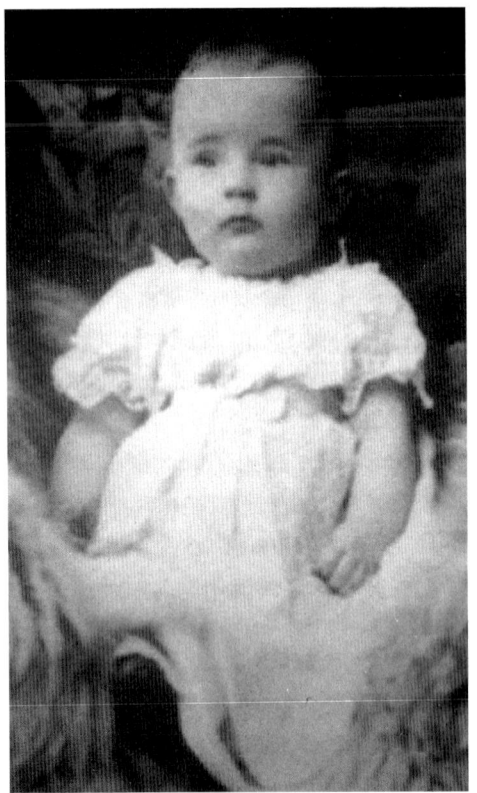

Baby Heinrich Himmler.

Heinrich with his father, a great influence on his personality.

The close-knit Himmler family. Ernst is next to Heinrich and Gebhard is seated right.

In this very early photograph, Himmler stands beside Hitler. The other main characters are Schreck, Pfeffer, Schaub, Esser, Bouhler and Schwarz.

Hitler departs, with Himmler in the rear seat.

Reichsführer-SS Himmler wearing the rank insignia of a SS-Oberführer.

Himmler with his new wife and daughter.

Himmler in a portrait produced for postcards.

Himmler in the Bavarian sunshine with his wife and a friend.

Himmler tenderly places a loving hand on his wife's back.

Himmler having relaxing fun at the top of a mountain in Bavaria.

Left: The SS remained subordinate to the larger SA and Himmler intrigued to step out from the shadow of Röhm.

Below: 30 January 1933, at the Hotel Kaiserhof in Berlin. Hitler's supporters await the news of Hitler's appointment as Reich Chancellor. Left to right: Wagener, Kube, Goebbels, Kerrl, Göring, Himmler, Röhm, Darré and Körner.

Following Röhm's murder, Himmler introduced a unique rank insignia for Reichsführer-SS.

Off-duty at home.

Himmler tries an unconventional method of striking a croquet ball in his garden at Gmund. Marga watches on the right.

The Reichsführer-SS with his wife.

Himmler has just arrived.

The SS group around Hitler at a Reich Party Day in Nuremberg. Present are von dem Bach, Waldeck, Darré, Heydrich, Wolff, Wittje and Himmler.

Above: Lütze and Himmler escort Hitler at the Reichsparteitag.

Left: A quick snack at the airfield.

Göring and Himmler remained bitter rivals in the Nazi hierarchy.

Himmler in Finland. Behind him is his close-protection officer, Sepp Kiermaier.

Birthday greetings from the Führer.

Clockwise from left:

At the Wolfsschanze on Himmler's forty-third birthday, 1943.

A rarely seen profile study of Himmler's features.

A formal Hoffmann portrait of the Reichsführer-SS.

The Reichsführer strikes a pose for the camera.

The military dreamer between Hermann Priess and Otto Baum.

15 August 1941, Himmler visits a POW camp in Minsk. He had just witnessed an execution of partisans and Jews, carried out by Einsatzkommando 8. On his right is Karl Wolff and on his immediate left is Otto Bradfisch. The Heer General appears to be Wilhelm Stubenrauch.

Himmler at the Fuhrer Headquarters. Left to right: Himmler, Buch, Stürtz, Dietrich and Schwarz.

Reichsminister of the Interior and Reichsführer-SS Heinrich Himmler.

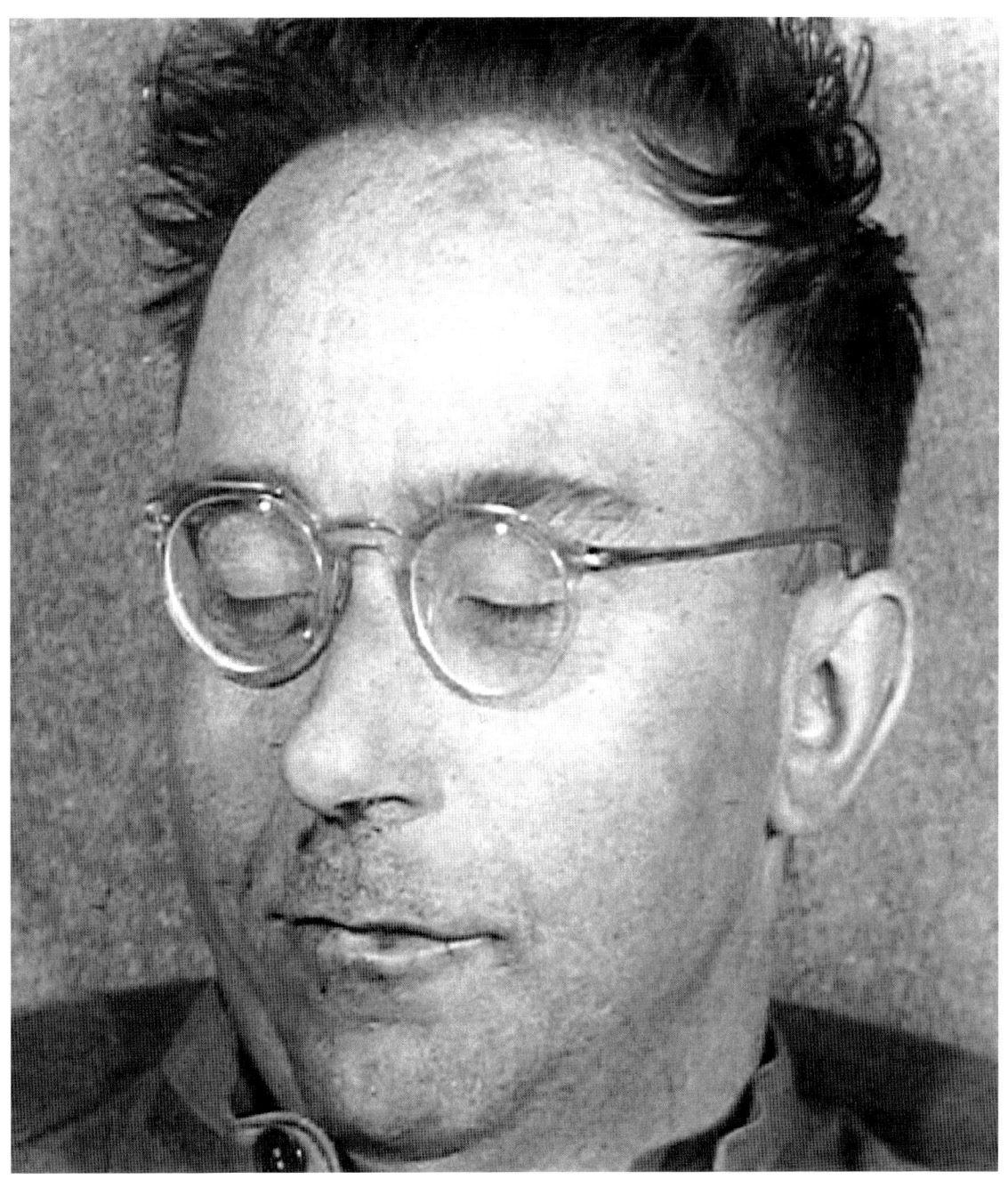

Himmler dead. Note the marks around his mouth where futile attempts were made to resuscitate him.

HERMANN JOHANN MATTHÄUS HÖFLE

I have done nothing to be ashamed of; I am not a criminal.

Hermann Höfle, 5 May 1945

HERMANN HÖFLE was born on 12 September 1898 in Augsburg, the son and only child of the Catholic Bavarian post inspector Johann Höfle (born on 13 February 1869 in Giggingen, died 3 April 1930 in Augsburg) and his wife, Maria (born Kuisel on 13 January 1874 in Holzheim, died of cancer in the summer of 1945).

Hermann attended the elementary school in Augsburg from 1905 until 1909, followed by the St Stephan Gymnasium, from where he matriculated in January 1916. He volunteered for active service and on 31 August 1916, he was posted to the 8th Bavarian Infantry Regiment as a Fahnenjunker.

Höfle trained as an aerial observer before being posted to Air Reconnaissance Squadron 18 of the Bavarian Flying Corps. In 1917, he was promoted to Fahnrich and then, on 1 October 1917, to Leutnant. He was seriously wounded during an aerial combat.

In March 1919, Höfle joined the Freikorps Epp and for a period in 1920 he was an ordnance officer to Hauptmann Ernst Röhm. He later saw service with the Reichskriegsflagge whilst with the 19th Infantry Regiment in Munich. He was one of that unit's officers who refused to terminate their membership. He was promoted to Oberleutnant on 1 April 1925.

Höfle was married on 20 November 1925 to Elizabeth Schaefer (born in Offenbach on 26 September 1898; NSDAP member 89 099; she was also a holder of the Golden Party Badge). They had two daughters: Helga (born on 26 September 1929) and Sigrid (born on 15 April 1934).

In the late 1920s, Höfle studied Spanish and passed an interpreter's course, gaining a profiency certificate in September 1930 and a diploma in Spanish in

1931. The same year he was appointed commander of the 7th Motor Transport Battalion. From 1 May 1932 until 15 June 1933, he was seconded to the Spanish government as a military attaché. During this period, on 1 April, he was promoted to Hauptmann. In June 1933, he was posted to the Military War Academy in Berlin.

On 9 November 1933, Höfle was accorded the rank of SA-Standartenführer, on the staff of the Senior SA Leadership. He became a military advisor to SA-Stabschef Ernst Röhm. He retired from the Army on 31 July 1934 with the rank of Hauptmann der Reserve. With his specialist knowledge of Army transport, he transferred to the NSKK on 1 October 1934 and was attached to the staff of the Corps Leadership of the NSKK. His rank became NSKK-Standartenführer and, at the same time, he took over command of the NSKK-Reichsführerschule. Höfle was promoted to NSKK-Oberführer on 20 April 1935 and to NSKK-Brigadeführer on 30 January 1936.

From January 1937 until May 1937, Höfle was an instructor with the Legion Condor in Spain, where he was promoted to Major der Reserve; he had to return to Germany as a result of ill health.

He joined the NSDAP on 1 May 1937 and was allocated membership number 3 924 970. Returning to duty with the NSKK, he was given command of Motor Brigade Ostmark on 14 June 1937. For one month, from 28 June, he simultaneously commanded Motor Brigade Berlin.

On 6 September 1937, he was promoted to NSKK-Gruppenführer and transferred to Munich as Inspector of Training for the NSKK Leadership. On 30 January 1939, Höfle was promoted to NSKK-Obergruppenführer.

He served for two weeks as a Reserve Major with the 5th Panzer Regiment in May 1939.

Höfle was appointed Leader of the Silesian Motor Brigade on 11 September 1939 and became NSKK Liaison Officer, with Governor General Hans Frank, in Poland the following month. On 2 August 1940, Höfle was appointed to the Peoples' Court. On 28 April 1941, he took command of NSKK-Motor-Obergruppe Ost.

In December 1942, Höfle complained to Himmler during a meeting that the HSSPF Russland-Mitte, Erich von dem Bach, had made derogatory comments about the NSKK in his area, stating that they were inactive in fighting partisans. Himmler ordered von dem Bach to apologise, but the meeting with Höfle had made a deep impression on Himmler, who was impressed with the NSKK man, and he determined to poach him for the SS.

Höfle transferred to the SS on 1 July 1943 as a member of the RFSS personal staff. He was given SS number 463 093 and the rank of SS-Gruppenführer und Generalleutnant der Polizei, with seniority effective from 30 January 1939. He was posted as commander of SS-Oberabschnitt Mitte and HSSPF Mitte on 15 September 1943.

On 20 April 1944, Höfle was promoted to SS-Obergruppenführer und General der Polizei, and on 1 July 1944 he also attained the rank of General der Waffen-SS.

Himmler appointed Höfle as HSSPF in Slovakia on 20 September 1944. In this role he supervised the suppression of the Slovakian revolt in October of that year.

An Army man, Höfle always wrestled with his loyalty to the SS. Himmler came to regret appointing Höfle as HSSPF in Pressburg and had reason to chastise him on several occasions—complaining that Höfle never paid any attention to his orders and ignored his letters. In one letter, Himmler threatened to dismiss Höfle if he continued to ignore his wishes.

Höfle was captured by American troops on 5 May 1945 near Kreuth, in Bavaria, and was interned at Dachau POW Cage 29. He was also held in the witness wing during the Nuremberg International Military Tribunal, but was subsequently handed over to the Czechs, who tried him for war crimes during his tenure as HSSPF. Found guilty, he was hanged in Bratislava on the morning of 9 December 1947, along with Hanns Ludin and Josef Tiso. In his last letter to his family, the day before his death, he wrote:

> ....you have always been my happiness and joy. Remain faithful to God. Know that I am beyond the stars, your adviser and protector forever. I salute you, my three loved ones and my country. I kiss you. I love you always. Your Vati.

His last words on the scaffold were: '*Long live Germany!*'

Although a steadfast National Socialist, evidence suggests that Höfle was an honourable man who believed he had genuinely not committed any crimes, as demonstrated by his parting words to his family upon his arrest. He remained unconvinced and rather lukewarm to the SS cause, but his belief in Hitler never waivered.

Hermann Höfle on his wedding day.

NSKK-Obergruppenführer Höfle.

Höfle in the Generalgovernment, standing behind Kurt Daluege. To the left is Paul Riege and on Daluege's left are Adolf Hühnlein, Herbert Becker and Odilo Globocnik.

SS-Gruppenführer Hermann Höfle.

Nový svet

Obrázkový, spoločenský, kritický týždenník • Bratislava, 18. novembra 1944 • Ročník XIX. • Číslo

(K)

Generál Höfle *veliteľ oslobodzovacieho vojska na Slovensku*

Foto: Archív

SS-Obergruppenführer Hermann Höfle on the front cover of a contemporary Slovakian magazine.

Höfle speaking at the rostrum.

Left to right: Jozef Tiso, Hermann Höfle and Wilhelm Trabandt

Höfle saluting a guard of honour.

Under a massive SS banner, Höfle listens to a speech by Jozef Tiso.

SS-Obergruppenführer Höfle in conversation with a Slovak official.

Höfle speaking. To the far right is Jozef Tiso, the Slovakian First Minister and Catholic priest who was hanged in 1947.

Höfle inspecting the Slovak guard.

Prisoner of war.

Höfle at his post-war trial.

Tiso and Höfle stand accused—both were hanged.

OTTO LUDWIG KARL ADAM HOFMANN

O TTO HOFMANN was born on 16 March 1896 in Innsbruck, the son of a German salesman, Adam Hofmann, and his wife, Hermine (born Rosmanith). At the age of eight years, young Otto went to live with his grandfather and the retired Major became responsible for his upbringing. From 1902 until 1907, Hofmann attended elementary primary school before transferring to the Theresien Gymnasium in Munich, where he remained until 1914.

He enlisted with the 9th Bavarian Field Artillery Regiment on 28 August 1914. He underwent initial training before changing to the 8th Bavarian Reserve Field Artillery Regiment on 11 January 1915. Hofmann was dispatched to the front on 21 January 1915, assigned to the 2nd Battery of this regiment. He was promoted on 5 May 1915 to Gefreiter and on 13 August 1915 to Unteroffizier.

On 22 March 1916, Hofmann became an Officer Applicant and was promoted to Vizewachtmeister on 9 July 1916. By March 1917, he was an Offiziersstellvertreter and was commissioned on 6 March 1917 as a Leutnant der Reserve. He transferred to an Austrian flying unit, Field Flight Company 39, as an observer and liaison officer, on 26 March 1917. He was shot down and captured by the Russians on 30 June 1917, but escaped from Cernowitz on 3 August. He returned to his first regiment as a member of the Ersatz Abteilung (*Replacement Unit*) on 20 September 1917. On 5 December 1917, Hofmann was posted for training with Flight Reserve Unit 1 at the XXV aerial gunnery course, followed by basic pilot training. He was then attached to the 2nd Reserve Flight Section on 25 January 1918 and on 22 March 1918, he attended Flight School number 3. From 1 May 1918, Hofmann was with the Bavarian Reserve Flight Section 2; he finished the war under the command of Flight Section Sonthofen, having transferred on 4 October 1918. He was discharged from Army service on 3 February 1919. From 1 April until 30 September 1919, Hofmann was a member of Freikorps Battery von Axthelm.

Hofmann was married on 16 July 1918 to the daughter of the Nuremberg wine wholesaler Carl Giessing, for whom Hofmann went to work in 1920. He rose to the position of company secretary, but was forced to leave when his marriage ended in divorce in July 1925, with both parties accepting fault for the breakdown of the relationship. The marriage produced a daughter on 24 June 1919.

From 1925 until April 1933, Hofmann was employed as a freelance representative for large wine companies both in Germany and abroad. He remarried on 6 January 1927 to a railway official's daughter, Gertrud Maria Strerath (born on 15 February 1900 in Rheydt-Rheinland). The couple had one daughter, born on 24 June 1929, and they adopted two sons, born 20 April 1935 and 5 June 1936.

Hofmann joined the NSDAP on 1 August 1929, with membership number 145 729. There is some evidence that he had been a member for a short period in 1923, before the NSDAP was banned.

He joined the SS on 1 April 1931 and was allocated SS number 7 646. He became a SS-Mann on 20 May 1931 and was promoted to SS-Truppführer on 30 July 1931, when he was posted the staff of SS-Standarte 3 in Nuremberg. On 17 December 1931, Hofmann was given command of the motorised unit of SS-Standarte 3 and promoted to SS-Sturmführer.

Hofmann was further promoted on 9 September 1932 to SS-Sturmhauptführer. He transferred the same day to the command of the motorised units of SS-Abschnitt IX. During this period, Hofmann fell out with Gauleiter Julius Streicher, who accused him of lacking National Socialist ideals and intriguing against the Nuremberg SA-Standartenführer Philipp Wurzbacher. On 2 November, Hofmann demanded an apology from Streicher, or he stated he would take the matter further. Streicher's adjutant, Hanns König, replied the following day, stating that the Gauleiter did not respond to threats.

The argument did not hinder the progress of Hofmann, who was promoted to SS-Sturmbannführer on 30 January 1933 and made honorary commander of the motorised units of SS-Abschnitt IX. In April 1933, Hofmann became a full-time SS officer. He was transferred on 20 April to SS-Gruppe Süd and was assigned as adjutant to the commander of the Bavarian Auxiliary Political Police.

On 10 August 1933, Hofmann transferred to become staff officer of SS-Gruppe Nordwest, redesignated as SS-Oberabschitt Nordwest on 16 November 1933. He was promoted to SS-Obersturmbannführer on 1 January 1934. He took temporary command of SS-Standarte 21 on 15 March 1934, with the appointment becoming permanent on 20 April 1934, when he was promoted to SS-Standartenführer. Hofmann transferred again on 2 April 1935 to the command of SS-Standarte 28, in Hamburg. He was appointed as temporary commander of SS-Abschnitt XV on 25 May 1935. This post was made permanent on 15 September 1935 when he was promoted to SS-Oberführer.

On 29 March 1936, Hofmann was unsuccessful in his bid to become a Reichstag representative. He tried again in April 1938, but again without success.

His next move was significant; he was posted to the SS-Rasse-und

Siedlungshauptamt on 1 January 1937 and became the main SS representative for SS-Oberabschnitt West in the RuSHA. Hofmann was appointed as chief of the Sippenamt (*Ancestry Office*) in the RuSHA on 1 February 1939, and deputy to the chief of the RuSHA on 17 July. With the outbreak of hostilities in September 1939, Hofmann's boss, Günther Pancke, was occupied with other duties in Poland and consequently Hofmann effectively ran the Hauptamt. He was promoted to SS-Brigadeführer on 10 September 1939 and was appointed as head of the Race Office on 16 December 1939.

Hofmann was confirmed as permanent chief of the RuSHA on 9 July 1940. He was promoted to SS-Gruppenführer on 20 April 1941. In September 1941, Hofmann undertook an inspection tour of Lublin, Kiev, Mogilev and Riga. He was invited by Reinhard Heydrich to attend a working breakfast meeting at the villa Am Grossen Wannsee 56–58, in the Berlin suburb of Wannsee, on 20 January 1942; Hofmann represented the SS-RuSHA at what was to become known as the Wannsee Conference.

He was accorded the rank of Generalleutnant der Waffen-SS on 21 June 1942. On 14 September 1942, Hofmann attended a meeting with Heinrich Himmler concerning the Germanisation of children from Weissruthenien. Hofmann was removed from the RuSHA on 20 April 1943 as a result of difficulties in processing racial examinations due to lack of manpower. He was posted as HSSPF Südwest and chief of SS-Oberabschnitt Südwest, and became head of the Police Branch of the Württemberg Ministry of the Interior. On 21 June 1943, he was promoted to SS-Obergruppenführer und General der Polizei. He received Waffen-SS promotion to General on 1 July 1944.

In September 1943, Himmler had reason to reprimand Hofmann for disloyalty and weak leadership. Again, on 29 November 1944, Himmler wrote to the HSSPF Südwest complaining that he (Hofmann) was not displaying strong leadership in a time of crisis. The local SS and Sipo (*security police*) units in Alsace were panicking and needed taking in hand. Himmler pointed out that he had authorised the shooting of a Sipo leader in Paris under similar circumstances.

Hofmann was captured in May 1945 and was subsequently held at Nuremberg Prison pending trial. He appeared as a defendant in Case VIII (the RuSHA Case) on 20 October 1947. He was found guilty of war crimes and crimes against humanity, and was sentenced to twenty-five years in prison on 10 March 1948. This sentence was reduced on 21 January 1951 to fifteen years' imprisonment, on recommendation of the clemency board. Hofmann served his sentence at Landsberg am Lech Prison and was released on 7 April 1954. Following his release, Hofmann found employment as a business clerk in Württemburg. He died in Bad Mergentheim on 31 December 1982.

Otto Hofmann.

Otto Hofmann (left) attends a local farmers' festival near Detmold. He listens as a local man points out something to Georg Martin.

Hofmann joins in the festivities by running in the egg-and-spoon race in full SS uniform and greatcoat.

Himmler held a presentation on settlements in the East on 20 March 1941 in Berlin. Hofmann (far left) attended as chief of the SS-RuSHA. Others included Meyer, Todt, Greifelt and Hess.

In this photograph Himmler explains the layout on a model. Left to right: Bouhler, Greifelt, Hess, Daluege, Hofmann, Todt and Meyer.

SS-Brigadeführer Otto Hofmann, chief of the SS-Rasse- und Siedlungshauptamt and attendee at the Wannsee Conference on 20 January 1942.

Hofmann (far left) during an inspection visit.

Hofmann salutes.

SS-Gruppenführer Otto Hofmann.

Left: SS-Obergruppenführer Hofmann.

Below: Hofmann (left) with Günther Pancke.

A visit by SS-Obergruppenführer Hofmann with SS-Brigadeführer Hansen.

Hofmann inspecting Italian troops.

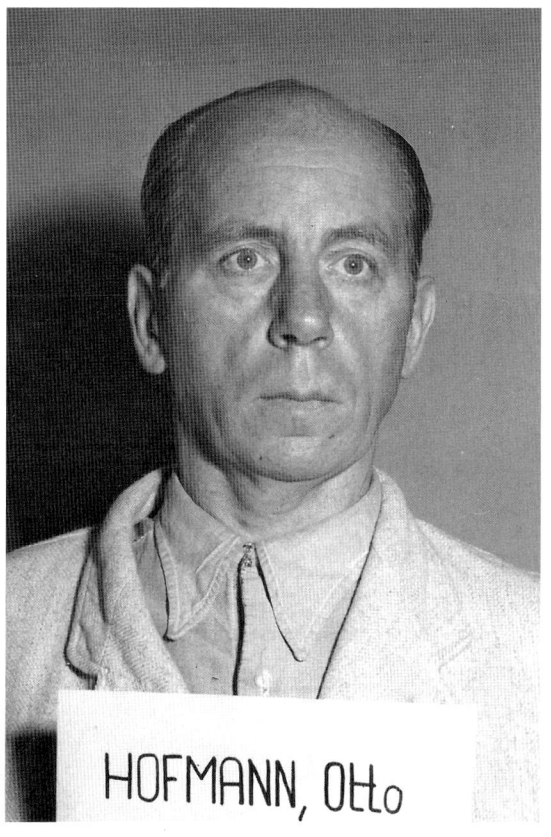

Prisoner of war.

Hofmann dressed for his trial.

Hofmann prepares paperwork for his defence at Nuremberg. On his left is Richard Hildebrandt.

Above: Hofmann pleads at Nuremberg. On his right is Werner Lorenz and on his left is Richard Hildebrandt.

Left: Otto Hofmann in 1954.

Above: Hofmann's eighty-first birthday celebrations; Hofmann conducts the band.

Right: The grave of Otto Hofmann.

FRIEDRICH AUGUST JECKELN

F RIEDRICH JECKELN was born on 2 February 1895 in Hornberg, Baden, the son of a wealthy factory owner. He attended the local elementary primary school, followed by the Oberrealschule in Freiburg am Breisgau until 1913, when he studied engineering at the polytechnic college in Köthen.

He enlisted for one year on 1 October 1913 with the 76th Field Artillery Regiment, based in Freiburg. He saw action with this unit on the Western Front after hostilities began in August 1914. Jeckeln remained with this detachment until March 1915. He was then commissioned as a Leutnant der Reserve and was appointed as adjutant of Fusilier Regiment 40. One year later, he transferred back to his original unit whilst undergoing pilot training. This was before being posted to the 5th Replacement Flight Detachment as a pilot in early 1917.

Jeckeln was married on 13 May 1918 to Charlotte Hirsch—whose father was a Jew, but whose mother was a gentile. Jeckeln and Charlotte were divorced on 15 December 1927, and a bitter relationship developed between the couple. The marriage produced three children (his son Klaus, born on 20 January 1920, was killed in action in 1944). Charlotte complained in a letter to Adolf Hitler in 1932 that her ex-husband was not supporting his family. Hitler passed the complaint to Himmler and Jeckeln promptly blamed everything on his ex-father-in-law, declaring that he was a Jew.

On 20 January 1919, Jeckeln was discharged from military service. (*Note: Some sources state that Jeckeln served with a Freikorps unit, but he clearly states on three separate questionnaires in his SS file that he experienced no Freikorps service*). He found employment in Trappenwalde, working for his father-in-law as an estate administrator. He spent a period from 1922 until 1924 as a member of the Jungdeutschen Ordens (Jungdo—*German Youth Order*). Jeckeln left his job with Herr Hirsch in 1925 and became self-employed as an engineer in Braunschweig.

Jeckeln was married on 4 July 1928 to Annemarie Wienss (born in Danzig on 12 August 1907). The couple had a further five children between 1929 and 1941. Jeckeln also had at least one other daughter, Renate, who was born outside marriage in the Lebensborn programme at Steinhöring, in Bavaria. (*She was the subject of a TV programme in the 1990s, when she revisited certain locations in her father's life*).

Jeckeln joined the NSDAP on 1 October 1929 and was issued Party membership number 163 348. His first Party organisation was the SS. He officially joined in Hannover, on 1 December 1930, as member number 4 367. He was promoted to SS-Sturmbannführer on 31 March 1931, with seniority to date from 15 March 1930. (*Note: the explanation for this to pre-date his entry into the SS is not recorded in his file*). He was the leader of the 1st Sturmbann of the 12th SS-Standarte and was entrusted with forming and running the 17th SS-Standarte simultaneously. Jeckeln was promoted to SS-Standartenführer on 22 June 1931 and gained control of the 12th SS-Standarte. He was posted as Führer on the staff of SS-Abschnitt IV on 20 September 1931 and was promoted to SS-Oberführer.

On 31 July 1932, Jeckeln was elected to the Reichstag as NSDAP representative for Südhannover-Braunschweig.

He was assigned as commander of SS-Gruppe Süd on 30 January 1933, and gained promotion to SS-Gruppenführer on 4 February 1933. He transferred to the command of SS-Gruppe Nordwest on 10 August 1933; this was redesignated as SS-Oberabschnitt Mitte from 1 April 1936.

During 1933, Jeckeln was appointed to several police posts in Braunschweig. He was nominated as Polizeimajor from 1 October 1933 and he took control of the Braunschweig Political Police in April 1934. On 29 November 1933, he was involved in a car accident and suffered burns to his face and hands.

Jeckeln was promoted to SS-Obergruppenführer on 13 September 1936. Himmler appointed him as Keeper of the Blood and Life Law of the SS on 25 January 1938. On 28 June 1938, he was nominated as HSSPF Mitte. During a car journey from Braunschweig to Bremerhaven on 22 August 1938, Jeckeln's vehicle was involved in a collision with a truck. Jeckeln sustained light injuries, but SS-Standartenführer Hans-Georg von Waldow was killed. It is not clear who was driving in this particular accident, but Jeckeln's involvement in several road incidents throughout his career indicates the strong possibility of driving under the influence of alcohol.

On 8 November 1938, Jeckeln organised the anti-Jewish action against the Jewish population of Braunschweig during Reichskristallnacht.

Jeckeln developed a close friendship with the commander of Totenkopf units, Theodor Eicke. For three months from March 1940, he was commander of the 1st Battalion 2nd SS-Totenkopf Infantry Regiment and saw active service in the western campaign. At the same time, Jeckeln was appointed to the Braunschweig State Council.

He was appointed as HSSPF West and commander of SS-Oberabschnitt West on 9 July 1940. On 1 April 1941, he was promoted to General der Polizei. He transferred to the RFSS staff on 1 May 1941, to prepare for the Russian campaign. Himmler appointed him HSSPF South Russia on 29 June 1941.

Several battle groups fell under his jurisdiction as HSSPF. In July 1941, acting on orders from Generalfeldmarschall von Reichenau, Jeckeln commanded the 1st SS Infantry Brigade (Motorised) during a three-day-long operation which claimed the lives of seventy-three Russian troops, 165 communist activists and 1,658 Jews—as subsequently reported to C-in-C 6th Army. A few days later, the same unit was responsible for the execution of 439 Jews in Starokonstantinov. At the end of August 1941, Jeckeln directed the mass execution of 23,600 Jews in Kamenets-Podolsky with the assistance of members of Einsatzgruppe C. This was followed by an action in Berdichev, where 1,303 Jews were shot.

Towards the end of September 1941, a meeting took place between Jeckeln, Generalmajor Eberhard, SS-Brigadeführer Rasch and SS-Standartenführer Blobel. This resulted in the massacre of 33,771 Jews in the ravine of Babi-Yar, at Kiev, during 29 and 30 September 1941. SS-Oberführer Kroeger of Einsatzkommando 6 carried out further orders from Jeckeln to execute another 15,000 Jews on 13 October 1941.

Although Jeckeln was excelling at carrying out the policy of ridding his area of Jews, his methods were attracting criticism. Himmler perceived a tendency of Jeckeln to subordinate himself to the commanders of the Einsatzgruppen. Also, complaints were being received from the Reich Governor of the Ukraine, Erich Koch, that his relationship with Jeckeln was deteriorating to the point of impossibility. Jeckeln's blunt and rude manner had not been well-received. Himmler decided to replace him and proposed a direct exchange between Prützmann and Jeckeln. Consequently, on 1 November 1941, Jeckeln was appointed HSSPF Ostland in Riga and Prützmann became HSSPF Russland-Süd.

Jeckeln immediately set about his new duties with vigour. On 7 November 1941, he directed the shooting of 15,000 victims in Rowno. On 29 November 1941, he commenced the liquidation of the Jewish ghetto in Riga. Jeckeln insisted during his interrogation that this action was on a direct order from Himmler, on or around 10 November, to liquidate all the Jews of the Ostland. On 30 November 1941, a train arrived in Riga carrying the first German Jews from Berlin. Jeckeln ordered that they be taken to the Rumboli Forest, just outside Riga, and executed immediately; 1,035 were shot in about forty-five minutes, just after 8 a.m., by the Einsatzkommando under Rudolf Lange. By 8 December 1941, a total of 26,000 Jews from the Riga Ghetto had been shot or gassed using mobile gassing vans. Rudolf Lange had overseen the killing operation, and it was for this reason that Heydrich included him in the list of invites for the conference in Wannsee on 20 January 1942, in order that he might impart his experience.

On 12 December 1941, Jeckeln was appointed commander of SS-Oberabschnitt Ostland. He commanded Polizei Kampfgruppe Jeckeln from 17 February 1942 until 13 August 1942, subordinate to Army Group North. In June 1942, he was wounded in action. On 7 August 1942, Himmler ordered that the defeat of local partisans was fundamental to the victory in Weissruthenien, and he directed that anti-partisan actions would be under the command of Jeckeln. From 22 August until 21 September 1942, Jeckeln carried out Action Swamp Fever. This was followed by various other actions carried out under Jeckeln's orders during the following year. He commanded a number of battle groups carrying the name Jeckeln until he was given substantial command in the final months of the war.

On 22 February 1944, Jeckeln was appointed HSSPF Ostland and Russland-Nord in Riga. He gained Waffen-SS General rank on 1 July 1944. From 22 September 1944 until 18 January 1945, Jeckeln was also HSSPF Belgien und Nordfrankreich—but in name only. His home was destroyed in an Allied air raid on 15 October 1944 and he lost all his belongings.

With the Red Army advancing, Jeckeln withdrew, and was assigned as commander of all Reserve Units within the area of HSSPF Südost from 18 January 1945. On 15 February 1945, he took command of the 5th SS-Volunteer Mountain Corps. He held this command until he was captured near Halbe on 28 April 1945.

Friedrich Jeckeln was one of the most highly decorated SS officers who held a Higher SS and Police Leader post. He won the Knights Cross of the Iron Cross, the Oakleaves to the Knights Cross of the Iron Cross (*as 802nd recipient*) and the German Cross in Gold. Probably as a result of his direct connections to the final solution in his capacity as HSSPF, many contemporary historians refer to him as an incompetent military leader. His long list of military decorations for leadership and bravery tends to disagree with this synopsis. It has been suggested that he relied heavily on his subordinates, but evidence of such an argument is equally balanced by his obvious successes in operations where he took personal command.

His responsibility of the massacre of partisans, communists and Jews, and his overall responsibility as HSSPF for crimes committed in the Riga Ghetto cannot be denied; his own admissions are recorded both in print and on film. To answer for these crimes, he was tried in Riga on 26 January 1946, along with six Wehrmacht generals; he was convicted on the morning of 3 February 1946. The large audience greeted the verdict of guilty against all the defendants with applause. That same afternoon, the guilty were taken out to the site of the ghetto and placed on the backs of lorries, under wooden beams, with a noose about their necks. The lorries then drove off, leaving their victims to be strangled, hanging from the beams.

Jeckeln (left) and Sepp Dietrich during the period of the ban on political uniforms.

SS-Gruppenführer Jeckeln.

Himmler at the SS-Junkerschule Braunschweig. Behind him are Klagges, Jeckeln and Wolff.

The 1,000th anniversary of the death of King Heinrich I in Quedlinburg, 1936. Himmler salutes the empty tomb while Wolff, Heydrich, Heissmeyer and Jeckeln look on.

SS-Obergruppenführer Jeckeln.

Hitler visiting a new housing development. Schreck drives with Krause, Wagner, Jeckeln and Brückner as passengers.

Jeckeln at a street parade of police officers.

Jeckeln (left) attended the wedding of Bruno Gesche, Hitler's bodyguard unit commander. SS-Oberführer Unger is on the right.

SS-Obergruppenführer Friedrich Jeckeln.

Awaiting the arrival of a parade, Jeckeln stands between Heissmeyer (left) and Berkelmann (right).

Jeckeln during anti-partisan operations.

Jeckeln personally supervised some actions carried out by Einsatzkommandos.

Jeckeln was posted to Riga as HSSPF and ruthlessly carried out the racial policies of the Reichsführer-SS.

Left and right: SS-Obergruppenführer Jeckeln.

Himmler had total faith in his loyal HSSPF in Riga.

Jeckeln gained a reputation as a strong and brutal SS leader.

Jeckeln at Riga airfield, awaiting the arrival of Himmler.

Himmler was pleased with Jeckeln's dedication to duty in Riga.

The Latvian General Bangerskis and Jeckeln, talking to Artur Silgalis.

Jeckeln photographed at Feldkommandostelle Hochwald.

Jeckeln stands trial in Riga.

Jeckeln was publicly hanged off the back of a lorry in Riga on 3 February 1946.

HUGO JURY

HUGO JURY was born in Mährisch-Rothmühl on 13 July 1887, the son of Roman Catholic senior teacher Hugo Jury and his wife, Julia. His brother, Richard Jury (born on 4 September 1889 in Mährisch-Rothmühl), later joined the SS and rose to a senior position in the NSDAP. Hugo Junior attended the local elementary school from 1893 until 1897, before moving on to the Gymnasium in Mährisch-Trübenau, from where he matriculated in 1905. He then attended the faculty of medicine at the Karl Ferdinand University in Prague from 1905 until 1911. During this time he volunteered for military service for one year, in 1908, as a military medical practioner. He was discharged from military service when he contracted tuberculosis.

In 1912, Jury obtained employment as a ship doctor with the Austrian Lloyd shipping line. He was appointed as public health doctor in Franconia on 15 January 1913 and retained this position until 1919, gaining his medical doctorate on 31 October 1913. During the First World War, he was called up for service as a civilian doctor at a military hospital in Petrinje. He was also responsible for three officers' prisoner-of-war camps at Pucherstuben, Wienerbrück and Mitterbach. From 15 January 1919, he was a lung expert in St Pölten, specialising in tuberculosis.

Jury was married on 17 January 1913 to Karoline Roppert (born in Karbitz on 24 May 1891). They had one daughter, born on 9 January 1914, and one son, born on 9 April 1918.

From 1927 until 1931, Jury was a member of the Austrian Heimwehr. He joined the NSDAP on 15 February 1931, and held Party card number 410 338 as a member (and eventual leader) of NSDAP Ortsgruppe St Pölten. In 1932, he was the NSDAP leader on the municipal council. In 1934, Jury was appointed as Kreisleiter for Upper Wiener Wald, and, as a result of his illegal NSDAP affiliation, he was interned with Gauleiter Josef Leopold from 8 January 1934 until 1935 in 'prevention' camps, including the infamous camp at Wöllersdorf. Following his release in 1935, Jury was appointed as Organisation Leader on the Leadership Council of the NSDAP in Austria. He was re-arrested early in 1936 and again interned at Lager Wöllersdorf, until his release on 30 July 1936.

Jury was the deputy leader of the illegal NSDAP in Austria from 11 July 1936 until 13 March 1938. On 20 February 1937, he was elected as chairman of the Committee of Seven for the Absorbtion of Austria into the Greater Reich. On 22 February 1938, he was appointed State Councillor and deputy to Arthur Seyss-Inquart, the Austrian Interior Minister.

Jury joined the SS on 12 March 1938 as a SS-Sturmbannführer, holding membership number 292 777. He was attached to SS-Oberabschnitt Donau.

From 13 March 1938, Jury was chosen as Austrian Minister for Social Affairs and he held this position for two months. He was elected to the Reichstag on 10 April 1938. He was promoted to SS-Standartenführer on 20 April 1938. On 21 May 1938, Hitler appointed Jury as Gauleiter of Niederdonau and three days later, he was designated Landeshauptmann of Lower Austria. Jury was appointed DRK-Generalhauptführer in the German Red Cross on 28 May 1938 and became the area commander for Wien on 16 June.

He was promoted to SS-Oberführer on 25 July 1938, and to SS-Brigadeführer on 30 January 1939. He was appointed as Reich Defence Commissioner for Lower Austria on 22 September 1939.

On 30 January 1940, he was selected to head the Party Liaison Office in the Protectorate of Böhmen Mähren. He was appointed as Reichsstatthalter of Niederdonau on 15 March 1940. Jury was promoted to SS-Gruppenführer on 9 November 1940. On 1 January 1942, he transferred to the staff of the RFSS and he received his final promotion, to SS-Obergruppenführer, on 21 June 1943.

On 23 March 1945, Jury attended a conference with other Austrian NSDAP leaders and Franz Ziereis, the commandant at Mauthausen, at which Himmler ordered the evacuation of all camp inmates from various camps in Austria. He directed that no prisoners were to fall into Allied hands. Hundreds died in the ensuing death marches from the camps. On 15 April 1945, Jury ordered the execution of forty-four prisoners from Vienna at the Stein Jail. They were individually killed by a single shot to the nape of the neck. Jury continued to call for armed resistance and led a Volkssturm unit during the final days of the fighting.

Hugo Jury was a committed National Socialist, and decided to take his own life at the end of the war. During the night of 8–9 May 1945, in a house at Gerungserstrasse 10 in Zwettl, he shot himself in the head with his pistol.

Hugo Jury was interned by the Austrian government for his political beliefs and for agitating. Here, he is photographed at the Wöllersdorf camp.

Jury was a member of the NSDAP from 1931 and held senior political posts in Austrian politics.

Left and right: Gauleiter Jury.

Foto : O. Stibor, Brünn

Die deutschen Menschen erfühlen vielleicht mehr als sie erkennen, daß das Schicksal der heutigen Generation eine unendlich beglückende, weil grandiose und einmalige Aufgabe gestellt hat: Den alten Sehnsuchtstraum der besten Deutschen aller Generationen, den Traum vom großen heiligen deutschen Reich zu verwirklichen. Alle guten und starken Kräfte sind am Werke. Die Tatsache aber, daß hunderttausende deutscher Menschen auf den Ruf des Führers in ein Vaterland zurückkehrten, das sie zum Großteil gar nicht kannten, ist ein Beweis dafür, daß sich etwas Einmaliges in der Geschichte des deutschen Volkes vollzogen hat!

Above: Gauleiter Jury stands far right.

Left: A page from a NSDAP calendar.

A pencil sketch of SS-Sturmbannführer Hugo Jury.

A portrait of Jury at his desk.

A smiling Gauleiter Jury (second from left) with young admirers.

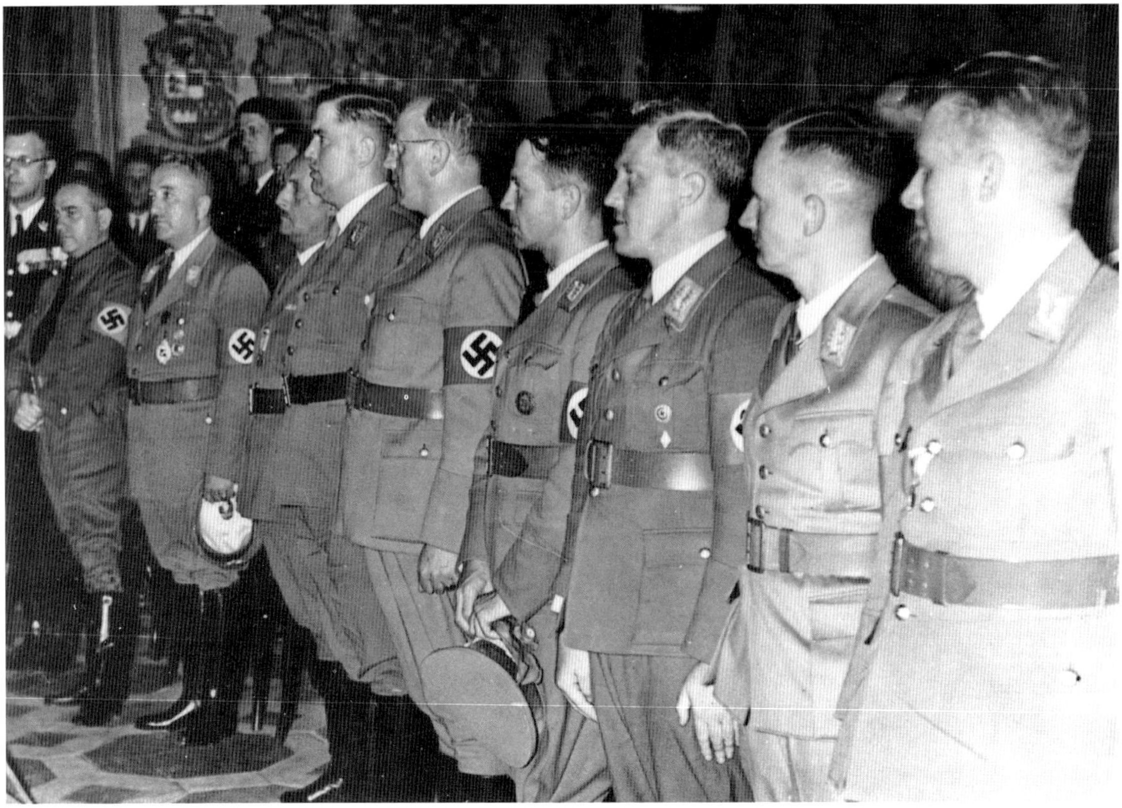

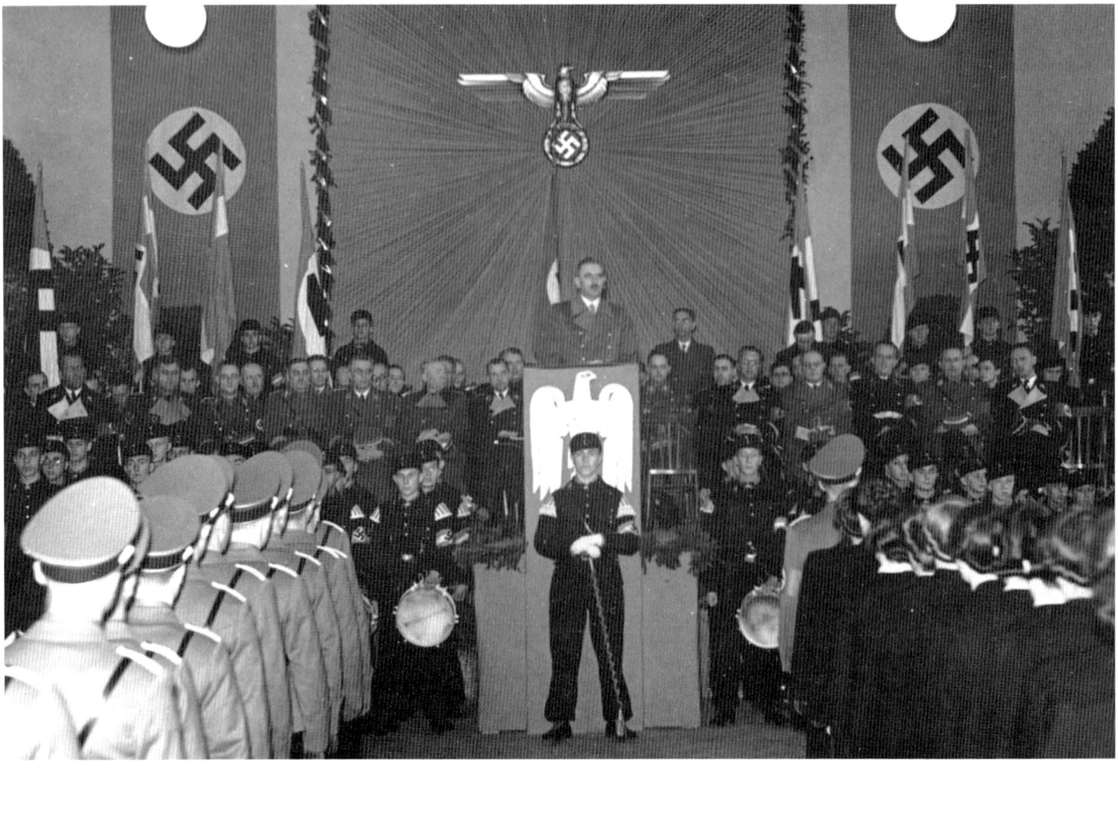

SS-Gruppenführer Jury (left) visiting Heydrich and Henlein in Prague.

Opposite page:

Above: The Austrian Gauleiter. Left to right: Seyss-Inquart, Bürckel, Ley, Klausner, Hofer, Jury, Uiberreither, Eigruber, Rainer and Globocnik.

Below: Bernhard Rust speaks. Behind him are numerous NSDAP senior officials, including (from the left) Kaltenbrunner, Heissmeyer, Seyss-Inquart, Jury and Wächter.

Gauleiter Jury emerges from behind Bruno Streckenbach to take his place in the guard of honour for Heydrich's coffin.

Hradcany Castle, Prague, 7 June 1942. Jury is behind Streckenbach in the guard of honour.

The funeral cortege outside the castle gates, preparing to move off.

SS-Obergruppenführer Hugo Jury with Reichsprotektor Wilhelm Frick.

Opposite page:

Above: SS-Obergruppenführer Jury seated beside Karl Hermann Frank, Wilhelm Frick, and Hans Lammers.

Below: SS-Obergruppenführer Jury with his wife, talking to Friedrich Rainer.

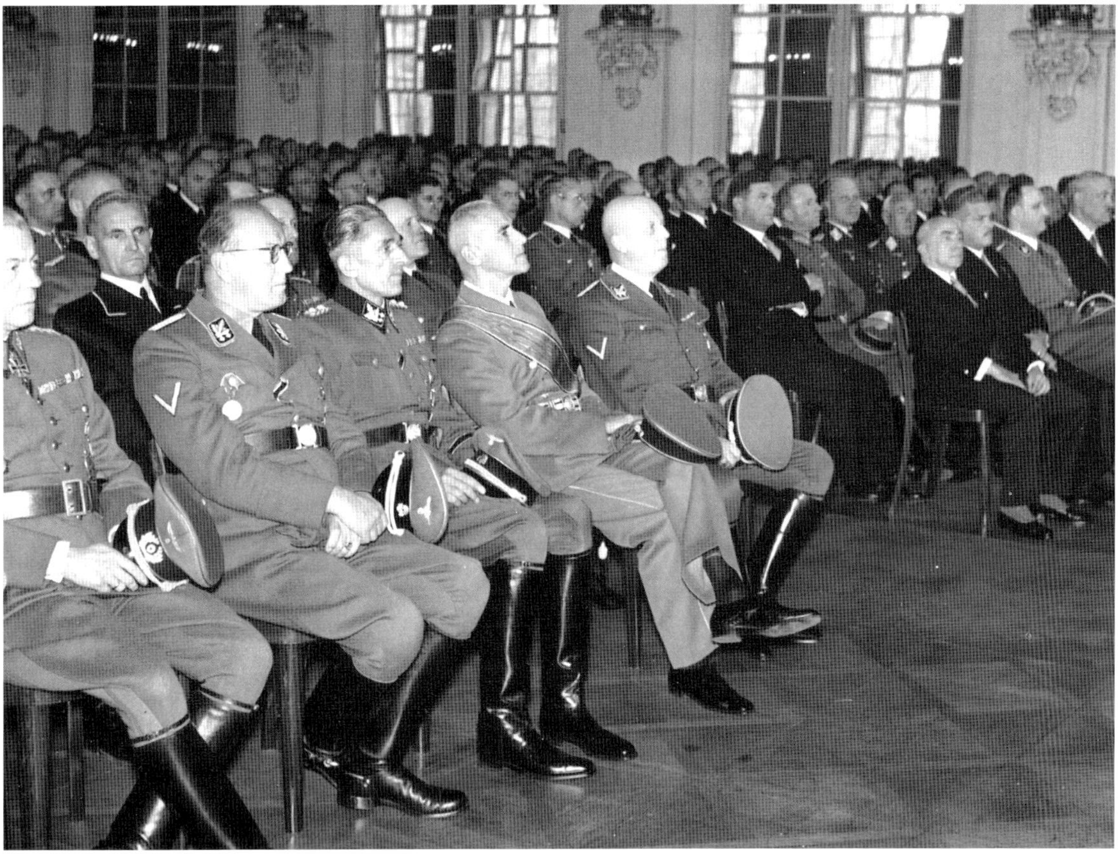

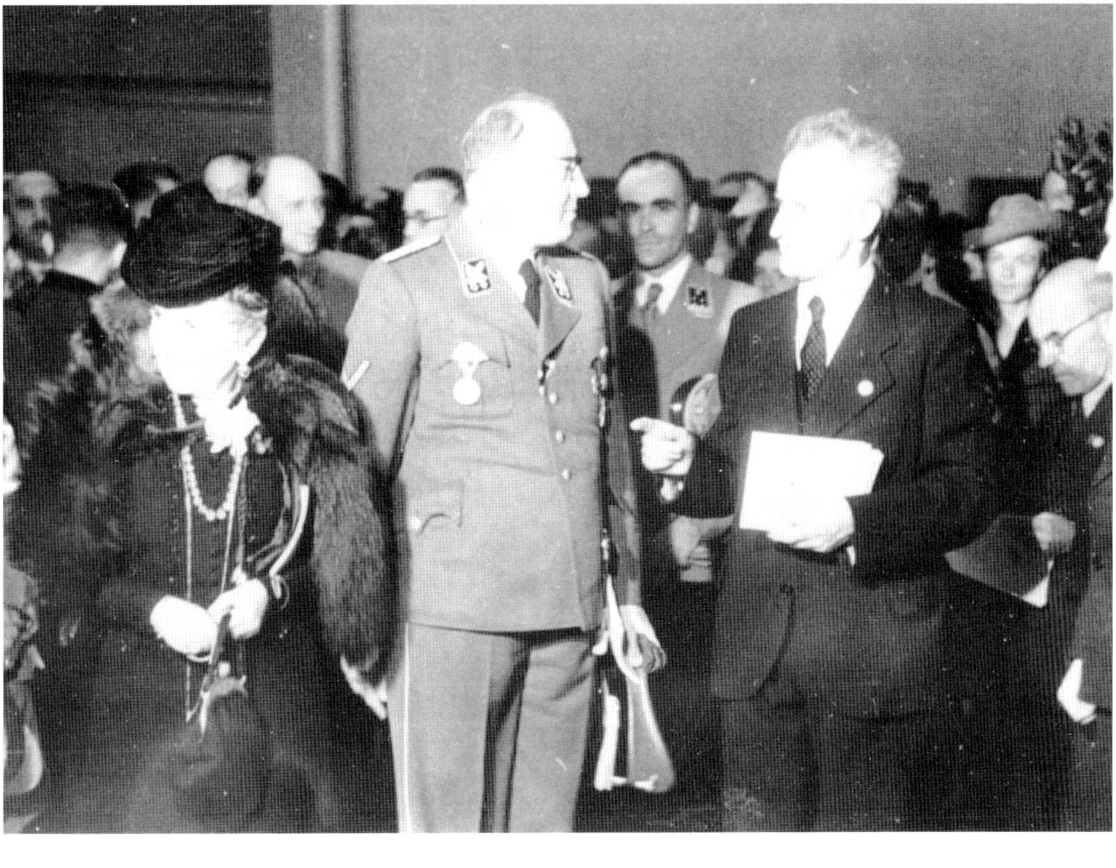

A candid photograph of Jury wearing his SS uniform.

A newspaper photograph of Jury and Frank.

Hugo Jury lies dead in his SS uniform, having just shot himself.

HANS GUSTAV GOTTLOB JÜTTNER

Hᴀɴs Jüᴛᴛɴᴇʀ was born on 2 March 1894 in Schmiegel, Posen. His parents, the teacher and vice-principal Paul Robert Jüttner (born on 8 October 1864 in Gross-Kauer) and Hedwig Ottilie Christine Jüttner (born Hoffmann in Schmiegel on 3 April 1870) were evangelists. After his initial education at elementary school in Krotoschin, from 1900, he attended the local Wilhelms-Gymnasium. He left school in 1913 and found work as a bank apprentice until August 1914.

Jüttner volunteered for war service on 7 August 1914, enlisting with Fusilier Regiment 37. He first saw action on 29 September 1914. He was commissioned as a Leutnant der Reserve on 14 May 1915 and joined the 264th Reserve Regiment at the front. He was shot in the upper thigh on 18 June 1915 and spent some months recovering. From 18 November until 8 December that year, he was at the Military Education Establishment at Altengrabow. On 22 January 1916, he was posted to the NCO School at Weissenfels as an instructor. On 11 November 1916, he transferred to the NCO School at Wetzlar. Jüttner returned to an active service unit on 18 April 1917, when he was posted to Ersatz-Abteilung 153.

He underwent machine-gun training at Torgau from 1–16 May 1917. Later that summer, on 26 July 1917, he was posted to Turkey. On 19 August, he was assigned the command of the Ottoman Empire 22nd Motorised Column. From 6–22 July 1918, he was the column's legal officer and deputy adjutant for the Motorised Columns in Iraq. On 26 October 1918, he became adjutant for Motorised Columns in Iraq and commander of Motorised Column Jüttner.

He returned to Germany after the armistice, disembarking from the steamship Kerkyra in Wilhelmshaven on 23 March 1919. On 3 May 1919, he was assigned command of Motor Staff Schneidemühl, the Motor Depot Schneidemühl and the Motorised Border Troops East. He was commander of the Motorised Replacement Battalion 2 from 1 September 1919. At his own request, Jüttner was discharged from the Army on 6 January 1920 with the rank of Oberleutnant der Reserve.

Jüttner was married on 24 March 1923 to Marga Fischer (born in Königsberg on 13 June 1894). She died at 12.15 p.m. on 8 December 1943 and was buried on 10 December at the Berlin-Dahlemer Waldfriedhof. They had one foster child.

From 1920 until 1929, Jüttner found employment in the business world and in 1929, he began a period of self-employment. He continued his association with the Army, being posted as the company commander for Fortress Battalion Breslau in 1930. During the winter of 1930–1931, he ran tactical training courses for the battalion under General von Sichard. Until February 1933, he was responsible for battalion training. That month, he became commander for the battalion machine-gun section.

Jüttner joined the NSDAP on 1 February 1931 and was allocated Party membership number 541 163. He joined the SA the same day as becoming instructor with SA-Standarte 11 and was commissioned as SA-Sturmführer. He later became staff officer of SA-Brigade 20 and was promoted to SA-Sturmbannführer on 15 April 1933.

In April 1934, he was the SA senior instructor at Breslau in SA Regional Command VIII. On 1 July 1934, Jüttner was assigned to SA-Gruppe Schlesien. On 15 October 1934, he transferred as staff officer and referent (*consultant advisor*) of SA Area Command VII in Munich, remaining in this post until he was discharged from the SA on 15 April 1935.

Jüttner enrolled in the SS on 17 May 1935 as SS-Hauptsturmführer and was allocated SS number 264 497. He was initially placed in charge of the 6th Sturm/ II Sturmbann of SS-Standarte 'Deutschland'. On 3 October 1935, he was appointed adjutant of the Standarte.

On 1 April 1936, he transferred to the staff of the SS-VT Inspectorate in the SS-Hauptamt. He was promoted to SS-Sturmbannführer on 13 September 1936. Jüttner became the SS-Verfügungstruppe (SS-VT) Inspectorate Chief of Staff in October 1937.

He was promoted to SS-Obersturmbannführer on 9 November 1937, and to SS-Standartenführer on 30 January 1939. He was chief of Inspectorate (E) of the SS-VT and Inspector of SS-Totenkopfverbände from September 1939. On promotion to SS-Oberführer on 1 December 1939, he was assigned to head the Operations Office of the SS-VT.

Jüttner was promoted to SS-Brigadeführer on 20 April 1940 and gained Waffen-SS rank on 3 May 1940, when he was granted the rank of Generalmajor der Waffen-SS. On 11 May 1940, he was appointed Chief of Staff of the Waffen-SS Command in the SS-Hauptamt. On 15 August 1940, he was designated as official deputy to the chief of the SS-Führungshauptamt. On 23 October 1940, Jüttner was also appointed as Chief of Amt VI (Allgemeine-SS) in the SS-Führungshauptamt.

On 16 April 1941, Jüttner participated in a meeting in Graz between Himmler, Daluege, Wolff, Heydrich and the General Quartermaster of the Army, Eduard Wagner. Guidelines were drawn up over the responsibilities of Waffen-SS, Security

Police and the Army in the forthcoming invasion of Russia. Four days later, Jüttner was appointed Chief of Staff of the SS Operational Headquarters. He was further promoted to SS-Gruppenführer and Generalleutnant der Waffen-SS on 28 April 1941.

As nominal head of the SS-Führungshauptamt, Jüttner held a position of extreme power and his manner of administering his department often brought him into conflict with other SS leaders. In November 1942, Maximilian von Herff complained to Karl Wolff about the attitude of Jüttner and some of his associates in the SS-Führungshaupamt—namely von Jena, Petri and Hansen. He complained that they did not have the best interests of the SS at heart, and were only interested in military matters. Subsequently, the SS-Führungshauptamt was re-organised and on 30 January 1943, Jüttner was appointed as chief of the SS-Führungshauptamt.

Jüttner was promoted to SS-Obergruppenführer and General der Waffen-SS on 21 June 1943. On 21 July 1944, he was appointed Chief of Staff to the Commander-in-Chief of the Replacement Army. On 16 August 1944, Jüttner was nominated as a member of the Control Board under the HSSPF Hungary. For his organisational talents towards war work, he was awarded the Knights Cross of the War Service Cross with Swords.

The British arrested Jüttner in Arenholz on 17 May 1945 and he was interned. He appeared as a witness in the Nuremberg International Military Tribunal. On 4 March 1948, he was sentenced to ten years in prison by a de-Nazification court, but this was subsequently reduced to four years on appeal. Jüttner was released in 1950. In 1961, he bought a sanatorium in Bad Tölz. He was an active member and supporter of HIAG, the Waffen-SS veterans' organisation, and he appeared as a defence witness for Karl Wolff during his trial in September 1964. After the war Jüttner married Frau Herta Martha Jüttner (born Winter, died on 7 March 1971 in Reit im Winkl). Hans Jüttner died on 24 May 1965 in Bonn.

Left and right: SA-Sturmbannführer Jüttner.

SS-Sturmbannführer Jüttner; a photograph from his SS file.

Jüttner rose swiftly up the promotion ladder. Here he is a SS-Brigadeführer.

Clockwise from right:

Himmler was quick to recognise Jüttner's skills and seize upon them. This photograph shows Jüttner talking tactics with General Hoepner.

Jüttner during an inspection visit.

SS-Gruppenführer Hans Jüttner.

Jüttner is about to begin an inspection of this SS facility. To the far left is Julian Scherner.

Note the Turkish Gallipoli Star on Jüttner's right breast pocket.

Jüttner's inspection is over for this particular barrack.

Jüttner quizzes this Totenkopf man. Julian Scherner is in the background.

Another inspection and more questions.

A look inside a classroom.

Jüttner watching a machine-gun demonstration.

'Any complaints?'.

The Gruppenführer listens in on the radio set.

Jüttner with Ernst Robert Grawitz.

A signed photograph of SS-Gruppenführer Jüttner.

Jüttner speaking in Prague.

SS-Gruppenführer Hans Jüttner.

Jüttner in conversation with Kurt Daluege in Prague.

SS-Obergruppenführer Jüttner.

The SS-Obergruppenführer at Feldkommandostelle Hochwald.   Jüttner visits the front.

Jüttner with Karl Maria Demelhuber (left).

Left to right: Friedrich Christiansen, Jüttner and Demelhuber.

Jüttner at Hitler's headquarters, July/August 1944. Note that Hitler shakes hands with his left arm as a result of his injury to his right elbow in von Stauffenberg's bomb blast. Himmler is to the right.

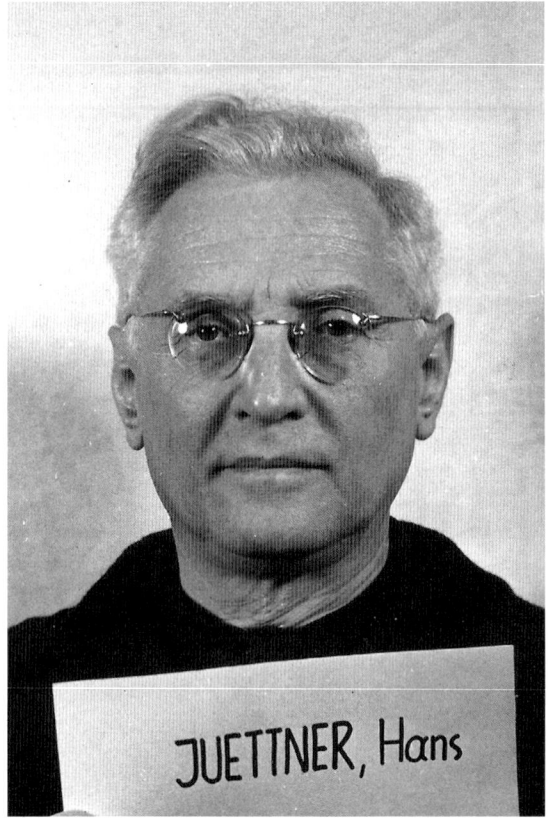

JUETTNER, Hans

HEDWIG JÜTTNER
*3.4.1870 +6.9.1951
HANS JÜTTNER
GENERAL A.D.
*2.3.1894 +24.5.1965
GRETE TILLWICHS
GEB. JÜTTNER
*14.7.1890 +19.3.1969
IN MEMORIAM
PAUL JÜTTNER
*8.10.1864 +3.1.1944
HUGO TILLWICHS

Clockwise from top left:

A photograph issued to mark the award of the Knight's Cross of the War Service Cross with Swords. The award in this particular image has been subsequently added.

Prisoner of war.

Jüttner's gravestone.

COMPARISON OF OFFICER RANKS

SS	GERMAN ARMY	BRITISH ARMY
Reichsführer	Generalfeldmarschall	Field Marshal
Oberst-Gruppenführer	Generaloberst	No equivalent
Obergruppenführer	General	General
Gruppenführer	Generalleutnant	Lieutenant General
Brigadeführer	Generalmajor	Major General
Oberführer	No equivalent	No equivalent
Standartenführer	Oberst	Colonel
Obersturmbannführer	Oberstleutnant	Lieutenant Colonel
Sturmbannführer	Major	Major
Hauptsturmführer	Hauptmann	Captain
Obersturmführer	Oberleutnant	Lieutenant
Untersturmführer	Leutnant	Second Lieutenant

BIBLIOGRAPHY

Agoston, *Blunder! How the US Gave away Nazi Supersecrets to Russia*, (Kimber & Co. 1985).

Allen, *Oswald Pohl: Chef der SS-Wirtschaftsunternehmen; in* R. Smelser (Ed.): *Die SS-Elite unter dem Totenkopf: 30 Lebensläufe* pp. 394-407, (Ferdinand Schöninger 2000).

Black, *Ernst Kaltenbrunner, Ideological Soldier of the Third Reich* (Princeton University Press 1984).

Deschner, *Heydrich, The Pursuit of Total Power*, (Orbis 1991).

Dornberg, *The Putsch That Failed*, (Weidenfeld & Nicholson 1982).

Ford, *German Secret Weapons Blueprint For Mars*, (Pan/Ballantine 1969).

Frank, *Mein Leben für Böhmen*, (Arndt 1994).

Frischauer, *Himmler*, (Odhams Press 1953).

Fröbe in Smelser/Syring, *Die SS—Elite unter dem Totenkopf*, (Schöningh 2000).

Hamann, *Winifred Wagner*, (Harcourt Trade 2005).

Höffkes, *Hitlers politische Generale: Die Gauleiter des Dritten Reiches*, (Grabert-Verlag 1986).

Hutton, *Hess, The Man and His Mission*, (David Bruce and Watson 1970).

Kershaw, *The End: The Defiance and Destruction of Hitler's Germany, 1944-1945*, (Penguin, 2011).

Koch (Ed.), *Himmlers Graue Emminenz: Oswald Pohl und das Wirtschaftsverwaltungshauptamt der SS,* (Facta Oblita 1988).

Koop, *Himmlers letztes Aufgebot—Die NS-Organisation Werewolf*, (Böhlau 2008).

Lang, *Bormann, The Man Who Manipulated Hitler*, (Book Club Associates 1979).

Lilla, Döring, Martin & Schulz, *Statisten in Uniform. Die Mitglieder des Reichstags 1933-1945*, (Droste Verlag 2004).

Löbsack, *Danzigs Gauleiter Albert Forster*, (Hanseatische Verlagsanstalt 1934).

Matlok, *Dänemark in Hitlers Hand*, (Husum Verlag 1988).

Meissner, *Magda Goebbels*, (Sidgwick and Jackson 1980).

Miller, Schulz, *Gauleiter, vol. 1*, (Bender 2012).

Neufeld, *The Rocket and the Reich*, (Harvard 1995).

Padfield, *Hess, the Führer's Disciple*, (Papermac 1993).

Padfield, *Himmler, Reichsführer SS*; (Papermac 1991).

Peterson, *The Limits of Hitler's Power*, (Princeton University Press 1969).

Pohl, *Credo, Mein Weg zu Gott*, (Alois Girnth, Landshut 1950).

Preradovich, *Die Generale der Waffen SS*, (Vowinckel 1985).

Rainer, *My Internment and Testimony at the Nuremberg War Crimes Trial*

Reischle, *Reichsbauernführer Darré*, 1933.

Rose, *Julius Schaub—In Hitlers Schatten*.

Sauer, *Wilhelm Murr. Hitlers Statthalter in Württemberg*, (Silberburg Verlag 1998).

Schenk, *Hitlers Mann in Danzig*, (Dietz 2000).

Schmitz-Köster, *Kind L 364: Eine Lebensborn-Familiengeschichte*, (Rowohlt Berlin 2007).

Schneider, *Verleihung Genehmigt!*, (Bender 1993).

Scholtyseck, *Die Führer der Provinz: NS-Biographien aus Baden und Württemberg*, (Univ. Verlag 1999).

Smelser, Syring, Zitelmann, *Die braune Elite II*, (Wissenschaftliche Buchgesellschaft 1993).

Sydnor, *Soldiers of Destruction*, (Princeton University Press 1977).

Tiscenko, *Strawberries with the Führer*, (Shoal Bay Press 2000).

Wahl, *Aus Liebe zu Deutschland*, (Arndt 1997).

Weiss, *Biographisches Lexikon zum Dritten Reich*, (Fischer 1998).

Whiting, *The Hunt For Martin Bormann*, (Leo Cooper 1996).

Williams, *Heydrich—The Biography (in two volumes)*, (Ulric Publishing 2001 & 2003).

Yerger, *Waffen SS Commanders*, (Schiffer 1998).

Yerger, *Waffen-SS Commanders*, (Schiffer 1997).

Das Deutsche Führerlexikon 1934-1935, (Stollberg).

Der Deutsch Reichstag 1936, (Decker's Verlag 1936).

Der Dienstkalender Heinrich Himmlers 1941-42, (Christians 1999).

Grosse Prüfung, (Jomsburg-Verlag 1995)

The Stroop Report, (Pantheon Books 1979)

Documents on German Foreign Policy, (London 1950)

OTHER SOURCES

Illustrierte Beobachter

After the Battle magazine, no. 56

After the Battle magazine, no. 14

Völkischer Beobachter

Private correspondence with Hartmut Heissmeyer

Decision of the Staatskommissariat für die politische Säuberung Land Württemberg-Hohenzollern, File N1841, 4 May 1950

Registrar of Births and Deaths, Ulverston, Cumbria

RSHA Operational Reports

Correspondence with Standesamt Bad Godesberg-*Bonn*

Private correspondence with Kurt Knoblauch

UNPUBLISHED SOURCES

Cadle, *My Honor is Loyalty—the Biography of SS General Kurt Daluege*, (Princeton University 1979), thesis.
Miller, Michael D., *Notes on Werner Lorenz*

ARCHIVES

Bayerisches Hauptstaatsarchiv, Nachlass von Eberstein
Stadtarchiv Halle
Landeshaupstadt Munich
Stadt Essen Oberbürgermeister
Stadtarchiv Bonn
Czech Security Service Archive Prague
SS Personnel files BDC
Geoff Walden's archives
Author's archive
Private archives
d'Alquen archive, in anonymous private hands
The former Berlin Document Centre, US Mission Berlin
National Archives and Records Administration, College Park, Maryland
Auschwitz Memorial Museum Archive
Hoover Institute, Stanford University
Burg Stadtarchiv Fehmarn
Halle Stadtarchiv
Detmold Stadtarchiv
Imperial War Museum London
National Archives Kew
The archives of Hermann Historica GmbH Munich

OTHER SOURCES

Hanseatisches Auktionshaus für Historica Ringel OHG
Axis History Forum
Alexander Historical Auctions